"MYSTICISM" IN IRAN

Studies in Comparative Religion
Frederick M. Denny, Series Editor

"MYSTICISM" IN IRAN

The Safavid Roots of a Modern Concept

ATA ANZALI

THE UNIVERSITY OF SOUTH CAROLINA PRESS

Published by the University of South Carolina Press
Columbia, South Carolina 29208

www.sc.edu/uscpress

Manufactured in the United States of America

26 25 24 23 22 21 20 19 18 17 10 9 8 7 6 5 4 3 2 1

Library of Congress Cataloging-in-Publication Data can be found at
http://catalog.loc.gov/.

ISBN: 978-1-61117-807-4 (hardcover)
ISBN: 978-1-61117-808-1 (ebook)

تقدیم به فهیمه، همدم و همراه، سنگ صبور

و نرگس و اسرا، دو فرشته زندگی

To Fahimeh, Narges, and Esra

CONTENTS

SERIES EDITOR'S PREFACE

This deeply researched book provides a detailed history and analysis of the ways in which Iranians have defined and understood Shiʾite Muslim beliefs and practices from their origins in early Islamic history down to the present. Central to the study is how the broad modern concept of "mysticism" relates to the traditional Muslim concept of *ʿirfan*, a term that is widely expressed in English as "Islamic mysticism." The study explains the traditional term *Sufism,* also widely translated as Islamic mysticism, and the ways it is thought to relate to *ʿirfan* as the two traditional terms have been understood.

The two terms are thoroughly compared by the author as he leads us on an enthralling tour of how Sufism can be understood with respect to the central beliefs, values, and practices that Muslims have universally embraced since the earliest history of Islam. We also learn of the serious differences Muslims have experienced between those who have deep mystical dimensions in their beliefs and practices and those who regard mysticism as essentially unIslamic. Ata Anzali has brought the contemporary understanding of Islamic mysticism and Muslim beliefs and practices generally to a rich new level that will be a true blessing for the study of Islam globally as well as in Iran.

Frederick Mathewson Denny

ACKNOWLEDGMENTS

My adventure with ʿirfan started long before the research for this book, beginning eighteen years ago, when I moved to Qum to follow a rigorous course of study in the traditional Islamic disciplines. I had the good fortune to find an erudite mentor there who graciously accepted me into his circle of students. He was a generous and kind human being and an undisputed master of Islamic philosophy and ʿirfan. With his help, I immersed myself for four years in the writings of Suhravardi, Ibn Turka, Ibn ʿArabi, Mulla Sadra, Tabataba'i, and other great masters. My education took a sharp turn when I moved to the United States to begin graduate studies in religion at Rice University, but my fascination with ʿirfan did not subside. In fact, the strong emphasis on the study of mysticism in the religion department at Rice broadened my scope significantly and allowed me to view ʿirfan from a comparative perspective. I am very grateful to the people who taught me there. I was as encouraged by their continuous support as I was educated by their breadth of knowledge. They introduced me to a new way of looking at religion, one that I found troubling and at the same time profoundly liberating. For that liberation, I am indebted most of all to Jeffrey Kripal, my adviser and mentor. He is among the most generous and insightful human beings I have ever known. The support that I received from Rice University's Humanities Research Center was also instrumental at the initial stages of the research project that culminated in the publication of this book. The HRC provided funding that helped me spend two years in full-time research and writing at Harvard University's Widener Library.

I am also grateful to Professor Carl Ernst for his continuous support and encouragement over the course of my research. Special thanks go to Professor Bruce Lawrence, who, without having met me in person, kindly provided immensely helpful feedback. I am also profoundly grateful for the help of Professor Alireza Doostdar and Professor Matthew Melvin-Koushki. Both were extremely generous with their time, carefully reading the entire manuscript at different stages and giving invaluable feedback. I extend my gratitude to my fellow Iranian academics as well, first and foremost to Professor Shahram Pazouki. I am thankful to have had the opportunity to discuss my ideas with him in the early stages of formulating my questions about ʿirfan, and he provided much-needed guidance. I would also like to thank the peerless scholar Rasul Jaʿfariyan, whom I have never had the pleasure of meeting in person. His vast, unrivaled scholarship and his leadership at the Majlis Library facilitated and guided my research agenda in important ways. The library's amazingly rich manuscript collection was put online through his initiative, making it possible for me to browse a treasure trove of archival material from half a world away, in the OL section on the sixth floor of Widener Library. This material was critical for my research, and the world of Iranian studies has few better friends than Professor Jaʿfariyan.

The generous support of my new institutional home, Middlebury College, has been instrumental in ensuring that the present book is the best possible scholarly work that I can offer my audience. I am grateful for that support and, more important, for the friendship, support, and collegiality of my religion department colleagues, who have been nothing short of exceptional.

Special thanks go to Laurie Pierce, who generously agreed to help smooth out the rough edges of my English prose. I am fortunate to have had her beside me as an editor on the long road to publishing a work that I hope readers will find clear and coherent. I have also been very fortunate to have enjoyed a close friendship with the Pierce family, especially Matthew, who has been a constant source of support. I would also like to thank Jim Denton, the acquisitions editor for the University of South Carolina Press, who has patiently worked with me to ensure the proper publication of this work. I am, of course, solely responsible for the content of this book.

Although this project was carried out at a great distance from my family, their support and love have been crucial. I am thankful for my dear brother Amin, always the first person to whom I turn with my problems, technical and beyond. Mom and Dad, thank you for your endless support, for your unconditional love, and for forgiving me for taking your sweet grandchildren to the other side of the world, where you can't experience the joy of holding their hands and telling them the stories you told me.

Finally, the most important thank you, the attempt to express an ineffable gratitude. I feel obliged by convention to say these final words, even though saying them does not feel right. Acknowledgments in a book are usually accompanied by the assumption that the written work belongs to the person whose name is on the cover. But another person is behind every sentence of this book as much as I am, despite not having written the words herself. I have had the great blessing of spending the past nineteen years of my life with this person. She and I began our journey together in a humble basement in Qum, with little money and much love. Nothing looked impossible or even difficult in the face of our passion for learning and our deep love for each other. When we decided to embark on a new adventure and come here to the United States, she became a *sang-e sabour* not only for me but for our two wonderful daughters, Narges and Esra. All the while, she graciously put up with a perfectionist graduate student turned novice teacher who was a less than perfect husband. I thank you, Fahimeh, for all of this and so much more.

NOTES ON TRANSLATION AND TRANSLITERATION

The term *ʿirfan* has been translated into English by scholars variously and often inconsistently as Islamic "mysticism," "mystical knowledge," "Islamic theosophy," "gnosis," and "gnosticism." The semantic field of the term *ʿirfan* can overlap, sometimes significantly, with all of these, depending on the context in which it is used. Given, however, that the subject of this book is the history of the use of the term *ʿirfan* and the formation of ʿirfan as a concept, I have kept the word untranslated throughout the work for clarity and to help the reader better understand the rationale of scholars who choose to translate it using the English terms listed. With the same rationale and for the sake of consistency, I have left *ʿarif* (pl. *ʿurafa* or *ʿarifin*) and other cognates of the root ʿ-r-f untranslated throughout the book as well.

Because of the overwhelming Persianate context of the subject of this book, I have followed a simplified form of IJMES Persian transliteration scheme throughout, even with Arabic terms, with the following important adjustments:

I have italicized non-English terms only in their first appearance in the book. All non-English phrases, however, have been italicized throughout. Only the first words of phrases in Persian and Arabic, such as book titles, have been capitalized.

I have omitted all diacritical marks, except for hamza and ʿayn, for the sake of simplicity. Initial and final hamzas, and the final 'h' for the silent ه, both in *nisba* endings and cases of *ta marbuta,* are omitted as well (for example, ʿurafa, not ʿurafaʾ; Zahabiyya, not Zahabiyyah; *andisha,* not *andishah*). Similarly, the 'w' for the silent *vav* has been omitted throughout the book (for example, Khansari, not Khwansari). Readers can find full transliterations of names and book titles in the bibliography.

Regarding personal names: I have dropped the definitive article *al-* from all surnames. More important, I have followed AIS transliteration rules for names of people who died after 1900 (for example, Kazemzade, not Kazimzadah). Finally, when the abbreviated form MS appears after the short title of a referenced work in the footnotes, it indicates an unpublished manuscript.

INTRODUCTION

The Question of ʿIrfan in Contemporary Iran

On October 5, 2011, channel four of the state-run Islamic Republic of Iran Broadcasting (IRIB4) network televised a debate between Mahdi Nasiri and Mohsen Gharaviyan.* The former is an independent commentator on religious and social issues and the editor-in-chief of *Semat,* a quarterly journal established to provide "a platform to explain and defend the teachings [*maʿarif*] of the Qurʾan and the family of the Prophet, peace be upon them."† The latter is a well-known and somewhat controversial ayatollah from Qum, a lecturer in Islamic philosophy, and the author of several books on theology, philosophy, logic, and other subjects.‡ The theme of the debate, which was broadcast nationally in Iran, was the relationship between *ʿirfan* and Islam. Nasiri has long been known for his adherence to a puritanical reading of Shiʿism and for his passionate promotion of the idea that the true face of Islam and the original doctrines of the twelve Shiʿi imams have been obscured by various "curtains" over the course of the centuries.§ One of these curtains, he believes, is Sufism, and another is philosophy.** In contrast to Nasiri, Gharaviyan, who studied under prominent teachers of philosophy and ʿirfan in Qum, is a firm believer that ʿirfan is not only compatible with but also an integral part of the teachings of the imams.

* IRIB4 caters primarily to well-educated Iranians interested in subjects related to the humanities, arts, and sciences. The debate can be accessed online at *Munazara-yi janjali-yi Nasiri va Gharaviyan darbara-yi ʿirfan va din,* 2011, http://www.youtube.com/watch?v=I-DZIQHdfsg&feature=youtube_gdata_player (accessed March 29, 2016).

† See http://www.sematmag.com/index.php/about-us (accessed March 29, 2016).

‡ For his personal website, see http://www.gharavian.ir (accessed March 29, 2016).

§ His views are deeply influenced by a school of thought called *maktab-i tafkik,* established by Mirza Mahdi Esfahani (d. 1946). For more on this school of thought and its similarities to the Akhbari school see Gleave, "Continuity and Originality." For their attacks on philosophy see Rizvi, "'Only the Imam Knows Best.'"

** A third curtain is modernity.

Many aspects of this debate would be interesting to discuss, but the feature that goes to the heart of the question this book asks is the terminology used by the two men. Throughout the hour of back-and-forth debate, Gharaviyan consistently uses the word *ʿirfan*—a term that generally has positive connotations among Persian speakers—to refer to the mystical tradition of Islam. Nasiri, on the other hand, insists on using either the term *tasavvuf* (Sufism) or the pejorative *ʿirfan-i mustalah* (the so-called ʿirfan). Nasiri's semantic choice strikes the native speaker of Persian as strange, but it is deliberate: he wishes to make the point that what is called ʿirfan in Iran today is in fact Sufism—a term imbued with negative connotations and sometimes used as a pejorative, especially among religious people.

This televised debate, in particular Nasiri's word choices and their implications, is one of many examples of a dispute in larger Iranian society over the status of ʿirfan and Sufism and their relationship to "authentic" Islamic teaching. No in-depth study of the intensification of this debate has been carried out, but having tracked publication trends in Iran in recent years, I find that the argument between proponents and opponents of Sufism and ʿirfan has escalated over the course of the past decade.* I believe this can be traced to sociocultural developments in Iran following the Islamic Revolution.

After the success of the Islamic Revolution of 1979 and the subsequent takeover of major branches of government by conservative religious circles led by Ayatollah Ruhollah Khomeini (d. 1989), a new form of religiosity came to be promoted and idealized in Iran. This religiosity was based primarily on a framework laid out by Khomeini and his students, particularly the prominent religious intellectuals Morteza Motahhari (d. 1980) and Hoseyn-ʿAli Montazeri (d. 2009).† ʿIrfan was a major component of this revolutionary religiosity. This was related to the fact that Khomeini, the architect and leader of the Islamic Revolution, was not only a jurisconsult (*mujtahid*) and source of emulation (*marjaʿ-i taqlid*) of the highest caliber but also an acclaimed *ʿarif.*

From the early years of his education in Qum during the third decade of the twentieth century, Khomeini was strongly inclined toward mysticism. He studied both philosophy and ʿirfan at the highest level possible with Mirza Mohammad-ʿAli Shahabadi (d. 1949) and Mirza ʿAli-Akbar Hakim (d. 1925).‡ He became famous not only as an outstanding jurist but also as a teacher of Islamic ethics (*akhlaq*) and an unofficial guide for seminary

* See page 8, note *.

† These two men played a fundamental role in constructing the framework on which the Islamic Republic's ideology rests.

‡ Knysh, "*Irfan* Revisited," 634. Khomeini frequently referred to Shahabadi in his writings as "our shaykh," "our master in divine knowledge," and "the perfect ʿarif." See, for example, Khomeini, *Sharh-i chihil hadith*, 20, 67, and 653.

students (*talaba*) on matters of their spiritual quests (*sayr va suluk*). His early publications established him as a commentator on works of speculative mysticism by Ibn ʿArabi (d. 1240), the Islamic philosopher-mystic par excellence, and as a student of the mystical philosophy of the Shiʿi philosopher and theologian Mulla Sadra (d. 1635).*

Those in the seminaries, however, were not always inclined to embrace the mystical elements of the new ideology. Khomeini's penchant for ʿirfan was an exception, not the norm, in the upper echelons of the Shiʿi hierocracy in Qum. Most high-ranking religious scholars were suspicious of philosophy and ʿirfan, to say the least, and they were disinclined to give ʿirfan a free pass to enter the seminary curriculum. Granted, Ibn ʿArabi's speculative mysticism and Mulla Sadra's philosophy had been taught in the seminaries for more than two centuries, but the teachers who propagated their thought had always been marginalized (if not demonized or opposed outright) by traditionalist jurists intent on safeguarding orthodoxy. In fact, during the 1950s, Khomeini himself was at odds with Ayatollah Borujerdi (d. 1961), the most prominent marjaʿ-i taqlid of the time, over the issue of teaching the mystical philosophy of Sadra openly in the Shiʿi seminary system (*hawza*).† Nor were his mystical views well received among Arab religious scholars when he was exiled by the shah to Iraq. Khomeini's followers often speak of how exoteric and literalist jurists despised him to the extent that they even considered his son ritually impure because of his father's indulgence in the heretical teachings of Ibn ʿArabi and his teaching of Mulla Sadra's books.‡ Khomeini was not shy about his political views or his ʿirfani inclinations, but in view of such strong opposition he took pains to distance himself from Sufis and to emphasize the difference between ʿirfan and Sufism. For example, in his highly esoteric work *Sirr al-salat* (*The Mystery of Prayer*), he responded to the prevailing culture of excommunication (*takfir*) against the mystically minded in these words:

> And among the important points that bear repeating and that our pious brethren, especially the people of knowledge—God increase their numbers—need to keep in mind is that if they see or hear some words from the ulama of the soul [*ʿulama-yi nafs*] and the folk of *maʿrifat,* they should not consider it false or corrupt simply just because it is not familiar or is based on a vocabulary they do not share. They should not insult

* For more on Khomeini's ʿirfan, see Knysh, "*Irfan* Revisited," 631–53.

† Mottahedeh, *Mantle of the Prophet,* 242–43.

‡ The story, which is probably a myth, is continually repeated. For an informed discussion of Khomeini and his opponents in this regard (and one that mentions this story), see Bojnordi, "Imam Khomeini."

> or belittle such folks without proper Islamic legal [*sharʿi*] proof. They should not think that whoever talks about the levels of the soul, the stations of the saints and ʿurafa, manifestations of God, love, affection, and similar concepts—vocabulary popular among the folk of maʿrifa—is a Sufi or someone who is promoting the claims of Sufis, or that he is just making things up by himself and has no rational or legal proof . . . the point being, our brethren in faith need to become more familiar with divine knowledge and to remove this suspicion that has taken a hold in their hearts regarding the great ulama of Islam, [leading them to] accuse them of Sufism.*

Even after the revolution, Khomeini was forced to cancel a series of nationally broadcast lectures due to mounting pressure from traditional seminary authorities who were outraged by the strong mystical and philosophical coloring of his esoteric (*batini*) interpretation of the Qur'an.

Despite such opposition, proponents of philosophy and ʿirfan have gradually, in the years since the revolution, changed the status quo. Mulla Sadra's mystical philosophy is now an accepted element of the official seminary curriculum, and the works of Ibn ʿArabi and his followers on speculative mysticism are taught with greater frequency, freedom, and openness. This is largely thanks to the efforts of Mohammad-Hoseyn Tabataba'i (d. 1981) in the prerevolutionary period† and to structural reforms in the administration and curriculum of the seminary introduced by Khomeini's supporters after the revolution. The gradual move of both philosophy and ʿirfan into the mainstream is perhaps best demonstrated by the adoption into the hawza curriculum of two textbooks written by Tabataba'i for students of philosophy as well as by the production of the first-ever textbook on speculative mysticism.‡

Exclusive, unlimited media access enabled Khomeini's students to pro-

* Khomeini, *Sirr al-salat*, 39–40.

† Tabataba'i was the twentieth century's most prominent Twelver Shiʿi philosopher. For more on his life and thought and for an overview of Islamic philosophy in Iran in modern times, see Nasr, *Islamic Philosophy*, 254–77. See also Aminrazavi, "Islamic Philosophy" 1037–50.

‡ The two textbooks on Sadra's philosophy, *Bidayat al-hikma* (*The Beginning of Philosophy*) and *Nihayat al-hikma* (*The Conclusion of Philosophy*), were adopted as textbooks in the first decade after the revolution in response to the demand in the hawza that novice seminarians be educated in accordance with the Khomeini-approved model. The textbook of speculative mysticism mentioned earlier was published only within the past several years, and the late date is an indication of how problematic Ibn ʿArabi's school of thought remains in circles of leadership in the hawza. See, for example, Yazdanpanah, *Mabani va usul*.

mote an Islamic ideology that combined the modernist, juristic, and mystical elements reflected in their leader's religious outlook. The invasion of Iraqi forces in the summer of 1980 and the ensuing disastrous war that engulfed both nations for eight years heightened the relevance of this ideological rhetoric, one that portrayed the invading force, backed by the imperialist West, as the enemy of Islam rather than of Iran. This casting of the conflict as a holy war reinforced to the Iranian public the mystical aspects of this ideology, which drew on foundational Shiʿi narratives of the martyrdom of the Prophet's grandson Husayn (d. 680) at the hands of the Umayyad Caliph Yazid (d. 683) during the Battle of Karbala in 680.*

In advocating ʿirfan, ideologues of the revolution presented a spirituality and a grand framework of meaning that resonated deeply with the passionate young generation of Iranians known as the children of the revolution. But the promotion of ʿirfan as the true essence of Islam's mystical tradition also entailed casting aspersions on institutional Sufism and questioning the authenticity and orthodoxy of Niʿmatullahi and Zahabi Sufis, among others. However, due to Khomeini's deep and personal investment in the tradition of high Sufism (represented by Ibn ʿArabi and his school of thought) and despite the fact that he clearly distanced himself from anything that could be labeled Sufi, organized Sufism remained—for a while—safe from outright persecution.

The end of the war with Iraq and the liberal economic and cultural policies pursued under the presidencies of Akbar Hashemi Rafsanjani (d. 2017) and Mohammad Khatami brought dramatic changes in the sociocultural landscape of Iran. One aspect of this change was a rapid increase in the number of syncretistic, New Age–inspired religious movements.† Scientific theories, alternative medicine, traditional esoteric sciences like alchemy, and modern forms of spirituality began to be mixed with orthodox Islamic beliefs in various ways to cater to (for lack of a better term) middle-class Iranians in major urban centers who have increasingly resisted the state-sponsored religion forced down their throats.‡

In contemporary Persian discourse, these new spiritual movements are generally described by the adjectives *ʿirfani* or *maʿnavi* (spiritual).§ This

* For more on mysticism, martyrdom, and the youth, see Varzi, *Warring Souls.*

† For more on this, see Behdad and Nomani, "What a Revolution!"

‡ For more on these developments, see Doostdar, "Fantasies of Reason."

§ For example, a new school of mysticism known as *ʿirfan-i kayhani* (inter-universal mysticism) or *ʿirfan-i halqa* (ring mysticism) has recently become wildly popular in major urban centers of Iran. The founder of this school, Mohammad-ʿAli Taheri, published a number of books explaining his vision, all of which were eventually

designation highlights their place in a modernist trajectory of religious thought and practice that began in the early twentieth century and that has led to the formation of a distinct category to which the word *ʿirfan* now refers. The present-day proponent of ʿirfan in Iran tends to be wary of institutional forms of Sufism, which are often viewed as despotic, corrupt, and superstitious. Instead, modern-minded intellectuals in Iran embrace the category of ʿirfan as a realm distinct from that of traditional Sufism. In doing so, they construct a modern discourse of spirituality (often called *maʿnaviyyat*) that picks and chooses from the long history of Persian Sufism those aspects that are deemed sufficiently modern to meet the needs of a new generation of highly educated Iranians who aspire to a spirituality compatible with science, modern philosophy, and contemporary lifestyles.*

Such alternative readings of religion and mysticism cause the ideologues of the revolution an immense amount of anxiety, and the Islamic regime has proven increasingly intolerant of independent and popular religious/spiritual movements, no matter how much they emphasize their allegiance to Shiʿi orthodoxy. The regime has become increasingly obsessed with drawing clear and fast boundaries between "genuine," Khomeini-style ʿirfan and "pseudo-ʿirfans" (*ʿirfan-ha-yi kazib*). The task of combating these "deviant" mysticisms both ideologically and physically is relegated to the large, quasi-militia branch of the Revolutionary Guards known as the Basij. In a clear shift of policy from Khomeini's time, a brutal and unyielding policy of persecution against traditional Sufis and the New Age movements has accelerated under ʿAli Khameneʾi, Iran's current supreme leader.

As noted, because of Khomeini's personal sympathy with Sufi tradition, a "don't ask, don't tell" policy was followed during his leadership with regard to organized Sufism. As a result, the Niʿmatullahis and Zahabis, who had generally been considered orthodox and who subjected themselves to clerical

---

banned by the authorities, who were alarmed by the increasing number of people joining his school of thought. For a fascinating anthropological study of this group, see Doostdar, "Fantasies of Reason," 130–94.

* Sorush Dabbagh, son of the famous Iranian intellectual and religious reformer Abdolkarim Sorush, has recently published two consecutive articles on the subject. In these two articles he attempts to lay out the philosophical foundations of what he calls "*ʿirfan-i mudirn*" (modern ʿirfan) in contradistinction to "*ʿirfan-i sunnati*" (traditional ʿirfan). See Dabbagh, "ʿIrfan-i mudirn." In contrast, Mostafa Malekiyan, another prominent contemporary intellectual and philosopher in Iran, has put more emphasis on the category of maʿnaviyyat in his construction of a modern Persian spiritual discourse in which traditional mysticism is put in conversation with a modern form of rationality. Hence the title of his major project: "ʿAqlaniyyat va maʿnaviyyat" ("Rationality and Spirituality"). For a sociopolitical understanding of Malekiyan's context see Sadeqi-Boroujerdi, "Mostafa Malekiyan."

hegemony, were left to practice and preserve their centers.* Times changed, however, after Khomeini died. His heir, Khamene'i, lacked his predecessor's strong background in ʿirfan, and he had no sympathy for traditional Sufi groups. The liberal tendencies of Presidents Rafsanjani and Khatami did not initially provide Khamane'i with amenable circumstances for attacking the Sufis. However, following the election of Mahmud Ahmadinejad as president in 2005, Khamane'i was able to consolidate his power over the upper echelons of the political system, and the inherent tension between the totalitarian interpretation of Shiʿism centered around the idea of the guardianship of the jurist (*valayat-i faqih*) on the one hand and the Sufi demand for total submission to the will of the spiritual master (*murshid* in Arabic or *pir* in Persian) on the other became readily apparent. The first major clash between the regime and the orthodox Sufi networks happened in May 2006, when one of the most important Niʿmatullahi centers, located in the holy city of Qum, was confiscated and razed to the ground in the aftermath of a bloody clash between the Niʿmatullahi dervishes and the Basij militia.† The pressure on the Niʿmatullahis and other Sufi groups has been increasing ever since.‡

As mentioned, amid the heightened political and social tensions of the past several years, scholars have increasingly focused their attention on the ʿirfan-versus-Sufism debate and the question of the relationship of each with "authentic" Islam. For the first two decades after the revolution there was little debate on the issue. One of the few (and perhaps the sole) discussions on the topic in that period can be found in a 1994 issue of *Kayhan-i andisha* that contains two essays dealing with the difference(s) and similarities between Sufism and ʿirfan.§ In contrast, recent years have seen a dramatic surge in the

* Other Sufi groups that were deemed heterodox, like the Nurbakhshi branch of the Niʿmatullahi network, were not so fortunate. They were brutally persecuted and pushed underground soon after the revolution. Their leader, Javad Nurbakhsh, fled to London and died there in 2008.

† Although authorities have denied Niʿmatullahi claims regarding the death of several dervishes, officials confirmed the arrest of more than 1,200 members of the Niʿmatullahi khanaqah.

‡ The annual Human Rights Watch report designates the Niʿmatullahis as a religious minority under discrimination. See its "World Report 2011." For Amnesty International's report, see "Amnesty International | Working to Protect Human Rights." A more detailed report listing instances of illegal detainments, torture, and intimidation can be found in a document by the International Organization to Preserve Human Rights in Iran titled "Human Rights Violations against Dervishes." I am not in a position to confirm the details of this report, but there is little question in my mind that most of the information found in it is factually correct.

§ See, for example, Saduqi Soha, "Yaganagi ya duganagi," and Haqiqi, "ʿIrfan va tasavvuf."

number of articles and books dealing with the issue of Sufism versus ʿirfan.* As a result, Niʿmatullahi leaders, long suspicious of the ʿirfan/Sufism dichotomy, have grown increasingly aware of the danger posed by this seemingly innocuous semantic distinction, which allows proponents of state-sponsored ʿirfan to marginalize institutional Sufism and persecute Sufis without appearing to be opposed to spirituality. This has led the Niʿmatullahis to argue more vehemently in favor of using the two terms synonymously.†

In this book, I attempt to identify the cultural trajectories and intellectual trends that contributed to the formation of this dichotomy, one that has been exploited by secular and religious authorities in several episodes of Iranian history, including the present time, as an effective discursive tool to legitimize the persecution of Sufis. This semantic, intellectual, and social genealogy is well overdue in a scholarly sense, but more importantly, it also helps give a voice to the subaltern Sufis of Iran.

This book follows the story of ʿirfan across a time span of nearly four hundred years, from the seventeenth to the twentieth century. Scholarship on some of these periods from the angle I pursue is virtually nonexistent, and many important figures related to the historical trend I research remain unstudied, their work unpublished. I have tried to do my share by bringing some of these figures into the light, but important gaps in the story will remain until further research is done. Additionally, some important aspects of the story of ʿirfan have been left out simply because it is impossible to cover everything in one book. I have done what I could, however, to create a coherent, systematic, scholarly narrative. In the daunting task of picking and

* The following works are among many that address the issue in detail or are devoted to it entirely: Arab, *Tasavvuf va ʿirfan;* Tehrani, *ʿArif va sufi;* Aqa Nuri, *ʿArifan-i musalman;* Javdan, "ʿAliman-i shiʿa va tasavvuf;" and Movahhedian ʿAttar, *Mafum-i ʿirfan.* For a fascinating, informative, and erudite scholarly debate on the issue, however, see Pazouki, "Paraduks-i tasavvuf," 93–108, and a response by Ghaffari in "Tasavvuf ya ʿirfan?" 109–26. Additionally, a recently established publication house, Rah-i nikan, has been very active in publishing works that deal with the distinction between "true" and "false" versions of ʿirfan and/or the relationship between the latter and Islam. The majority of these can be considered part of the anti-Niʿmatullahi propaganda encouraged by state policy. See, for example, Tavana, *Sarchashma-ha-yi tasavvuf;* Madani, *Irfan-i islami,* and Rusta, *Tafavut-i ʿirfan va tasavvuf.* The amount of crude polemics on this topic on the Internet dwarfs the number of published books and articles mentioned here.

† For the earliest arguments against this distinction, see Safi-ʿAli Shah, *ʿIrfan al-haqq.* Later and more elaborate arguments can be found in Tabande, *Ashina-yi ba ʿirfan va tasavvuf.* Additionally, several issues of the periodical *ʿIrfan-i iran,* edited by the scholar of Persian Sufism Seyyed Mostafa Azmayesh, who is affiliated with the Nʿimatullahi network, feature articles that deal with this distinction. See especially nos. 7, 10, 22, and 27–28.

choosing what to cover, I chose to focus on themes and practices that, I argue, best illuminate the transformations of religious sensibilities that led to the transition from Sufism to ʿirfan. I have anchored my broader treatment of the emergence and development of ʿirfan in the more specific discussion of the central issue of master/disciple relationship (which is, by definition, a social issue) and also of certain Sufi practices such as *zikr* (again, a communal practice). As such, although this book is primarily an exercise in intellectual history, it also borders, at times, on social history.

1 ʿIrfan in the Pre-Safavid Period

In Arabic, the root ʿ-*r-f,* from which the terms *ʿirfan, ʿarif,* and *maʿrifa** are derived, denotes "recognition" or "knowledge." Its beginnings in Arabic literature of the Islamic period are humble. The Qur'an does not contain the terms *maʿrifa* and *ʿirfan,* and when other words derived from the root ʿ-r-f appear, they generally correspond to recognition (which is opposed to forgetfulness), rather than knowledge.† Instead, beginning with the Qur'an, the concept of knowledge (which is opposed to ignorance, or *jahl*) is denoted by words derived from the root ʿ-*l-m,* from which come various verb constructions as well as nouns such as *ʿalim* and *ʿilm.* In contrast with the nonappearance of *ʿirfan,* the term *ʿilm* is used as to denote knowledge more than sixty times in the Qur'an.‡ Furthermore, it is important to note that constructs from the root ʿ-r-f are never used to denote something about the divine nature, acts, or attributes, whereas *al-ʿalim* (the Knower) is one of the most commonly used

* Although I have left this term and other cognates untranslated throughout this book for reasons mentioned in Notes on Translation and Transliteration, I believe that *maʿrifa* can be often legitimately translated as "gnosis." Both words are used overwhelmingly in reference to knowledge related to divine mysteries (see *Oxford Dictionary of English,* s.v. "Gnosis"). Although the term *gnosis* has other connotations rooted in its association with Christian Gnosticism, it has other bodies of meaning in common with maʿrifa, including those related to the unmediated nature of this knowledge, the fact that it is reserved for a few elite, and its realization through exploring the inner self (see *Dictionary of Gnosis and Western Esotericism,* s.v. "Gnosticism."). One major aspect of maʿrifa that differentiates it from gnosis, as will be shown, is that the former, in addition to its "noetic" denotations, to use James's terminology, is also frequently used to refer to an advanced spiritual station (*maqam*) that is associated with the profound realization of the true nature of reality (*al-haqq*) in nondual terms.

† See 2:89; 2:146; 5:83; 6:20; 6:46; 9:102; 12:58; 12:62; 16:83; 22:72; and 23:69, among others. This is the case for another repeatedly used construction of the root ʿ-*r-f* in the Qur'an, that is, the term *maʿruf,* which means "the recognized [way]."

‡ This count is specifically for the form ʿilm. If we count all the various derivatives of the root ʿ-l-m, there are more than six hundred cases.

names of God. In accordance with the Qur'an, Muslim authors have refused to acknowledge *al-ʿarif* as a divine name, arguing that the latter root signifies a prior knowledge that has been or is susceptible to being forgotten and then remembered. This *re*cognition, they explain, is not applicable to the omniscient God. Hence, Muslim authors have made several attempts to draw a clear line of distinction between ʿilm and maʿrifa. Any substantial discussion of such distinctions, based mainly on philological observations, as interesting as they might be, fall beyond the scope of this book.* What is important for this project is that Sufi authors, even when they theoretically distinguish between the two terms, have largely used them interchangeably.†

Sufis, Philosophers, and the Quest for Maʿrifa

It appears that the term *maʿrifa,* along with the active participle ʿarif, was first singled out as a distinct category in the Sufi lexicon around the middle of the ninth century.‡ The emergence of this category was connected to an important transformation in the early spiritual landscape of the Islamic heartlands—a shift in popular conceptions of what constituted the ideal religious life. The established mode of spirituality concerned with renunciation, or *zuhd,* and associated with a pietistic lifestyle centered on worship, or *ʿibada,* was challenged by a new spiritual vision focused primarily on the cultivation of the inner life.§ This new vision, according to Karamustafa, was an "inward turn [that] manifested itself especially in new discourses on spiritual states, stages of spiritual development, closeness to God, and love; it also led to a clear emphasis on 'knowledge of the interior' [*ʿilm al-batin*] acquired through ardent examination and training of the human soul. . . . For these 'interiorizing' renunciants, the major renunciatory preoccupation of eschewing this world [*dunya,* literally, the lower, nearer realm] in order to cultivate the other world [*akhira,* the ultimate realm] was transformed into a search for the other world within the inner self."**

A variety of spiritual movements in the early centuries of Islam contrib-

* For a basic summary of such efforts see Arnaldez, "Maʿrifa."

† In the case of Ibn ʿArabi, for example, see Chittick, *Sufi Path of Knowledge,* 149.

‡ Massignon credits Zu al-Nun Misri (d. 856) with singling out maʿrifa as a distinct category. See Massignon, *Essay on the Origins,* 143.

§ Historians and hagiographers have traditionally taken the early renunciants to be "Sufis-in-waiting" or "proto-mystics." See, for example, Schimmel, *Mystical Dimensions of Islam.* However, I am in general agreement with Nile Green that the two are better understood as representatives of rival visions of the spiritual path. See Green, *Sufism: A Global History,* 20–23.

** Karamustafa, *Sufism: The Formative Period,* 2.

uted to the development of this "inward turn." Not all who associated with those movements initially identified themselves as Sufis,* but the confluence of these different trends in the early Islamic spiritual landscape eventually led to the emergence of a more unified entity called Sufism (*tasavvuf*) in roughly the tenth century.† Early figures influential in the development of this "inward turn," including Zu al-Nun, Yahya b. Muʿaz (d. 871), Sari Saqati (d. circa 866), and others, used maʿrifa, among other concepts, to identify and distinguish the new paradigm of spirituality. For them, the ʿarif as an ideal type stood in contrast and was superior to the previous ideal of the *zahid,* or renunciant. Zu al-Nun, for example, is recorded as saying that "The renunciants are the kings of the afterlife, and the ʿurafa are the kings of the renunciants."‡ Similarly, Sari Saqati contrasted the two, saying that "a renunciant's life is not pleasurable since he is occupied *with* himself, but the life of a ʿarif is pleasurable because he is occupied with *other* than himself."§ In the same vein, Yahya b. Muʿaz said that "the renunciant is pure in appearance but dishevelled [*amikhta*] inside, [whereas] the ʿarif is pure inside and dishevelled in appearance."** He is also reported to have said, "The renunciant walks, while the ʿarif flies."††

In addition to these statements, popular hadith reports were circulated in order to provide a basis of legitimacy and authenticity for the introduction of this new term and, more generally, the new paradigm of the inward turn. The famous hadith "he who knows himself, knows his Lord,"‡‡ which was apparently put into circulation by Yahya b. Muʿaz, is a case in point.§§ The rise to prominence of such statements in Sufi literature in subsequent centuries played an instrumental role in popularizing the terms *ʿarif* and *maʿrifa* in later Sufi literature.

* For example, the Karramiyya and Malamatiyya seem to have been significant rivals of the early Sufi movement in the Khurasan region.

† Ernst has pointed out some problematic aspects involved in translating tasavvuf as Sufism (see Ernst, *The Shambhala Guide to Sufism,* 1–31). Nile Green has suggested that it might be better to use "Sufi Islam" instead of "Sufism" to emphasize how Islam and Sufism are inseparable for most Muslims (see Green, *Sufism: A Global History,* 18). This is an attractive suggestion, but it runs the risk of implying that "Sufi Islam" is another sect like "Shiʿi Islam" and "Sunni Islam." In line with Ernst and for simplicity's sake and lack of a better alternative, I keep to the convention of Sufism in this book.

‡ ʿAttar, *The Tadhkiratu'l-Awliya,* 1:128.

§ ʿAttar, *The Tadhkiratu'l-Awliya,*1:283.

** ʿAttar, *The Tadhkiratu'l-Awliya,* 1:307.

†† Sarraj, *al-Lumaʿ,* 365. Additionally, a full section of the book is dedicated to explaining what distinguishes an ʿarif from ordinary believers (35–40).

‡‡ Hadith Qudsi, "man ʿarafa nafsa-hu faqat ʿarafa rabba-hu."

§§ Massignon, *Essay on the Origins,* 83–88. Also see Böwering, "ʿErfān (1)."

From the beginning of its use in the ninth century, the concept of an ʿarif stands out as a descriptor of someone who has reached an advanced level of spiritual achievement. In the spectrum of spiritual stages and layers of inner realization, an ʿarif, to use Zu al-Nun's terms, "is among the Sufis, yet distinct from them."* In the sources, advanced levels of spiritual achievement have mainly to do with the realization of a state of union in which the agency of the wayfarer is subsumed and annihilated in the agency of God, who is the only true agent. Accordingly, Zu al-Nun developed a three-level hierarchy of maʿrifa in which the highest level is concerned with the attribute of unity (*sifat al-vahdaniyya*).† Abu Hafs of Nishabur (d. ca. 874) is reported to have said, "Maʿrifa necessarily entails for the man his absence [*ghayba*] from himself, in such a way that the memory of God reigns exclusively in him, that he sees nothing other than God, and that he turns to nothing other than to Him. For, just as the man who reasons has recourse to his heart, his reflection, and his memories in every situation presented to him and in every condition he encounters, so the ʿarif has his recourse in God. Such is the difference between he who sees through his heart and he who sees through his Lord." ‡

Likewise, Shibli (d. 946) is believed to have said, "When you are attached to God, not to your works, and when you look at nothing other than Him, then you have perfect maʿrifa."§ In a similar vein, Bayazid Bistami (d. 875) is recorded as saying, "The creature has its conditions, but the ʿarif does not have them, because his traits are effaced and his essence [*huviyya*] is abolished in the essence of the One. His features become invisible beneath the features of God." He is also said to have responded to a question about the station of an ʿarif with "There is no station there. Rather, the greatest benefit of the ʿarif is the existence of his Known."** Bistami is later remembered in Sufi literature as *sultan al-ʿarifin*.†† As one of the most celebrated Sufis, he is famous for statements in which he talks about shedding his "I"-ness like a snake's skin in the state of annihilation, or *fana*, only to gain a transformed self-consciousness in which there is no self but God. This was, in fact, what a ʿarif was supposed to achieve. Abu Bakr Vasiti (d. 932) is also worthy of quotation in this regard. He said, "An ʿarif is not authentic when there remains in the man an independence which dispenses with God and the need for God. For to dispense with God and to have need of Him are two signs that the man is awake and that his characteristics remain, and this on account of

* ʿAttar, *The Tadhkiratu'l-Awliya*, 1:126.
† ʿAttar, *The Tadhkiratu'l-Awliya*, 127.
‡ Arnaldez, "Maʿrifa."
§ Arnaldez, "Maʿrifa."
** Sulami, *Tabaqat al-sufiyya*, 69.
†† ʿAttar, *The Tadhkiratu'l-Awliya*, 1:134.

his qualifications. Now the ʿarif is entirely effaced in Him whom he knows. How could this—which is due to the fact that one loses his existence in God and is engrossed in contemplation of Him—be true, if one is not a man devoid of any sentiment which could be for him a qualification, when one approaches existence?"*

What is striking about these quotations is that they emphasize the consequences of attaining maʿrifa rather than focusing on the actual content of it. That is to say, maʿrifa, at least at this level of development, is not about a specific subject of knowledge, about the "what" of "what the mystic knows." Rather, it is indicative of a mystical station acquired as the ʿarif advances close to God. In such a state, we are told, the ʿarif realizes that what he thought was he himself, his acts and his attributes, are in fact those of God. The literature is thus concerned with what follows from acquiring such a state, rather than what is entailed, in noetic terms, in that knowledge. In fact, the distinction between being and knowing no longer applies at this advanced spiritual station.

As the older and rival paradigm of renunciation weakened and "Sufi" became more prevalent as an umbrella term, the term *ʿarif* came to be situated and understood in relationship to the term *Sufi*, rather than renunciant. In this process, however, it retained its elitist connotations, referring to a level of spiritual realization attained only by the select among the saints (*awliya*). In an early compilation of the sayings of the great Sufi of Khurasan, Abu Saʿid Abu al-Khayr (d. 1049), a certain Khaja Masʿad is said to have praised Abu Saʿid with these words: "I am not going to call you a Sufi or a dervish, but a perfect ʿarif."† Here, Abu Saʿid is identified as an accomplished ʿarif rather than as a Sufi or a dervish, implying that the former is superior to the other two terms. It is important to note, however, that this anecdote, when analyzed in the context of other similar anecdotes, does not appear to conceive of the ʿurafa as a group distinct from the Sufis, as Pourjavady argued, or as an antithesis to Sufis, as Ghaffari has suggested.‡ Rather, the former denotes a person who has reached a particularly advanced spiritual station, and it is used as a designation for accomplished saints, whether they identify as Sufis or not. For example, Khaja ʿAbdullah Ansari (d. 1088), in his biography of Tirmizi (d. ca 910), recognized the latter not as a Sufi but as a *hakim* who was also a ʿarif (*hakimi bud ʿarif*).§ Furthermore, in the early hagiographical

* Arnaldez, "Maʿrifa."

† Abu al-Khayr, *Asrar al-tawhid,* 231.

‡ Pourjavady, *Ishraq va ʿirfan,* 250–55; Ghaffari, "Tasavvuf ya ʿirfan," 109–26.

§ The term *hakim* ("wise man" or "sage"), rather than Sufi, was the most popular designation for a particular social type of mystically minded learned man in the

sources, discussions of the meaning of the terms *Sufi* and *Sufism* are often immediately followed by anecdotes about maʿrifa and ʿurafa.* Thus there is a strong sense of continuity and connection between the two sets of concepts, rather than opposition and contradistinction. In the few cases that the term *ʿirfan* appears in early classical Sufi literature, its range of meaning is indistinguishable from that of the term *maʿrifa,* indicating a lack of semantic independence and significance.†

Maʿrifa reached its climax in Ibn ʿArabi's thought as the pivotal concept of a trend usually known as high Sufism. As Sufism spread throughout the Muslim world, its adherents diversified. Many among the learned sought refuge in it after becoming disillusioned with the spiritual promise of other fields of religious knowledge. Experts in theology, jurisprudence, and other disciplines converted to Sufism, sparking conversation between and a synthesis of these branches of knowledge and significantly influencing the future trajectories of all of them, including Sufism, which developed a robust and systematic intellectual tradition. The thought and work of Ibn ʿArabi, otherwise known as *al-shaykh al-akbar* (the Greatest Master), are among the most remarkable products of this type of synthesis—so much so that even a basic understanding of his complexities of thought and mind-bogglingly vast writings requires familiarity with an array of Islamic disciplines from jurisprudence and theology to medicine and the esoteric sciences.

Through the school of thought founded by Ibn ʿArabi, the category of maʿrifa went through a major semantic evolution in Sufi usage that brought its noetic quality to the fore. Maʿrifa was now used more often to refer to the knowledge of the unseen worlds rather than the spiritual station that it entailed. The Greatest Master directed his formidable spiritual accomplishments and intellectual talents toward developing a technical vocabulary to talk systematically about the unseen realm (*ʿalam al-ghayb*). This led to the rise of a new paradigm called, in Chittick's words, "the Sufi path of knowledge," which contrasts with an equally strong and important paradigm

---

northeastern regions of the Muslim world during the ninth and tenth centuries. See Karamustafa, *Sufism: The Formative Period,* 47.

* For example, see the anecdotes in *Kashf al-mahjub* about Junayd (d. ca. 910) and the anecdotes in *Tazkirat al-awliya* on Bishr Hafi (d. ca. 850) and Zu al-Nun. See Hujwiri, *Kashf al-mahjub,* 161ff and ʿAttar, *The Tadhkiratu'l-Awliya,* 106–34.

† In the eleventh century, for example, the term *ʿirfan* appears only three times in the entire volume of *Kashf al-mahjub,* a relatively early classical Sufi hagiography written by Hujviri (d. 1072). Fast forward two centuries, and the term appears only twice in ʿAttar's classic Sufi hagiographical work, *Tazkirat al-awliya.* One of the two occurrences is a reference to nonreligious knowledge; in the other, *ʿirfan* is interchangeable with *maʿrifa.*

known as "the Sufi path of love."* The following paragraph is a good illustration of the path of knowledge, written by Ibn ʿArabi himself:

> God never commanded His Prophet to seek increase of anything except knowledge, since all good [*khayr*] lies therein. It is the greatest charismatic gift [*karāma*]. Idleness with knowledge is better than ignorance with good works . . . By knowledge [maʿrifa] I mean only knowledge of God, of the next world, and of that which is appropriate for this world, in relationship to that for which this world was created and established. . . . Knowledge [ʿilm] is an all-encompassing divine attribute; thus it is the most excellent bounty of God. Hence God said, "[Then they found one of Our servants, whom We had given mercy from Us], and whom We had taught knowledge from Us" [18:65], that is, as a mercy from Us. So knowledge derives from the mine of mercy.†

Ibn ʿArabi spoke of the ʿurafa as the greatest saints and defined maʿrifa as "any knowledge which can be actualized only through practice [*ʿamal*], godfearingness [*taqva*], and wayfaring [*suluk*]."‡ Maʿrifa is one of the most prominent concepts in his oeuvre. By contrast, ʿirfan is a marginal term, not only in Ibn ʿArabi's corpus but also in other classical Sufi works from this period. In the rare cases that Ibn ʿArabi used the word *ʿirfan*, it did not signify an -ism such as Sufism. Rather it denoted the advanced spiritual station at which one becomes capable of receiving divine knowledge. ʿIrfan remained an obscure term in Ibn ʿArabi's time and the centuries that followed, despite the monumental influence of the Greatest Master's speculative mysticism and its heavy dependence on the category of maʿrifa. There was, however, another intellectual tradition, that of Islamic philosophy, in which the term *ʿirfan* seems to have played a more prominent role.

Ibn Sina and His Legacy of ʿIrfan

The elitist nature of the concept of maʿrifa made it popular not only among those associated with high Sufism but also among another elite group: phi-

* Obviously, constructed dichotomies like "intellectual Sufism" versus "love Sufism" simplify and thus to some extent distort the complex dynamics of the huge tradition of Sufism. They are useful insofar as they can help us understand, classify, and account for the apparent differences that we see in Sufi literature and the different ways various Sufi masters approach fundamental questions of the spiritual path. Actual Sufis are always a mixed bag of all these "ideal types," to use Weber's terminology. As a case in point, Ibn ʿArabi wrote an entire treatise on the subject of love, titled *Tarjiman al-ashvaq*.

† Ibn ʿArabi, *al-Futuhat al-makkiyya*, 2:370, quoted in Chittick, *Sufi Path of Knowledge*, 148.

‡ Chittick, *Sufi Path of Knowledge*, 149.

losophers. Ibn Sina (d. 1037), the philosopher par excellence of the Islamic world, dedicated an entire chapter of his classic *al-Isharat va al-tanbihat* to a systematic exposition of the spiritual stages traversed by the ʿarifin. In this chapter, which is titled "Maqamat al-ʿarifin," he contrasts the ʿarifin with renunciants and worshippers. Ibn Sina says that while the latter two are mostly concerned with avoiding the lower realm of this world and its attachments, the ʿarif is entirely absorbed in the unseen world, the world of pure intellect, and is constantly receiving divine knowledge. The goal of the ʿarif is nothing but God's ʿirfan (*ʿirfani-hi*).* One of the earliest commentators on *al-Isharat,* Fakhr Razi (d. 1210), began his comments on this chapter by saying that it is the most noble among the chapters of this book and that in it Ibn Sina "has systematized the disciplines of the Sufis [*ʿulum al-sufiyya*] in a way no one had done before him."† There is no question from the unique vocabulary and style of writing used in this chapter that Ibn Sina had in mind an audience very familiar with Sufi discourse. Yet it is anachronistic and incorrect, in my view, to describe the chapter as one in which " the discipline of Sufism" is discussed, as Razi and other commentators who followed him said. At the very least, to say that "Sufism" is the best descriptor of the chapter's contents flies in the face of Ibn Sina's avoidance of any reference to such a term or to names or works associated with Sufism, despite their relation to the themes he addressed. In other words, by forgoing explicit reference to the original web of concepts from which key terms such as *maʿrifa* had emerged, Ibn Sina consciously approached the set of questions and themes that interest Sufis on his own terms and from his own disciplinary perspective.

This comes as no surprise given the sour relationship between philosophers and Sufis throughout much of the history of the Islamic world. Sufis overwhelmingly disapproved of discursive philosophy. "There is no one more distant from the law of the Hashemite Prophet than a philosopher," said ʿAttar Nishaburi (d. 1221), echoing Sanaʾi Ghaznavi's (d. 1131) sentiments that "From words [prevalent in philosophy] like 'primary matter' and 'primary cause' you will not find the way into the presence of the Lord."‡ The story of the alleged meeting between Ibn Sina and Abu Saʿid Abu al-Khayr, although almost certainly apocryphal,§ is a reflection of how the rational method was often disdained (though not completely rejected) by Sufis. In the story of their encounter, the two are said to have met and engaged in a three-day private conversation. At the end, each was asked his impression of the

* Ibn Sina, *al-Isharat,* 3:369 and 375.
† Ibn Sina, *al-Isharat,* 3:363.
‡ Schimmel, *Mystical Dimensions of Islam,* 18–19.
§ See Ritter, "Abu Saʿid Fadl Allah ibn Abi'l-Khayr," and Nicholson, *Studies in Islamic Mysticism,* 42.

other, and Abu Saʿid replied that everything that he could see, Ibn Sina knew. In turn, Ibn Sina said that everything he knew, Abu Saʿid could see.*

The Avicennan ideal of the perfect ʿarif, therefore, stands independent of and in contrast to the ideal espoused by many Sufis. It presupposes thorough training in the rational sciences, especially in discursive metaphysics. Epistemologically, it rejects the centrality of the mystical vision (*mukashafa*) as the primary source of knowledge in favor of the faculty of reason and its capacity to attain new knowledge through syllogism.† This is not to say, of course, that philosophy for Peripatetic philosophers was limited to syllogism. Quite the contrary, it was a way of life that included practices of mortification and purification of the soul.‡ To the Peripatetic philosophers, philosophy was composed of two branches, the practical and the speculative, which together provided the adept with a wholesome, integrated, and complete vision of the meaning of life and its final goal.§ The perfect philosopher, in other words, was one who educated his mind in discursive reasoning while at the same time striving to establish virtues in his soul and uproot the vices. It was only then, with a sharp and purified intellect, that he reached the stage of acquired intellect (*al-ʿaql al-mustafad*), which mirrored the source of all knowledge, the active intellect (*al-ʿaql al-faʿʿal*), from which the prophets gained their knowledge.

A good signifier of the independence of Ibn Sina's discourse from that of Sufism is expressed in his redefinition of the concept of the spiritual master, or pir, in a treatise titled *Hayy ibn Yaqzan* (*The Living, Son of the Wakeful One*). This symbolic, enigmatic story tells of the soul of an adept meeting its spiritual master and asking it about the mysteries of the world. The master is none other than the active intellect, or "the living," as it is called in the treatise, which emanates, in the metaphysical scheme of Peripatetic philosophy, as a "son" from "the wakeful one," that is, the penultimate pure intellect. Both metaphysical entities are discussed in great detail in the theory of creative emanation professed by Farabi (d. 950) and Ibn Sina. In the latter's story, the active intellect surpasses the perceptible world through knowledge, the soul's guide toward its prime principle, which is the being that shines forth

* Abu al-Khayr, *Asrar al-tawhid*, 159.

† More specifically, as Gutas has argued, Ibn Sina's epistemology is based on the concept of *hads* rather than anything resembling mystical visions. Hads, according to Gutas, is "the capacity to hit spontaneously upon the middle term in any syllogism," and all that is contained in the active intellect. See Gutas, "Avicenna V. Mysticism."

‡ Rizvi, "Philosophy," 8–10.

§ On the philosophical origins of this classification, see Giladi, "On the Origins," 81–93.

above all others. Some scholars have tried to make sense of the story by interpreting it as an indication of Ibn Sina's inclination toward an Illuminationist (*ishraqi*) epistemology or an explicitly Sufi treatise,* but the story makes perfect sense within the confines of Peripatetic principles, as Goichon has convincingly argued.†

As Pourjavady has pointed out, this symbolic story is probably the first treatise in which the term *pir,* which refers to a human guide in Sufi literature, is redefined as an abstract, heavenly entity—in this case the active intellect—that appears to philosophers or mystics, guides them, and provides them with divine secrets.‡ This transformation of the idea of the pir from a human master to an abstract heavenly entity is, in my mind, a significant confirmation of the fact that Ibn Sina approached mysticism on his own terms, refusing to submit his discourse to the alternative paradigm of understanding the master/disciple relationship within a Sufi worldview that required the spiritual master to be a human being.

One must, I believe, understand the meaning of the term *ʿirfan* in Ibn Sina's thought within this context. Far from confirming his Sufi inclinations, ʿirfan functions in this chapter as a concept that contrasts with Sufism. Ibn Sina used it to describe what might be called a mystical program, to define, on his own terms, the process of human flight from the material world toward the pure world of abstract entities. ʿIrfan, to Ibn Sina, was the process of ascetic practices of detachment from this world and unity with the divine world through which one goes to become a ʿarif:§ "ʿIrfan begins with differentiation [*tafriq*], invalidation [*naqz*], abandonment [*tark*] and rejection [*rafz*]. It continues with an integration [*jamʿ*] that is the integration of divine attributes into the essence of the true seeker. It ends in the One [*al-vahid*], and then stillness [*vuquf*].** . . . Whoever prefers ʿirfan for the sake of ʿirfan has associated a second with God, and whoever realizes ʿirfan is not realizing it [ʿirfan] but is realizing the one who is known, and thus he has plunged into the abyss of intimacy."††

Ibn Sina continued with an enigmatic allusion to further stages that are "unknowable and indescribable . . . whoever wants to know them must to ascend gradually until he is among the folk of *mukashafa* (vision) rather than dialogue and among the ones who have reached reality rather than those

* See, for example, Corbin, *Avicenna,* 23–27, and Anawati, *Mu'allafat ibn sina,* 213–44.
† See Goichon, "Ḥayy B. Yakẓān."
‡ Pourjavady, *Ishraq va ʿirfan,* 147–50.
§ Similarly, *tasavvuf* literally means becoming a Sufi and, as such, refers to a process rather than a stable essence.
** Ibn Sina, *al-Isharat,* 3:389.
†† Ibn Sina, *al-Isharat,* 3:390.

who have heard of its vestiges."* While Gutas has made a strong case against understanding this reference to this ineffable stage of mukashafa in Sufi terms,† there is no question that Ibn Sina's successors and followers, as mentioned, interpreted remarks like this in a framework overwhelmingly influenced by Sufism.

This is understandable when we take into account the contexts in which they lived and wrote, which were vastly different from the one in which Ibn Sina found himself. The religious, intellectual, and social landscape of the Islamicate world changed dramatically in the centuries after the great philosopher's death.‡ Sufism grew rapidly, effectively conquering the cultural landscape of the Middle East on both the elite and the popular levels. It became omnipresent in all layers of Muslim society through the establishment of local, regional, and transregional social networks of Sufi brotherhoods. In the words of Nile Green, "Having established their institutional footholds across a wide region, the period between 1100 and 1500 . . . saw the Sufis achieve an extraordinary ascent to a position in which, from Morocco to Bengal, they acted as the social and intellectual linchpins of the very different communities that they penetrated across this vast area. By 1500, not only were Sufis at once the patrons and clients of kings, they were also central to the lives of lower class groups in town as well as country, a position consolidated by their role in the conversion of nomadic and cultivator groups to Islam in expanding frontier regions."§ The establishment of Sufi networks followed the emergence of the Sufi lodge—variously called a *khanaqah, ribat, zaviya,* or *dargah*—as a significant center of medieval social life alongside the madrasa and the mosque. In the aftermath of the Mongol invasion and the downfall of the caliphate in 1258 and the attendant blow to the unity of the worldwide Muslim community (*umma*), these brotherhoods "gave the ordinary Muslims who joined them both the conceptual and institutional framework with which to connect themselves to a contemporary community of fellow believers and a past tradition of blessed forerunners."** The Sufi ethos went beyond the walls of the khanaqah, entering the fabric of society in the form of men's clubs and guild organizations built around the notion of chivalry (*futuvva*),

* Ibn Sina, *al-Isharat,* 3:390.

† For a detailed analysis of this passage, see Gutas, "Intellect without Limits," 366–72.

‡ At the same time, *al-Isharat* quickly became an indispensable textbook of philosophy, a fact that is attested by the considerable number of commentaries written on it and their wide distribution. As early as the late twelfth century it had become known as *mushaf al-falasifa,* literally, "the scripture of philosophers." See Michot, "La pandémie avicennienne," 287–344.

§ Green, *Sufism: A Global History,* 71.

** Green, *Sufism: A Global History,* 87.

which functioned as regulators and maintainers of the social order. As a result, Sufism gradually began not only to dominate the religious life of the people but also to provide an important basis for social order.* In Hodgson's words, "[T]he Sufi tie at once deepened the local moral resources, and tied them into a system of brotherhoods in some ways as universal as the old caliphal bureaucracy had been, which had disappeared. . . . Thus Sufism supplemented the Shariʿa as a principle of unity and order, offering the Muslims a sense of spiritual unity which came to be stronger than that provided by the remnant of the caliphate."†

It was therefore only natural that later commentators on Ibn Sina who lived and breathed in a Sufi-dominated intellectual environment interpreted the ninth chapter of *al-Isharat* as a distinct section discussing the science of Sufism rather than as an independent piece of philosophical discourse. For example, almost two centuries after Ibn Sina, Khaja Nasir al-Din Tusi (d. 1274), one of the most important philosophers of the time, a prominent commentator on *al-Isharat,* and a man of politics during the tumultuous times that followed the Mongol invasion, wrote a small treatise titled *Awsaf al-ashraf* (*Attributes of the Nobles*). In the opening remarks of *Awsaf,* Tusi says that after writing a treatise on ethics titled *Akhlaq-i Nasiri* according to the principles of philosophers, he desired to write one based on the principles of the wayfarers of the spiritual path (*salikan-i tariqat*). The latter phrase is an unmistakable reference to Sufi adepts, and the author used such terminology throughout the work.‡ Tusi devoted a chapter of *Awsaf* to the notion of maʿrifa, but, instead of according with Ibn Sina's notion of ʿirfan, his understanding of the term lay totally within the framework of Sufism.§ Tusi provided a more detailed schema of the progressive spiritual stages in his *Awsaf al-ashraf,* drawing heavily upon the *manazil* genre of Sufi literature, a body of texts describing the spiritual stations and best represented by ʿAbdullah Ansari's *Manazil al-saʾirin.*** In fact, he seems to have been unimpressed by Ibn Sina's concept of ʿirfan, as the term does not appear in *Awsaf.* In other words, it is clear that Tusi gave up his forebear's ambition to establish and promote an independent mystical program under the title of ʿirfan based in philosophy rather than Sufism. The fact that Tusi, unlike Ibn Sina, felt compelled to write a treatise using the technical vocabulary of Sufism speaks to the radical shift in the balance of power when it came to the relationship of the discipline of Sufism and

* Hodgson, *Venture of Islam,* 2:204.
† Hodgson, *Venture of Islam,* 221.
‡ Tusi, *Awsaf al-ashraf,* 28–34.
§ Tusi, *Awsaf al-ashraf,* 133–34.
** For an informative analysis of Tusi's *Awsaf* see Pourjavady, *Ishraq va ʿirfan,* 224–47.

the discipline of philosophy in his time. In Madelung's words, "It is thus not surprising that he felt competent to compose a treatise on the Sufi path. Both he and the vizier Juwayni, a Sunni and firm supporter of Islam, must have sensed the growing tide of Sufi sentiment throughout Islam, which was to reach its peak in the Mongol age. They must have been aware that Sufism, if anything, could break down the barriers between schools and sects and unite all Muslims under the banner of the great Sufi networks. Tusi thus conceived his treatise on Sufi ethics as a complement, addressed to the common Muslim, to his philosophical ethics, addressed to the elite."*

Although the dominance of the Sufi tradition largely prevented Ibn Sina's notion of ʿirfan from gaining primacy, it was taken up in sixteenth-century Safavid Shiraz after half a millennium in a small treatise titled *Manazil al-saʾirin va maqamat al-ʿarifin,* written by the prominent philosopher and dignitary of early Safavid Shiraz Ghiyas al-Din Mansur Dashtaki (d. 1542). This work offers a fresh look at the ninth chapter of *al-Isharat* and draws heavily upon Tusi's commentary on that chapter as well as on the latter's *Awsaf.* The title of the work, which is a precise combination of the title of the ninth chapter of *al-Isharat* and that of Ansari's classical work *Manazil al-saʾirin,* is an explicit restatement of Ibn Sina's definition of ʿirfan in terms of Sufi stages of spiritual advancement, just as found in Tusi's *Awsaf.*† The heroes of Dashtaki's *Manazil,* however, are the ʿarifin, and their special gift is ʿirfan. Sufism and Sufis are not mentioned at all; if they are, they are disapprovingly called pseudo-Sufis.‡ Dashtaki's definition of ʿirfan in this work is taken verbatim from *al-Isharat.*§ What represents a development from the latter work, however, is Dashtaki's increasing use of ʿirfan as a substantive term that sometimes refers to a distinguished group of people, the lords of ʿirfan (*arbab-i ʿirfan*).** To further reinforce ʿirfan as a distinct category and the folk of ʿirfan as a distinct group of the learned, Dashtaki provided us with a short list of terms used by the folk of ʿirfan.†† Although he did not mention this fact, the list was taken, almost word for word, from Suhravardi's (d. 1191) *Kalimat al-tasavvuf,* in which the terms are listed under the heading "Mustalahat al-sufiyya" ("Technical Terminology of the Sufis").‡‡ That is to say, in spite of his indebtedness to Sufi literature, Dashtaki eschewed any mention

* Madelung, "Nasir al-Din Tusi's Ethics," 11.

† For a fuller analysis of Dashtaki's sources in his *Manazil,* see Pourjavady, *Ishraq va ʿirfan,* 248–62.

‡ Dashtaki, *Dashtaki va falsafa-yi ʿirfan,* 169 and 178.

§ Dashtaki, *Dashtaki va falsafa-yi ʿirfan,* 179–80.

** Dashtaki, *Dashtaki va falsafa-yi ʿirfan,* 150 and 159.

†† Dashtaki, *Dashtaki va falsafa-yi ʿirfan,* 180.

‡‡ Dashtaki, *Dashtaki va falsafa-yi ʿirfan,* 229, note 59 and 251, note 150.

of Sufis or Sufism in his exposition, perhaps with the aim of creating an aura of discursive autonomy and independence for ʿirfan in contrast to Sufism.

This semantic move by Dashtaki, whatever the reasons behind it, failed to attract much attention, at least in the short run. It would take another hundred years for the notion of ʿirfan to be picked up again, this time by another Shirazi religious scholar, Shah Muhammad Darabi. Darabi's works, I argue, were a significant source of inspiration for later constructions of the concept of ʿirfan that stood in opposition to Sufism. It is not unlikely, however, that Dashtaki's premature attempt stemmed from his awareness of an enormous transformation in the air: the rise of Safavid Shiʿism and its dominance in Iran.

2 The Safavid Opposition to Sufism

The Safavid Sufi network is said to have been founded by Shaykh Safi al-Din Ardabili (d. 1334). Sometime during the fifteenth century the network took on a strong political-military agenda, and both Shaykh Junayd (d. 1460) and Shaykh Haydar (d. 1488), the grandfather and father, respectively, of Shah Ismaʿil (r. 1501–1524), died on the battlefield in their fight against Qaraquyunlu rulers. With the help of Anatolian Sufi tribes known as the Qizilbash (literally, the "Red Heads") who acted as their military and ideological backbone, the Safavids' struggle culminated in the enthronement of Shah Ismaʿil as the first Sufi king of Iran.

Sufism and the Safavids

Qizilbash religiosity was marked by a mixture of shamanistic ideas, Sufi ideals, and a distinct messianic vision. Each of the early Safavid rulers was venerated by the Qizilbash not only as a perfect spiritual master (*murshid-i kamil*) but also as the reincarnation of heroic figures of the past who had fought for the cause of the family of the Prophet. These rulers were believed to have acquired divine qualities and powers that even made them worthy of worship.* At the nascent stage of the Safavid revolution, the symbolic and charismatic role played by Shah Ismaʿil prompted many of the Qizilbash Turkish tribes to pay allegiance to him, guaranteeing their unconditional submission and support.† The syncretistic, revolutionary, and popular form of religiosity to which the Qizilbash adhered, although extremely helpful in the initial stages of the Safavid revolution, was a liability in later phases, when rulers focused their efforts on the stabilization and institutionalization of the newly established kingdom. At this stage bureaucrats and the landed elite

* See the fascinating report of an anonymous Venetian merchant who was in Tabriz in 1518 in Barbaro et al., *Travels*, 206–7.

† For an interesting attempt to understand the religious relationship between the Qizilbash and Shah Ismaʿil in light of the former's cannibalistic rituals see Bashir, "Shah Ismaʿil and the Qizilbash."

were needed more. Additionally, the establishment of a new religious orthodoxy capable of providing society with law and order was a necessity.

Although it is not entirely clear why Shah Ismaʿil chose Twelver Shiʿism as the state-sponsored religion of his kingdom, it is abundantly clear that in the following decades, with only a brief exception, Safavid religious policy consisted of promoting Twelver orthodoxy, which provided the kingdom with legitimacy and a basis upon which to construct and maintain social cohesion. Hand in hand with this policy went the suppression of dissident religious and political movements that threatened this unifying tendency. The Safavid kings claimed legitimacy as the shadows of God on earth, guardians of the true faith, and upholders of Twelver tradition. As such, it was imperative that they fight Sunnism (most notably the Sunni Turks and Uzbeks) and combat movements that did not conform to the prevailing orthodoxy. Although several brutal massacres took place during the late sixteenth and early seventeenth centuries, particularly involving adherents to the Nuqtavi and Hurufi heresies, the political elite appears to have been aware of the problems entailed in killing its way to conformity and social cohesion.* Establishing a strong and popular religious orthodoxy proved a more attractive method of suppressing and preventing such deviations. In other words, identifying and suppressing heresy in a systematic way requires a systematic notion of orthodoxy and an organized group of guardians who patrol the boundaries between heresy and orthodoxy. With the support of the royal court, such a group came into being: a class of Shiʿi ulama that emerged in the early seventeenth century and grew in size and strength as newly established Twelver centers of learning in Iran produced exponentially increasing numbers of graduates.

It is an irony of history that the demise of organized Sufism came about under the Safavids, who themselves came to power as a Sufi network. In the beginning of the sixteenth century, when most of Iran fell under the control of the Safavids, many active Sufi networks existed throughout Persia. By the end of Safavid rule, there is little evidence of active organized Sufi networks in Iran. In attempting to account for the considerable decline of organized Sufism, historians of the Safavid period have largely assumed the existence of a royal policy of active, targeted, and systematic persecution of Sufi networks, enforced more or less consistently throughout the dynasty's rule. This

* For an overview of the religious views of the Hurufis and their founder, see Bashir, *Fazlallah Astarabadi*. For the Nuqtavis, see Kiya, *Nuqtaviyan ya pasikhaniyan*. The suppression of the Nuqtavi movement, for example, seems to have been explicitly linked to the political ambitions of this group. See Babayan, *Mystics, Monarchs, and Messiahs*, 101 and 377–78.

assumption, which I call the suppression model, is convenient and sounds plausible, and thus it has been repeated time and again as an explanation for the eclipse of organized Sufism in Iran.* My reading of the sources, however, leads me to believe that it is misguided to cite systematic royal persecution as the most important factor in the decline of organized Sufism in Safavid Iran. A detailed critique of the suppression model is beyond the scope of this book, but I would like to devote a bit of space here to sketching the outlines of an alternative model for analyzing and understanding the disappearance of organized Sufism in Iran. This decline, I believe, can be more accurately attributed to the conversion of Iran's masses to Shiʿism in the sixteenth century, the crown's ferocious propagation of anti-Sunni Twelver ideology by way of Qizilbash zealots, and the way in which existing Sufi networks responded to the changing religious environment.

Dina Le Gall's fascinating study of the history of the Naqshbandi network, although not concerned with Safavid history per se, is (as far as I am aware) the first major step in Western scholarship toward questioning the assumptions traditionally made by historians and constructing a new framework for understanding this period.† Naqshbandis were among the Sufi networks disinclined to adopt the Safavid version of Twelver Shiʿism. As Le Gall explains in her work, in the first half of the sixteenth century, several

* See, for example Arjomand, *Shadow of God,* 112–19, and Nasr, "Religion in Safavid Persia," 279–80. The suppression model is much older, however, going back to late nineteenth- and early twentieth-century Iranian scholars of Persian literature. In his *A Literary History of Persia,* Edward Browne defers to the authority of his "learned and scholarly friend," Mohammad Qazvini, to whom he wrote to inquire about the "decline" of Persian poetry during Safavid times. The latter attributed this decline to the connection between "poetry and belle lettres" on the one hand and "Sufism and mysticism" on the other. Since the Safavids brutally and systematically suppressed the latter, it is no surprise that the former declined as well. See Browne, *Literary History of Persia,* 4:26–28.

† As far as I know, Babayan was the first to note the challenge that Le Gall's narrative poses to the dominant paradigm of suppression. See Babayan, *Mystics, Monarchs, and Messiahs,* 114, note 91. In addition to Le Gall's valuable contribution, Algar and McChesney pushed for a new direction in understanding sixteenth-century Safavid Iran as well (see McChesney, "Central Asian Haj-Pilgrimage," 129–56, and Algar, "Naqshbandis and Safavids," 7–48). Much earlier, and within the realm of Persian language scholarship, Zabihollah Safa offered his own alternative reading, one that, in spite of some important points of disagreement, I find much more accurate when it comes to the roots of the decline of organized Sufism in Iran. See Safa, *Tarikhi-i adabiyyat,* 5:201–22. The fact that in a recently published textbook Newman offered a balanced narrative that does not overly emphasize the suppression assumption is a good sign of a general readiness to revisit the problem. See Newman, *Safavid Iran.*

outstanding members of the network traveled as missionaries from Greater Khurasan to major urban centers such as Qazvin in the Iranian plateau with the intent of establishing Naqshbandi centers there.* These missions faced increasing hostility because of their emphasis on their Sunni roots. By the second half of the century, this antagonism had forced them to move to the fringes of the Safavid realm, where the central government had little muscle to bother them, or to leave entirely and settle in Ottoman lands. Le Gall's analysis of the decline of the Naqshbandiyya provides us, I believe, with a good starting point for a sounder analysis of Safavid attitudes toward Sufism. She says,

> The picture that emerges from sixteenth-century Naqshbandī sources is somewhat more complex. The Safavids may well have sought to extirpate the ṭariqa, as well as other manifestations of Sunnism, but this was not easily achieved in central Iran, and certainly not in border areas such as Khorasan or Azerbaijan. In time, the Naqshbandī presence did disappear throughout the country. However, this was the product of a protracted process that lasted some fifty years in Herat and Qazvin and over a century in Tabriz and its environs. It involved instances of outright repression, of flight or emigration to Sunni territories beyond the border, and of shaykhs who simply withdrew from teaching or proselytizing. Nor was emigration out of Iran always a response to direct and outright repression by the regime: it might be induced by the inauspicious atmosphere that the establishment of a Shiʿi state entailed, or by the actual or anticipated loss of patrons, or simply by the towering difficulty of living among Shiʿi neighbors who became increasingly arrogant as Safavid rule was becoming more entrenched.†

In other words, when the Safavid policy of religious coercion started in the sixteenth century with an emphasis on the two central pillars of *tavalla* (love for the family of the Prophet) and *tabarra* (disassociation from the enemies of the family of the Prophet, especially the first three caliphs), many Sufi religious scholars who had no problem with the first pillar refused, as standard-bearers of Sunni religiosity, to compromise on the second, which involved cursing revered companions of the Prophet whose legacy was central to that religiosity.‡ Under the social pressure caused by the *tabarra'i* Qizilbash, they had no choice but to keep a low profile. In order to do that, many chose leaving the heartlands of the Iranian plateau either for the fringes of the Safavid

* Le Gall, *Culture of Sufism.*

† Le Gall, *Culture of Sufism,* 24–25.

‡ Safa, *Tarikh-i adabiyyat,* 5:157–62.

realm or for Ottoman and Mughal realms, where the environment was much more hospitable. And, like the Naqshbandi shaykhs, some of the important Kubravi masters preferred to continue their activities in Uzbek territory or northern Mughal regions.

The suppression model also fails to provide an accurate account of the history of another major Sufi network of pre-Safavid Iran: the Niʿmatullahi network. Contrary to Nasr's assertions,* the Niʿmatullahiyya were clearly in decline long before the advent of Safavid rule. It is baffling to see historians reference, as if it were an established fact, Safavid suppression of the Niʿmatullahi network.† During the fifteenth century, Niʿmatullahis in Kerman lost their two major leaders, one to India and the other to death. What remained of the network in Iran soon became an aristocratic familial entity interested primarily in preserving its material interests and forging profitable political alliances. As such, when the Safavids established their power, the Niʿmatullahis forged close relationships with the court by arranging strategic marriages between the two families, and they held important official posts in the Safavid dynasty, especially in Yazd.‡ The cozy relationship between the Niʿmatullahis and Safavid monarchs began to sour only in the first decades of the seventeenth century, when a member of the Niʿmatullahi family known as Mirmiran became involved in a rebellion against the shah in Kerman.

Other groups of Sufis, such as the Kubraviyya, had a religious outlook that included distinctly Shiʿi aspects, such as belief in the sanctity of the twelve imams, the occultation of the twelfth imam, and his return as the Mahdi.§ These groups were naturally more prone to adopting elements of the increasingly dominant Shiʿi religious outlook of the state-sponsored ulama at the expense of a corporate Sufi identity that, from a sociological point of view, set them apart from mainstream mode of piety propagated by

* Nasr and Jahanbegloo, *Dar just-va-ju-yi amr-i qudsi*, 393–94.

† For example, see Terry Graham's sensational title choice for an article that appeared in the third volume of *The Heritage of Persian Sufism* ("The Niʿmatu'llāhī Order under Safavid Suppression and in Indian Exile"). The author presents not a single piece of evidence to substantiate his claim that the Niʿmatullahis were suppressed by the Safavids, depending totally on Arjomand's narrative in *The Shadow of God.* In fact, Graham's own narrative often provides us with evidence that such suppression could not have happened in the first place because by 1450, as Graham notes, what remained of the Niʿmatulllahi Sufi network had already declined "from a dynamic spiritual institution into a moribund dynastic family tradition." Graham, "Niʿmatu'llāhī Order," 178.

‡ See Algar and Burton-Page, "Niʿmat-Allāhiyya."

§ Molé, "Les Kubrawiya," 61–142.

the ulama. The suppression model, therefore, cannot adequately explain the decline of various branches of the Kubravi network in Iran.

There is no question that some prominent Nurbakhshis ran into trouble because of their perceived political ambitions. The descendants of Sayyid Muhammad Nurbakhsh (d. 1464) had a cozy relationship with early Safavid rulers including Shah Isma'il and Shah Tahmasp I (r. 1524–1576), but this ended when the latter decided to imprison and then execute Shah Qavam al-Din (d. 1537, a grandson of Nurbakhsh) because of a combination of his political ambitions and his associations with members of the Aqquyunlu and the Timurids.* The decline of the Nurbakhshis in the aftermath, however, was not as precipitous as has been assumed. I argue that the Nurbakhshis were a visible presence in the cultural and religious landscape of Iran up to the mid-seventeenth century. The gradual decline of their corporate identity, I believe, can more soundly be attributed to a comparatively smooth transition to Twelver Shi'ism resulting from the already described Shi'i elements in their worldview than to Safavid suppression. Other branches of the Kubravi network, such as the followers of 'Abdullah Barzishabadi (d. 1452), who later came to be known under the title of the Zahabiyya, made a similar smooth transition into Twelver Shi'ism and were intimately involved in the invention of the concept of 'irfan.

With the constant drain of Sunni Sufi leaders from the central Safavid realm and the transition of some others into Twelver Shi'ism, often at the expense of their corporate identity, Sufism was increasingly dominated by Qalandars, wandering dervishes, and low-profile populist shaykhs with little knowledge of Islamic disciplines, to say nothing of the jugglers, magicians, and entertainers who posed as dervishes to give themselves a holy and enigmatic aura. In such circumstances, the newly emerging class of Shi'i ulama was able to paint its conflict with the Sufis as a war between knowledge and superstition, discipline and laxity, and observance and antinomianism.

Shah 'Abbas, the Decline of the Qizilbash, and the Rise of the Ulama

The reign of Shah 'Abbas I (r. 1588–1629) saw the transformation of the Safavid rule "beyond an agrarian-based military-fiscal polity into what Mann calls a 'territorial empire,' one in which ideology and culture rather than raw military power provide cohesion," as Matthee eloquently put it.† It is probably true, as Matthee points out, that the Zuhab treaty, signed in 1639, during the reign of 'Abbas I's successor, Shah Safi (r. 1629–1642), which acknowledged in perpetuity the Ottoman claim to Mesopotamia, sealed this transformation.

* Bashir, *Messianic Hopes*, 189.

† Matthee, *Persia in Crisis*, 251–52.

It symbolized the end of war as the natural condition of the state, which in turn spelled the end of its many practical and symbolic functions, including keeping tribal forces engaged, acquiring booty and slaves, enhancing the shah's heroic aura, and forcing him to patrol his realm.* A major component of this transformation was the entrance on the political scene of a corps of Caucasian slaves, (*ghulam*) which ʿAbbas I introduced for the purpose of supplanting the influence of and assuming rule over the Qizilbash.† As a result, by the time of Shah Safi's coronation, Caucasian slaves of the Safavid household were in full control of the political arena.‡

The decline of the Qizilbash was concomitant with the ascendance of alternative status groups of a different disposition. Most important among these were the bureaucrats ("men of the pen," most of whom were ethnic Persians), the clerical class (composed of Persians as well as Arab immigrants from Lebanon and Bahrain), and, eventually, the eunuchs, who came to dominate court politics in the later seventeenth century.§ As this new clerical elite consolidated power and became a prominent class, it was able, with the help of the political center, to impose its desired version of orthodoxy upon the populace, objecting to aspects of popular religiosity that it found objectionable, especially those represented in the religious outlook of Qalandars, the Qizilbash, and many wandering dervishes.

The process of institutionalizing clerical power began to get under way in the early decades of the seventeenth century. By that time, a critical mass of the populace, especially in the heartlands, had converted to Shiʿism. With the official sponsorship of Safavid kings and the favorable new social situation, an emerging class of Shiʿi ulama began to coalesce. Meaningful consolidation of power, however, did not occur until the second half of the seventeenth century, and thus to speak of a hierocracy prior to that time is anachronistic. The century between 1620 and the abrupt end of the Safavid Empire in 1722 is thus the time period in which the ulama evolved from a heterogeneous and in some cases syncretistic group in which prominent figures

* Matthee, *Persia in Crisis,* 251–52.

† For a fascinating and detailed account of this new elite class, see Babaie, *Slaves of the Shah.*

‡ For more on this transformation, see Babayan, "Safavid Synthesis" and "Waning of the Qizilbash."

§ Babayan, "Waning of the Qizilbash," 251–52. Andrew Newman has called the migration of a significant number of Arab ulama from Jabal ʿAmil to Iran a myth. See Newman, "Clerical Migration." His arguments have not been persuasive to the majority of historians of the Safavid era, and counterarguments have been offered. See, for example, Farhani Monfared, *Muhajirat-i ʿulama-yi shiʿa;* Abisaab, *Converting Persia;* and Stewart, "Notes on the Migration."

such as Shaykh Baha'i (d. 1621) and Majlisi Sr. (d. 1659) depended more on Sufi-inspired personal charisma than on institutional power to a hierarchical and institutionalized social class. This transition resulted in a clerical hierocracy, to use Arjomand's terminology, that was, at least initially, highly dependent on the power of the state and its vast financial resources. An important key to this evolution was religious education. Thanks to financial support from the Safavid court, numerous madrasas were built and endowed in major urban centers. This process gained momentum especially after ʿAbbas I transferred the capital to Isfahan. Hundreds of students flocked to these madrasas to study under prominent Shiʿi religious scholars. Some of these teachers were brought in from Lebanon and Bahrain—long Twelver strongholds—and others were local Persian scholars. A new, energetic, and idealistic generation was now in charge of educating the masses, and this generation took it upon itself to attack various forms of deviance.

Abu Muslim, Storytelling, and the Ulama

Such attacks were not initially targeted against Sufism proper, since, in the early decades of the seventeenth century the Sufi legacy of the Safavid dynasty was still strong. By the early seventeenth century, remnants of the Sufi past, such as referring to the shah as the murshid-i kamil and using the prayer mat of guidance (*sajjada-yi irshad*) in coronation ceremonies, had lost much of their original significance and meaning, but their symbolic connection to Safavid discourses of legitimacy and authenticity meant they could not be discarded.* Rather than attacking Sufism generally, the puritan defenders of God aimed their ire at practices related to Sufism that they considered deviant, calling them impermissible innovations (*bidʿa*). One such deviation was the popular practice of storytelling. At the time, storytelling (*qissa-khani*) was a significant and effective medium for creating, guiding, and expressing religious, economic, and social aspiration and discontent. Stories were performed by professional storytellers (*qussas* or *qissa-khanan*) in public venues including coffee houses and bazaars. These narratives were major sources of public entertainment, but they were also frequently used as powerful political tools.

The story of Abu Muslim, as told in its many versions across Iran and Anatolia right before the advent of the Safavid rule, was one such narrative. It was

* It was only decades later, during the reign of Shah ʿAbbas II (r. 1642–1666), that there seems to have been a conscious effort on the part of the Safavid monarch to disentangle Safavid political discourse from the remnants of Sufi-infused symbols. One example is the decision, for the first time, not to use the *sajjada* in ʿAbbas II's coronation. See Quinn, "Coronation Narratives," 327–28.

an alternative history of the Abbasid revolution that overthrew the "tyrannical" rule of the Umayyads (661–750), who had usurped the right of the family of the Prophet to rule over the Muslim community. The death of the Prophet's grandson Husayn at Karbala is the drama that sets the tone of the Abu Muslim epic (the *Abu Muslim-nama*) as a genre. The martyred members of Muhammad's family are portrayed as victims of the aggression of the Umayyads, who had usurped the right of leadership. Most of the epics composed in Turkish that would have been transmitted by the Qizilbash begin with Husayn holding his half-brother Muhammad b. Hanafiyya (d. 700) in his arms. Husayn designates this half-brother as heir and the next imam, envisioning a line of imams that differs from that of Twelver Shiʿism. The genealogy promised by Husayn, says the story, can be reactivated at various points in history, when Muhammad b. Hanafiyya returns miraculously in other human forms, including that of Abu Muslim, who led the Abbasid revolt.* Inspired by the followers of Husayn and Abu Muslim, the Qizilbash devotees entered the battlefield and sacrificed their lives for the beloved family of the Prophet, considering Shah Ismaʿil's grandfather, Junayd, another reincarnation of Ibn Hanafiyya.† As such, in the epic that tells Junayd's story, the *Junayd-nama,* Junayd is said to have been a descendant of ʿAli and a contemporary of Abu Muslim. At the end of this epic, the reader is referred to the *Abu Muslim-nama* to learn more about the story of Junayd.‡

Storytellers, tapping into widespread sentiments of what Marshall Hodgson aptly called "ʿAlid loyalty,"§ recounted the chivalric struggles of Abu Muslim and his companions as supporters of the family of the Prophet in the face of Umayyad injustice. As Safavid missionaries traveled throughout Eastern Anatolia during the late fifteenth and early sixteenth centuries to propagate their cause among the Qizilbash, the story of Abu Muslim was used to draw parallels between the mythical figure and the actual struggles of their time. As such, it functioned as the myth that grounded the worldview of the Qizilbash and their recruits, orienting their religious, social, and political sensibilities and actions.

Storytelling was not a practice confined to the Anatolian tribes. Rather,

* Babayan, *Mystics, Monarchs, and Messiahs,* 126. My narrative on the subject of storytelling heavily draws on Babayan and, to some extent, Jaʿfariyan; both provide fascinating analyses. See Jaʿfariyan, *Safaviyya,* 2: 520ff

† Babayan, *Mystics, Monarchs, and Messiahs,* 138. Also see Safa, *Tarikhi-i adabiyyat,* 5:148.

‡ Babayan, *Mystics, Monarchs, and Messiahs,* 140. Primary sources tell us that a group of Sufis, referred to as "Sufiyan-i Ardabil," recited the stories of Ibn Hanafiyya and Abu Muslim. See Babayan, *Mystics, Monarchs, and Messiahs,* 121.

§ Hodgson, *Venture of Islam.*

it was a widespread practice and a major source of entertainment and inspiration for urbanites and nomads alike. As such, stories were transmitted by many different types of people. Genres also varied. Religious stories about the family of the Prophet were popular—passionate poetic narratives that detailed their unique and heavenly qualities, their heroic acts in defense of the true faith, and the sufferings they endured in their noble cause. This type of narrative was widely known as *maddahi* or "eulogizing [the imams]." Other types of stories included tales from secular epics like Firdawsi's *Shah-nama,* which covered the history of the kings of Persia from the beginning of time up to the Islamic conquest.* Storytellers themselves varied in their affiliations, but they functioned within a widespread, popular, loosely defined but highly visible social phenomenon that has sometimes been called dervishism. Indeed, many were wandering dervishes, and though not all were Sufis, some had loose connections to organized Sufism or at least utilized paraphernalia and a technical vocabulary that suggested such an affiliation. Thus the common people, learned scholars of the madrasa, and foreign travelers widely perceived them to be a Sufi-related group despite the fact that many who donned the dervish cloak and traveled from town to town with fantastic stories did not have slightest adherence to any otherworldly and ascetic lifestyle.†

It would be wrong to draw a firm dividing line between "dervishism"—the conglomeration of eclectic and syncretistic forms of belief and practice represented by individual free-ranging dervishes—and the organized, institutional Sufism of established khanaqahs. Members of organized Sufism were also involved in practices like storytelling. We are told, for example, that the renowned Nurbakhshi Sufi shaykh Qazi Asad Quhpa'i (d. 1638), who oversaw the Nurbakhshi khanaqah in Kashan in the early seventeenth century, was fond of Abu Muslim.‡ Even some of the Sufi-minded ulama of the early seventeenth century, luminaries like Majlisi Sr., are reported to have been comfortable with storytelling practices. Sufis are also portrayed in various sources as fans of *Shah-nama* storytelling. The pseudo-Ardabili tells us in *Hadiqat al-shi'a* of a certain group of Sufis in the mid-seventeenth century called the Jawriyya (or Juriyya), who were fond of listening to the stories of the Zoroastrians (*gabran*) and those of the *Shah-nama.*§ Even much

* Ja'fariyan, *Safaviyya,* 2:859.

† Zarrinkub, *Dunbala,* 228–29. James Morier's account in *The Adventures of Haji Baba Isfahani,* although it dates to the early eighteenth century, is a good example of how a suspicious outsider might have seen the wandering dervishes. See Morier, *The Adventures.*

‡ Ja'fariyan, "Si risala," 255.

§ Pseudo-Ardabili, *Hadiqat al-shi'a,* 2:777.

later, when such practices were supposed to have been marginalized, another elite Nurbakhshi Sufi, Mirza Abu al-Qasim Sukut (d. 1822), nearly lost his life when a mob attacked his house, accusing him of reading the *Shahnama* with his disciples.* As these examples demonstrate, so-called popular or folk aspects of Sufism often coexisted with elite or high Sufism in organized Sufi networks centered in the khanaqah. It was perhaps this intermingling of popular and elite elements that made it possible for puritan mullas, once their concern with storytelling had abated, to initiate the next phase of their religious crusades: a fierce anti-Sufi campaign. As the power of the Qizilbash in court began to wane in the early seventeenth century and their form of religiosity was seen as a liability, the court did nothing to stop and sometimes actively supported attacks on the practice of storytelling, especially that of Abu Muslim, that inspired the masses and could be (and were) used to manipulate them. Attacks on storytelling not only were politically beneficial for the state but also were in the interest of the newly emerging clerical class, for which identifying forms of heresy and deviation was the easiest means to define orthodoxy (albeit in a negative way).

While there are examples of ulama opining against the practice of storytelling (especially telling the story of Abu Muslim) in the sixteenth century, the wave of coordinated attacks came only later. Examples from the sixteenth century include a religious edict (*fatva*) by the great Arab mujtahid Shaykh ʿAli Karaki (d. 1533), who came to Iran upon Shah Ismaʿil's invitation. Karaki encouraged followers of the imam to curse Abu Muslim and other enemies of the family of the Prophet.† A short time later, a student of his named Muhammad b. Ishaq Hamavi (d. after 1531) wrote a treatise called *Anis al-mu'minin* against Abu Muslim epics. Babayan's view is that these early attacks constitute the first of two waves of anti–Abu Muslim propaganda in which representatives of Twelver orthodoxy tried to suppress what they considered to be heretical renditions of the sacred history of the infallible imams.‡ Her reconstruction of this so-called first wave is based entirely upon Hamavi's work. Many details of Hamavi's assertions, including the

* Maʿsum-ʿAli Shah, *Tara'iq al-haqa'iq,* 3:249. He was, according to the reverend missionary Henry Martyn, "one of the most renown Soofies in all Persia" and "a large proportion of the people of Shiraz, it is computed, [were] either the secret or avowed disciples of Mirza Abulcasim." Sargent, *Memoir,* 300.

† The fatva is mentioned in a number of early sources, including *Anis* itself. It is reproduced in Jaʿfariyan's valuable report of the content of his work, along with a lengthy and brilliant discussion of the practice of storytelling in Safavid times. See Jaʿfariyan, *Safaviyya,* 2:862–69.

‡ Babayan, "Waning of the Qizilbash," 204.

destruction of the tomb of Abu Muslim by Shah Tahmasp I in Khurasan,* are not mentioned in any of the chronologies dedicated to the life of the first two kings of the Safavid house, as Babayan herself acknowledges.† Given Hamavi's strong bias against the folk of Abu Muslim, it is very unlikely that the early attacks constituted a coordinated and widespread attempt—a wave, so to speak—to undermine such a popular practice. Even if we accept his claim about the destruction of Abu Muslim's tomb in the vicinity of Nishabur, the fact that, according to Hamavi himself, the tomb was soon rebuilt by Abu Muslim's fans indicates that during the sixteenth century public opinion was still overwhelmingly in favor of this legendary figure; thus, a strong and coordinated attack against his myth is very unlikely to have occurred.‡ The fact that the Shiʿi ulama still lacked effective organization and had yet to establish a discourse of orthodoxy that would function as a base for attacking heterodoxy gives us further reason to doubt the existence of anything beyond scattered and isolated attempts to attack the practice.

It is only toward the end of the reign of Shah ʿAbbas I, when the initial foundations of the clerical hierarchy were being laid, that we witness the emergence of what can be called a concerted campaign against Abu Muslim and the storytellers who recited his epic, one that ignited a major debate in seventeenth-century Iran. These polemical writings, which took the form of refutations (*rudud*), were authored by a group of religious scholars from Isfahan, Mashhad, and Qum.§ Among the earliest of such writings was a work called *ʿUmdat al-maqal,* written by the son of Karaki, Hasan (d. after 1559). There is also a small treatise against the practice of reciting Abu Muslim epics, *Sahifat al-rishad,* written by the vehement enemy of Sufis in Mashhad, Mir Muhammad-Zaman Razavi Mashhadi (d. 1631).**

In his introduction to the work, Mashhadi tells how he learned of a certain *sayyid* (a descendant of the Prophet) in Isfahan known as Mir Lawhi (d. after 1671), who evoked a strong reaction from the people there because

* Jaʿfariyan, *Safaviyya,* 2:864.

† Babayan, "Waning of the Qizilbash," 204.

‡ Hamavi, *Anis al-muʾminin,* 182.

§ Jaʿfariyan has dealt extensively with various aspects of this cultural phenomenon, its underlying reasons, and its connection to Sufism, messianic and apocalyptic movements, and "exaggerationist" (*ghulat*) trends within Shiʿa society at the time. See Jaʿfariyan, *Safaviyya,* 1:37–39 and 2:851–79 as well as Jaʿfariyan, *Qissa-khanan.*

** This treatise, along with two other important examples of the same genre, has been published by Jaʿfariyan under the title *Si risala dar bab-i abu muslim va abu muslim-nama-ha.* For more on Razavi Mashhadi see Hurr ʿAmili, *Amal al-amil,* 2:273. Also see Zanuzi, *Riyaz al-janna,* 4:439.

of his controversial public comments against Abu Muslim. He goes on to say that took it upon himself to write the treatise in order to support Lawhi and to guide the people of Isfahan.* Many other ulama followed the same tack, and at least seventeen works were written in Lawhi's support over a two-decade period, *Sahifat al-rishad* being one of the earliest.† The attack on Sufism followed immediately on the heels of this anti–Abu Muslim campaign, and Mir Lawhi was a leading figure in the attacks against Sufism as well. The puritan activists were eventually successful, in both cases, in marginalizing what they perceived to be a threat to true Islam. The attacks on storytellers and later on Sufis and a host of other movements seen as heretical are only half of the story. For such popular and widespread practices to be marginalized, the emerging class of Shiʿi ulama needed to provide both the populace and the learned with an alternative worldview within which such practices would lose their appeal—an attractive sacred canopy, to use Berger's terminology, built upon foundational myths and reaffirming rituals that provided a sense of meaning that oriented their lives. To that end, they directed their efforts to the traditions of the imams, the hadith literature, as an alternative source of authority that could provide a new religious framework that met the worldly and otherworldly needs of everyday people. The seventeenth century saw immense activity by Twelver religious scholars, with the financial and political support of the Safavid monarchs, to gather and "discover" such literature on the imams from all existing sources in every corner of the Shiʿi world and to comment upon and distribute it. One of the most striking features of Shiʿi intellectual life in Safavid Iran from the early decades of the seventeenth century till the fall of Isfahan in 1722 is the stunning pace at which the study of hadith became the dominant business of the ulama. In the frantic race to contribute to the formation of a new religious framework for the newly converted people of Iran, the most pressing issue was not the reliability of the collected sayings but the need to find and popularize enough of them to replace the Sunni canon with a new foundation of legitimacy and authority.

The Anti-Sufi Campaign

Seventeenth-century refutations of organized Sufism are best understood against the backdrop of major doctrinal and political shifts touched upon earlier. Strong early connections between Sufism and Safavid rule help account for the fact that few (if any) anti-Sufi treatises were written in the

* Razavi Mashhadi, "Sahifat al-rishad," 268–69.

† Tehrani, *al-Zariʿa*, 4:152.

sixteenth and early seventeenth centuries.* Twelver Shiʿism and its network of religious authorities were not powerful enough at that time to initiate anti-Sufi campaigns and compel the political authorities to join. A religiopolitical power structure with a vested interest in maintaining a version of orthodoxy to which Sufism was a threat had not yet arisen. This changed, however, after the reforms of Shah ʿAbbas I. The changes that took place during his rule led to the demise of existing religious and political power structures and the rise of new ones based on clerical authority. The political landscape of Persia was now ripe for an organized and sustained attack against Sufism.

Of course, this was neither the first nor the last time in history that Sufis would come under attack.† What makes the anti-Sufi campaign of the Safavid era noteworthy is its unique religious and political context.‡ The established equilibrium between the Sufis and their opponents was destroyed by state-sponsored propaganda that promoted a militant and exclusive version of Twelver Shiʿism as the official religion of Safavid Persia—a version defined and understood primarily in anti-Sunni terms. The central political power sought a new equilibrium, and much was at stake.

In this context and with the approval (implicit or explicit) of the Safavid kings, some mid-ranking religious scholars seized the opportunity to launch a sustained and public literary attack on Sufism that began in the first half of the seventeenth century and lasted for one hundred years. The outpouring of polemical works began immediately after the anti–Abu Muslim campaign discussed earlier. The attacks against Abu Muslim were mostly limited to the two decades between 1626 and 1649,§ but the anti-Sufi campaign, which

* We are told that Karaki, a Lebanese jurist of the early Safavid times, wrote a treatise called *Mataʿin al-mujrimiyya* that included a refutation of Sufism. The work has not survived, and, as scholars have noted, it is doubtful that it contained anything beyond a refutation of the story of Abu Muslim. We are also told that in the middle of the sixteenth century, Karaki's son wrote a treatise called *ʿUmdat al-maqal* that contained anti-Sunni and anti-Sufi rhetoric. This work has likewise not survived. See Jaʿfariyan, *Safaviyya,* 2:520–21.

† As Von Ess and Böwering have demonstrated, a considerable number of polemical works and acts of persecution against Sufis were written and carried out by Sufis themselves. Thus, many polemics directed against specific Sufi groups were the product of intra-Sufi debates over controversial doctrines and practices. See, for example, Von Ess's "Sufism and Its Opponents," and Böwering's "Early Sufism."

‡ I use the term "campaign" because of the sustained and coordinated nature of these anti-Sufi polemics.

§ This is based on Babayan's estimations. See Babayan, *Mystics, Monarchs, and Messiahs,* 421. For her rationale, see page 158, note 73, of the same work. Newman, however, maintains that two decades of writing polemical works against Abu Muslim picked up steam around the same time, was sustained for a much longer period. Its longevity is indicative of the strength and significance of the target and its deep roots in the society.*

The next section contains a bibliographical summary of anti-Sufi treatises written in Safavid Persia from 1633 to 1733. This is followed by a detailed description and analysis of a select number of works from that list. Most of the treatises chosen for analysis remain in manuscript form and have received little or no scholarly attention prior to this point. My hope is to demonstrate how these works increase our understanding of the religious, political, and intellectual history of this period.

A Bibliography of Anti-Sufi Works (1633–1733)

In my attempt to compile a comprehensive list of anti-Sufi works, I have consulted a number of bibliographical compendia of Shiʿi writings, including Aqa Bozorg's *al-Zariʿa,* Hurr ʿAmili's *Amal al-amil,* and various supplements to it such as Qazvini's *Tatmim.* I have likely missed works that belong to this genre, but I believe the bibliography here is a nearly comprehensive list of anti-Sufi treatises from this period of Safavid Persia. Compiling the list would have been much more difficult had it not been for newly developed digital databases that allowed me to design complex strategies for searching the enormous amount of information contained in the compendia. To that end, I made extensive use of the database software *Tarajim va kitab-shinasi* produced recently by Noor Incorporated in Qum. I encountered two main difficulties in making this list. First, the precise date of many of the works cannot be assigned with confidence. That said, I have done my best to evalu-

began in 1633. See Newman, *Safavid Iran,* 131. This discrepancy can be explained by the fact that Babayan focuses on the beginning of any form of debate on Abu Muslim, which was apparently initiated by Mir Lawhi's oral attacks from the pulpit, while Newman's dating reflects the start of the essay-writing campaign, which, according to information provided by Sayyid Ahmad ʿAlavi's son at the end of the latter's polemical work *Izhar al-haqq,* started a bit later. See Tehrani, *al-Zariʿa,* 4:150–51.

* Interestingly, a similar phenomenon occurred at the same time in Ottoman domains, where a coordinated campaign against Sufis was launched by the middle-class religious scholar and preacher Kadizade Mehmet b. Mustafa (d. 1635), the figurehead of what is known as the Kadizadeli movement. The success of the Safavid anti-Sufi campaign and the eventual failure of the Ottoman one speak to the dramatically different religious and cultural contexts in which the two operated. A comparative historical analysis of the two movements might answer important questions and shed light on some hitherto neglected cultural dynamics shared by both the Safavids and the Ottomans. For more on the Kadizadeli movement, see Zilfi, "The Kadizadelis." Also see Semiramis Cavusoglu, "The Kâdîzâdeli Movement."

ate internal and external evidence and on that basis to establish a time frame in which a given text was likely composed. Second, some of the main anti-Sufi authors had a vested interest in making up titles of nonexistent anti-Sufi works as a campaign strategy to scare their enemies. Therefore, I do not include titles of works that have not survived unless I found corroborating evidence from multiple sources that they in fact existed.*

Works Composed (Approximately) between 1633 and 1650

1. *Risala-yi radd-i sufiyya,*† by Muhammad-Tahir Qummi.

2–4. *Tawzih al-mashrabayn,*‡ *Salvat al-shiʿa,*§ and *Usul fusul al-tawzih,*** all either edited works or abridgements by Mir Lawhi††

5. *Hadiqat al-shiʿa,* anonymous‡‡

* For example, I have left off two oft-mentioned works from the sixteenth century, *al-Mataʿin al-mujrimiyya* by Karaki (written sometime in the first half of the sixteenth century) and *ʿUmdat al-maqal* by his son Shaykh Hasan (finished in 1565), because they have not survived. Moreover, it is not clear that they were written primarily against Sufis. See Jaʿfariyan, *Safaviyya,* 2:512 and 521.

† The surviving manuscripts of this work do not have a title. I refer to it as Qummi's *Radd-i sufiyan,* following the example of Jaʿfariyan *(Safaviyya, 573).* This treatise somehow garnered the attention of Majlisi Sr., who who wrote a gloss refuting its anti-Sufi arguments. Later, in *Tawzih al-mashrabayn,* Mir Lawhi reproduced Qummi's treatise, Majlisi's response, and Qummi's rebuttals to that response, along with his own comments, which are mostly in support of Qummi. More on this to come (see Lawhi, *Kifaya* MS, f. 186b).

‡ Written before 1650; no known manuscripts of this work survive. We can surmise from other reports, however, that it was an edited volume by Mir Lawhi composed of (1) Qummi's *Raddi-i sufiyan,* (2) Majlisi Sr.'s glosses on *Radd-i sufiyan,* (3) Qummi's supra-gloss in response to Majlisi's comments, and (4) Mir Lawhi's own remarks at the end of each chapter evaluating Qummi and Majlisi's arguments and counter-arguments (see Jaʿfariyan, *Safaviyya,* 2:573).

§ Finished in 1650. For a recently edited version, see Lawhi, *"Salvat al-shiʿa,"* 339–59. For some helpful contextual information and analysis, see Jaʿfariyan, *Safaviyya,* 2:559–67.

** This is an abridged version of *Tawzih al-mashrabayn.* Only a single, incomplete manuscript survives. Jaʿfariyan has commented extensively on this manuscript. See Jaʿfariyan, *Safaviyya,* 2:572–75. For a partial English translation see Anzali, "Opposition to Sufism." Given the fact that only a single incomplete copy has survived, Lawhi's assertion in *Kifaya* that, at the time of the writing (1670–1673), there were "thousands of copies" of this work circulating in Isfahan must be hyperbole. See Lawhi, *Kifaya* MS, f. 186b.

†† His full name is said to have been Muhammad b. Muhammad Lawhi Husayni Musavi Sabzavari, but Mostafa Shariʿat has recently produced evidence that "Muhammad" was not the given name of the author, saying that his full name was simply Mir Lawhi Musavi Sabzavari. See Shariʿat, "Introduction," 21–26.

‡‡ Members of the ulama have debated the attribution of *Hadiqa* to the famous early Safavid jurist and religious scholar Ahmad b. Muhammad Ardabili (d. 1585),

Works Composed (Approximately) between 1651 and 1666

1–4. *Munis al-abrar,*[*] *Hikmat al-ʿarifin,*[†] *Fatava zamm al-sufiyya,* and *Tuhfat al-akhyar,*[‡] all by Muhammad-Tahir Qummi

---

otherwise known as Muqaddas Ardabili, from early on. *Hadiqa*'s impact as a foundational source for later anti-Sufi polemics cannot be overemphasized. A great number of anti-Sufi hadiths appear for the first time in this work, and their attribution to Ardabili, a well-known and respected scholar, lent them authenticity and helped ensure that they would be widely circulated. As Babayan has pointed out, *Hadiqa* is also unique in that it is the only substantial refutation of Sufism that begins with an attack on Abu Muslim (see Babayan, *Mystics, Monarchs, and Messiahs,* 421–22). Several studies in recent decades by both Iranian and Western scholars have investigated the problem of *Hadiqa*'s authorship, and modern scholars are unanimous in rejecting its attribution to Ardabili. Some, like Babayan, speculate that Mir Lawhi may have written it, while others, including Daneshpazhuh, identify Qummi as the real author (see Tadayyon, "Hadiqat al-shiʿa," 105–21). Newman offers an extensive argument for the latter position (see Newman, "Sufism and Anti-Sufism," 95–108). Newman's argument is based on the similarity (and sometimes identicality) between *Hadiqa*'s anti-Sufi section and a section of Qummi's *Radd* that enumerates and condemns "heretical" practices of some twenty Sufi groups. I do not find Newman's argument convicing: Given the fact that some early manuscripts of Qummi's *Radd-i sufiyan* do not include the section mentioned, it is questionable whether it was an orginial part of Qummi's treatise at all. In fact, the *Tawzih,* in which Qummi's *Radd* is reproduced as the base, also does not include this section. Furthermore, closer attention to Mir Lawhi's vocabulary and style of writing leads me to believe that, as Babayan suggests, it is more likely that he was the author of this section of *Hadiqa.* He probably added it between 1648 and 1650 to Mulla Muʿizz Ardistani's discussions of Abu Muslim in his *Kashif al-haqq,* which was completed in the Deccan in 1648. Also, keep in mind that the proponents of Sufism at the time specifically accused Mir Lawhi, not Qummi, of writing anti-Sufi works and spreading them under fake names. See Tabib Tunikabuni, *Tabsirat al-muʾminin* MS, fol. 58a.

* A long ode on the virtues of the Household of Muhammad and the vices of Sufism was written before 1664 and dedicated to Shah ʿAbbas II (some parts, especially the polemics against philosophy, are probably later additions, either by Qummi himself or his collaborators). An edition (not critical) was published recently. See Qummi, "Munis al-abrar," 423–37.

† An important work, primarily against mainstream philosophy as well as Sufi metaphysics of Ibn ʿArabi, written in Arabic between 1657 and 1664 for a scholarly audience. For a critical edition of the work with a lengthy introduction that contexualizes the status of philosophy in the late Safavid period see Anzali and Gerami, *Opposition to Philosophy.*

‡ Completed in 1664, this popular anti-Sufi work was written in Persian for a general audience as a commentary on *Munis al-abrar.*

5–7. *Aʿlam al-muhibbin,** *Idra al-ʿaqilin,*† and *Tasliyat al-shiʿa* (an expanded version of *Salvat al-shiʿa*), all by Mir Lawhi
8. *Suqub al-shihab,* anonymous
9. *Shihab al-muʾminin,* anonymous‡
10. *Hidayat al-ʿavam* (also known as *Nasihat al-kiram*), by ʿIsam al-Din Muhammad b. Nizam al-Din§
11. *al-Radd ʿala al-sufiyya,* by Ahmad b. Muhammad Tuni**
12. *al-Siham al-mariqa,* by Shaykh ʿAli b. Muhammad ʿAmili (d. 1692)††

Works Composed (Approximately) between 1667 and 1699

1. *Dirayat al-nisar,* by ʿAlam al-Huda b. Fayz Kashani‡‡
2–3. *Muhibban-i khuda* and *al-Favaʾid al-diniyya,* by Muhammad-Tahir Qummi§§
4. *al-Isna ʿashariyya,* by Hurr ʿAmili
5. *al-Arbaʿin fi mataʿin al-mutasavvifin,* by Mulla Zu al-Faqar***

* No surviving manuscripts. It is mentioned, however, in Isam's *Nasihat al-kiram* and Mir Lawhi's *Kifaya.*

† An incomplete manuscript survives in the Marʿashi Library. For a brief report on the content of the work see Jaʿfariyan, *Safaviyya,* 2:565–67.

‡ Mentioned and extensively quoted in *Nasihat al-kiram.* The author claims to be a student of Mir Damad. Aqa Bozorg mentions Sayyid b. Zayn al-ʿAbidin ʿAmili (the author of *Izhar al-haqq*) as the potential author. See Tehrani, *al-Zariʿa,* 5:9. This is unlikely, however, as Zakeri has demonstrated. Although there is no way to be certain, I agree with Zakeri that the author of this work might be Mir Lawhi himself. See Zakeri, "Akhbari-gari."

§ An important Persian work; a reproduction of *Tuhfat al-akhyar* with an introduction and extensive conclusion in which the author adds valuable historical information about the anti-Sufi campaign. On the basis of internal evidence, most of the work must have been written between 1664 and 1666. Some of the marginalia, however, were added later (1672). More on this later.

** See Hurr ʿAmili, *Amal al-amil,* 2:23, and Khansari, *Rawzat al-jannat,* 4:246.

†† This Arabic work was written at 1664. See ʿAmili, *al-Siham* MS, 60. Also see Tehrani, *al-Zariʿa,* 12:260 and multiple other cross-references related to anti-Sufi literature throughout this work.

‡‡ Finished around 1695; see Tehrani, *al-Zariʿa,* 8:56.

§§ *Muhibban* was dedicated to Shah Sulayman (r. 1666–1694). See Tehrani, *al-Zariʿa,* 16:336, and Jaʿfariyan, *Safaviyya,* 2:569. While we have no concrete date for *al-Favaʾid,* internal evidence indicates that the content was written between 1667 (the beginning of Shah Sulayman's rule) and 1680 (before the death of Fayz Kashani). See Qummi, *al-Favaʾid* MS.

*** For a summary of the content and information on the author, see Jaʿfariyan, *Safaviyya,* 2:580–83.

6. *al-Jamiʿ al-ardabiliyya fi radd al-sufiyya,* by Muhammad ʿAli Shafiʿ Mashhadi*

Works Composed (Approximately) between 1700 and 1733

1. *Radd-i bar sufiyan,* by Razi Qazvini†
2. *Radd-i sufiyya,* by Jadid al-Islam‡
3. *al-Radd ʿala ahl al-shuhud,* by Mulla Muhammad-Saʿid Lahiji§

It is worth noting that nearly all of these works were written in Persian rather than in Arabic, the primary language of religious scholarship. This made the writings more accessible to the Persian-speaking public under Safavid rule, and it reveals the authors' desire to reach a broader audience. The anti-Sufi campaign was not aimed primarily at elite learned circles. Its goal was to change public perceptions of Sufism, thereby creating a hostile environment for the dervishes and Sufis who occupied and controlled public spaces such as bazaars, central squares, and coffeehouses. The most intense period of attack, deduced from the number of works produced, was the period between 1651 and 1666 under the reign of ʿAbbas II (r. 1642–1666). A purely quantitative assessment is somewhat misleading, however, because two prolific polemicists—Muhammad-Tahir Qummi (d. 1689) and Mir Lawhi—were particularly active during this period. Each man penned several refutations, often recycling older material in abridgements or expanded versions or with new glosses. The end of the seventeenth century saw a decline in the number of works written against Sufism, but the number of religious scholars contributing to the campaign actually increased. This is a sign of the success of early attempts spearheaded by Qummi and Mir Lawhi to spread an anti-Sufi agenda. Their efforts to recruit others to their cause induced high-ranking ulama including Hurr ʿAmili (d. 1693) and Mulla Khalil Qazvini (d. 1678) to join the campaign. Given their importance, a few words about Mir Lawhi and Qummi are in order.

Mir Lawhi, the Preacher

According to his own statements, Mir Lawhi (d. after 1671) was trained in Isfahan under the most prominent scholars of the period, Shaykh Bahaʾi and Mir Damad (d. 1631).** A mid-ranking mulla, Mir Lawhi had little taste for

* See Tehrani, *al-Zariʿa,* 21:354.
† Jaʿfariyan, *Safaviyya,* 2:579.
‡ See Jaʿfariyan, *Safaviyya,* 2:600–605. The full text of Jadid al-Islam's treatise has also been reproduced in this work: 2:659–97.
§ Tehrani, *al-Zariʿa,* 10:187.
** He refers to both as his teachers in several places in *Kifaya.*

scholarship. His puritan spirit, however, was unwavering, and he had immense aptitude for preaching that mobilized his audience in extraordinary ways. He represents what I call the populist front of the attacks on Sufism, and his sway with the public greatly impressed the French traveler John Chardin (d. 1713), who had this to say about an incident he witnessed firsthand:

> In the year 1645, at the corner of an old tomb, they found a marble slab inscribed with the name of Shaykh Abu al-Futuh. Everyone presumed that it was the epitaph of the famous Shaykh Abu al-Futuh Razi, the author of the famous commentary on the Qur'an in Persian. He was a saint in their eyes, and they soon built a mosque there and a tomb within it, which the people adorned with their offerings and other devotions. But all this devotion soon came to an end, for at the same time there was a famous mulla called Mir Lawhi, a popular preacher in the country whom I met and who often preached in open spaces. He began to prove with traditions and passages of history that the real Shaykh Abu al-Futuh had been buried in the small town of Rayshahr, and that this Abu al-Futuh was a Turkish Sunni and a great enemy of the Imams. He persuaded the people of this, and one day after hearing him preach, two thousand of them went to the mosque and tomb and plundered and razed the building. I later saw that the place had been reduced to a public latrine. This demonstrates how far the Muslim clergy remain from the prudence and authority of the Roman church, which is careful not to permit examination of the subjects it presents to people for worship and veneration.*

Mir Lawhi's attacks from the pulpit were largely responsible for starting the heated debate on Abu Muslim in both public spaces and learned circles. His extending his criticism to Sufism had even greater repercussions. He faced significant opposition and came under increasing pressure, even receiving threats to his life.† After his initial attacks, mounting harassment

* Chardin, *Safarnama,* 4:1519–20. For the French original, see Chardin, *Voyages,* 8:20–21. This was in fact a popular shrine complex that contained the tomb of Abu Nuʿaym Isfahani (d. 1038), the famous author of the classic hagiography of Sufi saints *Hilyat al-awliya,* as well as Abu al-Futuh ʿIjli Isfahani (d. 1204), a Shafiʿi jurist, among others. It is worth noting that Majlisi Sr. considered the former among his maternal ancestors. Mir Lawhi's enmity toward Majlisi, then, might have played some role in his incitements. See Mahdavi, *Zindagi-nama-yi ʿallama majlisi,* 1:150.

† Lawhi, "Salvat al-shiʿa," 354–56. See also Jaʿfariyan, *Miras,* 2:269 and 274–77, and Lawhi, *Kifaya* MS, f. 9b.

from the Sufi camp forced Mir Lawhi to keep a low profile for a time, and for two decades he published his anti-Sufi rhetoric pseudonymously. The mood of the time is reflected vividly in one of his own treatises, *Salvat al-shiʿa,* which was written under the pen name Muhammad b. Mutahhar al-Miqdadi. Here, in a reference to an anonymous sayyid (himself), he says "they [Sufi sympathizers] forged so many lies against him. . . . Every single day they would make one of their followers famous as one cursed [*malʿun*] by him.* Thus, from the end of the year 1050 [1640–1641] to the present time, which is the middle of 1060 [1650–1651], in order to avoid any trouble and keep them quiet, he [Mir Lawhi] has not added the epithet 'cursed' [*laʿin*] even when mentioning Satan's name. He has not cursed Yazid, Muʿaviya, or Banu-Umayya, so careful is he that no one should hear the term 'curse' from him."†

The strong reaction of Sufi-minded people should come as no surprise. Granted, by the time anti-Sufi rhetoric accelerated, the power of the Qizilbash in the Safavid court had waned, and the Sufi ethos of a dynasty that positioned the shah as the murshid-i kamil had become, for the most part, a hollow legacy rather than a meaningful and practiced reality. But Safavid legitimacy was still tied to a past replete with Sufi symbols that could not quickly be forgotten. The memory of the founding fathers of the Safavid dynasty, men like Safi al-Din Ardabili, Shaykh Junayd, Shaykh Haydar, and Shah Ismaʿil, still inspired public imagination. In the face of this legacy, attacks on Sufism could easily be seen or portrayed as an attack on the roots of the Safavid dynasty. Many high-ranking ulama had favorable views towards Sufism. Even those who had intellectual objections to Sufism were affiliated with the court or had other connections that made activities like those of Mir Lawhi too politically risky to entertain. For the time being, the minority of ulama who had objections found it more prudent to spend their time consolidating their power in the court or working toward the academic credentials necessary to join the ranks of the elite.

Even at the peak of anti-Sufi polemics in the second half of ʿAbbas II's reign, Sufism in both its popular and its elite forms still had a vibrant and strong social presence.‡ Fierce debate on the issue broke out not only in the

* That is, they would spread the rumor that Mir Lawhi had cursed someone, and that person would immediately become popular among the Sufi-minded people.

† Lawhi, "Salvat al-shiʿa," 356. In perfect harmony with this account, Najib al-Din Zargar, who later assumed the role of pole in the Zahabiyya Sufi network, wrote of an "ignorant" mulla nicknamed "Mulla Laʿnati" (the cursing mulla) for his unrelenting insistence on cursing prominent Sufis in public. See Tabrizi Isfahani, *Sabʿ al-masani,* 362.

‡ There were at least twenty-one active khanaqahs in Isfahan alone during Shah Sulayman's reign (1668–1694). See Mahdavi, *Zindagi-nama-yi ʿallama majlisi,* 201–2.

capital but also in other major urban centers such as Mashhad.* ʿAbbas II, who was sympathetic to the Sufis, was disturbed by the fact that some dared to publicly denounce the heritage upon which the Safavid dynasty based its legitimacy, and he threatened to physically punish and cancel the stipend of people involved in the campaign.† In an additional gesture of explicit support for Sufis, in 1660 he ordered a Sufi center to be built on the banks of the Zayanda River.‡ The center was called Takiya-yi Fayz after the Sufi-minded religious scholar Mulla Muhsin Fayz Kashani (d. 1680).

Sufis were not the most dangerous targets for passionate puritan preachers like Mir Lawhi and religious scholars like Qummi. Far more hazardous was taking a stand against some of the most prominent, politically well-connected, and charismatic religious scholars of the time. These included Shaykh Bahaʾi, Majlisi Sr., and (later) Fayz Kashani. Shaykh Bahaʾi was a celebrated polymath and one of the most significant religious scholars in Iranian popular imagination, but to his foes his faults were legion. He is said to have enjoyed the company of dervishes and Sufis, and his works, such as *Arbaʿin* and *Kashkul,* contain strong mystical overtones. There are even tales that he traveled around in a Sufi cloak.§ Criticizing him was risky, but the fact that he was deceased gave his detractors a measure of safety when it came to portraying him to the public in a negative light. By contrast, taking on the likes of Majlisi Sr. and Fayz, whose syncretistic religious outlook the puritans abhorred, portended a long, nasty fight among the ulama over who would get to define orthodoxy.

Muhammad-Tahir Qummi

Mir Lawhi was neither the only nor the most erudite member of the ulama to object to Majlisi Sr.'s popularity, strong connection to the court, and mode of piety.** In fact, while Mir Lawhi was the populist face of the anti-Sufi front, the intellectual force driving the anti-Sufi campaign in the second half of the seventeenth century was another figure—Mulla Muhammad-Tahir Qummi (d. 1689).

* See Najib's report of this debate in Mashhad in Tabrizi Isfahani, *Sabʿ al-masani,* 360–66. Relevant pages from a manuscript I accessed have also been consulted for the sake of accuracy. In this case, see Tabrizi Isfahani, *Sabʿ al-masani* MS, f. 328a–334a.

† Tabrizi Isfahani, *Sabʿ al-masani,* 365.

‡ Qazvini, *ʿAbbas-nama,* 256.

§ For more about Shaykh Bahaʾi's mystical tendencies see Lewisohn, "Sufism and the School of Iṣfahān," 88–89.

** For a more detailed analysis of Qummi's works see Anzali and Gerami, *Opposition to Philosophy,* 1–46.

Qummi was born to an ordinary family in the province of Fars sometime in the early seventeenth century. For reasons the passage of time has obscured, his family moved to the shrine city of Najaf in present Iraq when he was very young. We know little about this important period of his life, but some years later, around 1638, Qummi fled Najaf for Iran, fearing the repercussions of the imminent Ottoman takeover of Iraq.* As an intellectual figure, Qummi is perhaps best categorized as a theologian (*mutakallim*) and a hadith scholar with Akhbari leanings. He became a prolific writer after he settled in Qum.† His writings demonstrate both his erudition as a scholar and his passion for defending the teachings of the twelve imams, as he understood them. Qummi's earliest treatises, written in the first decade of his residence in Qum, contain no polemics against Sufism or signs that their author was concerned with this issue.‡ Instead, these writings are focused mainly on classical theological problems such as divine attributes, predetermination, and sectarian apologetics. As might be expected given the subject matter, Sunni theologians and philosophers bear the brunt of Qummi's criticism in these early pieces.§ Notably, Qummi expressed astonishment and dismay that his prominent contemporary, the Shiʿi philosopher Mir Damad, followed the "unorthodox" beliefs of earlier figures like Avicenna on the issue of free will. Nonetheless, Qummi did not attack Mir Damad directly.**

Indirect criticism of his contemporaries evolved into a full-blown ideological war as Qummi rose to prominence and became one of the most influential religious scholars of his time. His rapid rise was evidence of his exceptional talent for navigating the sociopolitical landscape of Safavid Persia. Like many other ulama of the time, he sought to establish close links with the Safavid court, and he was extraordinarily successful in doing so. He was initially appointed as the Friday prayer leader of Qum, and, by the time Shah Sulayman claimed the throne, he had risen to the position of judge and *shaykh al-islam*, the highest religious office in a major shrine-city.††

* See Tehrani, *Tabaqat*, 8:303. For a fairly detailed account of his life and works see Goli-Zavare, *Sitaragan-i haram*, 14:132–74.

† For a fairly comprehensive list of works attributed to Qummi available, see Dargahi and Taromi, "Pishguftar."

‡ In their earliest editions, neither *Safinat al-najat* (written in 1643) nor *Bahjat al-darayn* (written in 1645), both among the earliest datable treatises written by Qummi, included noticeable polemical reference to Sufism. Some anti-Sufi polemics were incorporated into later manuscripts of *Safinat al-najat*. The published edition is based on these later manuscripts.

§ For example, see Qummi, *Bahjat al-darayn* MS.

** See, for example, Qummi, *Bahjat al-darayn* MS, f. 9b–10a.

†† For a detailed account and analysis of Qummi's life and works see Anzali and Gerami, *Opposition to Philosophy*, 1–46.

As mentioned earlier, Qummi's scholarly nature contrasted sharply with the populist stance that earned Mir Lawhi the title of "*Lawhi ma'raka-gir*" among his detractors,* and the former's initial foray into the fight against Sufis appears to have been a reluctant one. The story of Qummi's entrance into the dispute is recorded by none other than Mir Lawhi, who tells us that, as a young, mid-ranking religious scholar (that is, sometime around 1650), Qummi wrote a short treatise against Sufis known to us as *Radd-i sufiyya*. According to Lawhi, Qummi had no intention of distributing the treatise widely. A certain disciple of Hallaj (d. 922) called ʿAli Beg, however, reputedly "stole" Qummi's *Radd* and circulated it among the ulama in Isfahan in order to provoke them against the author. When the work came to the attention of Majlisi Sr., it set off a high-profile controversy. Majlisi Sr. took it upon himself to write a gloss refuting its assertions,† and Qummi, in turn, wrote rebuttals. The original treatise, Majlisi's glosses, and Qummi's supra-gloss were then combined by Mir Lawhi in a treatise titled *Tawzih al-mashrabayn va tanqih al-mazhabayn* (*An Explanation of the Two Paths and Examination of the Two Schools*), which contained Lawhi's own judgments (*muhakamat*) at the end of each chapter.‡

While he may have been dragged reluctantly into the initial debate with his teacher, it is clear that Qummi came to embrace the role of polemicist. He went on to write numerous treatises that outlined the heretical views of Sufis such as Hallaj and Ibn ʿArabi and functioned as the intellectual underpinning of the anti-Sufi campaign. At the beginning, however, Qummi was on the defensive; the anti-Sufi campaign was in its nascent stage, and pro-Sufi forces still had a tremendous amount of social and political capital. This

* Tabib Tunikabuni, *Tabsirat al-mu'minin* MS, fol. 58a. The author was a Sufi and the personal physician of the Safavid king. *Maʿrakah-gir* was a common epithet used in this period to refer to public performers and entertainers, including storytellers, eulogizers of the imams, jugglers, athletes, and so on. Mir Lawhi was apparently given this title because of the populist and passionate nature of his lectures from the pulpit. For more on this epithet see Zabihollah Safa, "Dastan-guzari," 466.

† Lawhi, *Kifaya* MS, f. 187a. The unlikelihood of a junior religious scholar like Qummi engaging in a direct dispute with a senior teacher is part of Aqa Bozorg's argument against ascribing the marginalia to Majlisi Sr. See Tehrani, *al-Zariʿa*, 4:497. Mir Lawhi's explanation, however, makes it clear that Qummi did not initially intend to directly challenge a senior and highly respected scholar. There is no reason, therefore, to doubt the authenticity of the ascription.

‡ Later, Mir Lawhi compiled a shorter version that left out his own analyses. This abridged version is titled *A Summary of the Explanation (Mukhtasar al-tawzih) or Essential Portions of the Explanation (Usul fusul al-tawzih)*, the chapters of which have only three sections. Only this version of the work survives. For excerpts from this fascinating debate in English, see Anzali, "Opposition to Sufism."

is clearly reflected in how Qummi responded to Majlisi Sr.'s criticisms in the abridged version of *Tawzih al-mashrabayn.* Qummi went out of his way, for example, to reject Majlisi Sr.'s accusation that, as an anti-Sufi, he (Qummi) must be opposed to a spiritual journey based on love and desire. Qummi's words on the subject are revealing and deserve to be quoted at length:

> [I]t is fitting for me to outline my views on love [*mahabbat*] and desire [*shawq*], which are necessary for the folk of ʿirfan, so that my reason for writing the treatise is made clear to the respected cleric.
>
> Let it be clear that what I believe, and what is evident from the teachings of the Prophetic Household, is that God's servants worship him in three ways. Some worship Him in order to attain paradise, which is the worship of a hired laborer. Others worship Him fearing hellfire, which is the worship of slaves. Still others worship Him out of love and desire, which is the worship of free men.* The path of the ʿarifs and those close to God, and the goal of the wise and sagacious in their mortifications and struggles, is to reach this path . . . only those who have followed the Prophetic Household, those guides on the path of love, have reached the final destination. . . .
>
> This humble servant has gathered many hadith reported by the Prophetic Household on the topic of love and desire. Some time ago, I began compiling a treatise on the subject, which I have titled *Maqamat al-muhibbin,* and which I hope to have the good fortune of completing. However, the pietists [*ʿabidan*] and practitioners of mortification among the Sunnis who oppose the Prophetic Household have issued misguided personal opinions [*ijtihadat*] and reveled in corrupt fantasies as they traverse the valley of divine love, adding misguidedness to deviance, and creating innovations on the path of obedience.
>
> . . . In the treatise, I mentioned signs of Sunni practitioners of mortification who follow Hallaj and Bayazid. Among the signs that I did not mention is that [members of] this group call themselves *ʿashiq* [literally, lover] and attribute *ʿishq* [literally, love] to God Almighty. The [members of] the Household of the Prophet, may God bless him and his descendants, who are the guides on the path of love, have avoided using this term in their supplications and hadith because it is the name of a melancholic illness [*sawdavi*]. Rather, they are content to use the terms *mahabbat* [literally, love] and *shawq* [literally, desire], and their followers do the same. The path of love and desire that this humble servant has chosen is the path of the perfect ʿarif Shaykh Safi [al-Din Ardabili], as

* For one version of this hadith see Kulayni, *Kafi,* 1:84.

> well as that of Shaykh Varram b. Abu Furas, Ibn Tawus, Ahmad b. Fahd Hilli, Mulla Ahmad Ardabili, and other Shiʿi ʿarifs, may God bless them. It should be clear from what I have said that my aim in writing this treatise is not to reject love and desire [for God] as the respected cleric [Majlisi Sr.] has supposed, unleashing words of derision upon me.*

In this rebuttal, Qummi rejects out of hand the notion that he is a rigid literalist theologian who knows nothing about divine love and intimacy, an image often (and perhaps unfairly) associated with people who are opposed to Sufism even today.† Qummi's emphasis on the concept of mahabbat in contrast to ʿishq is a perfect example of the semantic strategy he used to challenge Sufi discourse.‡ His quotation of the famous hadith in the section quoted is an acknowledgment that there is a hierarchy in modes of worship and that the highest forms of worship are possible only if they are performed the sake of God and out of the worshipper's intense desire for Him. At the same time, Qummi objected to the use of the term *ʿishq,* which is absent from the Shiʿi canon, to describe this mode of worship. He argued that in its stead, terms such as *mahabbat,* which are actually found in the Qur'an, should be used. Qummi's objection was not merely a matter of semantics. His brief attacks on the "Sunni followers of Hallaj and Bayazid" make clear his belief that those followers have neglected the teachings of the imams, relying instead on their "misguided" personal opinions to formulate the concept of ʿishq. Qummi refuted the concept not only because the word *ʿishq* was not a part of the vocabulary of the Qur'an or reports of the imams but because

* *Usul fusul al-tawzih,* quoted from Jaʿfariyan, *Safaviyya,* 2:607–9.

† In fact, Qummi's writings, prose and poetry, demonstrate an intense desire to cultivate an inner life with the ultimate aim of subduing the carnal soul and attaining eternal salvation in proximity to God. His many quatrains, for example, express Qummi's desire to be subsumed in divine love play a crucial role in countering this image. They are a challenge to the hegemony of Sufi love poetry and an assertion that Sufis and Sufi-minded ulama do not have sole ownership over the concept of love. (For some of his quatrians with this theme see Qummi, *Safinat al-najat,* 111–12 and 134–44.) The ideals and practices entailed in his introspective mode of piety bear a greater resemblance to those of the *zuhhad* (renunciants) in the early centuries of the development of Islam than they do to later, more explicitly Sufi modes of piety (see, for example, his *Muʿalajat al-nafs, Mubahasat al-nafs,* and *Tanbih al-raqidin,* all published in Qummi, *Shish risala,* and Qummi, *Safinat al-najat,* 125–33). The piety of the *zuhhad* was marked by an extraordinary obsession with subduing the carnal soul, lack of attachment to worldly pleasures, a constant reminder of the proximity of death, and the fear of eternal damnation in hellfire (for more on the early renunciants see Karamustafa, *Sufism: The Formative Period,* 1–7).

‡ For another example of this strategy, see his definition of the concept of *hikma,* discussed in chapter 3, see pages 122–25 and 134–35.

it was part of a discourse that was not—for Qummi—sufficiently informed by the "authentic" Twelver canon. In Qummi's writings, the concept of love (mahabbat) is invoked primarily in reference to the Shiʿi notion of tavalla, or loving the imams. This love is expressed through devotional practices such as visiting their shrines, recounting their virtues, eulogizing their deaths, and cursing their enemies. At its essence, tavalla is total obedience to the will of the imams as expressed in their hadiths and interpreted by the righteous ulama. For Qummi, it was impossible to talk about loving God without first loving his most beloved creatures, the imams, and expressing that love through action. The term *ʿishq* is part and parcel of the larger discourse of Sufism that is based on epistemological and theological assumptions that are at odds with Qummi's espoused version of Shiʿism. This is why Qummi was so adamant about replacing such terms—and their entire discursive register—with "indigenous" terms of the Shiʿi canon, such as *mahabbat,* that are already present in what he saw as canonical, orthodox Shiʿi discourse.

Finally, and more important, Qummi's use of the terms *ʿirfan* and *ʿarif* in the passage and in some of his quatrains that I discuss elsewhere is an example of the same semantic trend.* My research leads me to make the significant claim that this is one of the earliest instances in Safavid literature in which the concept of ʿirfan was used in contrast to the term *Sufism,* though I stop short of asserting that the use of this term in this sense originated with Qummi. In contrast to the writings of Sufi-minded scholars, Qummi did not pursue the contrast between ʿirfan and Sufism except in passing. It seems likely to me, however, that Sufi-minded, Akhbari-leaning scholars such as Qutb al-Din Nayrizi and perhaps Fayz Kashani were influenced by Qummi's polemics as they began to use the concept of ʿirfan as the semantic center of a more explicitly Shiʿi mode of Sufi thought. Qummi's reference to foundational figures of Safavid Shiʿism such as Shaykh Safi al-Din Ardabili, Hilli, and Tusi as ʿarifs was crucial to this development. His conceptualization of these foundational figures as exemplars of ʿirfan was adopted and expanded on by Sufi-minded ulama who played a crucial role in the Safavid domestication of Sufi thought. This was a significant step toward establishing an imagined community of like-minded, well-respected Shiʿi luminaries of the past who presumably all believed in ʿirfan.

Qummi's semantic choices helped construct an alternative regime of truth in which the infallible imam takes the place of God as the primary subject of maʿrifa, or knowledge of God. For example, in *Hikmat al-ʿarifin,* one of Qummi's most important works, the foundational *qudsi* hadith ("he who knows himself, knows his Lord") ubiquitous in Sufi literature is replaced by

* See Anzali and Gerami, *Opposition to Philosophy,* 26–9.

an exclusively Shiʿi hadith on the imamate: "One who dies not knowing his imam has died a *jahili* death [that is, as a non-Muslim]."* The importance of this shift in focus cannot be overemphasized,† and it was at the heart of a broader epistemic shift in seventeenth-century Safavid Persia that forced proponents of-long established traditions of knowledge, including philosophy, Usuli jurisprudence, and Sufism, to formulate new intellectual and social ways of legitimizing their discourse. Akhbari scholars such as Qummi were on the offensive, criticizing the extensive connections between these traditions of knowledge and old regimes of truth.‡ Given this dynamic, it should not surprise us that the Sufi-minded scholars discussed herein adopted the semantics of their nemesis and began to use the term *ʿirfan* as the signifier of a newly imagined discourse on spirituality.

Qummi's Attacks on Philosophy

As Qummi became more famous and forged closer connections to the Safavid court, he expanded his attacks beyond Sufism to other disciplines "tainted" by Sufi ideas, most notably the tradition of Islamic philosophy as represented in the teachings of Mulla Sadra. This led to a curious turn of events in which the author of the earliest anti-Sufi treatise himself became the target of anti-Sufis. In his writings, Qummi expressed surprise that "some among his contemporaries" were trying to synthesize philosophy and Sufism (a clear reference to the school of Mulla Sadra), given the fact that Sufis had abhorred and ridiculed the philosophical quest from the earliest centuries of Islam.§ He quoted and criticized Sadra's understanding of the concept and reality of existence (*vujud*) in the penultimate chapter of *Hikmat al-ʿarifin*, connecting it seamlessly to a critique of Ibn ʿArabi and the idea of Oneness of Being in the final chapter.**

As a highly technical Arabic work, *Hikmat* was meant for an elite audience. Beginning around 1669, however, Qummi supplemented his antiphilosophy polemics with two more accessible works in Persian, namely *al-Favaʾid al-diniyya* and *Tuhfat al-akhyar*. The latter is a popular work, primarily a critique of Sufism, with a final chapter, most probably added later, targeting philosophers. The former was written during the reign of Shah Sulayman (r. 1666–1694) in a question-and-answer format, and its content sheds light on the context of the antiphilosophy discourse of that era. One question

* Qummi, *Hikmat al-ʿarifin* MS, 4–5.

† See Lawson, "Hidden Words," 430, note 13.

‡ I take up this important issue in more detail at the end of chapter 3.

§ Lawson, "Hidden Words," 229.

** For a more extensive discussion see Anzali and Gerami, *Opposition to Philosophy*, 33–43.

Qummi answers is why, if philosophical ideas are so dangerous and heretical, none of the ulama bothered to declare philosophers infidels. This question reveals the author's concern with the lack of precedence for attacking philosophy. Qummi appears to have found no examples of contemporary religious scholars writing refutations of philosophy, for he resorted to mentioning Ghazali's famous critique of philosophy. This is particularly remarkable given the fact that as a Sufi and a Sunni, Ghazali was widely criticized by Qummi and other polemicists, including Shaykh ʿAli ʿAmili.* Despite this, Qummi adopted and summarized the arguments and opinions against philosophy reflected in Ghazali's *al-Munqiz* and *al-Tahafat*.† Qummi's antiphilosophy treatises are significant because they represent the first serious attempt by a high-ranking religious scholar to take opposition to philosophy beyond intellectual circles to a more general audience. Contemporary reports indicate that popular preachers began to condemn philosophy as a foreign discipline and a heresy around the same time.‡ This brings us to the final treatise I analyze in this chapter, a Persian work that combines anti-Sufi and antiphilosophy polemics and contains interesting information about the intellectual milieu of the time.

Nasihat al-kiram

Nasihat al-kiram va fazihat al-liʾam, alternatively known as *Hidayat al-ʿavam va fazihat al-liʾam,*§ is a unique and unstudied treatise written between 1664 and 1670 by Muhammad b. Nizam al-Din ʿIsam (d. after 1670).** The work has largely been neglected by scholars except for a brief but valuable report by Jaʿfariyan, who examined an incomplete manuscript at the Marʿashi Library

* At one point, he calls Ghazali "the head of the enemies of the family of the Prophet." See ʿAmili, *al-Siham al-mariqa* MS, f. 8a.

† Qummi, *al-Favaʾid* MS, 724–28.

‡ Muhammad-Baqir Sabzavari, the appointed *shaykh al-islam* of Isfahan after Majlisi Jr., expressed his concern over preachers who present an image of philosophy to the public that is totally opposed to Islamic teachings. See Sabzavari, *Rawzat al-anvar-i ʿabbasi,* 599–602. Quoted in Jaʿfariyan, *Safaviyya,* 2:532. The two tracts mentioned earlier in this chapter, *Shihab al-muʾminin* and *Suqub al-shihab,* are part of this novel polemical development.

§ Tehrani, *al-Zariʿa,* 24:182.

** My dating is based on two observations. First, the marginalia on folio 128b (apparently added later, probably by the copier of the manuscript) was written to announce and thank God (!) for the death of Muʾazzin in 1671–1672, which clearly signifies that the main body of the text was written before Muʾazzin's death. See ʿIsam, *Nasiha* MS, f. 128b. Second, the reference to *Nasiha* in Mir Lawhi's *Kifaya* is immediately followed by an explicit reference to the year 1671–1672. See Lawhi, *Kifaya* MS, f. 11b.

in Qum.* We know nothing about the author from bibliographical sources,† and no other work written by him seems to exist. This lack of information is the primary reason behind some scholars' conjecture that the author's name is a pseudonym for Qummi.‡ In my view, however, such assertions are based on an incomplete reading of the text.§

Nasihat al-kiram is a reproduction of Qummi's *Tuhfat al-akhyar,* to which ʿIsam added a lengthy and important epilogue containing critical information about the anti-Sufi campaign, an overview of the debate on Sufism and philosophy, and extensive quotes from polemical works against Sufis and philosophers. ʿIsam sets the stage for his critical attacks by categorizing his targets into two groups: philosophers (*falasafa*) and innovators (*mubtadiʿa*). The second group, he explains, includes Sufis and all other kinds of heretics, including Nuqtavis and members of other movements that he views as intimately connected to Sufism. In calling the Sufis innovators, he was simply

* Jaʿfariyan, *Safaviyya,* 2:570–72. Unfortunately, Jaʿfariyan's report does not cover the most important part of the manuscript, its lengthy epilogue. This is apparently a result of the fact that the copy he consulted is missing a substantial part of the epilogue. In the Majlis copy, the epilogue begins at folio 112b. The Marʿashi copy, according to the information provided by the cataloguer, ends abruptly at a place that corresponds to folio 120b of my copy (Hoseyni, *Fihrist,* 5:154–56). The Majlis copy's prologue continues to folio 144b.

† The one scant piece of biographical information comes from the epilogue, in which the author identifies Shaykh ʿAbdullah Shushtari and Shaykh Bahaʾi as masters of his masters.ʿIsam, *Nasiha* MS, f. 141b and 120a.

‡ See Jaʿfariyan, *Safaviyya,* 2:570–71. According to Jaʿfariyan, the real author must be Qummi, whom he believes wrote under a pseudonym as a safety measure.

§ First, it is not clear why Qummi would write anti-Sufi treatises under his real name, sending one of them (*Munis al-abrar*) to the Safavid monarch, and then suddenly decide to hide behind a pseudonym. As far as we know, in terms of scholarly fame and respect as well as his relationship with the royal court, Qummi's star was rising rapidly at this time. Indeed, he would soon be appointed the chief judge of Qum and the Friday prayer leader of the city. Furthermore, in the epilogue of *Nasihat al-kiram,* to which Jaʿfariyan apparently did not have access, the author of this work explicitly acknowledges that the twelve chapters of the book are copied from another work, that is, Qummi's *Tuhfat al-akhyar.* Throughout the chapters, there are instances in which ʿIsam adds a couple of lines or paragraphs, making a clear distinction between his voice and the voice of Qummi by adding "va ʿIsam guyad . . ." ("and ʿIsam says . . ."). See, for example, ʿIsam, *Nasiha* MS, f. 3a, 15a. In addition to these points, the author explicitly references his differences of opinion with the author of *Tuhfat al-akhyar* in the epilogue, saying, "know . . . that many conversations crossed the mind of this humble [man], whose name is Muhammad and who is known as ʿIsam, throughout the previous twelve chapters, but I held my tongue so that absolutely nothing is added to the statements of the author of the book on those subjects, and they are left untouched." See ʿIsam, *Nasiha* MS, f. 113a.

following in Qummi's footsteps; in *Tuhfat al-akhyar,* this designation is used many times in reference to "the followers of Hallaj and Bayazid."*

The author of *Nasiha* gives us unique insight into the dynamics of the anti-Sufi campaign. First, his work clears up confusion about the authorship of a number of polemical works of this period.† ʿIsam also provides us with the most detailed picture of how the anti-Sufi camp viewed the activities of Mu'azzin and other active Sufis. Although the basic framework of his narrative is similar to that of *Kifayat al-muhtadi,* ʿIsam adds detail to Mir Lawhi's account.‡ More important, he provides us with brief descriptions and sometimes extensive quotes from polemical works against Sufism that would otherwise have been completely lost. Among these are two works written by an anonymous Sayyid, probably Mir Lawhi himself,whom ʿIsam describes as "one of the renowned men of knowledge and exalted sayyids of the time, whose erudition and knowledge are matched by no one known to me in our age."§ ʿIsam goes on to recount two of this anonymous Sayyid's works written against Sufis and philosophers: *Shihab al-mu'minin fi rajm al-shayatin al-*

* Qummi, *Tuhfat al-akhyar. bidʿa,* normally translated as "innovation," is a common term used in reference to beliefs and practices that contradict conceptions of orthodoxy. Qummi seemed to be particularly fond of the term, which he used extensively in his criticism of Sufism. Both *Nasihat al-kiram* and *Kifayat al-muhtadi* refer us, on several occasions, to another polemical work called *Fazayih al-mubtadiʿa.* Although the author of the latter is not named, it is not unlikely that the work was authored by Qummi.

† He explicitly states, for example, that works like *Tasliyat al-shiʿa* and its abbreviated form, *Salvat al-shiʿa,* were written by a certain sayyid (Mir Lawhi) who, out of concern for his own safety, wrote under the pseudonym Mutahhar b. Muhammad Miqdadi. See ʿIsam, *Nasiha* MS, f. 121a–121b. While Jaʿfariyan was not aware of this explicit statement, he came to the same conclusion on the basis of other evidence. See Jaʿfariyan, *Safaviyya,* 2:559–60. ʿIsam also mentions that the same author, Mir Lawhi, is responsible for two other polemics against Sufism, *Tawzih al-mashrabayn* and *Aʿlam al-muhibbin.* See ʿIsam, *Nasiha* MS, f. 124a–124b.

‡ ʿIsam, *Nasiha* MS, f. 126a– 129a. Mir Lawhi actually refers to *Nasiha* for further information about Muʿazzin. Mir Lawhi, *Kifaya* MS, f. 11b.

§ ʿIsam, *Nasiha* MS, f. 114b. The quotation extends from f. 115a to f. 121a. In one of the excerpts quoted from his works, this anonymous sayyid claims to be a student of (among others) Mir Damad, whom he calls *ustaz al-kull,* or "the universal teacher," and whose anti-Sufi stance he references. ʿIsam, *Nasiha* MS, f. 120a. Aqa Bozorg speculates that this particular sayyid could be only Sayyid Ahmad al-ʿAlavi (d. after 1644), the prominent philosopher student of Mir Damad. See Tehrani, *al-Zariʿa,* 5:8. This does not seem to be supported by the content of *Suqub* that is quoted here, for the author of *Suqub* is unapologetically and vehemently against philosophy. Also, ʿIsam demonstrates his explicit approval of Sayyid Ahmad's work later, in his discussion of *ghina,* or illicit music, feeling no need to conceal his identity. See ʿIsam, *Nasiha* MS, f. 134b.

mubtadiʿin and *Suqub al-shihab fi rajm al-murtab.* The former has not survived in any form, and the only part of the latter that exists is an extensive passage from its introduction that is quoted in *Nasiha.* In this passage, the anonymous sayyid mentions that he wrote *Suqub* because he noticed that lay people were being led astray by the lure of Sufi music and dance. He notes that *Shihab al-muʾminin,* his other work refuting innovators and philosophers, was too laden with technical vocabulary to be suitable for a general audience.*

Perhaps the most important features of *Nasiha* are its coupling of philosophy and Sufism in its attacks and its focus on (nonsurviving) treatises that, according to the author, were written against both philosophy and Sufism. The closing section of the epilogue is quite revealing in this respect. Most of the extant anti-Sufi treatises from this period are relatively unconcerned with philosophy. They mention it, if at all, in passing remarks or brief chapters that are dwarfed in length by the anti-Sufi material. *Tuhfat al-akhyar,* the work reproduced in *Nasiha,* is an apt example; philosophers are targeted only in its last chapter, which evidence suggests it was added later to the book.† It appears that by adding the epilogue, the author of *Nasiha* wanted to expand his critique to cover philosophy in more detail alongside Sufism. Accordingly, he builds upon Qummi's critique of philosophers by devoting the first few pages of the epilogue to an extensive quote from *Suqub* that contains a strong rebuttal of philosophy. He follows the quotation with the usual anti-Sufi rhetoric and then returns to philosophy as his primary target.‡ This closing section offers several quotes from Safavid luminaries including Shaykh Bahaʾi, Fayz Kashani, and Majlisi Jr. in condemnation of the study of philosophy.§

ʿIsam maintains that philosophy and Sufism are inextricably linked, asserting that "the masters of Sufism and the apostates [*mulhidin*] have been

* ʿIsam, *Nasiha* MS, f. 117b.

† This chapter is also curiously missing from the print version of *Tuhfat al-akhyar.*

‡ In the part specifically dedicated to attacks against Sufism, several figures are explicitly named. Among them is a certain Mir Taqi Sudani, who is said to have been a student of Mahmud Pisikhani, the leader of the Nuqtavi movement. According to the author, the former was declared an infidel by Shaykh ʿAli-Naqi Kamaraʾi, a judge from Shiraz who was promoted as the *shaykh al-islam* of Isfahan during the reign of Shah ʿAbbas II. One Sufi Nawruz is also said to have been murdered in Shiraz after being declared an infidel (ʿIsam, *Nasiha* MS, f. 119a). Other Sufi names include Mir ʿAskari Rikhtagar, Husayn Rikhtagar, and ʿAbdullah Mutajannin. The last of these also looms large in Mir Lawhi's rhetoric in *Kifayat al-muhtadi.* It is unlikely, however, that this was his real name. Rather, Mutajannin appears to be a derogatory epithet that Mir Lawhi has chosen to describe this ʿAbudullah as a lunatic. Unfortunately, I was unable to identify these figures from other sources.

§ ʿIsam, *Nasiha* MS, f. 133a–139a.

often philosophy-minded."* This position is a reflection of how influential Qummi's critique of philosophy and his focus on Mulla Sadra and his students in *Hikmat al-ʿarifin* was. He also complains that philosophy has defiled and led astray many madrasa students:

> In these times, there are many people of corrupt belief . . . there is a group of them who call themselves seekers of knowledge and, by doing so, soil the name of the seekers of [religious] knowledge. That is because they embark upon reading the books of philosophers and Sufis without [first] having the power of certainty and without seeking the knowledge of religion. Thus, they have become corrupt in their beliefs, and most of them go on to deceive ignorant people . . . [however,] let me emphasize that it is permissible for those among the Twelver ulama who possess divine souls and the perfect power of certainty to study books of philosophy and other books after finishing their studies in religious sciences in order to break the glasses of misgivings [*shubahat*] and corrupt imaginings with stones of refutation thrown from the sling of reasoning and syllogism . . . [as] for others, it is better for them to turn away from reading and hearing such books so that they do not come to grievous ends.†

These remarks, I believe, represent a new stage in the long war waged by the emerging guardians of Safavid Twelver orthodoxy against different types of heterodoxy. The first battle was against the Nuqtavis and storytellers, but the war soon encompassed Sufism and then another major enemy, philosophy. The latter seems to have become the favorite target of attacks in the last three decades of the Safavid rule. The fact that *Hadiqat al-shiʿa* contains very little criticism of philosophy helps put into perspective the later growth of antiphilosophy sentiment in clerical circles. The magnanimity of *Hadiqa*'s author(s) toward major figures in the history of Islamic philosophy contrasts with the book's general aggressive tone. Authors including Ibn Sina and Sayyid Haydar Amuli (d. 1385) are excused for their support for Sufism on the grounds that they were tricked by Sunnis. "Everyone is subject to mistakes, except for the infallible imams," says the writer(s).‡

Ultimately, however, philosophy proved a much different target than Sufism. Because of the efforts of intellectual giants of Shiʿism such as Nasir al-Din Tusi and Hilli (d. 1325), philosophical vocabulary had become an integral part of traditional madrasa discourse, especially in the field of rationale

* ʿIsam, *Nasiha* MS, f. 120a.

† ʿIsam, *Nasiha* MS, f. 120a–120b.

‡ Pseudo-Ardabili, *Hadiqat al-shiʿa,* 2:795.

theology (*kalam*). Prominent teachers of traditional Peripatetic philosophy were among the most respected members of the madrasa elite, and they had a congenial and warm relationship with the higher echelons of the political order. This being the case, such teachers constructed and sustained a powerful philosophical orthodoxy, controlling the relevant discourse and the prestigious philosophy chairs in the madrasas. The prominent members of this establishment, for obvious socioeconomical and intellectual reasons, did not welcome "innovations" of the sort that Mulla Sadra, for example, was eager to introduce into philosophical thinking.

This explains, to a large extent, why philosophy came onto the radar of puritans so late in the Safavid period, despite its obviously "foreign" roots. Another important development that facilitated the turn against philosophy at the end of this period was the gradual rise of Akhbarism in madrasas as an alternative framework of legal thought in which the Usuli methodology (and its Aristotalian foundations) for juristic inquiries was completely rejected. The jurists adhering to the Akhbari legal school, in a move they described as a return to the way of the original hadith scholars (*tariqat al-qudama*), rid themselves of an Usuli vocabulary that was thoroughly indebted to Peripatetic philosophy and logic. This gave them freedom to attack philosophy as a foreign element that needed to be purged from the madrasas.

In spite of the increasingly hostile and heated rhetoric against philosophy, philosophers remained highly influential in the court well into the early decades of the eighteenth century, and thus their high social status was preserved. In fact, philosophy was taught and learned partly because of its prestigious position in the madrasa curriculum and the possible links it could provide for the students as well as the teachers to the Safavid court.* Examples of this include the prominent role played by Mulla Muhammad Baqir Sabzavari (d. 1679) in Sulayman's accession to the throne. The philosophically oriented Aqa Husayn Khansari (d. 1678 or 1679), a student of Mir Damad, Majlisi Sr., and Sabzavari, was also among the trusted members of the court ulama, and the shah erected a mausoleum for him upon his death. Finally, we know from a fascinating anectode in *Tatmim* that Muhammad Baqir Khatunabadi (d. 1715), the first cleric to occupy the position of *mullabashi*, appointed Shah Sultan Husayn, thus holding the highest religious office in the land as the "Mujtahid of the times" (*mujtahid al-zaman*), was compelled to

* For fascinating firsthand testimony of an Augustinian friar named Antonio, a native of Portugal who converted to Islam in Isfahan in 1696 and wrote several treatises against Christianity and Judaism under his new name, Ali-Quli Jadid al-Islam (d. after 1722). His account is quoted in Ja'fariyan, *Safaviyya*, 2:677–78.

teach philosophy in spite of his obvious lack of competence in the rationale disciplines.*

Although the polemical works met with a certain degree of success, especially as the influence of Akhbarism increased during the final decades of Safavid rule, the most significant disruption of the teaching and study of philosophy did not occur until the fall of Isfahan, when many elites fled the city they adored. This dispersal of scholars and the accompanying lack of financial resources had a marked impact on the city's intellectual circles, and particularly on the status of philosophy.†

Philosophy against Sufism

Exoteric jurists and puritan preachers such as Qummi and Mir Lawhi may have been the strongest and most influential wing of the anti-Sufi campaign, but they were not alone in objecting to Sufism. Elitist philosophers in Isfahan also expressed contempt for popular beliefs and practices associated with Sufism. Mir Findiriski (d. 1640) is one example. Though he was reportedly sympathetic toward dervishes,‡ he did not hesitate to condemn popular manifestations of the Sufi spirit that he considered problematic, including the Qalandar phenomenon. In an analogy that compares different classes

* See Qazvini, *Tatmim amal al-amil,* 78. For more on the office of *mullabashi,* see Ja'fariyan, *Safaviyya,* 2:241–44. For more on Khatunabadi, see Ja'fariyan's introduction to Khatunabadi's *Tarjama-yi anajil-i arba'a.* It is important to note, therefore, that romantic narratives of persecution of philosophers constructed by some modern scholars who focus on the Safavid era, Islamic education, and the madrasa system do not hold up when our primary sources are examined critically. In these accounts, philosophers have often been cast as noble guardians of rationalism and reason who were as threatened by bigoted literalists and exotericists as the Sufis, who are portrayed as incarnations of tolerance and universal peace. For a more detailed discussion of this romantic view and a thorough analysis of the status of philosophy during the last decades of the Safavid period see Anzali and Gerami, *Opposition to Philosophy,* 1–15. This perspective is by no means limited to his work. In fact, it has become the standard view of scholars working on the intellectual and cultural history of late Safavid Iran, with few exceptions. For a few examples see Zarrinkub, *Tasavvuf-i iran,* 262–66; Luizard, "Confreries Soufies," 283–315; Arjomand, *Shadow of God,* 151 and 158–59; and Nasr, *Islamic Philosophy,* chap. 12. The last two sources subscribe to a limited version of the persecution thesis in which philosophers are seen as having been under heavy attack only in the last couple of decades of Safavid rule. I argue that even at that period, perceptions of persecution are heavily exaggerated.

† Corbin's appraisal of the situation seems relatively accurate in this regard. See Corbin, *Islamic Philosophy,* 348–49.

‡ Lewisohn, "Sufism and the School of Iṣfahān," 99–100.

and groups of society to different parts of the human body, Mir Findiriski likened the Qalandars to pubic hair. Disdainful of their refusal to support themselves and their penchant for living off charitable donations, he remarked that they should share the fate of such hair, which the Islamic tradition known as *sunan al-fitra* says should be removed from the body.*

The philosophers' ridicule extended beyond popular expressions of Sufism. Mir Damad, an early seventeenth-century philosopher so eminent that he was called the Third Teacher (after Aristotle and Farabi), dismissed some of the metaphysical teachings of high Sufism as well.† For example, he held that the signature metaphysical postulate of the Sufis, the existence of the *mundus imaginalis,* an intermediate imaginal world between the material and abstract worlds, was a poetical fancy that could not be proved by reason.‡ He also authored a well-known critique§ of famous lines by Rumi that liken philosophers to lepers dependent on the shaky and unreliable leg of reasoning.**

This is not to deny that Mir Damad had mystical visions or a penchant for the spiritual and the occult. After all, he left behind an autobiographical account of his extraordinary mystical visions,†† and, as Melvin-Koushki has demonstrated, he was an accomplished occultist.‡‡ Instead, my argument is that his spiritual quest can be analyzed squarely within the Peripatetic philosophical framework in which mystical visions are not considered to be valid epistemological sources of knowledge. This is a framework in which even prophecy is construed as a special function of *hads,* a purified form of reason often translated as "intuitive judgment."§§ What remains to be explored in detail is the possibility that Mir Damad's views of rational reasoning and mystical visions evolved over time. Early works such as *al-*

* Findiriski, *Risala-yi sinaʿiyya,* 19. Although there appears to be a clear distinction between Qalandarism as an antinomian social movement on the one hand and organized Sufism on the other, it is not quite clear whether the two could be distinguished when it came to the popular mode of Sufi religiosity known as dervishism. See Jazaʾiri, *al-Anvar al-nuʿmaniyya,* 2:308.

† See Lewisohn, "Sufism and the School of Iṣfahān," 93–95.

‡ Damad, *Jazavat va mavaqit,* 62–67.

§ For Mir Damad's response to Rumi and a passionate rebuttal by Nayrizi, see Nayrizi, *Qasida-yi ʿishqiyya* MS, f. 98b.

** See Rumi, *Masnavi-i maʿnavi,* 1:lines 2125–53.

†† For the account and an analysis see Corbin, "Confessions Extatiques."

‡‡ Melvin-Koushki, "Quest for a Universal Science."

§§ See Damad, *al-Ravashih al-samaviyya,* 32. For a succinct presentation of Ibn Sina's theory of prophecy, which Mir Damad adopted, see Gutas, "Avicenna," 420–21. For Nasr and Dabashiʿs position see, for example, Nasr, "Spiritual Movements," and Dabashi, "Mīr Dāmād."

Qabasat paint a picture of their author as a pure and rigid Peripatetic philosopher, while works written at the end of his career, including *al-Jaʿliyya* and *al-Khalsa al-malakutiyya,* reveal an author more interested and invested in mystical visions.*

Mir Damad's skeptical orientation toward Sufism was shared by many of his students. One of the most prominent of these, Sayyid Ahmad ʿAlavi ʿAmili (d. after 1644), was an established philosopher who composed a work titled *Izhar al-haqq va miʿyar al-sidq* to refute the practice of storytelling.† A lengthier treatise against Abu Muslim, *Khulasat al-fava'id,* was written by another notable student of Damad, ʿAbd al-Muttalib b. Yahya Taliqani (d. after 1633).‡ Taliqani says that he repeatedly heard Mir Damad speak highly of Mir Lawhi.§ In fact, and as mentioned earlier, Lawhi himself claimed that he was a student of Shaykh Baha'i and Mir Damad, citing his great respect for both men.

Other prominent students of the Third Teacher were at the forefront of the attacks against Sufism. None among them had more influence on the course of rational and mystical Shiʿi thought than Mulla Sadra, the author of one of the earliest polemical works against Sufism. His *Kasr asnam al-jahiliyya* (*Breaking the Idols of Ignorance*), which was completed in 1618, during the reign of Shah ʿAbbas I, rails against a group its author called pretend Sufis (*mutasavvifun*).** Mulla Sadra had two basic critiques of the pretend Sufis. First, he accused them of hypocrisy and pursuing worldly pleasures such as lust and fame and of deceiving the simpletons and ignorant people around them in order to succeed in their abominable goal. Second, he portrayed them as staunch enemies of learning, as a bunch of ignorant charlatans too lazy and immersed in worldly pleasures to attempt the pursuit of knowledge. This scathing analysis might lead one to believe that Sadra was targeting low-profile, wandering dervishes with no ties to institutionalized

* As far as I know, Nayrizi was the first to raise this possibility. See Khuyi, *Mizan al-savab,* 3:1211.

† ʿAlavi ʿAmili, "Izhar al-haqq."

‡ The treatise was written two years after the death of the aforementioned Mulla Muhammad-Zaman in 1633. Taliqani also provides us with a long list of books and treatises written in Lawhi's support by the ulama.

§ Taliqani, "Khulasat al-fava'id."

** As Nasr reminded us many years ago, "The term *mutasavvif* is perfectly legitimate in most schools of Sufism, where it refers to the person who follows the path of Sufism, but in Safavid and post-Safavid Iran it gained a pejorative connotation as referring to those who 'play' with Sufism without being serious, in contrast to the real sufis who were called *sufiyya.* It thus acquired the meaning of *mustasvvif,* a term used by some of the earlier sufis to designate those who know nothing about Sufism but pretend to follow it." Nasr, "Spiritual Movements," 679, note 4.

Sufism, who spent their days entertaining people by juggling, telling stories, and the like. Yet Sadra made it clear that his critique also applied to institutional Sufism: "Woe to the ignorance of these tail-less and earless donkeys, who have all become shaykh-fabricators and shaykh-sellers," he said. "Every few days they become the disciples of a different fool, bereft of both their religion and their intellect."* He continued, saying that "the majority of those who retreat to the monasteries to be praised and who sit in the khanaqahs to become famous as ascetics and performers of miracles are deficient, damned fools imprisoned by the fetters of lust."†

Sadra's criticism of the Sufism of his time, however, should not be categorized with the anti-Sufi treatises written decades later, in the middle of the seventeenth century. His intellectual outlook, the two decades of separation between his *Kasr* and the anti-Sufi campaign, and the content of his work are enough to persuade any astute observer of Safavid Iran that his criticisms are part of a distinct intellectual trajectory. Sadra's unique intellectual outlook sets his writings (including *Kasr*) apart even from those of his contemporaries. Sadra was not a participant in the mainstream philosophical discourse of his time. He was no ordinary philosopher, and his views were very costly for him socially and intellectually. Nothing speaks to his marginalization from the intellectual circles of his time more than his self-imposed exile to the small village of Kahak near Qum and the correspondence with his teacher that dates to that time, in which he complained about the hostilities he faced.‡ His uneasy relationship with mainstream philosophers, exoteric jurists, and puritan fundamentalists is detailed in *Si asl,* in which he rails against a group of "hypocritical and worldly scholars" composed of philosophers, theologians, and jurists who were, according to him, completely obsessed with fame, worldly gain, rivalry, and envy.§

Another reason his critique of Sufism should be treated separately is that, despite Sadra's vehement opposition to Sufi pretenders, the teachings of high Sufism remained sacred to him. In fact, he used the terms *sufi, dervish,* and *tasavvuf* in a relatively positive sense in his *Si asl,* which was written primarily to defend an enlightened group of ʿarifin and saints against the attacks of exoteric, literalist jurists and theologians.** Similarly, in *Kasr,* Sadra was careful to carve out space for real Sufis whose spiritual states remained

* Shirazi (Mulla Sadra), *Kasr,* 176.

† Shirazi (Mulla Sadra), *Kasr,* 177–78. I am indebted to the translation of Mahdi Dasht-Bozorgi and Seyyed Khalil Toussi. See Shirazi (Mulla Sadra), *Breaking the Idols of Ignorance.*

‡ Ashtiyani, *Mulla Sadra,* 6–7.

§ Shirazi (Mulla Sadra), *Si asl,* 9–10.

** Shirazi (Mulla Sadra), *Kasr,* 39, 43, 113, and 122.

hidden from the eyes of people. "A Sufi," he claimed, "remains hidden from the eyes of the mind as a Sufi even though his body and other aspects of his personality might be visible to the [physical] eyes."*

From Sadra's perspective, Sufis were not the only group that could be divided into "real" and "pretend" categories. Such a distinction should also be made when it comes to philosophers. "Real" or "divine" philosophers, alongside the "lords of truth and ʿirfan" (*arbab-i haqiqat va ʿirfan*), were pitted not only against exoteric jurists and theologians but also against mainstream philosophers and their customary discursive philosophy (*al-hikma al-rasmiyya*). In keeping with his status as a student of Ghazali (d. 1111), Sadra did not consider discursive disciplinary scholarship to be highest form of knowledge. That honor was reserved for the unmediated knowledge of mystical visions (*ʿilm al-mukashafat*), which leads one to esoteric knowledge of the Qur'an and hadith literature.† The only true field of knowledge is the knowledge of unity (*ʿilm al-tawhid*), also known as the divine knowledge (*al-ʿilm al-ilahi*).‡ Sadra's magnum opus, *al-Asfar al-arbaʿa,* reaffirms this conception. In it, Sadra quotes Ibn ʿArabi and other Sufis whom he held in high regard, calling them "the realizers among the Sufis" (*al-muhaqqiqun min al-sufiyya*) or simply "ʿarifin."

Despite the prevalence of the terms *ʿarif* and *maʿrifa,* the category of ʿirfan does not appear frequently in Sadra's own works. Nor do they appear to be used explicitly in contrast to Sufism. In other words, in Sadra's framework of thought, maʿrifa and ʿirfan were still understood largly as signifiers under the broader umbrella of high Sufi thought. This is precisely, I argue, what makes him a target of Qummi's vehement critique.§ Similarly, Sadra's *Kasr* might best be understood not as an outsider attack meant to destroy the foundations of Sufism but as an elite critique from the margins of philosophy and speculative mysticism aimed at reforming both Sufi and Twelver thought. As a basis for such reform, Sadra presented a new mystical ideal that synthesized Twelver Shiʿa hadith literature, Ibn ʿArabi's speculative mysticism, Peripatetic discursive philosophy, Illuminationist principles, and theology. For the revolutionary Qummi, this was a misguided and futile attempt at best and a dangerous heresy at worst.

The innovative philosophical system outlined in Sadra's *al-Hikma al-mutaʿaliya* (*Transcendent Philosophy*) became a primary reference point when

* Shirazi (Mulla Sadra), *Kasr,* 177.

† Shirazi (Mulla Sadra), *Si asl,* 96 and 104.

‡ Shirazi (Mulla Sadra), *Kasr,* 122. To say that the only true field of knowledge is the knowledge of unity does not preclude, for Sadra, the necessity of preparing oneself by pursuing madrasa-based disciplines as prerequisites.

§ Rizvi has made a similar argument (see Rizvi, "The *takfir* of philosophers").

the category of ʿirfan was subsequently established. *Al-Hikma al-mutaʿaliya* was a bold attempt and an original contribution toward integrating major Sufi concepts, including the oneness of being and the validity of mystical visions, as sources of knowledge into a single, coherent philosophical system. Sadra's adoption of these mystical elements affirms the notion that in the final analysis, rationality and reason can take the wayfarer only so far toward understanding the mysteries of God. For Sadra, the afterlife, knowledge of the self, and other crucial aspects of the human condition and experience lie outside the realm of reason and rationality. Attaining true knowledge of such areas requires mystical visions and prophetic injunctions. These must necessarily precede rational arguments to establish the philosophic validity of such ideas and ideals.

Sufis, in their own turn, wrote polemical works against mainstream philosophy. A number of unstudied manuscripts written in Persian during the reign of Shah Sultan Husayn, the last Safavid king, directly attack the rational-philosophical method and question its legitimacy as a tool for understanding questions of faith like the principle of *tawhid*. There is one caveat, however. These polemical works seem to exclude, impilcitly or explicitly, Sadra's philosophical innovations from their critique.*

Conclusion

The relationship between Sufism and Islamic rationalist discourses has often been an uneasy one. By rationalist discourse, I mean disciplinary practices in which the process of human reasoning, understood within the framework of Aristotelian logic and syllogism at its center, is considered a valid and unavoidable epistemological source for deducing "truths" related to religious questions and debates. Early Muʿtazilite theology,† Usuli jurisprudence, Islamic discursive philosophy, and classical Ashʿarite theology (which is practically indistinguishable from discursive philosophy, especially in fundamental questions of the metaphysics of being) are all considered rationalist discourses from this perspective.

Sufism has also had an uneasy relationship with puritan discourses, by which I mean movements within Muslim learned society that are marked by (1) a desire to free Islamic knowledge from "foreign" influence and (2) an anti-

* These include Hasan Husayni's *Tawhid-nama* or *Tuhfa-yi tawhid-khana* and *Jala al-qulub* as well as Sayyid Husayn Tafrishi's *Bavariq mushriqa va sava'iq muhriqa*. For a brief and useful report on the first two works see Sadra'i Khuyi, "Tawhid-nama," 113–22.

† From very early times, the Muʿtazili rationalists ridiculed Sufis for being ignorant, superstitious, and irrational. See, for example, Sobieroj, "The Muʿtazila and Sūfism."

establishment orientation that challenges the authority and validity of certain traditional Islamic disciplines and favors a return to the fundamentals of the faith traced back to the "golden age" of the Prophet and his companions.* The *ahl al-hadith* movement of the early Abbasid period, pioneered by scholars of hadith such as Ibn Hanbal and later Ibn Taymiyya, and the Akhbari School of legal thought that emerged during the Safavid era are considered puritan discourses for the purposes of this analysis.

For their part, Sufis did not hesitate to express their disdain for philosophy, dismissing rational methods of inquiry about God as limited and futile.† At the root of this disdain was the fact that in Sufi epistemology, reason was a subordinate and ultimately unnecessary faculty, limited in its ability to apprehend ultimate truth and a hindrance to spiritual progress. For most Sufis, disciplinary knowledge—especially rational discourse—was irrelevant at best and a major obstacle and distraction at worst.

For philosophers and jurists, the cult of Sufi saints was an aberration of superstitious and uneducated minds or, worse, an example of evil at work. Experts in Islamic law, whose efforts are geared toward regulating social spaces and transactions as well as providing ritual guidelines, place the utmost importance on predictability and rationality as defined within the limits of religious law. Jurisprudence as a discipline is based upon the rationalist science of usul al-fiqh, and many jurists were also trained as theologians. This meant that their intellectual outlook was similar to that of the philosophers, especially when it came to fundamental concepts that defined God and shaped the way Muslim intellectuals thought about divinity and its relationship to humanity. Philosophers and jurists, concerned with crafting rational frameworks to explain the order of the universe and to regulate human interactions, were deeply troubled by the prospect of chaotic and spontaneous mystical experiences, which undermined the social structures supported by their efforts. Their tightly sealed systems of legal interpretation and metaphysical speculation stood in contrast to a Sufi world where boundaries between the unseen realm and the conscious mind were blurred, threatening established norms.

These competing conceptions had real-world ramifications for religious,

* I intentionally avoid using the term *fundamentalism* here since, as Bruce Lawrence and others have shown, it is essentially a modern phenomenon. See Lawrence, *Defenders of God.* There are, however, considerable similarities between the outlook, structure of thought, and ideals of what I call "puritan" movements and modern fundamentalist discourse.

† The story of the alleged meeting between Avicenna and Abu Saʿid Abu al-Khayr, mentioned earlier, is merely one example of how the rational method was often disdained, though not rejected, by Sufis.

political, and social power structures. The immanent and easily accessible God whom the Sufi shaykh of the khanaqah and the syncretistic wandering dervish claimed to mediate through their charisma was a formidable threat to the authority the jurists claimed as interpreters of God's will, commandments, and preferences. The promise of an ever-present, immanent God whose presence could be experienced in fresh and tangible ways was perhaps the most powerful aspect of the Sufi message—one that made Sufism popular with the lay masses who found little solace in the philosopher's dry notion of God or the jurist's obsession with obedience to a remote and often demanding God. Saintly Sufi figures offered what neither the philosopher nor the jurist could. They promised a direct connection to the supernatural and the possibility of tapping into the infinitely abundant resources of the unseen realm to meet worldly and other-worldly needs. They brought heaven and earth and the mundane and the sublime together in the present moment—here, now, embodied.

Puritan critiques usually stem from the struggle of an anti-establishment minority in a learned society to topple existing, knowledge-based power structures and replace them with an alternative, utopian model. The successful resistance of ahl al-hadith to state-sponsored Muʿtazilite theological thought in spite of a brief but intense period of inquisition under Caliph Amin is an apt example. More relevant examples are found in the efforts of Mir Lawhi and Qummi. Both were mid-ranking religious scholars, and neither had strong ties to or a considerable stake in the political establishment either early in their careers or in midcareer.* In fact, both vehemently opposed and entered a costly debate with Majlisi Sr. and Fayz Kashani, allies of the monarch who played a significant role in promoting and preserving the state-sponsored religious power structure. In waging a war not only against Sufis but also against syncretistic readings of Islamic sources by the ulama, Mir Lawhi and Qummi aspired to replace the existing paradigm of scholarship in madrasas with a new one that they considered authentic and true to how Islam was understood and explained by the imams and the Prophet.

Both esoterically and exoterically inclined ulama trained in the madrasa system consistently portrayed the Sufis of this period as ignorant and opposed to learning and education. Mulla Sadra's critique of Sufism, for example, claimed that the real pursuit of spirituality can happen only after one

* Qummi declared his fealty to the political establishment by writing a treatise on the necessity of Friday prayers in the time of occultation as a religious obligation in 1558. See Newman, "Sufism and Anti-Sufism," 101–2. For a case study of the political implications of the hotly debated issue of Friday prayers during the Safavid period, see Newman, "Fayd al-Kashani."

has thorough training in disciplinary sciences. According to Sadra, the quest to attain maʿrifa cannot result in valid outcomes if one refrains, as many dervishes and Sufis did, from participating in the disciplinary discourse housed in the madrasa.* He accused the "pretend Sufis" of having slid into the abyss of imaginary illusions by neglecting the study that would have allowed their discursive and rational faculties to flourish: "Most, nay all, of those in our time who have put themselves in the position of guidance and vice regency [*khalafa*] are fools ignorant of the paths of knowledge and maturity . . . they have largely shunned conceptual understanding [*al-suvar al-idrakiyya*] and have barred the doors of science and knowledge . . . thinking that doing so prepares the seeker to focus his/her attention on the Bountiful Origin. They have not understood that preventing the perceptory, rational, and imaginative faculties from . . . reaching maturity inclines them toward distorted concepts fabricated by the imagination."†

The same line of attack against institutional Sufism and its anti-intellectual position was pursued by ʿAbd al-Razzaq Lahiji (d. 1661 or 1662), a prominent theologian and student of Sadra. In his introduction to *Gawhar-i murad,* a theological work that stresses the importance of the spiritual path and is dedicated to Shah ʿAbbas II, he wrote, "The reality of Sufism is nothing but the travelling of the esoteric path . . . and we already said that to embark upon such a path, the exoteric path is a pre-requisite. So, a Sufi should first become a philosopher or a theologian. To claim to have become a Sufi before getting a solid grounding in philosophy and theology, that is, without completing the way of reason, whether it is according to the terminology of the ulama or not, is charlatanism and deceiving the masses. My concern is not with the word Sufism or Sufi. Rather, my goal is the spiritual quest and the pursuit of real union."‡ In a reiteration of his teacher's critique of non-madrasa-trained Sufis and dervishes, he said, "Sufis and Qalandars who do not have a firm grounding in discursive philosophy, who lack acquaintance with theology, traditional commentaries and exoteric knowledge about ontological origins and the end point of creation [*mabda va maʿad*], and yet still present themselves as masters and spiritual guides of the people—like the poles of our own period and previous epochs—are nothing but brigands who waylay the common folk. Sadr al-Mutaʾallihin [Mulla Sadra], in his treatise *Kasr asnam al-jahiliyya,* took such people to task and exposed the [un]learning of this group, revealing the extent of their decadence."§

* Shirazi (Mulla Sadra), *Kasr,* 26–46.

† Shirazi (Mulla Sadra), *Kasr,* 39.

‡ Lahiji, *Gawhar-i murad,* 38–39.

§ I have slightly changed Lewisohn's translation of Lahiji's remarks, which can be found in Lewisohn, "Sufism and the School of Iṣfahān," 112.

Other madrasa-based scholars, even though they were fundamentally opposed to Sadra's mystical and philosophical vision, shared his and his students' derision of this alleged anti-intellectual tendency of Sufis. Later, for example, Sayyid Niʿmatullah Jazaʾiri (d. 1701), a high-ranking religious scholar, a student of Majlisi Jr., and a vehement critic of Sufism, explained in his *al-Anvar al-nuʿmaniyya* that one of the reasons behind the popularity of Sufis is that their path is much easier than that of disciplinary knowledge, for the former promises the same results in a much shorter period of time!* Shaykh Hurr ʿAmili, another prominent Akhbari scholar and the author of the influential anti-Sufi treatise *al-Isna ʿashariyya,* made a similar point when he wrote: "And it has come to a point regarding those who claim to have had visions that they say the seekers of knowledge are wrong, that they are only concerned with exoteric matters and that they do not know God and his religion, and that the Sufis are the folks of esoteric matters and they are the ones who know God as He deserves to be known. Therefore, [in their minds] Sufism has become the opposite of the pursuit of knowledge, so they say: are you a Sufi or a seeker of knowledge?"†

The Sufi quest versus disciplinary knowledge as an either/or conception surfaces in anti-Sufi literature no matter the intellectual outlook of the author. This debate can be understood, of course, as a rivalry between two alternative hegemonic systems, that of the khanaqah and that of the madrasa. In the former the adept must totally submit himself to the shaykh "like a corpse in the hands of the washer," as the famous Sufi saying goes. In the latter, the student is disciplined by the mentor in accordance to a very specific interpretation of selected texts. This educational discipline secures "conservative" mystical experiences and rules out the possibility or validity of alternative experiences, providing controlled venues through which the erratic and unruly eruptions of the mystical may be channeled.‡

* Jazaʾiri, *al-Anvar al-nuʿmaniyya,* 2:293.

† Hurr ʿAmili, "Risala fi al-ghina," 1:183.

‡ Drawing rigid boundaries between the "genuine" and the "false" pursuit of gnosis emphasized by Sadra guarantees that the "noetic" content of the mystical experience, to borrow from Willam James, will not be understood and interpreted against his understanding of orthodoxy. Of course, all such efforts meet with only partial success, as a certain degree of innovativeness marks the mystical in all contexts. I believe constructivist interpretations of mystical experiences fail to account for this. For more on the "conservative" nature of mystical experiences, see Katz, "The 'Conservative' Character of Mysticism" and "Languauge, Epistemology, and Mysticism." The author's views have been influential and have recently been taken up by scholars of Sufism as an interpretive framework for understanding Sufism. See Green, *Sufism: A Global History,* 3–4. Katz's view, however, have been challenged by

Given Sufism's strong tradition of seeing the disciplinary sciences as obstacles to wayfarers, it should not surprise us that Sadra and his students framed their antagonism toward institutional Sufism as an opposition between madrasa training and the regimen of the khanaqah, in which discursive knowledge is highly suspect and underemphasized, if not rejected outright, in favor of a set of meditational steps a novice takes under the supervision of his shaykh.

To conclude, then, the jurist, theologian, and philosopher can all be seen as trainees of the madrasa system who were dependent on that system's rational discourse and elaborate curriculum. Together they formed a block in a power struggle against the Sufis, whose primary *modus operandi* was the khanaqah, socially speaking, and the claim to mystical visions, epistemologically speaking. The Sufi master, located at the center of the khanaqah as the intermediary visionary through whom a community of followers received divine guidance, represented a challenge to the mujtahid, located at the center of the madrasa as an intermediary hermeneut through whom the community of followers gained access to the divine, present in the form of sacred letters and words in the canonical scripture.* It must be noted, however, that the debate cannot be reduced to economics or politics. It was also a genuine religious debate in which both parties fought for what they considered to be the original message of Islam as embodied in the sayings and acts of the Prophet and, more important, the imams. To reduce this rivalry to a temporal power struggle would be a mistake, I believe, and a distorted view of how religious subjects construct their world and live their religion.

---

several counterarguments. See, for example, Forman, *Mysticism, Mind, Consciousness,* and Anzali, *Sakhtgira-yi sunnat va ʿirfan,* 232–98.

* I recognize that such a broad statement can be read as a warrantless oversimplification of the actual, messy situation on the ground. It is true, for example, that there are many Sufis who were at the same time theologiams and jurists and vice versa. My intention is not to suggest otherwise. Rather, inspired by Weber's conception of ideal types, I present the opposing ideals of madrasa and khanaqah to help the reader make sense of the real tensions that existed between Sufis and their opponents as demonstrated by examples in this and the following chapters.

3 The Sufi Response

By the middle of the seventeenth century, the Safavid project of converting Iran to Shiʿism had successfully pushed Sunnism to the fringes of the realm. Major Sufi networks present at that time had already converted to Shiʿism, though not necessarily to the state-sanctioned Twelver version. The marginalization and conversion of Sufi networks, however, did not stop their enemies, who continued to question the validity and authenticity of the Sufi quest because of its Sunni past. As far as critics were concerned, the ostensibly Shiʿi Sufis had preserved major Sunni elements in their thought. They were Sunnis disguised in the trappings of a tainted and distorted Shiʿism.* The allegedly uneasy relationship between the imams and early Sufi figures such as Sufyan Sawri (d. 778) and Hasan Basri (d. 728)† and the unorthodox teachings and practice of ecstatic figures including Hallaj and Bayazid were proof to the critics of the problematic Sunni origins and heretical teachings of Sufism.‡ Traditions from canonical hadith collections and additional traditions taken from *Hadiqat al-shiʿa* on the authority of Ardabili were circulated to substantiate the claim that the imams took an active stand against the Sufis of their time.§ The problem was not that Sufism was incompatible with Islam. For these detractors, Sufism was indeed compatible with Islam—just with the wrong version.

The detractors had a point. The Sufi networks remaining in Safavid heartlands in the mid-seventeenth century may have transitioned to a version of

* Qummi, for example, questions the sincerity of the Nurbakhshi Sufis, saying their claim to Shiʿism was merely a bluff. Qummi, *Shish risala,* 303.

† For examples of traditions from canonical hadith collections pertaining to Sawri's strained relationship with the imams, see Kulayni, *al-Kafi,* 1:393–94 and 5:65–70. For similar traditions related to Basri, see 1:51, 2:222, and 5:113. See also Qummi's long and damning diatribe based on these traditions: Qummi, *Tuhfat al-akhyar,* 30–36.

‡ See, for example: Hurr ʿAmili, *al-Isna ʿashariyya,* 15ff.

§ One of the most comprehensive compilations of traditions from *Hadiqa* and other sources is Hurr ʿAmili's *al-Isna ʿashariyya.*

Twelver Shiʿism more or less in line with the emerging Safavid orthodoxy, but their past was deeply embedded in a Sunni world. Any viable response to charges of Sunnism necessitated revising and redefining the past. The earliest and most thorough example of a revisionist attempt is Nurullah Shushtari's *Majalis al-mu'minin,* which was written at the turn of the century (1602). Shushtari was a Kubravi Sufi affiliated with the Nurbakhshi branch, and he argued that the Kubravi masters, along with many other prominent scholars of the past, were Shiʿa who practiced dissimulation (*taqiyya*) out of the fear of persecution. *Majalis* is among the hagiographical sources most frequently quoted by Sufis and Sufi-minded ulama of the seventeenth century.

Central to the revisionist agenda exemplified by *Majalis* is a categorical denial that any major Sufi figure (for example, Rumi, Ibn ʿArabi, Safi al-Din Ardabili, ʿAttar, Najm al-Din Kubra, ʿAla al-Daula Simnani) had any affiliation with Sunnism. The revisionist hagiography took centuries to complete, but the results are astonishing. Two centuries later, Shirvani (d. 1838), a prominent Niʿmatullahi Sufi traveler and historian of the early Qajar period, was able to proclaim, with no appreciable irony, that "A Sufi cannot be a Sunni."* A sea change had occurred since the time Sa'in al-Din Turka (d. 1427), an eminent Sufi and occultist of the fifteenth century, who stated with confidence that "All the Sufi shaykhs follow the Sunni denomination. In fact, no one who is not a member of Sunni denomination can grasp this science [of Sufism]. Hence, anyone who comes to a Sufi master [*murshid*] in pursuit of this science will not be offered any spiritual direction until he or she converts to Sunnism."†

* Shirvani, *Bustan al-siyaha,* 292–93.

† Quoted from Lewisohn, "Sufism and Theology," 66. Ibn Turka's statement, however, should be taken with a grain of salt. As mentioned in previous chapters, his time was one of confessional ambiguity and porous sectarian boundaries. Many elements of Shiʿi modes of piety were present in Sunni religious expressions, most significantly a strong sense of devotion to the Alid lineage of the family of the Prophet. Boundaries were even less defined when it came to elite esotericists. As Melvin-Koushki has demonstrated, Ibn Turka, the foremost occult philosopher of early Timurid Iran, was committed to a highly elitist, esoteric, trans-sectarian, lettrist system of thought that informed his worldview and guided his quest to "comprehend the cosmos using all available means, whether rational or mystical, scientific or magical." His quest, says Melvin-Koushki, "exemplifies the 'will to synthesis' that characterizes so much of later Islamicate intellectual history" (Melvin-Koushki, "Quest for a Universal Science," i). Such sectarian statements by Ibn Turka, therefore, should be understood in the broader context in which the philosopher faced serious charges of heresy and was forced to defend himself in Shahrukh's court. For more on Ibn Turka's apologies, see Melvin-Koushki, "Quest

In order to better understand this transformation and the way organized Sufism came to terms with fundamental changes in the religious landscape of Iran, it is helpful to explore the case of a Persian Sufi network known as the Zahabiyya. This was by no means the most prominent Sufi network in seventeenth-century Persia. To the extent that the primary sources provide an accurate picture of organized Sufism in the second half of the seventeenth and the beginning of the eighteenth century in Iran, it appears that the Nurbakhshi Sufis were the best known network in the period, and the only major Sufi network known to both proponents and opponents of Sufism in the heartlands of the Safavid Empire. Despite the prominence of the Nurbakhshi network, I have chosen to focus on the Zahabiyya because, as I have argued elsewhere, the Zahabi project was *at its inception* both Shiʿite and Safavid in nature. The adoption of the designation Zahabiyya and the construction of a spiritual lineage for the network happened in the late seventeenth and early eighteenth centuries.* Thus a study of this network best exemplifies the discursive shift in Shiʿi Sufism that was part of the larger transformation in the religious landscape of Safavid Iran. Moreover, the formation of the Zahabi Sufi network in the seventeenth century was very much intertwined with the history of Nurbakhshi network. As the Nurbakhshis gradually ceased to operate as a distinct Sufi network in the post-Safavid religious landscape of Persia, many of their prominent figures, works, and teachings were claimed by the Zahabis. I hope, then, to shed light on both Zahabi and Nurbakhshi traditions.

My analysis of the emergence of the Zahabiyya as a Shiʿi Sufi network emphasizes the uniquely Safavid nature of the phenomenon. This emphasis highlights the rise of an important religious and political outlook in which Safavid Twelver discourse stood in polar opposition to (Ottoman and Uzbek) Sunni discourses—a dichotomy in which tabarra and cursing the enemies of the imams were necessary accompaniments to tavalla, love of the imams.† But it also draws attention to the formation of a discourse of legitimacy that supplanted a Sufi discourse rooted in a Sunni past. The new discourse was based on Twelver hadith sources and the discursive tradition built upon those sources by Twelver ulama.

A number of important works written during this time provide us

---

for a Universal Science," 428–33. Nevertheless, the very fact that his apology contained such sectarian statements confirms my point that the guardians of orthodoxy sought to confine Sufism firmly within the framework of Sunnism.

* Anzali, "Emergence."

† In the Sunni world, this phenomenon was known as rejection (*rafz*), and the Shiʿa were labeled rejectors (*rafizis*). See Jaʿfariyan, *Safaviyya*, 1:32–36.

with a detailed picture of the Sufis' innovative attempts to legitimize and authenticate their tradition on the basis of a new canon composed of the four early Shiʿi compendiums of hadith along with other, less universally accepted hadith compilations that they found helpful. Such attempts involved the partial or complete expunging of problematic aspects of the previous narrative of sacred history, which was rooted in Sunni hadith sources and drew on the teachings of Sunni scholars and shaykhs. As a result of this shift, many of the established markers of identity for Sufi networks that had informed the connections and distinctions between rival Sufi networks and between Sufi discourse and other learned Islamic discourses became increasingly irrelevant. New distinguishing markers were adopted by innovative Sufi masters, markers founded on new myths and enacted with new rituals. These helped forge the emerging identity of Sufi networks, including that of the Zahabiyya.* New myths and rituals connected Sufi discourse to Sufi elements of Safavid sacred history (going back to the foundational figure of Safi al-Din Ardabili) and to sources of Twelver tradition that lent themselves to being used as evidence of the authentically Twelver nature of Sufi discourse.

In order to demonstrate more concretely how these new priorities, sacred narratives, and markers of identity were authenticated in works written by Sufis and Sufi-minded ulama, I turn to an analysis of important texts that exhibit the changes that took place in seventeenth-century Safavid Persia.

The *Tafsir* of Mu'min Mashhadi

The first work to which I would like to draw the reader's attention is a commentary (*tafsir*) on the thirtieth and final part of the Qur'an, known as the *ʿamma juz*. The commentary was written in Persian by Shaykh Mu'min Mashhadi and dedicated to Shah ʿAbbas I on the occasion of his travel to Mashhad.† The style and the content of the work suggest that it was written in the early seventeenth century, and its mention of the shah coming to Mashhad may be a reference to ʿAbbas I's journey on foot from Isfahan to Mashhad to visit the shrine of the eighth imam. This famous walk took place in 1601, which would place the writing of the work at the turn of the century.‡

* By *myth,* I mean "a sacred story that founds and grounds a particular world." By *ritual,* I mean "the re-enactment of the myth that makes that world come into being through scripted and repeated action." See Kripal et al., *Comparing Religions,* 115–16.

† Mu'min Mashhadi, *Tafsir,* 1. Given this dedication, the date that appears at the end of the manuscript (1678) must be a scribal error or a reference to the date this particular manuscript was copied from the original.

‡ The symbolic significance of this trip occupied Iranian imagination for centuries to come. See, for example, Shaykh ʿAbbas Qummi's detailed account in his extremely popular devotional work, *Mafatih al-jinan.*

The identity of the author is a more difficult question, as several Sufi masters active in Safavid Khurasan in this period were known by the title Shaykh Mu'min.* Unfortunately, sufficient evidence does not exist to permit us to determine which of these figures authored this small treatise. It is evident, however, that the text was written by an erudite Sufi shaykh. References to Twelver Shiʿism as the saved sect (*firqa-yi najiya*) indicate at least a nominal adherence to Twelverism, but a closer examination of the content of book reveals that the author was quite distant from the Shiʿi orthodoxy of mid-seventeenth-century Isfahan. The work is heavily based on *al-Kashshaf*, an important commentary by Zamakhshari (d. 1144). It quotes Sunni canonical sources extensively, rarely making use of specifically Shiʿi sources of hadith. The author's knowledge of the Shiʿi exegetical tradition is superficial, and the dearth of references to canonical Shiʿi hadith collections is a strong indicator that he speaks from the vantage point of a Sunni-dominated intellectual world and educational curriculum.† The network of authorities and references used to support the points raised in the treatise is similar to that of Sufi works written in Central Asia in the mid- and late sixteenth century.‡ As such, the work belongs to a nascent stage of the transformation of Sufism in Iran, one in which Sufi teachings remain deeply embedded in traditional Sunni frames of reference despite nominal adherence to Safavid Twelverism.

* For example, the author of *Qisas al-khaqani* speaks of a prominent Sufi of the time, Shaykh Mu'min Mashhadi (d. 1652), recounting that the latter was the most respected and prominent Sufi shaykh (*shaykh al-mashaiykh*) in the entire Khurasan region. Shamlu also mentions the considerable financial resources at Shaykh Mu'min's disposal and the many charitable constructions built at his behest. See Shamlu, *Qisas al-khaqani*, 183–84. Given the strong presence of the Nurbakhshi Sufi network in Khurasan at the time, it is quite possible that this Shaykh Mu'min was in fact a Nurbakhshi master. Another possible author is the Shaykh Mu'min, whose mausoleum, known in modern times as the Green Dome (*gunbad-i sabz*), is located in the vicinity of the shrine of Imam Riza in Mashhad. According to the gravestone on display inside, construction of the tomb was finished in 1626. The author of *Mutakhab al-tavarikh* states that "it is not clear whether he was a Sunni or a Shiʿi, which would make it all the more possible that he is the actual author. (See Khorasani, *Muntakhab al-tavarikh*, 472. Note that the author has miscalculated the *abjad* value indicating the completion date of the tomb, stating that it was finished in 1191 rather than 1036.) It is common knowledge that the mausoleum was formerly at the center of a khanaqah complex demolished during the Pahlavi reign to allow for urban development. An active Khaksar khanaqah remains across from the traffic roundabout that encircles the mausoleum.

† See, for example, the references to Sunni tafsir works on pages 14, 30, 61, 149, 171, and 172.

‡ See, for example, Kharazmi, *Adab al-muridin* MS.

Bayan al-asrar

Just a few decades later, however, a different kind of Sufi writing emerged in the Safavid cultural domain, especially in major cities that had larger populations of Twelver Shiʿa or were more central to the Safavid agenda. This new type of writing was marked by a conscious effort to draw on hadith literature associated with Shiʿism. *Bayan al-asrar,* a fascinating short monograph, is such a work. The text was written by Shaykh Husayn Zahidi (d. after 1648), who is known primarily as the author of another small but significant treatise, *Silsilat al-nasab safaviyya* (*The Genealogy of the Safavids*).* *Bayan* is best understood as part of a revisionist attempt by the Safavid court to reimagine and reframe the roots of the Safavid family after the fallout with the Qizilbash. Zahidi belonged to a prominent family descended from Shaykh Zahid Gilani (d. 1301), the purported master of Safi al-Din Ardabili. The family had close ties to the royal court as custodians (*mutavalli*) of the shrine of Safi al-Din in Ardabil,† which was arguably the most important sacred space in Iran after Imam Riza's tomb in Mashhad. Zahidi's writings, therefore, can be seen as broadly in line with the official propaganda of the Safavid house.

In addition to frequent references to Safi al-Din as the founder of the Safavid Sufi network, Zahidi also makes numerous references to two early seventeenth-century Sufi figures from Khurasan: Pir Palanduz (Master Packsaddlemaker)‡ and Zahidi's own master, Shaykh Mu'min Mashhadi. Interestingly, evidence suggests that both of these figures were officially affiliated with the Nurbakhshi Sufi network.§ Zahidi himself notes that the Nurbakshiyya were a "very famous" Sufi network throughout the region of Khurasan.** It is clear from the way the text moves fluidly between past and present that the author considered his ancestors in the Zahidi lineage and the more contemporary Sufi network that connected him to pir Palanduz and Shaykh Mu'min Mashhadi to be part and parcel of a unified spiritual constellation. At the same time, he makes clear distinctions between the corporate identity and communal rituals of the two Sufi networks. For example, Zahidi says that the Nurbkahshis follow the hidden zikr (*zikr-i khafi*) as opposed to vocal zikr (*zikr-i jali*), which, according to him, is a hallmark of the

* This important work was first published by Edward Browne in 1924.

† Zahidi, *Silsilat al-nasab,* 3.

‡ Pir Palanduz's mausoleum was built in 1577–1578 during the reign of Shah Muhammad Khudabanda (r. 1578–1587), Shah ʿAbbas I's father. See Khorasani, *Muntakhab al-tavarikh,* 471–72. This is enough to cast doubt on later Zahabi claims that prominent figures such as Fayz Kashani were his disciples.

§ For more on this see Anzali, "Emergence."

** Zahidi, *Bayan al-asrar* MS, 108.

Safavid Sufi network.* He makes no mention of the Zahabi Sufi network in this work, a noteworthy point in light of the fact that later Zahabi hagiographies claim not only him but also Pir Palanduz and Shaykh Muhammad Mu'min Mashhadi as a part of their own lineage.†

Bayan is written as a commentary on *Misbah al-shariʿa va miftah al-haqiqa*, a work composed of one hundred chapters on the spiritual levels and qualities of the wayfarer. The work is heavily laden with Sufi vocabulary. The earliest appearance of content from what came to be known as the *Misbah* in works by learned Sufis is found in *al-Amali* by Ibn Babuya (d. 991), better known as Shaykh Saduq.‡ Ibn Babuya makes no mention of a book called *Misbah;* instead, he credits transmission of the material to a well-known Sufi, Shaqiq al-Balkhi (d. 809), who in turn ascribes it vaguely to "some learned people" (*baʿz ahl al-ʿilm*).§ Two centuries later, in a remarkable development that speaks to the Sufi–Shiʿi cross-pollination process that is a hallmark of this period, the prominent Twelver scholar ʿAli b. Tavus Hilli (d. 1266) mentions the name of the book, *Misbah,* in his *al-Aman,* confidently ascribing it to the sixth imam, Jaʿfar Sadiq, and strongly recommending that devout Shiʿa take it as a companion on their travels.** Despite this mention and recommendation, the work seems to have been unknown to all but a few Sufi-minded religious scholars of Shiʿism. Not until the advent of the Safavids did the work begin to circulate widely among Twelver Sufis. *Misbah* provided Shiʿi Sufis as well as Sufi-minded Shiʿi religious scholars with an important source for legitimizing their teachings on the basis of what they considered to be an authentically Shiʿi work. A brief look at the number of manuscript copies of the work preserved in libraries in Iran tells us much: only two extant copies of the book can be dated to the sixteenth century, and not a single copy dating to previous centuries has survived. The situation changes dramatically when it comes to the seventeenth century, as fifty-seven manuscripts can be dated, precisely or approximately, to that century and twenty-five to the subsequent one (see Table 1).†† This marked increase demonstrates

* Zahidi, *Bayan al-asrar* MS, 105. Furthermore, he associates Pir Palanduz with the silent method of zikr, quoting him as an authority in this respect and giving us more reason to believe that the latter was in fact a Nurbakhshi Sufi master (110–11).

† For further analysis of this important revisionist attempt by the Zahabis see Anzali, "Emergence."

‡ Ibn Babuya Qummi, *Al-amali,* 638–40. Majlisi Jr., *Bihar al-anvar,* 1:32.

§ It appears that the work continued to be attributed to Shaqiq in the mainstream Sunni literary tradition. See Balkhi, *Misbah al-shariʿa* MS.

** Ibn Tavus, *Al-aman,* 91–92.

†† This chart was produced after consulting the massive index of Islamic manuscripts recently published in Tehran under Mostafa Derayati's supervision. See Derayati, *Fihristvara,* 9:656–64.

TABLE 1: The distribution of the surviving manuscripts of *Bayan al-asrar* during the Safavid period

Date	*Number of surviving manuscripts*
1500–1550	0
1551–1590	2
1591–1640	8
1640–1688	30
1689–1737	11
1738–1785	2

the important role the work played in the cultural and religious landscape of the second half of the Safavid rule.

A noteworthy Arab Shiʿi scholar of the early Safavid era played an important role in the transmission and preservation of this work. Zayn al-Din al- Jubbaʿi ʿAmili (d. 1558), otherwise known as the Second Martyr, appears to be the link through whom Sufi authors of the seventeenth century came to know *Misbah.* The author of *Bayan,* for example, states in his introduction that Zayn al-Din was responsible for naming the collection *Misbah al-shariʿa va miftah al-haqiqa,* even though he does not question the attribution of its content to the sixth imam.* There is also a unique manuscript of *Misbah* copied in 1671 by none other than Mu'azzin Khurasani (d. before 1672), a purportedly Zahabi master, whom I discuss in detail later. In this manuscript, the author claims that he copied, through two intermediary links, from an original penned by the Second Martyr himself.† As reflected in some of his writings, especially *Munyat al-murid,* Zayn al-Din was inclined toward Sufism. His scholarly credentials and especially his position as a Shiʿi scholar tragically executed by Ottoman authorities gave him an impeccable aura of sainthood and authority. Sufi authors in Safavid Iran took advantage of the combined Sufi–Shiʿi elements in his character and writings as an important source of legitimacy for their teachings.

The question of who wrote *Misbah* deserves an independent inquiry, but it is not of direct concern here. Rather, the importance of *Bayan* lies in the fact that it represents one of the earliest examples of Sufi writings in which

* Zahidi, *Bayan al-asrar* MS, 3.

† See Shirazi, *Fihrist,* 1:308–10.

authors began to focus on traditions of the twelve imams rather than the Prophet, his Companions, and the early and foundational figures of Sufism. That is to say, *Bayan* is an early example of an emerging Shiʿi–Sufi discourse validated through an alternative set of authoritative sources. Accounts of the imams effectively served as the new *hagiographica,* and sacred stories about them provided the stuff of reoriented or new myths and rituals that grounded the Safavid subject in time and space. For the Sufis of the Safavid era, unlike their predecessors, Shaqiq could do little to respond to questions posed by opponents regarding the authenticity of the Sufi mode of piety. The same sayings, however, when attributed to the sixth imam, become immediately relevant and tremendously helpful in establishing the legitimacy of the newly emerging Shiʿi–Sufi discourse.

Muʾazzin Khurasani and the Making of the Golden Lineage

According to our sources, Muhammad-ʿAli Mashhadi (d. before 1672),* better known as Muʾazzin Khurasani, was initiated into a Kubravi- Barzishabadi Sufi lineage and trained by Shaykh Hatam Zaravandi (d. ca. 1647). After the latter's death, he emerged as one of the most influential Sufi figures of his time in Iran, especially in Mashhad and Isfahan.† Contemporary biographical accounts represent him as a popular and charismatic shaykh and a devout lover of the family of the Prophet. Vali-Quli Shamlu (d. after 1665), a Sufi-minded chronicler of late Safavid times, wrote the most extensive extant report on Muʾazzin in his *Qisas al-khaqani.*‡ According to Shamlu, Muʾazzin left for hajj in 1652 along with a large group of pilgrims from across Khurasan. The author notes that he sponsored many poor people on this journey, saying that he "heard from a reliable source that after this peerless shaykh returned from that trip, he owed fourteen hundred *tuman.* In a short while, it was granted to him as a freely bestowed gift from the divine treasury [*khazana-yi ʿamira*]."§ According to the same source, Muʾazzin made a

* He was definitely alive in 1665, as Shamlu's report indicates (see Shamlu, *Qisas,* 185). It is also clear from a note added to the margin of the manuscript copy of *Nasihat al-kiram* to which I had access that he died in 1671 or 1672 or shortly before. See ʿIsam, *Nasiha* MS, f. 129b.

† Other significant Sufi figures of the time included Darvish Muhammad Salih Lunbani (based in Isfahan and d. 1662), Shaykh Muʾmin Mashhadi (based in Mashhad and d. 1652), Muhaqqiq Bidguli (based in Kashan and d. after 1665), and Darvish Adham Khalkhali (based in Ardabil and d. 1643).

‡ Babayan gives a partial report of this section of *Qisas al-khaqani* in *Mystics, Monarchs, and Messiahs,* 453–55.

§ Shamlu, *Qisas,* 187. This translation is based on Babayan's, but I believe that the phrase "the royal treasury" is a mistranslation of the original (*khazana-yi ʿamira*). In some instances the phrase can indeed be translated in this way, but the context

second hajj trip in 1655 during the reign of ʿAbbas II and stayed in the capital for an extended period of time on his way back home. His scholarship and charismatic personality soon made him a member of elite society in Isfahan as well as a popular prayer leader and preacher, and his erudition helped him forge connections with members of the ulama such as Fayz Kashani, as well as members of the royal court, including the king himself.*

Mu'azzin's connections with prominent political and religious figures and his popularity as a Sufi master made him a primary target of the anti-Sufi campaign. Mir Lawhi portrayed him as a skilled charlatan who fooled people into giving him large sums of money by fabricating fantastic stories of the miracles and dreams of the imams he had experienced.† Lawhi pulled no punches in his description of Mu'azzin, calling him an "infidel," "a human satan," and "the herald of the caravan of misguidedness" (*pishahang-i karavan zalalat*). Lawhi's frustration with Mu'azzin's popularity is clearly reflected in this sarcasm-laden analysis:

> Is there no one more righteous, more knowledgeable, or more pious than this Shaykh Muhammad ʿAli? Compared to him, who among the ulama, the learned, or the worshippers of the time has captured the people's interest to this extent? Insightful people who know the state of that herald of the caravan of misguidedness know that this destroyer of religion busies himself with nothing but making accusations [*iftira*] about God, the Prophet, and the immaculate imams, and that he occupies himself with songs and illicit music in the mosque. Even though many among the trustworthy believers and reliable folk of religion have officially signed a document certifying his infidelity, none of his deceived followers have turned their back on him. Instead, they grew even more interested in that satan . . . for why should the common folk concern themselves with the teachings of the ulama?‡

---

of this passage leads me to believe that what the author has in mind is better translated as "the divine treasury." See Babayan, *Mystics, Monarchs, and Messiahs,* 428 and 454. Cf. Shamlu, *Qisas,* 185.

* In one report, he is said to have been present at a special session convened by ʿAbbas II to meet with two prominent dervishes from the Ottoman lands, Dervish Mustafa and Dervish Majnun, who requested a meeting with their Safavid counterparts. Mulla Rajab-ʿAli Tabrizi (d. 1669) and Dervish Muhammad Salih Lunbani, who had just received grants from the monarch, were introduced to them. In this courtly assembly, Mulla Muhsin Fayz Kashani is also said to have been present. See Qazvini, *ʿAbbas-nama,* 255. Also see his *Tarikh,* 662–63.

† A more extensive and detailed account of charges of financial fraud and other accusations can be found in ʿIsam's *Nasiha* MS, f. 126b–129b.

‡ Lawhi, *Kifaya* MS, f. 10a–11a. Also in Lawhi, *Arbaʿin* MS, 17. Babayan's understanding and translation of this passage are flawed and lead to unwarranted statements

Mu'azzin's own writings naturally paint a different picture. Two substantial pieces of his work survive. One of these is a collection of his poems, his *Divan.** Most of the poetry it contains belongs to Mu'azzin's early years as a Sufi master, prior to his extended stay in Isfahan.† He spent the final decade of his life in the Safavid capital, where he composed a book of greater consequence, a substantial work on Sufism titled *Tuhfa-yi ʿabbasi. Tuhfa* was finished around 1666 and, as the title suggests, was dedicated to the Safavid monarch ʿAbbas II.

The religious outlook reflected in the *Divan* is that of a devout Shiʿa, a passionate lover of the family of the Prophet and the imams, whom Mu'azzin understood in an unmistakably Twelver Shiʿi way. But the poems also reflect the perspective of a genuine Sufi who defends controversial practices such as ritualistic dance (*samaʿ*) and vocal, communal zikr. Furthermore, the *Divan* frequently and explicitly references Mu'azzin's beloved master, Shaykh Hatam. In keeping with the norms of Sufi poetry, the concept of love (ʿishq) pervades Mu'azzin's verse, but he infused the concept with an overwhelmingly Shiʿi tone by emphasizing the primacy of the love of the imams and its importance for those who undertake the Sufi path.‡ ʿAli b. Musa al-Riza, the eighth imam and patron of what came to be known as the Zahabi Sufi network, looms especially large in this poetry.

Tuhfa-yi ʿAbbasi

Mu'azzin's *Tuhfa-yi ʿabbasi* differs from his *Divan* in numerous ways, including the extent to which it reflects the religious, intellectual, and political environment of Isfahan. *Tuhfa* must have played a major role in transitioning Safavid Sufism away from the Sunni foundations of traditional Sufism and replacing them with the newly developed and expanding platform of Shiʿi

about Mu'azzin's religious outlook. Instead of "making accusations (*iftira*) about God, the Prophet, and the immaculate imams," she translates the text as "he made higher claims than God, the Prophet, and the immaculate Imams." Babayan, *Mystics, Monarchs, and Messiahs,* 452. This mistranslation paves the way for her to argue for a nonexisting *ghuluvv* (heretical exaggeration) in the religiosity of Mu'azzin and men like him (455).

* *Mu'azzin, Divan MS.*

† I found no mention of Isfahan or figures and events associated with his adventures in the post-hajj period in the poems. It is clear that some poems recorded in the *Divan* belong to the early years of his career as a master of this Sufi network. One particular lyric, in which he mourns his master, was most likely written soon after the death of his master, Shaykh Hatam (see f. 121a). Another lyric refers to the year 1651, before his first hajj trip (see f. 116a). It should be noted, however, that the Majlis manuscript is incomplete (see f. 136a).

‡ Mu'azzin, *Divan* MS.

hadith literature, and numerous editions of the work have been printed in Iran in the past century.* Unfortunately, none of the print editions are reliable enough for a critical analysis. They contain many errors and, more important, outright redactions.† My analysis, therefore, is based primarily on two early manuscripts.‡ The content of the book gives us unique insight into the dramatic transformation of Sufism in this critical period.

Before getting into details, I would like to make two general observations about the content of the book. First, the author is clearly preoccupied with responding to the attacks of the anti-Sufi campaign, which was at its peak when he wrote. In fact, the attacks constitute the very raison d'être of penning *Tuhfa,* as Mu'azzin states in his opening remarks.§ The main accusation that Mu'azzin seeks to address is that of being Sunni. To counter this accusation, he argues that the scarcity of Shiʿi traditions in mainstream Sufi sources is, for the most part, a result of the practice of taqiyya. By writing *Tuhfa,* Mu'azzin claims, he is making the first attempt in Shiʿi literature to demonstrate how the basics of the Sufi path and its precepts and practices are fully rooted in and in compliance with the teachings of the infallible imams.** This is followed by a discussion in twelve chapters (the number is not a coincidence) in which he draws upon Shiʿi hadith sources such as Kulayni's (d. 941) *Usul al-kafi,* Ibn Babuya's *al-Majalis* and *Iʿtiqadat,* Sayyid Razi's (d. 1015) *Nahj al-balaqa,* Tusi's (d. 1067) *al-Amali,* and Ibn Abi Jumhur's (d. 1501) *ʿAvali al-la'ali.*

This takes us to the second striking feature of the work, which is the plethora of quotations from Shiʿi hadith collections and the writings of well-

* Seyyed Hossein Nasr was the first scholar of Persian Sufism to emphasize the importance of *Tuhfa,* something he did in the 1980s. See Nasr, "Spiritual Movements," 663–65. Mu'azzin's work has recently been translated into English by Faghfoory with the title *Tuḥfah-yi ʿAbbāsī: The Golden Chain of Sufism in Shīʿite Islam.* This excellent translation is marred only by the fact that it is based on an early twentieth-century print edition of the work that was "corrected" by Zahabi editors.

† For examples, see Anzali, "Emergence," 163, note 53.

‡ Mu'azzin, *Tuhfa* MS1 and *Tuhfa* MS2. A 2002 edition published under the auspices of the Ahmadi khanaqah of the Zahabiyya in Shiraz came to my attention after my research was done. The anonymous editor claims to have made use of several early manuscripts, including the earliest one, which is dated 1657. This manuscript is currently held in Tbilisi, Georgia. For a brief description of this early manuscript see Afshar and Daneshpazhuh, *Nashriyya,* 8:177. I have not examined this edition to see how accurate or useful it is.

§ In the introduction, the author says that he was compelled to write the book because of the onslaught of a fierce anti-Sufi campaign that was initiated by those who know nothing of exoteric or esoteric knowledge. See Mu'azzin, *Tuhfa* MS2, 11.

** Mu'azzin, *Tuhfa* MS2, 11–15.

known Sufi-minded Twelver scholars of the past. The ubiquity of such material in *Tuhfa* is a sign of its time, a period in Safavid religious history that, as discussed earlier, was marked by intense scholarly activity in hadith studies. It also clearly speaks to Sufi authors' urgent need to develop an alternative framework of reference to legitimize their teachings. Shamlu's astute and important remark that Mu'azzin busied himself during his years of residence in Isfahan with the study of hadith literature should be understood in this context.*

Moving beyond these general features to more specific aspects of the work, we should note that the prologue contains a number of important points about the situation of the nascent Zahabi network at this time. First, much like the author of *Bayan*, Mu'azzin writes as both an affiliate and proponent of the Safavid Sufi order and a member of the specific Sufi tradition he has inherited from his master. Neither in *Divan* nor *Tuhfa* does Mu'azzin use the term *Zahabiyya* in reference to the Sufi network to which he belongs. Rather, he employs labels like *silsila-yi khassa-yi muqaddasa-yi nabaviyya* (the special and sacred prophetic order) and *tariqa-yi marziyya-yi mukhtassa-yi murtazaviyya* (the unique and praiseworthy ʿAlid path). The term *murtazaviyya* (ʿAlid) also appears in his *Divan* as a title for this path, or tariqa.† He emphasizes that his order (silsila) is connected genealogically to the Safavids, the "house founded on the caliphate" (*khanadan-i khalafat bunyan*), and he boasts of being trusted as "gatekeeper" and "treasurer" of the secrets of this royal Sufi order.‡ To make this connection even clearer, he provides a chain of transmission that connects him and the order to the legendary figure of Shaykh Safi al-Din Ardabili as a supplement to the primary Barzishabadi chain of spiritual transmission, which he lays out in detail.§ This dual lineage allowed him to distinguish his lineage from that of the Safavid order, while also providing a much-needed source of legitimacy.

Mu'azzin's attempt to connect his spiritual lineage through an additional

* Shamlu, *Qisas*, 2:187.

† *Mu'azzin, Divan MS, f. 128a.*

‡ Mu'azzin, *Tuhfa* MS2, 10. The exact phrase appears in Shamlu, *Qisas*, 2:186, which indicates that Shamlu had access to the book or the author—a confirmation not only of Shamlu's mystical proclivities but also of how well received Mu'azzin's work was among the elite members of the Safavid house.

§ Mu'azzin, *Tuhfa* MS1, f. 27b–30a. For more on Mu'azzin's spiritual genealogy see Anzali, "Emergence." The purported link between Mu'azzin's primary Kubravi lineage and the Savafid lineage is Shah Qasim Anvar (d. 1434), a student of Shaykh Safi's son, Shaykh Badr al-Din. Criticism of Shaykh Safi was off limits for even the most outspoken opponants of Sufism. Instead of denigrating him, critics presented revisionist pictures of his life in which his Shiʿi identity eclipsed his Sufi religious outlook.

alternative line to the Safavid network is by no means a unique phenomenon, as we saw in the case of *Bayan.* Irrespective of the historical value of such claims, forging such connections or emphasizing existing ones was crucial to a Sufi network's survival in the new Shiʿi milieu of Iran. Karbala'i, for example, claimed that Shah Ismaʿil spared his branch of the Barzishabadi network in Tabriz from persecution by Qizilbash zealots partly because of the ruler's awareness of the connection between the two networks.* Putting aside the question of whether such accounts exaggerate Qizilbash persecution, it is easy to see how these genealogical links were perceived as advantageous. Such connections helped the Nurbakhshi Sufi network flourish in Khurasan in the early Safavid period, before the falling out between Shah Tahmasp I and Shah Qavam al-Din Husayn, the grandson of Nurbakhsh the messiah.† Using adjectives like *nabaviyya, murtazaviyya,* and *razviyya* (explicit references to the Prophet, ʿAli, and the eighth imam, respectively) and tracing one's history to the Safavid Sufi network represent not only the formation of a new identity based on the personality and teachings of the twelve imams but also its compliance with the hegemonic Sufi discourse of the Safavids.

As we transition from the prologue to the content of *Tuhfa,* we encounter a lengthy introduction divided into five disparate chapters that constitute more than one-third of the whole book. The author begins with a discussion of the meaning of the terms *Sufi* and *Sufism,* departing little, if at all, from the traditional Sufi discourse of past masters. The trajectory soon changes, however, and Mu'azzin explains that the majority of the Sufis and dervishes of his day are imposters. He devotes nearly ten pages to the vices and dangers of such people. This is followed by a lengthy discussion of what Mu'azzin believes constitutes a real Sufi. He lists the attributes and qualifications of such people, noting how scarce they are. For more than sixty pages he quotes traditions, primarily from the imams but also from the Prophet. In each case, the original Arabic text is accompanied by its Persian translation, an important indication of the intended audience for the book. Most of these traditions are taken from Shiʿi hadith collections and pertain to the extraordinary spiritual accomplishments and qualifications of true believers (*mu'minin;* in this case, true Shiʿa). For Mu'azzin's purposes, however, they double as descriptions of real Sufis since, we are told, one cannot be a true Shiʿa without following the path of Sufism (and vice versa). The author presents a paradigmatic human being, a person who perfectly embodies both

* Karbala'i, *Rawzat al-jinan,* 2:105 and 159. He belonged to a branch of the Barzishabadi network called the Lala'i after its founder, Sayyid Badr al-Din Ahmad Lala'i (d. 1506).
† For more on this, see Bashir, *Messianic Hopes,* 186–94.

Sufi and Shiʿa ideals. He does this through copious quotations of Twelver sources accompanied by extensive commentaries on how these passages affirm the validity of the Sufi path.

After a cursory discussion of the two main precepts of the faith, the unity of God (*tawhid*) and the resurrection (*maʿad*), the remaining sections of the introduction are dedicated to explaining the Sufi perspective on that most crucial of doctrines, the imamate. The brevity of the author on the subjects of tawhid and maʿad and the length of his treatment of the imamate is a clear indication of the concerns of the time. After clarifying the meaning of *imam* from a Sufi point of view, the author brings this section to a close with a general discussion of how Sufis trace their teachings back to the imams. He then outlines his spiritual genealogy, which connects him to the imams and, through them, to the Prophet.* Throughout this lengthy introduction, Mu'azzin takes every opportunity to emphasize the importance of Sufis observing the Shariʿa, again a clear indication of the sort of allegations he faced.†

The main body of the book begins with a lengthy discussion of knowledge, which points to the primacy of religious knowledge and epistemology for Mu'azzin. From the early times, Shiʿi intellectuals have concerned themselves with the nature of religious knowledge and its authentic sources. Shiʿi sectarian identity depends fundamentally on a number of significant epistemological claims. The most important of these is that the imams are the only valid sources of religious knowledge, the sole inheritors of the prophetic maʿrifa, and the only people who know the true meaning of the Qur'an. It is no coincidence, then, that the earliest and most celebrated work of the Shiʿi hadith canon, Kulayni's *Usul al-kafi,* begins with a chapter titled "Kitab al-ʿaql va-l-jahl" ("The Book of Intellect and Foolishness").‡ Kulayni wrote his magnum opus at a time when a new Twelver Shiʿi identity emerged after the crisis of the occultation forced a fundamental rethinking of the doctrine of the imamate.

Similarly, *Tuhfa* was compiled as a new Sufi–Shiʿi identity emerged in the

* Mu'azzin, *Tuhfa* MS2, 208–9.

† Mu'azzin, *Tuhfa* MS2, 183–91. At the end, the author specifically mentions that a group called the *malahida* claim that the burden of observing the law does not apply to accomplished mystics. Not surprisingly, Mu'azzin categorically rejects this claim. The term *malahida* (sing. *mulhid*) usually refers to Ismailis in classical sources, but it appears that in this context it has become a more general designation applied to any group deemed heretical.

‡ It is difficult to convey in English the meaning of *jahl* as used in *al-Kafi*. I have chosen "foolishness" rather than "ignorance," but neither word approaches the polysemy of jahl.

aftermath of the crisis that a new, ulama-established orthodoxy posed for traditional Sufi modes of piety. In this context, it is not difficult to see why the author of *Tuhfa* was concerned primarily with questions of epistemology. The debate over approved sources and methods for attaining ma'rifa was, as mentioned previously, at the center of the battle between Sufis and the ulama over what would define Twelver orthodoxy. The stakes of this battle were high, for the victors would control religious discourse. It should not surprise us, then, that this was an issue of great debate between pro- and anti-Sufi authors and that knowledge is the subject of one of the most extensive discussions of *Tuhfa*.*

This is partly why Mu'azzin insists on speaking of Sufism as a discipline and highlighting the distinction between formal disciplinary fields of knowledge (*'ulum rasmiyya*), in which reasoning plays an essential role in constructing arguments, and what he calls the true disciplines (*'ulum haqiqiyya*). The latter, for him, is the discipline of Sufism. Only through mastery of this discipline can a drop of the unfathomable ocean of divine ma'rifa be distilled in the heart. In treating Sufism as a discipline, Mu'azzin aligned himself not only with a long tradition of scholarly Sufism† but also with some of Twelver Shi'ism's most respected, Sufi-minded scholars, including his contemporary Fayz, his teacher Sadra, and the Second Martyr. In addition to his link to *Misbah*, the Lebanese scholar's *Munyat al-murid* is among the most-cited works in Sufi treatises of this period. A paragraph from this work classifying the branches of knowledge is frequently referenced by Sufis and Sufi-minded ulama of this period, and it deserves to be quoted in full.

> After learning the exoteric disciplines and all that earlier scholars have compiled in their books, including [rules] for daily prayers, fasting, recitation of the Qur'an and other prayers, there are other things necessary for the scholar to learn. In addition to the supererogatory rites, obligatory rituals, and duties compiled by jurisprudents that every individual who reaches the age of adolescence (*mukallaf*) is expected to observe, there are other disciplines more essential to learn and observe. These are also subject of great debate and controversy. They include purification

* Mu'azzin, *Tuhfa MS2*, 212–39.

† References to Sufism as a branch of knowlege ('ilm) date back to as early as the tenth century, most notably in the works of Abu Nasr Sarraj and Abu Talib Makki, among others. Later, Ghazali divided knowledge into the categories of exoteric and esoteric, and subdivided the latter into *'ilm al-mu'amalat* and *'ilm al-mukashafat*. When Ibn 'Arabi came on the scene, the latter expanded significantly and resulted in the establishment of a distinctly Sufi metaphysical school of thought, usually referred to as *al-'ilm bi-allah* or *'ilm ilahi* in contrast to *'ilm manazil al-akhira* or simply *'ilm al-manazil*, a reference to what Ghazali called *'ilm al-mu'amalat*.

> of the soul from vicious habits and traits such as pride, bigotry, jealousy, hatred, and other poisonous characteristics that have been discussed in relevant disciplines. . . . It is mandatory for everyone to learn these disciplines and put them to practice. These duties and obligations cannot be found in the books of jurisprudence or discussions of [the laws of] transaction and rent and the like. In order to acquire the knowledge of these disciplines every individual who reaches the age of adolescence is expected to seek scholars of the truth (*ulama-yi haqiqat*) and read books they have written in these fields. There is no pride more destructive for a divinely learned man than his preoccupation with the formal sciences and his negligence of his own soul and struggle to earn God's pleasure, blessed and exalted is He.*
>
> . . . After complete knowledge of exoteric sciences [*ʿilm al-zahir*] [the seeker of knowledge] moves forward to learn the true sciences [*al-ʿulum al-haqiqiyya*] and the true disciplines [*al-funun al-haqqiyya*]. Indeed, these are the kernel of the sciences and the essence of all that is known. Through these sciences one can attain the stations of those who were brought nigh to God and reach the station, as those [before you] who have reached the station of union [with the Beloved]. May God connect you and me to that threshold; verily He is the generous and the bestower.†

For Mu'azzin, there is no question that ʿAmili's emphasis on the "true" over the "official" disciplines can be interpreted in only one way, as a reference to the discipline of Sufism. The true religious scholars are none other than Sufis.‡ He concludes, "Therefore, it is prudent to say that by relying on formal knowledge based on reason one cannot attain the station of ʿirfan, which is the abode of those who are brought nigh to the Lord. One cannot witness the beauty of the true Beloved by any means other than the light of the sun of divinely inspired knowledge. Because on the path of reason there are many thorns of skepticism and doubt . . . and the end of most of the arguments is disagreement, and the basis of syllogism (*qiyas*) is often conjecture and exaggeration (*gazaf*).§

Mu'azzin also finds an ally in the Second Martyr on the subject of the traditional Sufi classification of the ulama into three groups: (1) those who

* Mu'azzin, *Tuhfa* MS2, 238–39. The original passage can be found in ʿAmili, *Munyat al-murid*, 154–55. I have used Faghfoory's translation of ʿAmili's passage with minor changes and corrections. See Mu'azzin, *The Golden Chain*, 103–4.

† Mu'azzin, *The Golden Chain*, 109. Originally in ʿAmili, *Munyat al-murid*, 389.

‡ Mu'azzin, *Tuhfa* MS2, 239.

§ Mu'azzin, *Golden Chain*, 107. Cf. Mu'azzin, *Tuhfa* MS2, 249.

are exclusively well versed in exoteric matters (*al-ʿalim bi-amr allah*); (2) those who are exclusively well versed in esoteric matters (*al-ʿalim bi-allah*); and (3) those who are well versed in both (*al-ʿalim bi-Allah va-bi-amr allah*).* The third type is the ideal from both Muʾazzin's perspective and that of the Second Martyr. This ideal human being is a true Sufi numbered among the "poles [*aqtab*] of the time," of whom only a handful exist in the east and west in each age. These are those whose patronage makes life possible for the populace.†

The Second Martyr was not the only Sufi-minded Twelver scholar whose work Muʾazzin found useful in laying a Twelver Shiʿi foundation for Sufi teachings. A long-standing affinity between Shiʿi and Sufi thought and the fact that most Twelver scholars throughout history had operated in a predominantly Sunni environment in which Sufism was a major and often dominant player meant that many well-known religious scholars with Shiʿi affiliations had written treatises that drew upon and resembled Sufi literature. In addition to quoting classical sources of Twelver hadith and well-known Sufi works, *Tuhfa* is filled with quotations from works such as Ibn Abi Jumhur Ahsaʾi's *ʿAvali al-laʾali,*‡ Ibn Fahd Hilli's *al-Tahsin fi sifat al-ʿarifin,*§ Nasir al-Din Tusi's *Awsaf al-ashraf,* ʿAllama Hilli's *Minhaj al-karama* and *Sharh al-tajrid,* Shaykh Bahaʾi's *Kashkul* and *Arbaʿin,* and ʿAmili's *Munyat al-murid.* By the end of the first chapter of the *Tuhfa,* the halfway point of the book has been passed.

Tuhfa and the Necessity of a Pir

I close my analysis of *Tuhfa* with a brief note on how Muʾazzin addressed the subject of the pir, or spiritual master. As suggested earlier, the way writings from this era handle this sensitive and fundamental aspect of traditional Sufi thought is a barometer of how transformations in the religious environment influenced Sufis' understanding of their heritage and social institutions. The necessity of a spiritual master for the wayfarer is addressed in the last chapter of *Tuhfa,* which contains a detailed discussion of (1) why one must seek a pir when embarking upon the mystical path and (2) the qualifications necessary for both disciples and masters. According to Muʾazzin, a

* This is a very old classification ascribed by Razi to Shahqiq al-Balkhi in the former's commentary on the Qurʾan. See Razi, *Tafsir,* 2:181. Zayn al-Din paraphrases Razi at some length here. See ʿAmili, *Munyat al-murid,* 123–25.

† ʿAmili, *Munyat al-murid,* 278–79.

‡ For his biography, seen from a late Sufi–Shiʿi perspective, see Maʿsum-ʿAli Shah, *Taraʾiq al-haqaʾiq,* 1:248–51.

§ See Maʿsum-ʿAli Shah, *Taraʾiq al-haqaʾiq,* 221–23.

person must attain five primary and twenty secondary qualities related to mystical capabilities and moral character in order to be worthy of being a shaykh.* His discussion of these qualities is taken, often word for word, from a classical Sufi source, *Mirsad al-ʿibad,* which was written by the Kubravi Sufi shaykh, Najm al-Din Razi Daya (d. 1256). It is quite normal for a Sufi master like Mu'azzin to paraphrase *Mirsad;* what interests me here is the places where he felt it necessary to edit or supplement Daya's comments.

The pertinent section of *Mirsad* begins with a list of five fundamental qualities necessary for the spiritual guide. Four of these have to do with the ability of the spiritual master to receive divine secrets and grace in an unmediated fashion.† This is a concrete demonstration of how the Sufi ideal of ideal religious authority differs fundamentally from that of the ulama, whose emphasis has always been on the mediation of religious knowledge through other human beings, namely prominent teachers of the past and present. In the corresponding portion of *Tuhfa,* Mu'azzin follows *Mirsad* with only minor additions and modifications.‡ However, he leaves out Daya's final remarks in which Daya discusses how the novice attains unmediated knowledge of the divine. Daya emphasizes the crucial role of falling in love with the beauty (*jamal*) of the master and giving up all personal preferences and choices in favor of those of the master. Such language, apparently, did not suit Mu'azzin as he sought to position his arguments within an orthodox Twelver framework. Another telling erasure can be seen in the following pages, where Mu'azzin has left out Daya's discussion of the proper mode of behavior in samaʿ and the correct manner of prostrating oneself before one's master.§

Moving on to the twenty additional qualities a true master must have, we find two important differences between *Mirsad* and *Tuhfa.* In the former work, Daya mentions the necessity of the Sufi master having a "minimal knowledge of Shariʿa," so that he can give appropriate advice to his disciples in "urgent cases."** Mu'azzin adds this provision to Daya's remark: "If the master reaches the station of leadership of the community, mastery of the exoteric sciences is necessary so that one can help solve the questions and problems of wayfarers and disciples."†† This additional provision, I believe, reflects the intellectual environment of Isfahan, which forms the context in which *Tuhfa* was written. Mu'azzin understood that as a resident of a

* Mu'azzin, *Tuhfa* MS2, 494–529.
† Razi, *Mirsad al-ʿibad,* 237–40.
‡ Mu'azzin, *Tuhfa* MS2, 512–16.
§ Razi, *Mirsad al-ʿibad,* 263; Mu'azzin, *Tuhfa* MS2, 527.
** Razi, *Mirsad al-ʿibad,* 244.
†† Mu'azzin, *Tuhfa* MS2, 515. Translation from Mu'azzin, *Golden Chain,* 208.

khanaqah, he would not be taken seriously by the ulama, who had increasing control over the social, financial, and political resources that major religious institutions needed to survive. Had he chosen to ignore the so-called official disciplines in favor of his "true discipline," he would have been dismissed as an ignorant dervish not only by puritanical anti-Sufis but also by mystically minded members of the ulama such as Sadra and Fayz. Given this reality, it is not difficult to understand why he decided to take up the study of hadith so late in his career. The mid-seventeenth century was the heyday of scholarly obsession with hadith, and such study provided him with the credentials needed to engage in a meaningful conversation with patrons of the court and his colleagues in the madrasas. The second striking, though not surprising, contrast between *Mirsad* and *Tuhfa* is Mu'azzin's departure from his predecessor's emphasis on the necessity for both master and disciple of adhering to the essentials of Sunni doctrine (*iʿtiqad-i ahl-i sunnat va jamaʿat*). Mu'azzin simply replaces this with an emphasis on the necessity of a pure and unwavering submission to the teachings of the imams.*

Mu'azzin was a important figure in the dynamic religious environment of Safavid Iran, and his intellectual and religious outlook provides us with a window into major changes of the era. In the early decades of his career (the pre-Isfahan era), he functioned as a popular Sufi shaykh, comfortable in his khanaqah, where he practiced zikr and samaʿ regularly with his disciples, much as the Kubravi masters had done before him. The second phase of his career, epitomized by *Tuhfa,* was markedly different. His time in Isfahan brought an acute awareness of and a concern with issues of religious authority and authenticity that were being debated in the lively intellectual environment of the capital. Mu'azzin's lifetime spanned two different worlds, and he made an original and innovative attempt to arbitrate their differences. He sought to build a bridge between the world of institutionalized Sufism and that of the new religious and political elite of Isfahan, where he engaged in scholarly conversation with mystically minded ulama and sought the sponsorship of the Safavid monarch by presenting himself as a devout Twelver and a guardian of the Safavid Sufi legacy.†

* Razi, *Mirsad al-ʿibad,* 244; Mu'azzin, *Tuhfa* MS2, 516.

† Mu'azzin, for example, is reported to have appealed to the authority of Fayz Kashani when questioned about the validity of the practice of samaʿ in his khanaqah. In response, we are told, Fayz denied having supported such a practice (see ʿIsam, *Nasiha* MS, f. 126b–127a). Babayan reports the same story based on Jaʿfariyan (see Babayan, *Mystics, Monarchs, and Messiahs,* 448). Although, as she has pointed out, Fayz's denial accords with the stand he takes against the practice of *zikr-i jali* in his *al-Muhakimat,* since the story appears only in anti-Sufi literature and serves an

Najib al-Din Riza and the Demise of Organized Sufism

During the final decades of Safavid rule, the pressure on Sufis and dervishes increased. The death, in 1659, of Majlisi Sr., whose popularity and explicit proclivity toward Sufism made him a valuable and strategic ally to Sufis facing heightened criticism, was a significant blow to the pro-Sufi front. Seven years later, Sufis lost another major ally with the passing of Shah ʿAbbas II, the last Safavid king to openly favor dervishes and Sufis. Four years later, Mu'azzin, one of the most prominent Sufi masters of the time in terms of his influence in the capital, passed away. Other prominent figures gradually distanced themselves from Sufism as a result of the impact of the anti-Sufi campaign and the weakening of royal support. The tide was turning rapidly against the Sufis.

Fayz Kashani is a good example of a figure whose support for Sufism waned over the course of his life. He initially wrote treatises favorable toward Sufism, at least in its learned forms, but gradually distanced himself from it in the final decades of his career, eventually writing a treatise in which he expressed regret for having spent his time on such inauthentic teachings.* This trend became more pronounced, culminating in the work of his son, Muhammad b. Muhsin (known as ʿAlam al-Huda), a prominent religious scholar who wrote several treatises against Sufism.† A similar trajectory is observable with Majlisi Sr. and his son. The former was unhesitating in his defense of certain elements of Sufi thought, but his son Muhammad Baqir Majlisi (d. 1699), who gradually rose to prominence after his father's death, vehemently opposed Sufism and wrote treatises against it. He was appointed to the office of *shaykh al-islam* in Isfahan, a posting that was followed by two similarly important appointments, in Qum and in Mashhad. By 1687, three of the most prominent and outspoken anti-Sufi critics, Muhammad-Tahir Qummi, Shaykh Hurr ʿAmili, and Majlisi Jr., had been appointed to the highest clerical positions in three major urban centers of Iran (Qum, Mashhad, and Isfahan, respectively). The emergence of this triangle of anti-Sufi *shaykh al-islams* was an important development in the anti-Sufi campaign. Only mid-ranking mullas had engaged Sufis in the early decades, but as the end

---

obvious polemical goal, it must be approached carefully. Irrespective of the facticity of the story, it is significant that Fayz, of all the ulama, was chosen to play the role of an advocate for Sufism.

* For a broad analysis of the evolving position of Fayz regarding Sufism see Jaʿfariyan, *Safaviyya,* 2:537–56. For a more recent and in-depth analysis of the same subject, see Zargar, "Revealing Revisions."

† For a bibliography of ʿAlam al-Huda's writings see Hoseyni, "Introduction," 1:18–29.

of the seventeenth century approached, high-ranking ulama had enough the power and authority to fight all forms of heresy, including Sufism.*

At the same time, the Safavids faced increasing difficulty managing the economy and the financial resources of the empire.† To add insult to injury, during the first decade of Shah Safi II's reign, Iran was struck by two bad harvests, a devastating earthquake in Shirvan, and several other calamities that were taken as proof that the shah had been crowned at an inauspicious time, necessitating that his coronation be done anew, this time with his name changed to Sulayman.‡ Despite this step, the economic hardship continued for most of Shah Sulayman's reign. The decade following his second coronation proved domestically troublesome, despite relative calm on the borders. The overall deterioration in the health of the empire did not check the rise of the ulama, who benefited from the unwavering support of the Safavid monarchs, especially the final king, Shah Sultan Husayn (r. 1694–1722).§ They were increasingly successful in securing the necessary financial and political resources to build their hierocracy. Madrasas continued to be built, and religious education flourished apace.** The half-century after the death of Shah ʿAbbas II was the apex of clerical power, a time that saw the consolidation of an elaborately structured religious hierocracy and the cementing of a strong alliance with the political establishment.††

In contrast, Sufi khanaqahs and dervish monasteries found it ever more difficult to secure the necessary financial resources to keep such centers operational. The Zahabi network is an excellent example of this struggle. According to later Zahabi sources, the leadership of the network passed during

* Sefatgol, *Sakhtar*, 452. The fact that the "archbishops" of the three most important urban centers of Iran, religiously speaking, were more or less Akhbari in their approach testifies to the dominant position of this legal school of thought in the final decades of Safavid rule.

† For a fascinating and in-depth analysis of this crisis, see Matthee, *Persia in Crisis*.

‡ The 1670s witnessed drought, harsh winters, locust swarms, famine, and earthquakes. In 1678–1679 some seventy thousand people are said to have perished from famine in Isfahan alone. Newman summarizes the devastation, which was widespread in most of the Safavid lands. He tells us of another poor harvest in 1669 and a plague in Gilan in 1684–5, which spread to Aradabil, where some eighty thousand were said to have died, and from there to Hamadan. It went on to strike Azerbaijan, Mazandaran, Astarabad, and Isfahan itself in 1686–1687. In 1689, the plague was said to have killed thousands in Shiraz, and it struck areas from Baku to Basra, Mosul, and Baghdad. See Newman, *Safavid Iran*, 94.

§ On his religious sensibilities and devotion, see Sefatgol, *Sakhtar*, 91–97.

** For a detailed and masterly analysis of the hierocratic structure of the late Safavid period see Sefatgol, *Sakhtar*, 397–458.

†† Sefatgol, *Sakhtar*, 184–234.

this period to an artisan named Najib al-Din Riza Zargar Tabrizi (d. ca. 1696), who lived in Isfahan for most of his life. Najib's autobiographical account of his miserable situation in Isfahan is a personal testament not only to the economic hardships he endured but also to his failure to reinvigorate the network after his master's death. Najib was unable to gain a significant number of followers in Isfahan. In the very last pages of *Sabʿ al-masani,* the magnum opus that he wrote in Isfahan around 1680, Najib complains that the city was "built by Judas" and devoid of manliness (*muruvvat*).* He explains that in the initial years of his residence in the capital, he was able to amass and disburse significant funding, and thus desperate people frequented his house in times of economic hardship. His resources, however, were rapidly depleted, and his inability to replenish them is an indication of the privation Sufi centers experienced because of a lack of wealthy and well-connected patrons, a reality that forced many such centers to cease operation. This stands in stark contrast the report Najib had written on Mashhad a decade earlier, which portrayed a prosperous khanaqah with a kitchen full of food.†

In spite of his dismal leadership record, Najib played a fundamental role in the history of his Sufi network. Alongside his master, he crafted the Zahabi spiritual genealogy, giving it the name by which it was known from the eighteenth century on, the Zahabiyya. I have written about this important development extensively elsewhere,‡ and thus I limit my comments here to noting that the increasing pressure from the anti-Sufi front and the concordant stigmatization of epithets like sufiyya, alongside the urgent need for an authentically Twelver outlook, meant that the title Zahabiyya, with its strong semantic association with the figure of the eighth imam, was a perfect choice for the network. The fact that the network had flourished during the previous century in Mashhad, where it maintained an active khanaqah located near the shrine, meant that the eighth imam was in effect the patron of this Sufi group from the early seventeenth century onward. The choice of Zahabiyya as a designation was also in accordance with the increasing role that the eighth imam played in the religious imagination of the newly converted Shiʿi population of Iran. It confirmed the Twelver nature of this Sufi network and preemptively responded to the charges of Sunnism usually leveled against Sufis during this time.

The designation Zahabiyya and the spiritual genealogy that claimed

* Tabrizi Isfahani, *Sabʿ al-masani,* 372–73.

† Three or four of his children died as a result of harsh economic conditions in Mashhad and then Isfahan. For a heartbreaking account of the loss, see Tabrizi Isfahani, *Nur al-hidaya* MS, f. 172b–173a. For a different version of the same story see Tabrizi Isfahani, *Sabʿ al-masani,* 372–73.

‡ Anzali, "Emergence."

both Safavid and Shiite descent were born out of a late seventeenth-century religious and spiritual culture that was distinctly Safivid in nature. The Zahabiyya were in full compliance with the hagiographical narrative that gave Safavid rule its spiritual legitimacy—a narrative that revolved around the figure of Safi al-Din Ardabili as the founding figure of the Safavid Sufi network.* As a sayyid and a pious and orthodox Sufi follower of the twelve imams, Safi al-Din stood at the center of an elaborate foundation myth. He embodied the Safavid spiritual ideal and served as a model to be emulated. His presence loomed large, overshadowing other Sufi figures of the past. Mu'azzin and others like him claimed authority by presenting themselves as gatekeepers to the secret teachings of the Grand Master Safi al-Din.

This silsila also incorporated into its worldview another key facet of the Safavid milieu: the fundamental elements of the new Twelver orthodoxy developed by the ulama. The clearest sign of this is the omnipresence of the twelve imams in the network's literature. The dazzling charisma and indisputable authority of these holy men pushed all other Sufi figures to the margins. The saintly figures of the past, the charismatic Sufis and dervishes at the center of public devotional rites, were eclipsed by the twelve imams and their descendants. Devotion to the latter replaced previous cults situated around the quasi-divine powers of past saints, and the powerful symbolism of the imams became the new focus of mass religiosity as well as the main theme of religious literature composed by the elite.

Despite his original contribution, the combination of a hostile environment and a lack of financial resources meant that Najib spent the final years of his life in isolation (he passed away around 1698).† For the next two decades, there is little record of any Zahabi social, literary, or intellectual activities or of Sufi activities more broadly. So tenuous was the situation of organized Sufism in general and the Zahabi network in particular that the very existence of the next Zahabi pole, 'Ali-Naqi Istahbanati (d. 1714), would be doubtful if not for the fact that his successor, Nayrizi, mentions him as his master.‡ Until recently, no text written by Istahbanati was known to have survived. A recently published monograph attributed to him and titled *Burhan*

* Therefore, the connection of the spiritual lineage of the Zahabi Sufi network to the Safavid network remains important. This is reflected in Najib's remarks, taken almost word for word from his master's *Tuhfa*. He says, first, that Shaykh Safi's silsila can also can be traced back to the eighth imam via Ma'ruf Karkhi and, second, that *silsilat al-zahab*, the golden lineage, is also connected to the founder of the Safavi network, Shaykh Safi al-Din. Once again, the connecting link is Shah Qasim Anvar. See Tabrizi Isfahani, *Nur al-hidaya* MS, f. 188a–189a.

† For his death date see Khavari, *Zahabiyya*, 287–89.

‡ Khuyi, *Mizan al-savab*, 3:1199.

al-murtazin, however, has shed light on the situation of the network during those difficult times.* Istahbanati gives us a glimpse of how difficult the situation had become for Sufis toward the end of Safavid rule: "The masses . . . because of their ignorance and misguidedness, have found the courage to be sarcastic and curse and harass God's servants to the degree that they consider such harassment the most important religious duty after the five daily prayers. They use swords, stones, and sticks if they are able; otherwise they consider backbiting, accusing, slander, sarcasm, and cursing obligatory upon themselves."†

In spite of this hostility and the weakness of the network, a shaping and important event took place during this period: the center of the network was permanently transferred to Shiraz. The city was a much more welcoming and tolerant environment for unorthodox figures than Isfahan. Istahbanati died in 1714, and his passing was barely noted by the learned circles of his time.‡ The Zahabi network, however, underwent a revival under the leadership of his successor, Qutb al-Din Nayrizi, who devoted a half-century to scholarly activities, becoming a prolific writer and respected teacher.§ For these efforts, he is known as a reviver (*mujaddid*) in Zahabi sources.** His intellectual outlook and social networks, however, were closer to those of a high-ranking member of the madrasa than to those of a Sufi shaykh of the khanaqah. He was an established teacher in the madrasas of Najaf, the study of hadith was his main occupation, and he even refused to be called a Sufi. This was a fascinating and important development for the future of Persian Sufism in general and the Zahabi network in particular.

Safavid Shiʿism as a "Sacred Nomos" and a "World Religion"

The previous pages have demonstrated Sufism's solid social position in the early seventeenth century, before a group of mid-ranking ulama began to challenge its legitimacy. In less than a century, this position had changed dramatically. Public opinion had turned against Sufis and dervishes by the early 1800s. Lack of sponsorship and a well-organized campaign carried out with the tacit approval of religious and political authorities did much to weaken Sufism, but this does not fully account for how the average denizens of the Safavid Empire, especially residents of urban areas, who had

* Khavari, *Zahabiyya*, 297.

† Istahbanati, *Burhan al-murtazin*, 1–2. The content of this work is examined more thoroughly in chapter 4.

‡ Khuyi, *Mizan al-savab*, 3:1199. On his death date see Khavari, *Zahabiyya*, 296.

§ For an account of later developments in Zahabi leadership see Lewisohn, "Modern Persian Sufism."

** Khuyi, *Mizan al-savab*, XVIII.

previously relied on the rich and diverse symbolism of Sufism to make sense of the natural and supernatural worlds, severed their ties with Sufis in less than a century. It also does not explain how the Safavid populace became Twelvers who turned to the ulama to meet their religious needs, accepting the latter as mediators of the power, grace, and knowledge of the divinely guided imams.

Why this shift occurred within the Iranian populous is a complex and difficult question to which I cannot pretend to have a complete answer. In the following analysis, however, I offer some thoughts and suggest an analytical framework that may undergird a good understanding of the significant transformation of the religious landscape of Safavid Persia. This requires a different methodological approach. The previous discussion has dealt primarily with intellectual history, which by definition is not well suited to provide insight into the religious traditions of the lay masses. A combination of historical and sociological approaches is more appropriate for exploring what shapes popular religious attitudes and the circumstances and influences that change them. Two sociologists of religion are relevant to the question at hand. First, I rely on *The Sacred Canopy* and the insights of its author, Peter Berger, into the role that religion plays in the social construction of reality. Because I use some of the latter's technical vocabulary in my own analysis, some brief introductory remarks about his terminology and understanding of religion are in order. Second, I draw on Said Amir Arjomand's example in *The Shadow of God and the Hidden Imam,* in which he applies Weber's sociological framework to the study of Shiʿism during the Safavid period.

Peter Berger and *The Sacred Canopy*

Essential to Berger's understanding of the way humans construct the world that they inhabit are the processes of "world-construction" and "world-maintenance." Berger holds that human beings, as social animals, are a distinct species insofar as they create the world they inhabit, rather than being born to it hardwired genetically. That is, they create a meaningful order of things—a nomos, as Berger calls it—based on language. This human construction is first "externalized" and then "objectivated" as a reality independent of the individual, and finally it is "internalized" by the individual. What is considered "objective knowledge," therefore, is a common order of interpretation imposed by society upon experience.*

A crucial feature of these social constructions is that, as human productions, they are inherently precarious. Therefore, if they are to remain effective

* Berger, *Sacred Canopy,* 20.

and "objective," they need continuous support and reinvigoration. Legitimation is one important way of stabilizing such precarious structures. Berger defines legitimation as part of "the socially objectivated 'knowledge' that serves to explain and justify the social order. Put differently, legitimations are answers to any questions about the 'why' of institutional arrangements."* Historically, says Berger, religion has been most effective instrument of legitimation, because "it relates the precarious reality constructions of empirical societies with ultimate reality. [As a result] [the tenuous realities of the social world are grounded in the sacred . . . which by definition is beyond the contingencies of human meanings and human activity."†

There are different levels of legitimation, to be sure. Although most of Berger's analysis is focused on pre-theoretical stages of the construction of such *nomoi,* he nevertheless recognizes the importance of theoretical levels of knowledge production. The learned elite play an important role in this work by producing the body of official interpretations of reality.‡ Through such official interpretations, the nomos of a society is legitimized in its totality, and all less-than-total legitimations are theoretically integrated into an all-embracing worldview. Religious elites provide this level of legitimation by "bestowing social institutions an ultimately valid ontological status, that is, by *locating* them within a sacred and cosmic frame of reference."§ Finally, the success of religion as an instrument of legitimation requires the existence of a broad "plausibility structure" or, in other words, a significant enough social base whose belief in the objectivity of a certain sacred nomos makes legitimation plausible.

While I agree broadly with Berger's analysis, I find his exclusive emphasis on knowledge and theory as sources of religious legitimation somewhat narrow. There is no doubt that the beliefs, theology, and worldview offered by a religion play a significant role in the process of legitimation. But human behaviors associated with myth and ritual, as captured by the study of religion, also maintain and reinvigorate the inherently precarious nomoi against the ever-present threat of anomie, especially at the level of mass religiosity. If we understand myth as sacred story that founds and grounds a particular world by offering an overarching narrative of why things have developed and remain in a certain order, then ritual, broadly speaking, is a reenactment of myth, repeated on a regular basis to reaffirm the objective reality of that world.**

* Berger, *Sacred Canopy,* 29.

† Berger, *Sacred Canopy,* 32.

‡ Berger, *Sacred Canopy,* 20–21.

§ Berger, *Sacred Canopy,* 33.

** Kripal et al., *Comparing Religions,* 112–16.

The legitimation of a sacred nomos, therefore, should be understood as a rich and complex serious of interactions between multiple classes and groups in a given society, none of whose members are solely passive receivers (as the masses are sometimes portrayed) or active producers (as elites are often depicted). The religious scholar may affirm, modify, or reject the validity of a popular myth and its reenactment, but the masses are likewise involved in their own process of confirming, modifying, or rejecting scholars' claims to authority and their ideas about what narratives ought to found and ground their collective world. Legitimation is a symbiotic process, the result of countless social interactions and individual calculations regarding what is or is not meaningful and what is or is not worthwhile. Stories, rituals, and institutions may be lost or forgotten because they are no longer relevant or are simply too expensive to maintain in the face of opposition. At other times they prove resilient, retaining such appeal in society at large that detractors are forced to modify or give up their opposition.

To borrow Berger's framework, I argue that, at its most basic level, the transformation of the Iranian society during the Safavid period was about constructing a new sacred nomos. This process necessitated the deconstruction of old structures, the jettisoning of some elements, and the salvage and integration of others into a new world order. A particularly important aspect of the new sacred nomos was that, unlike previous Shiʿi worldviews, which were embedded within the larger Sunni order, Safavid Shiʿism achieved an intellectual independence and social and institutional autonomy unprecedented in the Shiʿi experience. This takes us to another important analytical concept: Shiʿism as a world religion.

Shiʿism as a World Religion

In the very first page of *The Shadow of God and the Hidden Imam,* Arjomand, inspired by Weber's analytical framework, urges us to think about Twelver Shiʿism as a world religion. "Twelver Shiism," he says, "as a branch of Islam, can be fruitfully considered a 'world religion' as conceptualized by Weber—that is, as an autonomous intellectual pattern or belief system, which is embodied in meaningful social action and enfolded in sentiments."* I wholly agree with Arjomand's perspective and find the category of world religion helpful for the reasons laid out later. I am fully aware, however, that in the current climate of religious studies the use of the category of "world religions" can create some critical pushback. In the past couple of decades, scholars of religion have embarked on a soul-searching mission, questioning the validity and analytical usefulness of many of the foundational categories

* Arjomand, *Shadow of God,* 1.

of their field of study. The applicability of categories such as religion, mysticism, and world religion has been questioned, especially their suitability in non-Western, non-Christian contexts. Before I use the category analytically, then, I need to attend to this criticism.

In his remarkable critical study of the category of world religion, Tomoko Masuzawa demonstrates how this neutral-looking concept is in fact tied to a discourse constructed as "part of a much broader, fundamental transformation of European identity" during the nineteenth and early twentieth centuries.* As such, this supposedly universal and pluralist category is informed by the power dynamics of nineteenth-century Europe, when scholars produced a new set of comparative "scientific" systems of linguistic and racial classifications that were informed, at least in part, by colonial expansion and the "discovery" of the East. In Masuzawa's own words, "we have good reason to suspect that the discourse of world religions came into being precisely as a makeshift solution to the particular predicament that confounded European Christianity at the end of the nineteenth century, that is to say, as a covert way out of the profound conceptual difficulty confronting Europe and its imperial subject-position."† As such, a fundamental question arises: "whether the world religions discourse can be in any way enlisted, and trusted, on the side of historical scholarship . . . whether the idea of the diversity of religion is not, instead, the very thing that facilitates the transference and transmutation of a particular absolutism from one context to another–from the overtly exclusivist hegemonic version (Christian supremacist dogmatism) to the openly pluralistic universalist one (world religions pluralism)- and at the same time makes this process of transmutation very hard to identify and nearly impossible to understand."‡

Similar concerns have been raised by scholars regarding the power dynamics that contributed to the formation of major concepts in contemporary religious studies, such as religion, mysticism, and spirituality.§ This postcolonial critique of how many disciplines, including the study of religion, are entangled in a fundamentally unbalanced power relationship between researchers and the subjects of their study has been taken seriously by scholars, who have responded to it in at least two radically different ways.

* Masuzawa, *Invention of World Religions*, xii.

† Masuzawa, *Invention of World Religions*, 327.

‡ Masuzawa, *Invention of World Religions*, 326–27.

§ On "mysticism," see, for example, Jantzen, *Power, Gender, and Christian Mysticism*, and King, *Orientalism and Religion*. King offers a critical analysis of both mysticism and religion as categories of Western origin. On the latter category, Talal Asad's critique in *Genealogies of Religion* has been especially influential. Most recently, Brent Nongbri offers a similar criticism inspired by Asad in *Before Religion*.

One response is to question the very possibility of constructing analytical categories that are cross-culturally useful. Such categories for analyzing human behavior and thought across space and time, the reasoning goes, are doomed to distort the subjects of inquiry beyond hope. Scholars who hold to this line of thinking often avoid research that would require them to use comparative and cross-cultural constructs. They do not always object to cross-cultural scholarly analysis on principle, but they have little to offer when it comes to proposing an acceptable alternative model for scholarship on subjects like religion. To quote Masuzawa again, "If the scientific efficacy of the world religions discourse is put in doubt, what alternative method, what new strategies should be adopted in its stead in order to conduct basic research, or to teach an introductory course on various religions?"* She admits that she does not have a good answer to this question.† If the world religions discourse is entirely useless and cross-cultural analyses too fraught to be attempted, what then? An extreme outcome would be the shuttering of religious studies department, an option I hope gives scholars of religion pause. Others have suggested the less drastic step of repositioning religious studies as a subfield within the broader framework of cultural studies.‡

The problem with discarding a cross-cultural approach to world religions is a simple one, in my opinion. At its most basic level, scholarship is an exercise in using the familiar to make sense of the unfamiliar. Saying something meaningful, even in purely descriptive terms, about cultures, languages, and societies that are not our own requires the use of concepts and categories that are to some extent familiar. The same critique levied by Masuzawa against concepts in religious studies could be applied to postcolonial theorists and concepts such as culture, power, hegemony, and colonialism, which pepper their writings. It can be reasonably argued that these, too, are Western categories that maintain the same power dynamics they claim to fight. That is to say, aren't all academics, no matter their intellectual leanings, participants to some degree in the economic and political power of the West and its dominant role in the production of knowledge?

Another response is to take a more commonsense approach to postcolonial critiques. Some scholars take seriously the shadow cast by Western colonialism and liberal Protestantism on their fields of study, committing themselves to recognizing past mistakes and constructing more nuanced, accurate, and culturally sensitive categories for the present and future study of religion. They recognize, as J. Z. Smith has reminded us, that categories like

* Masuzawa, *Invention of World Religions*, 327.

† Masuzawa, *Invention of World Religions*.

‡ See King, *Orientalism and Religion*, 58–59, and Fitzgerald, "Religious Studies," 35, 47.

religion are not "native terms." Instead, they are "created by scholars for their intellectual purposes and therefore [are] theirs to define."* A thoughtful approach to creating such categories requires self-reflexivity and an awareness of the hidden biases we bring to our research.

In this spirit, and in agreement with Arjomand, I argue that it is analytically useful to understand Twelver Shiʿism during the Safavid period as a world religion. In other words, conceptualizing the transformation of the religious landscape of Persia as a shift from sectarian Shiʿism to Twelver Shiʿism as a world religion gives us insight into the comprehensive change that took place at both the elite and the popular levels.† By sectarian, I mean a religious identity defined by its rejection of some or all major elements of the mainstream construction of reality, one that cannot be properly understood without reference to the overarching sacred nomos. By world religion, on the other hand, I refer to a religious identity that is built on an overwhelmingly independent network of symbols, one composed of a set of sacred stories, ritual performances, intellectual discourses, and social institutions that constitute a new sacred nomos, whose intellectual traditions and institutions function autonomously.‡

* Smith, "Religion," 281.

† In using the terms *elite* and *popular,* I do not mean to suggest an essentialist dichotomy. Both modes of piety are interdependent and have significant overlaps, but categorizing them in this manner is the most useful (though not a perfect) way of describing a situation in which the overwhelming majority of the population lacked the literacy and access necessary to contribute directly to intellectual conversation between scholars. Scholars, in turn, were and are limited in their ability to define how the masses practice religion.

‡ Putting *world religion* in apposition to *sect* is somewhat reminiscent of the Church–sect model, especially as redefined by sociologists of religion such as Benton Johnson and Bryan Wilson. See Johnson, "On Church and Sect," 539–49, and "Church and Sect Revisited," 124–37. In contrast to the initial distinctions offered by Weber and Troeltsch, which are primarily based on the mode of membership, Johnson offers a new and, I believe, more helpful analysis of the dichotomy. He defines *church* primarily in terms of *acceptance* of the social environment, whereas *sect* is characterized by *rejection* of it. I find his insights applicable to the case of Twelver Shiʿism and its transformation in the Safavid era, but I avoid the term *church* not because of its strong association with Christianity but because it has been put to use primarily by sociologists in discussions of the social institutions and dimensions of religion. The phrase *world religion* does a much better job of capturing the pervasiveness and multidimensionality of an overarching world order created by religion. By *world religion* I mean something different from the textbook sense of major religions of the world, considered such due to geographical spread, number of adherents, or contributions to civilization. A brief and useful overview of the development of sociological thought regarding the church/sect dichotomy can be found in Swatos, "Church-Sect Theory."

I would like to offer tangible examples of how this lens helps make sense of the changes in popular religious sensibilities, stories, and rituals. First, I discuss the ritual of tabarra, the disavowal or cursing of the enemies of the family of the Prophet. Changes in this practice during the Safavid period are an illustration of the transition of Shiʿism into a world religion. As mentioned earlier, the establishment of the Safavid dynasty and the move by Shah Ismaʿil to make Twelver Shiʿism the official religion of the empire laid the groundwork for the gradual conversion of the predominantly Sunni population of Persia to Shiʿism. The initial phase of this process in the sixteenth century entailed a radical shift away from the sectarian ambiguity in the preceding centuries under Timurid rule. Fluid sectarian identities gave way to a highly sectarian Shiʿism defined as a rejection of Sunnism, and in the process, the parameters of the latter also became more clearly delineated. A striking marker of this process was a significant move in Shiʿi discourse away from the practice of taqiyya toward a theatrical and organized practice of cursing the companions of the Prophet, or tabarra. As Stanfield-Johnson demonstrates in her insightful study, we have reports of occasional cursing prior to this period, usually by dervishes or Qalandars, but only after the establishment of the Safavid dynasty did this practice become an organized ritual sponsored and protected by the political and military establishments and endorsed by the ulama. Multiple reports tell us that by the time of Shah Tahmasp I, an organized corps of cursers (tabarra'iyan) worked closely with the royal court and under the protection of the Qizilbash.* Official sponsorship and support were important factors in helping the ritual of tabarra to gain such prominence, but the practice of *laʿnat,* or cursing, was not exclusively carried out by the Qizilbash and the designated tabarra'iyan corps. This role was also assumed by popular public figures including dervishes, tradespeople, Qalandars, the ulama, and maddahs (eulogizers of the family of the Prophet).† This was less a dictatorial imposition of Shiʿism from the top than a fascinating collaboration between elites and nonelites to create a new moral and ideological framework.

As the seventeenth century approached, however, this ritual lost its prominence. This is not to say that anti-Sunni polemics did not remain an important part of the rhetoric of the religious and political elite or the religious practices of the populace. Quite the contrary, as demonstrated by the anti-Sunni bias demonstrated in the attacks on Sufism. At the same time, however, this period saw a clear shift in the function and goals of such polemics. In the sixteenth century, the polemics were produced largely in response

* Stanfield-Johnson, "The Tabarra'iyan."

† Stanfield-Johnson, "The Tabarra'iyan," 55.

to actual threats to the construction and implementation of the new Safavid-Shiʿi order. By the middle of the seventeenth century, however, ʿAbbas I's programs to stabilize his kingdom had been successfully implemented. A watershed moment was reached, and an alternative plausibility structure was in place. In other words, a significant enough social base believed in the objectivity of the Twelver sacred nomos to make legitimation plausible. At this point, polemical efforts like the anti-Sufi campaign can be understood largely as symbolic attempts to maintain Shiʿism as the organizing principle of the new sacred nomos, attempts that reminded its inhabitants of the ever-present threat of anomie. The anti-Sufism campaign of the mid-seventeenth century was not prompted by threats posed by Sunni Sufis from outside the sacred canopy of Shiʿism. Rather, it was a rhetorical and symbolic campaign that made use of a highly stigmatized association to marginalize alternative interpretations of Shiʿism from within.

Unlike the anti-Sufi campaign, the campaign against Abu Muslim storytellers, which had happened earlier in the seventeenth century and in tandem with other antiheresy campaigns, was a response to an actual threat to the establishment of the new sacred nomos. The Abu Muslim story was helpful in the revolutionary phase of the Safavid takeover, but it became obsolete at best and threatening at worse to the new Twelver nomos that gradually emerged. As the ulama made strides in redirecting the religious sensibilities of the populace, it was necessary to found new myths in order to ground people in a meaningful cosmic order. The story of Husayn's passion was the natural choice. The myth of Abu Muslim, given its syncretistic nature multitude of versions, had helped legitimize the concerns and aspirations of a variety of client groups. It lacked the potential, however, to create the overarching sacred canopy necessary for the establishment of a unifying Shiʿi-Safavi identity. The myth of Karbala, on the other hand, had already been domesticated by the ulama and the maddahs. As such, it was the perfect myth to legitimize the new order, the central pole capable of holding up the canopy of Shiʿism.

Imam Husayn's Passion as Founding Myth

The high-ranking ulama, even with the help of mid-ranking mullas, could not have brought the masses under the sacred canopy of Twelver Shiʿism without the assistance of their foot soldiers, the maddahs. The performers who eulogized the heroic lives and sufferings of the imams carried on a tradition that not only had enormous religious significance but also served as public entertainment. Public commemoration of pivotal moments in the lives of the twelve imams, especially the tragic death of Imam Husayn, grandson of Muhammad and son of the first imam, ʿAli, predates the Safavid period.

Such practices grew in popularity from the thirteenth to the fifteenth centuries, when the mainstream mode of piety in a wide swath of Muslim lands was marked by what Hodgson aptly called "ʿAlid loyalism."* Vaʿiz Kashifi's *Rawzat al-shuhada,* a passionate account of the suffering of the martyrs of Karbala that became immensely popular in Safavid Iran, was compiled in the nominally Sunni Timurid court prior to the advent of Shah Ismaʿil.† The Timurid period, in fact, was the pinnacle of the spread of ʿAlid loyalism as a marker of mainstream Sunni mode of piety. The line between Sunnis who were emphatic about their loyalty to the family of the Prophet, especially the twelve imams, and Shiʿis who downplayed their rejection of the other companions and eschewed the practice of cursing was very thin. The advent of the Safavids, however, took things in a different direction.

Performing/reciting the eulogies of the imams (*maddahi*) and recounting their martyrdoms (*rawza-khani*) played a significant role in forming the religious sentiments of the populace in Safavid Persia. Such stories and eulogies were often told by dervishes as part of their multifaceted entertainment skills. They would entertain people in coffeehouses, bazaars, and central squares by storytelling, juggling, snake charming, and selling exotic merchandise and herbal medicine. In the context of seventeenth century Safavid Iran, the propagation of Twelver Shiʿism was considered a prestigious and sacred duty and was not only the primary agenda of the ulama but also the major component of the Safavid ideological agenda. As such, a huge number of financial, political, and social resources flowed in that direction. Wandering mendicant dervishes found their storytelling and entertainment skills useful in a context that valued inspirational tales about the infallible imams.

Dervishes had widely varying religious outlooks; some were antinomian Qalandars who cared little for religious precepts whereas others were passionately devout Twelvers whose views were squarely within the boundaries of orthodoxy as drawn by the clerics. Zarrinkub touched on this diversity, saying, "the Jalali dervishes arriving from India were sometimes called Qalandars by the lay people, even though they did not have any relation to the old Qalandars. Maddahi was their main occupation, which they considered a religious obligation [*farz*]. . . . Haydaris and Shattaris would appear on the street with their strange appearance, sometimes nude and sometimes with

* Hodgson, *Venture of Islam,* 2:446. Molé's old yet still authoritative work on the Kubravi order between Shiʿism and Sunnism provides an excellent account of the general phenomenon that some scholars have called Twelver Sunnism (see Jaʿfariyan, *Tarikh-i Tashayyuʿ,* 2:726). It provides a detailed look at a specific Sufi network, a branch of which later came to be known in Iran as the Zahabiyya. See Molé, "Les Kubrawiya."

† For more on Kashifi, see Subtelny, "Kāšefi."

a piece of animal skin on their shoulders. The Jalalis would wander in the streets and bazaars . . . chant poems [eulogizing the imams] and collect donations. . . . In spite of the resentment of the jurists and puritans, the desperate appearance of the dervishes would inspire the generosity of lay people."*

These dervishes would often gather in a lodge, usually called a *tekke* in Anatolia and the Balkans, to share their donations, eat together, and have zikr and samaʿ sessions.† We have evidence that by the fourteenth century, in some Turkish tribes in Anatolia, Sufi zikr rituals had some degree of overlap with Muharram ceremonies.‡ In Safavid Persia, however, as the power of the religious hierocracy increased, attacks against antinomian and other "problematic" aspects of the dervish phenomenon helped stamp out diversity of religious outlook among dervishes, who increasingly served as auxiliaries of the clergy in propagating an orthodox version of the love of the family of the Prophet. As dervishes fell in line with the dominant religious orthodoxy, the name for their lodge, the tekke (or *takiya*), seems to have been used increasingly as a reference to a place where the passion of Husayn was commemorated and as a gathering place for other religious celebrations connected to the life and career of the imams.§ These men who gathered at the tekiyes gradually gave up their dervish paraphernalia, and their outlook and religious worldview came to be less defined by the traditional Sufi ethos and its notions of futuvva and blameworthiness (*malama*). Mir Lawhi's father, a well-known dervish-maddah called Mulla Lawhi, is a perfect example of the new class of eulogizers that appears to have emerged in the seventeenth century and functioned increasingly as an arm of the clerical hierarchy. Nasrabadi tells us that Lawhi's poetry eulogizing the imams was so elegant that most of his fellow dervish-maddahs used them.**

Similarly, although we have evidence of ritualized public processions during Muharram in places like Baghdad, it was only in the Safavid era that

* Zarrinkub, *Dunbala*, 242–45.

† The term was used at least as early as the sixteenth century as an equivalent for *khanaqah, zaviya,* and *ribat* to denote an establishment that belonged to a group of Sufis, especially in Ottoman Anatolia. See Clayer, "Tekke."

‡ Rahimi, *Theater State,* 211.

§ It was perhaps through the Turkish tribes of Anatolia, the Qizilbash, that this term migrated to Iran and began to be used in reference to dervish lodges. It became used as a synonym for *khanaqah,* but, as the establishment of Takiya-yi Fayz by Shah ʿAbbas II indicates, it was also used increasingly in reference to places where maddah and rawza-khan dervishes performed eulogies and told the story of Husayn's passion. Later, perhaps by the end of the eighteenth century, the semantic connotation of tekiya was restricted to the latter.

** Nasrabadi, *Tazkira,* 430.

a fully theatrical and ritualized form of such practices emerged.* Speaking of the history of the *ta'ziya,* or passion play, Babak Rahimi wrote, "While its pomp and spectacle appealed to both the Safavid population and foreign travelers, particularly Europeans, the pre-Safavid versions of the Muharram ceremonies were never entirely tied to state power, nor were they originally organized in the form of an elaborate public event."† In much the same way, some level of ritual violence seems to have occurred during early Muharram processions,‡ but the Safavid period seems to have been a time when ritualized violence became a greater and more consistent part of such public processions, especially on Ashura.§ Developments and elaborations on Muharram ceremonies continued apace into the late Safavid era:

> The progressive expansion of Muharram rites from 1641 to 1714 led to the diversification, popularization, and, hence, carnivalization of the rituals, performed within relational setting and social interactive ties, that is: networks of socio-professional groups, urban quarters, professional guilds [*asnaf*], futuvvat, and especially the poor sector of Safavid society. The travel reports of Tavernier (1667), Chardin (1667; 1673), Bedik (1670–75), Struys (1671), Kaempfer (1684–85), Careri (1694), Gaudereau (1695), de Bruyn (1704) and Krusinski (1714) demonstrate not only how Muharram grew in importance as a state ritual, but how the ceremonies also became a progressively common and familiar seasonal event of everyday Safavid life.**

The Ulama between "Superstition" and Religion

Such developments occurred in interaction with and were facilitated by the controversial support of influential figures among the religious elite. Throughout the seventeenth century, extremely popular figures, including Shaykh Baha'i, Majlisi Sr., Majlisi Jr., Fayz Kashani, and Shah Muhammad Darabi, played an important role in redirecting people's attention from charismatic Sufi shaykhs to the imams when they sought help in meeting worldly and otherworldly needs and aspirations. These hybrid scholarly figures acted as spiritual guides who led people to new ways of finding meaning and

* For a broad and rich overview of this ritual performance see Chelkowski, "Ta'zia."

† Rahimi, *Theater State,* 201.

‡ Nakash, "Rituals of 'Ashura'," 169. It is likely, as Nakash points out, that some manifestations of ritual violence, including flagellation, were also introduced to Persia through Anatolia.

§ For a brief report of some of these practices see Rahimi, *Theater State,* 218–30.

** Rahimi, *Theater State,* 233.

staying connected to the heavens. The infallibility of the imams and widespread fantastical accounts about their lives and deaths had accorded them quasi-divine status. All that remained was to develop ways for people to approach them as they had previously approached Sufi shaykhs and dervishes. In Arjomand's words,

> The basic religious predispositions and demands of the masses are marked by the congeniality of savior soteriology and the desire for solicitation of supernatural powers for earthly benefits such as good health and fulfillment of wishes. In the fourteenth and fifteenth centuries, the lay masses' demand for salvation was met by living saviors: the Sufi shaykhs and the claimants to mahdihood. For these the Shiʿite religious professionals had to substitute acceptable otherworldly saviors. These same otherworldly saviors could then be solicited and induced to use their supernatural powers from the worldly benefit of the believers.
>
> To establish their hierocratic domination over the masses in Iran, the Shiʿite doctors had to take two sets of factors into account: the predispositions and religious demands of the lay masses, and the services required by the rulers in exchange for which the indispensable royal political support could be secured. Under the impact of these two sets of factors, the "established" or orthodox Shiʿism that the doctors of the Safavid period sanctioned and propagated came to differ in some important respects form the Shiʿism of the sectarian phase, a religion of urban minorities that had borne the imprint of the outlook of their literate dominant strata.*

Popular figures among the ulama were loved not only for their personal piety but because, unlike proponents of puritanical discourse like Mir Lawhi and the elitist Peripatetic philosophers and exoteric Usuli jurists who advocated for rationalist discourse, they represented and promoted a syncretistic mode of religiosity that integrated popular belief and practices and was thus more accessible to the general masses. Their sycretism incorporated major elements of popular Sufism, using traditions from the imams that justified the inclusion of these elements into the new Twelver orthodoxy.

An important tactic in this vein was the endorsement and encouragement of the popular practice of visiting the tombs of the imams and their descendants (*imam-zada*), a practice known as *ziyarat.* The intercession of these figures was considered the key to success in this world and salvation in the hereafter, and one of the best ways to acquire it was to please them

* Arjomand, *Shadow of God,* 164.

by visiting their resting places. A visit to the tomb of an imam, some traditions held, was equal, if not superior, to the Hajj.* Many of the tombs designated as imam-zadas were doubtless former shrines of Sufi saints, and many more were "discovered" during the Safavid era and in subsequent centuries.† Such discoveries were often a considerable financial boon to the surrounding region, as they attracted pilgrims (and their purses) from afar. Ziyarat rituals were often elaborate, and pilgrims went so far as to circumambulate and prostrate themselves before the tomb, imploring the immaculate imams to intercede on their behalf so that God might grant their wishes, which usually pertained to worldly needs.‡ The belief in the ability of the imams and their descendants to perform such tasks was the cornerstone and raison d'être of this popular practice. Fantastic accounts of the supernatural powers of the imams and their miracles occupied the public imagination and filled thousands of pages in newly collected hadith compilations.

Such powers were by no means limited to the imams. The most sincere among their followers, especially those among the ulama (particularly if they were sayyids), were believed to be endowed with the same magical abilities. Such people became the foci of religious devotion, especially after their death. Dreams and visions were also important channels of connec-

* For an interesting preliminary comparison of the attention ziyarat received in later hadith collections verses the early canonical texts, see Arjomand, *Shadow of God,* 169. According to the data Arjomand retrieved from a number of classical sources, the number of pages dedicated to the matter of the Hajj ritual in early compilations dwarfs that for ziyarat by at least a factor of four. The equation is virtually reversed, however, in Majlisi Jr.'s *Bihar,* which features 387 pages dedicated to the Hajj and more than a thousand that deal with matters of ziyarat. It is also important to note that the major players who instigated and remained prominent in the anti-Sufi campaign were Iranian, although Arab scholars joined in later. I disagree with Ajormand's construal of this issue as a fight between the Persian ulama (the so-called sayyid notables), and the "clerical estate" made up of immigrant Arab ulama. In my view, the sources suggest a mixed and fairly unified ulama front against the dervish cult that was so deeply interwoven into the fabric of public life in Iran, especially in Isfahan.

† Many local and regional Sufi saints were considered sayyids as well. In the Safavid era, however, Sufi lineages and symbolism tended to be forgotten and Prophetic lineages emphasized. As a result, a given shrine that had previously been famous as that of a Sufi saint who also happened to be a sayyid might later become famous as the mausoleum of an imam-zada.

‡ The importance in popular religiosity of the shrines of real and putative imamzadas—a feature of popular Sufism taken over by Safavid Shiʿi sm—is clearly indicated in seventeenth-century European sources. See Arjomand, *Shadow of God,* 167.

tion to the imams, and they were instrumental in establishing authority and charisma.*

Similarly, quasi-magical and magical practices such as charm writing (*duʿa navisi*), prognostication based on the Qur'an (*istikhara*), and the use of talismans, which had previously been the domain of dervishes and Sufis, were increasingly taken up by a class of professional mullas who did not hesitate to claim exclusive authority over these practices. Arjomand provides the following succinct account of a treatise entitled *Ikhtiyarat,* written by Majlisi Jr.:

> [B]asing his prescriptions on a mixture of considerations drawn from astrology, geography, and sacred history, he determines the appropriateness of the days of the year for specific activities, the significance of natural and astral phenomena, the proper times, places, and conditions of copulation, the hours of *istikhāra,* and the days and manners of seeking help from the "men of the invisible world" [*rijāl al-ghayb*]. It is interesting that in conjunction with this last topic, Majlisī has to admit the absence of reference in the traditions gathered by the Shiʿite scholars to the "men of the invisible world," but opines that they must be the souls of the fourteen Immaculates (the Prophet, Fāṭimah, and the twelve imams), and of the prophets Khizr and Elīās, who are identified by the Sufis as the "poles" (of the universe; sing. Quṭb).†

Mir Lawhi's *Arbaʿin* is essentially a diatribe against the perspectives of Majlisi Sr. and his son, and it gives us an interesting perspective on what made them such popular and charismatic religious leaders and scholars.‡ Lawhi criticizes Majlisi Sr. and the "ignorant" people of Isfahan who followed him, accusing them of the same heretical exaggeration (ghuluvv) in belief and practice that had made the Sufis a target of attacks. According to Lawhi, at Majlisi's burial ceremony, the people "considered the Hidden Imam his servant and attributed miracles to his mule, and they broke his coffin and

* This important issue in seventeenth-century Safavid Iran needs further investigation. To mention one of many relevant example, Najib's argument for being the sole legitimate heir to the spiritual lineage of his master, Mu'azzin, is based in large part on dreams in which he relates that the imams instructed him to take on that role. See Anzali, "Emergence." For a recent and fascinating collection of essays on the role of dreams in Muslim societies, see Felek and Knysh, *Dreams and Visions.*

† Arjomand, *The Shadow of God,* 157–58.

‡ Kathryn Babayan gives a detailed report of the way Lawhi portrays Majlisi Sr. See Babayan, *Mystics, Monarchs, and Messiahs,* 461–73.

hung the pieces on their arms as talismans, looking for blessing and luck in this way."*

Lawhi goes on to claim that the masses prostrated themselves in front of Majlisi Sr.'s tomb and circumambulated it.† He also relates that the latter had a personal singer (*mutrib*) named Shah Mirak Zarkash in his service and engaged in the practice of zikr with a certain Mir Qasim Zakir as his master.‡ Lawhi was also furious over Majlisi's unapologetic support for and service to the Safavid house and the cozy relationship he had developed with the king, and he accused him of worldly ambitions and of being embroiled in politics for the purpose of material gain. In fact, the main reason for the writing of *Arbaʿin*, according to its author, was to respond to a treatise Majlisi Jr. had written not long before on *rajʿa* (the return of the most righteous and the most wicked at the end of time to participate in Armageddon).§ The latter treatise is a commentary on a collection of reports about *rajʿa* attributed to a prominent companion of Jaʿfar Sadiq, Fazl b. Shazan. Mir Lawhi's main point of contention with Majlisi Jr.'s commentary is the explicit and frequent attempts by the latter to link major events and important players in the reports to his own time in general and to the Safavid house in particular.

Such allegations might be easily dismissed as the fabrications of a hostile mind, and Lawhi's rhetoric against his opponents is admittedly full of hyperbole, if not outright lies. Yet other sources confirm, at least partially, what he says about Majlisi. Take, for example, Chardin's report of people visiting Majlisi's tomb: "[U]nder the dome bearing the name of the dervish's shrine [lies] the grave of a certain Mohammad Taqi, who was the priest of this mosque or Pich Namaz, during ʿAbbās II. He was recognized as a saint during his life, which he led in extreme detachment from the world; the populace venerated him as a prophet. He predicted his death, they say, three months before it occurred, while being in perfect health."**

Majlisi Sr. is among the religious scholars who argued for the permissibility of listening to beautiful tunes, provided that they remind the listener of God.†† His position favoring the consumption of hashish is often mentioned by later scholars, who debated the issue in works of jurisprudence.‡‡ Mir Lawhi also relates that Majlisi Sr. praised Abu Muslim and Hallaj from

* Lawhi, *Kifaya* MS, f. 9a.
† Lawhi, *Kifaya* MS, f. 185a. Also in Babayan, *Mystics, Monarchs, and Messiahs,* 465.
‡ Lawhi, *Kifaya* MS, f. 185b. Also in Babayan, *Mystics, Monarchs, and Messiahs,* 164.
§ Lawhi, *Kifaya* MS, f. 8a.
** From Babayan, *Mystics, Monarchs, and Messiahs,* 465.
†† Jaʿfariyan, *Safaviyya,* 2:700.
‡‡ Jazaʾiri, *al-Anvar al-nuʿmaniyya,* 4:55.

the pulpit.* Again, while it is difficult to know for certain whether Majlisi publicly defended such controversial figures, there is little doubt as to his strong Sufi proclivities.† In fact, throughout his glosses written in refutation of Qummi's attacks on Sufism in *Usul fusul al-tawzih,* Majlisi defends Rumi, Ibn ʿArabi, Bistami, and other significant Sufi figures as authentic Shiʿi saints while condemning Hallaj as a misguided Sunni who is reviled by "all the Sufis."‡ He frequently cites his teacher, Shaykh Bahaʾi, as the authoritative figure from whom he has learned about the path of the saints and repeatedly cautions against understanding their words literally or thinking that one can fathom the meaning of their words without proper guidance. He repeats a story told to him by Shaykh Bahaʾi, who said, "One day, a virtuous person in town, Mawlana Khaja Jan, came to me and said, 'Last night I pondered extensively until I understood the meaning of oneness of being.' I replied 'Akhund, who is your pir?' He responded, 'What does that word mean?' I continued, 'How many mortifications have you gone through?' and he answered, 'None!' I said, 'Clearly, the meaning that you have understood is different from the one Sufis have in mind, because they all agree that the meaning of oneness of being can only be revealed to someone who has served under a perfect master and undergone mortifications for forty years.'"§

Nevertheless, as a sign of changing times, Majlisi Sr.'s own son pursued a revisionist agenda regarding his father's legacy. Majlisi Jr. categorically denied his father's Sufi proclivities. In a well-known and widely circulated statement he says:

> Beware lest you suspect that my erudite father . . . was among the Sufis or believed in their path . . . far from it . . . among his contemporaries,

* Lawhi, *Kifaya* MS, f. 9a.

† Regarding Majlisi Sr.'s Sufi proclivities, it is worth mentioning a small treatise in defense of Sufism that is attributed to him, *Tashviq al-salikin.* It is highly unlikely that this attribution is correct. First, none of the pro-Sufi works written in the second half of the seventeenth century or early eighteenth century mention it. One would expect, given Majlisi Sr.'s status, that such a work would have been frequently cited by defenders of Sufism. Second, all surviving manuscripts of this treatise are very late, usually dating back to the nineteenth century. Third, the vocabulary used in the treatise all but rules out the attribution. For example, the text refers to the Zahabi tariqa as the best path toward God. The designation *Zahabiyya* was not applied to a particular Sufi network until the late seventeenth century. It appears to me that *Tashviq* was written sometime in the nineteenth century by proponents of the Zahabi network and intentionally attributed to Majlisi Sr. as a way of legitimizing the Zahabi mode of piety. Such myth-making efforts were quite common among the Zahabis during the nineteenth century.

‡ Lawhi, "Usul fusul al-tawzih," 616–46.

§ Lawhi, "Usul fusul al-tawzih," 656.

> it was he who was most familiar with traditions of the family of the Prophet . . . his path was the path of asceticism and abstention . . . and in the initial stages of his life he associated himself with the title of Sufism to attract the interest of Sufis and to prevent scaring them away, so that he might warn them against holding such beliefs. He was successful in guiding many of them to the path of truth . . . and, at the end of his life, as he realized that this provision had expired and that the flags of misguidedness [*zalal*] had been removed, and that [Sufis] are the explicit enemies of God, he distanced himself from them and declared them infidels . . . and I am most familiar with my father's path, and his writings about this are at my disposal.*

Contemporary Western historians have made much of Majlisi Jr.'s departure from his father's Sufi inclinations and have used his blunt criticism of Sufism to paint a picture of him as a bigot and fanatic.† There is no doubt that his position contrasts sharply with that of his father, and it is also true that, especially in the final decade of his life, he took up the fight against popular practices such as drinking, prostitution, juggling, and storytelling. Religious minorities might also have suffered persecution under his watch. Having said that, I believe that some of the criticisms of Majlisi Jr. reveal the biases of scholars. Too often we fail to contextualize and humanize figures we have difficulty liking. Two important points must be taken into consideration with regard to Majlisi Jr.'s opposition to Sufism. First, his stance should be seen in the larger context of the growing discontent with Sufism in this period. As a pupil not only of his father but also of Muhammad-Tahir Qummi, Majlisi Jr. was born into an environment characterized by hostility toward Sufism, and his positions make better sense when considered in this

* Majlisi Jr., *Sirat al-najat,* quoted in Jaʿfariyan, *Safaviyya,* 2:530–31. Interestingly, Mir Lawhi mentions the statement disapprovingly a number of times at the end of *Kifayat al-muhtadi,* saying that the senior Majlisi's Sufi proclivities were too obvious to be denied. See Lawhi, *Kifaya* MS, fol.187a–188a.

† A negative picture of Majlisi Jr. as bigoted and fanatical has dominated Western scholarship since E. G. Browne's groundbreaking writings. For a brief and refreshingly personal account of this bias against him, see Newman, *Safavid Iran,* ix. As Newman indicates, the stereotype has proven very resilient. It is discernible in Arjomand's *Shadow of God.* Lewisohn explicitly accuses Majlisi Jr. of bigotry (Lewisohn, "Modern Persian Sufism," 410). A more recent example of this view of Majlisi can be seen in Matthijs Van den Bos's otherwise valuable study of Niʿmatullahis during the nineteenth and twentieth centuries, which holds Majlisi responsible for "wiping out much of organized Iranian Sufism." See Van den Bos, *Mystic Regimes,* 51. A more balanced and informed analysis of his career can be found in Sefatgol, *Sakhtar,* 217–23.

context. It should also be said that the commonalities between father and son far outweighed their differences. As Zarrinkub has noted, Majlisi Jr. made a distinction between Sufis who complied with the percepts of Shariʿa and those with antinomian tendencies. His generalized condemnations of Sufism should not be taken entirely at face value,* because his writings incorporated many elements of Sufi thought, as I discuss later. Both Majlisis put great stock in their dreams and in mystical experiences that involved the imams, especially the Hidden Imam. Majlisi Jr. surpassed his father in gaining popular support and seizing the public imagination as a saint, and he was buried at his own request in a spot near his father, where his tomb was visited in the same manner. Majlisi Jr.'s burial wishes are a strong symbolic indication that the son did not see himself as having broken with his father's path. Instead, he viewed his father as an example whose legacy he wished to uphold.

The Hadith Movement and the Akhbari School

The lives of both Majlisis were devoted to one overarching concern: recovering the legacy of the imams. This expressed itself in their sincere and enthusiastic efforts to collect traditions dispersed across hundreds of canonical and noncanonical sources.† They sought to reorient the scholarly priorities of their colleagues by bringing the study of hadith from the periphery to the center of Shiʿi intellectual endeavor.‡ Both father and son were important players in a larger cultural and religious movement in which the emerging class of Shiʿi ulama engaged itself in studying the traditions of the imams. This hadith literature operated as an alternative source of authority that supported a new religious framework that met the needs of everyday people. These pioneering scholars and the many students they trained not only brought the study of hadith from the margins to the center of the madrasa curriculum but also broadened the audience for hadith by translating major canonical works into Persian. According to Majlisi Sr., prior generations of the ulama had paid little attention to the study of hadith, preferring to rely upon rationalist (*istidlali*) methods in jurisprudence in issuing their rulings. He notes that at one time, hadith books were difficult to find in Isfahan, and

* Zarrinkub, *Dunbala,* 260.

† Majlisi Jr. is said to have sent convoys to libraries around the Muslim world, as far as Yemen, to find unique manuscripts of early hadith works compiled by Shiʿa scholars. See Jaʿfariyan, *Safaviyya,* 2:751. He also collected many previously obscure works of hadith that had nearly been forgotten by history and others of unknown provenance that were authorized in miraculous (and convenient) encounters with the imams during the seventeenth century and early eighteenth centuries.

‡ Jaʿfariyan makes a similar remark. See Jaʿfariyan, *Safaviyya,* 2:1043.

he credits his teacher, Shaykh Baha'i, and Mulla Amin Astarabadi (d. 1036), the author of *al-Fava'id al-madaniyya,* for reversing the trend:

> About thirty years ago,* the great and learned Mawlana Muhammad Amin Astarabadi began to occupy himself with the examination and study of the traditions [*akhabar*] of the sinless imams. He studied the censure of opinion and evaluation [found in the traditions] and became acquainted with the method of the companions of the holy sinless imams. He wrote *al-Fava'id al-madaniyya* and sent it to this country. Most of the people of Najaf and the ʿAtabat approved of his method and returned to the traditions. The truth is that most of what Mawlana Muhammad Amin said is true. . . . I have now toiled for nearly forty years to ensure that the libraries, not only in Isfahan but also in the surrounding towns and other districts, contain several copies of all the books [of hadith]. The water that was gone from the river is back, and praise be to God, the majority of the learned of this time spend their time with the hadith literature. This increases every day . . . and praise be to God that the sovereign king and the exalted princes also spend much of their time reading and discussing hadith literature.†

The stunning pace at which the study of hadith became the dominant occupation of the ulama from the early seventeenth century to the fall of Isfahan in 1722 is one of the most striking features of Shiʿi intellectual life in Safavid Iran, and the phenomenon has not yet been given the study it warrants. This was perhaps the period in the history of Shiʿism that saw the greatest activity in gathering and "discovering" the sayings of the imams. In the frantic race to formulate a new religious framework for the recently converted people of Iran, the most pressing task was to find sayings of the imams to replace the Sunni hadith that had previously provided legitimacy and authority.

The radical increase in scholarly activity focused on Twelver hadith collections is perhaps nowhere more obvious than in the number of commentaries on the most important piece of the canon, *Usul al-kafi.* Of the twenty commentaries or glosses I identified using Aqa Bozorg's bibliographical compendium, sixteen were written between 1600 and 1737 (see Table 2).‡ One of

* This refers to the last years of Astarabadi's life.

† Majlisi Sr., *Lavami,* 45–48. Quoted in Jaʿfariyan, *Safaviyya,* 3:1058–60.

‡ The list of commentaries was compiled from the following pages in Tehrani's *al-Zariʿa:* 13: 95–100 and 14:26–28. For an interesting statistical analysis of the number of available copies of the works of Ibn Babuya, the author of one of what later came to be recognized as one of the four canonical books produced in this period, see Newman, "Recovery of the Past," 109–27 (esp. 112–14). Newman's findings accord with my own, affirming that scholarly activity focused on Shiʿi hadith

TABLE 2: The distribution of the commentaries of *Usul al-Kafi* during the Safavid period

Period	*Number of commentaries and glosses*
1500–1550	0
1551–1600	1
1601–1640	3
1641–1690	9
1691–1737	4
1738–1783	1

the most interesting facts about these is the diversity of their authors, who represent an amazing spectrum of intellectual leanings. They include the founder of the Akhbari school, Mulla Amin Astarabadi, as well as other Akhbari scholars who vehemently opposed philosophy and Sufism, including Mulla Khalil Qazvini. Also included are Usuli jurists such as ʿAli ʿAmili (d. 1691) and Muhammad Salih Mazandarani (d. 1670), as well as Sufi-minded philosophers such as Mulla Sadra, pure philosophers such as Mir Damad, and theologian-philosophers such as Mirza Rafiʿa (d. 1677). This diversity illustrates the centrality of Shiʿi hadith literature in the consolidation of orthodoxy and the competition between scholars and religious leaders of varying

reached its peak in the second half of the seventeenth century. As Newman points out, the concept of *sihah arbaʿa* (the four canonical books) was not widely known or used in the literature of that period. In the early seventeenth century, notes Newman, "Shaykh Bahaʾi's father Shaykh Husayn referred to Ibn Babawayh's Madinat al-ʿilm as one of the five usul" (Newman, "Recovery of the Past," 115). Nonetheless, based on on Amir-Moezzi's claim, Newman says that the thirteenth-century Twelver scholar Jaʿfar b. Hasan Hilli, al-Muhaqqiq (d. 1277) "may have been the earliest Twelver scholar to have referred to 'the four books'" (Newman, "Recovery of the Past," 112–13). Amir-Moezzi bases his claim on two of al-Muhaqqiq's works, *al-Muʿtabar* and *Nukat al-nahahya*. Upon checking these two sources per Amir-Moezzi's citation, I was surprised to find that none of them contained anything remotely resembling a reference to four canonical books. Amir-Moezzi seems to have corrected his position in a recent article written with Hasan Ansari. In a brief footnote, they note that the earliest use of this term appears during the sixteenth century in the writings of the Second Martyr (see Amir-Moezzi and Ansari, "MUḤAMMAD B. YAʿQŪB AL-KULAYNI," 227). It took another hundred years for this concept to become more popular in the writings of Shiʿi scholars.

perspectives to utilize that literature to legitimize their positions and bolster their authority. The fact that no Sufi shaykh is found among the commentators is a significant indicator that in this competition, Sufis lagged behind the ulama.

The exponential increase in hadith-related scholarly activities also meant that the number of traditions circulating in scholarly circles grew significantly. This resulted in the next generation of hadith scholars, including Majlisi Jr. and Shaykh Hurr ʿAmili, a prominent member of the Arab immigrant religious scholars from Lebanon, being urged at the end of the seventeenth century to compile massive encyclopedic works such as *Bihar al-anvar* and *Vasaʾil al-shiʿa.* The standard modern edition of the former is published in 110 volumes, and the latter, which is limited to matters of Shariʿa, contains enough material to span at least 30 volumes.

Along with the upsurge in the study of hadith came the establishment and rapid spread of the Akhbari (Scripturalist) legal school of thought, which eclipsed the traditional, Sunni-inspired, rationalist Usuli school in the second half of the seventeenth and most of the eighteenth century. Several attempts have been made to explain the popularity of the Akhbari school during this period in the history of Twelver Shiʿism. Robert Gleave has summarized these efforts succinctly, pointing out briefly why each explanation ultimately fails to account for the school's success and popularity. In general, Gleave says, such explanations fail to understand and appreciate "the multifarious intellectual interests and diverse academic careers of its various adherents."* This failure, I believe, has partly to do with a lack of attention to the larger context in which Akhbarism flourished, a context characterized by the increasing discursive autonomy of Twelver Shiʿi learned traditions, which signified the transformation of Shiʿism into a world religion. Prior to this period, the contours of Shiʿi learning were shaped by and in response to mainstream Sunni traditions. From the study of hadith and jurisprudence (*fiqh*) to kalam and philosophy, the methodology and subject matter of Twelver intellectual traditions were cast in the mold of Islamic learning writ large. In seventeenth-century Safavid Persia, however, this changed.

For example, the discipline of *dirayat al-hadith,* the critical examination of hadith reports, came into its own and flourished in the seventeenth century.† This discipline, however, had taken shape in the sixteenth century as a mirror image of its Sunni counterpart, *ʿilm al-jarh va al-taʿdil,* with little methodological difference between the two. A more significant development, one that represented a break with traditional ways of thinking about

* Gleave, *Scripturalist Islam,* 173–74.
† Modarressi, *Introduction to Shiʿi Law,* 6–7.

religious knowledge, was the evolution of the Akhbari movement into a distinct school of legal and doctrinal thought.* This fascinating development was based on reimagining of the nature of positive religious knowledge and the methods for gaining such knowledge. It was the product of a radical epistemic shift advocated by a group of Shiʿi scholars intent on moving Shiʿism away from traditional and disciplinary modes and toward a recognition of the exclusive authority of the imams over reason, consensus, and the Qurʾan. The relaxed and liberal approach of the Akhbari school toward authenticating hadith statements was valuable, because it maximized the number of traditions that spoke to different aspects of everyday life and provided needed guidance on pressing issues. It met an urgent need to find sources of legitimacy for the newly established Shiʿi nomos, and it was much better suited to this task than the traditional Usuli methodology, in which the elaborate disciplines of *ʿilm al-rijal* and *ʿilm dirayat al-hadith* were used to evaluate the reliability of the narrators involved in the chain of transmission of each hadith.† Finally, the Akbhari movement's categorical rejection of Sunni sources and Sunni methodology in the study of hadith and Islamic law, especially as reflected in the writings of its founder, Muhammad Amin Astarabadi,‡ was in line with Safavid propaganda, which made every effort to draw a sharp distinction between the Sunni Turks (Ottomans) and the followers of the family of the Prophet (the Shiʿa under Safavid rule).§

* This does not mean that traditionalist elements did not previously exist in the history of Shiʿi legal thought. Those elements, however, did not constitute a distinctive school of thought, and they did not form a part of a particular legal/doctrinal position, as was the case with the Akhbari School in the Safavid era. See Gleave, *Scripturalist Islam,* 30.

† In fact, as Arjomand has observed, the reemergence of an authentically Shiʿite Usuli school of jurisprudence at the end of the eighteenth century seems to have been predicated on the Akbhari movement's successful push to bring the study of hadith to the center of scholarly attention and activity. In his own words, "[T]he fruits of Akhbari traditionalism were fully appropriated by orthodox Shiʿism . . . in the closing decades of the eighteenth century, the collections of traditions such as Fayz's *Vafi,* Hurr ʿAmili's *Vasaʾil,* and Majlisi's own *Bihar* served as invaluable and indispensable new sources upon which the value-rational ingenuity of the Uṣūlī jurists in creation of new legal norms could be exercised. In fact, it does not seem to be an exaggeration to say that the accumulation of traditions in this period was a precondition for the revival of jurisprudence, which aimed both at the harmonization of the traditions as normative stereotypes and deduction of further positive (waḍʿī) norms." See Arjomand, *Shadow of God,* 153.

‡ Stewart, *Islamic Legal Orthodoxy,* 157.

§ Gleave argues against dominant scholarly perspectives that pigeonhole the Akhbari movement as anti-philosophy or anti-Sufism, saying, "there is no single Akhbari position on the role of philosophy and mystical experience in the discovery

The subject of this book—the emergence of the concept of ʿirfan in contradistinction to Sufism—is another example of how the Shiʿi discursive tradition gained increasing independence in this period.* The formation of an "ʿirfanian" discourse reveals the existence and authenticity of a distinct Shiʿi mystical discourse vis-à-vis the traditional Sufi–Sunni one. As Shiʿism established itself as a plausible structure in the seventeenth century, Sufi-minded ulama abandoned some elements of the Sunni–Sufi framework of thought and action, while restructuring other elements to help bolster the new sacred nomos. This process of religious and intellectual appropriation and synthesis happened concomitantly with the equally important process of sociopolitical "domestication." The idea of a pir or a pole (*qutb*), for example, was not merely a concept. It was a social reality that encompassed an extensive array of relationships and institutions that supported the world in which pre-Safavid denizens of Persia and beyond found and grounded themselves. This social reality—not the abstract concept—was what threatened the claims to authority of the emerging class of Shiʿi religious scholars. It should not surprise us, then, that the master/disciple relationship was the element of traditional Sufism that underwent the most dramatic reshaping at the hands of Sufis and Sufi-minded religious scholars.

---

of religious knowledge." Gleave, "Scripturalist Sufism," 158–76. I essentially agree with Gleave on this latter point, but when it comes to mainstream discursive philosophy, otherwise known as Peripatetic (*mashsha'i*) philosophy, an overwhelming number of Akhbari scholars condemned it as a foreign and un-Islamic discipline of knowledge because of its Greek roots and the heretical beliefs they claimed major philosophers held. Akhbari scholars such as Fayz Kashani who were well versed in Islamic philosophy usually differentiate between what they call official philosophy (*hikmat-i rasmiyya*), to which they object, and divine philosophy (*hikmat-i ilahi*), which, according to them, is derived from prophetic sources of revelation and the traditions of the imams. This aside, Gleave's astute observations on the nature of the Akhbari movement are a much-needed corrective to the misleading picture of Akhbarism that plagues primary sources of jurisprudence, which are mostly hostile to Akhbarism, as well as scholarly and nonscholarly expositions in Persian, Arabic, and English, in which proponents of this school are generally seen as rigid literalists and fanatical bigots. This picture has prevailed as a result of negative Usuli portrayals of Akhbari scholars in biographical and bibliographical resources. Since the Akbari school was effectively eradicated by the early nineteenth century, accounts of it come mainly from later Usuli ulama hostile to it.

* Another example of the move toward a more independent discourse is the field of Islamic philosophy. I lack the time and space to elaborate fully, but, despite the fact that Mulla Sadra's philosophy draws heavily on several pre-Safavid intellectual and spiritual traditions, his synthesis is a genuinely innovative work that laid the groundwork for the robust and distinct philosophical tradition that subsequently took root in Iran. That tradition still flourishes today, in marked contrast to the condition of indigenous philosophical discourse in many parts of the Muslim world.

4 The Invention of ʿIrfan

Thus far my discussion of the debate over Sufism has focused mainly on Isfahan, with good reason. In the post–Shah ʿAbbas era of Safavid absolutism, the bureaucracy, administration, and finances of the Safavid dynasty became increasingly centralized. Unparalleled amounts of wealth and power were concentrated in the capital, and Isfahan was not only the political center of Iran but also the intellectual, educational, and religious heart of the realm. Those who aspired to become scholars, especially in the religious disciplines, would spend a few years in their hometowns learning the basics, after which they would migrate to Isfahan to train under the most prominent scholars of their time. Anyone who wished to be taken seriously as a learned member of Safavid society had to forge connections with the Isfahani elite. Given the increasing interest of Safavid monarchs in religious disciplines and debates and the resultant flood of financial resources into the madrasas and the religious hierocracy, Isfahan was the dream city of aspiring clerics.

The Shiraz Circle

The autobiography of Hazin Lahiji (d. 1766) gives us a wonderful depiction of the vibrant cultural and intellectual environment of the Safavid capital in the late seventeenth and early eighteenth centuries. Hazin exemplified the urbane, cultivated, and cosmopolitan Shiʿa scholar educated in Isfahan. He was open minded and tolerant, seeking out fellow scholars among Christians, Jews, and Sabians. In return, according to Belfour, he was "equally admired and esteemed by the Muselman, Hindoo, and English inhabitants of India."* Born in 1691, he spent nearly two decades of his early life as an avid student in the city's educational institutions. His autobiography provides a colorful picture of the circles of learning in Isfahan, where he studied medicine, mathematics, astronomy, jurisprudence, hadith, philosophy, and mysticism with prominent teachers of the time.†

* Hazin, *The Life of Sheikh Mohammed Hazin*, v.
† Hazin, *Tarikh*, 168–72.

Among these was Mir Sayyid Hasan Taliqani (d. ?), Hazin's teacher in philosophy and mysticism who taught Ibn ʿArabi's *Fusus* and Suhravardi's *Hayakil al-nur.** According to Hazin, Taliqani was an outstanding scholar who synthesized philosophy and Sufism. Although Hazin complained about the charges of heterodoxy leveled by exoteric religious students against mystically minded scholars like Taliqani, it is clear from his overall account that it was possible for an interested student to pursue both philosophy and mysticism, at least in their speculative forms, with relative freedom in the context of the madrasa. After the fall of Isfahan, when many of the city's elites fled the city they loved, Hazin was among them. The exodus and drop in financial support took its toll on the study of philosophy and high mysticism.†

Isfahan, however, was not the only important cultural hub of the Safavid realm. Other major urban centers, such as Qum, Mashhad, Kashan, Ardabil, and Shiraz, were also active sites of learning and education. Shiraz in particular stood out as a vibrant intellectual center, especially for philosophically and mystically inclined students of religious disciplines. The sociocultural outlook of Shiraz was different from that of Isfahan in a number of ways. First, the city was marked by a liberal spirit and tolerant environment that was hospitable to forms of belief and practice that would have been identified, contested, and persecuted as deviant or heretical in other, more conservative urban centers, including Isfahan, Qum, and Mashhad. Second, because Shiraz had been the heart of Persian intellectual and aesthetic life for centuries before the advent of Safavids and because of its strategic geographic location, the intellectual outlook of many of its learned denizens was markedly cosmopolitan. This was a consequence in part of a fascinating cultural exchange between Shiraz and India.‡ As a result, a current of cosmopolitan thought ran deep and strong in Shiraz. The city had been host to the most prominent philosophers of the Islamic world in the fourteenth and fifteenth centuries. Figures such as Jalal al-Din Davani (d. 1502), Sadr al-Din Dashtaki (d. 1497), Ghiyas al-Din Mansur Dashtaki, and Muhaqqiq Khafri (d. 1550) formed the core of what has come to be known as the School of Shiraz.§ Shiraz was also home to prominent occultist scholars, especially of the

* Hazin, *Tarikh*, 169–70.

† Corbin's appraisal of the situation seems accurate in this regard. See Corbin, *History of Islamic Philosophy*, 348–49.

‡ The constant flow of scholars, poets, and dervishes between areas of Iran (especially the Caspian Sea region and Shiraz) and India is a fascinating phenomenon that deserves further attention.

§ This term has recently been used by some Iranian scholars to refer to the flourishing and vibrant period of Islamic philosophy in Shiraz in the late middle period. See, for example, Kakaie's remarks on maktab-i Shiraz in Kakaie, "Introduction."

Nuqtavi persuasion. The names of important figures such as Mahmud Dihdar (d. 1576), better known by his pen name ʿAyani, and his son Muhammad Dihdar (d. 1016), whose pen name was Fani, come to mind.

Not unrelated to this, the city was also a stronghold of organized Sufism.* The Nurbakhshi Sufi network in particular had had a major presence in Shiraz since the building of the Nuriyya khanaqah by a prominent student of Nurbakhsh, Muhammad Lahiji (d. 1506). Unfortunately, the history of Sufism in Shiraz in this period remains largely unexamined. We know virtually nothing about the fate of the Nuriyya khanaqah and the developments of organized Sufism there in the sixteenth and seventeenth centuries.

With the rise of prominent figures such as Mir Damad, the locus of philosophical learning shifted to Isfahan beginning in the early seventeenth century, but Shiraz remained an important cultural and intellectual center throughout the Safavid period. Hazin's remarks regarding a trip to the city demonstrate the liveliness of the educational system there. The scholar relates that after moving to Shiraz shortly before 1717, he studied the most celebrated canonical work of Shiʿi hadith, *Usul al-kafi,* with Shah Muhammad Darabi Shirazi, by some accounts the most prominent mystically minded religious scholar of Shiraz and a figure who is discussed extensively in the coming pages.† He also studied philosophy with Akhund Masiha Fasavi (d. 1715), a student of Aqa Husayn Khansari, the *shaykh al-islam* of Isfahan.‡ Hazin also provides a brief account of other prominent mystically minded figures whom he met there.§

The invention of the category of ʿirfan, I argue, can be attributed to a handful of religious scholars of the Safavid era who hailed from Shiraz. Several important trends and aspects of the intellectual environment of Shiraz contributed to the formation of this category. First, learned circles in the city continued to include syncretistic, open-minded, polymath scholars whose background in philosophy, Sufism, philosophical mysticism, and the occult informed their perspectives as they approached the foundational sources of Twelver Shiʿism, that is, the Qurʾan and hadith. Second, Shiraz was host to a reformed tradition of organized Twelver Sufism (represented by the Nurbakhshi and later the Zahabi networks) that had formulated a new Twelver-Sufi discourse that borrowed heavily from Sufi tradition but was purged of the "problematic" and "innovative" aspects of it. Third, there existed a strong

* Kakaie, "Introduction," 22.
† Hazin, *Tarikh,* 177–78.
‡ Hazin, *Tarikh,* 178.
§ These include Muhammad Baqir Sufi, who taught Hazin Suhravardi's *al-Talvihat,* and Muhammad ʿAli Sakaki, who was affiliated with organized Sufism and is discussed briefly in the coming pages.

poetic tradition exemplified by the cosmopolitan love poetry of Hafez that was instrumental in the formation of the discourse on ʿirfan. Finally, Shiraz was home to a strong and vibrant tradition of philosophical thought that informed the worldview of its intellectuals in significant ways and contributed to the making of the concept of ʿirfan.

These broad intellectual and literary trajectories might lead readers to believe that this chapter is concerned primarily with Mulla Sadra, his school of thought, and his students, because it is common among Iranian and Western intellectuals to see Mulla Sadra as a figure in whose work ʿirfan is most perfectly manifest. Gerhard Bowering, for example, contends that "*Erfān* reached its climax during Safavid times in the theosophical school of Isfahan with Mīr(-e) Dāmād (d. 1040/1630) and Ṣadr-al-Dīn Šīrāzī, known as Mollā Ṣadrā (d. 1050/1640)." Mulla Sadra's magnum opus, *al-Asfar al-arbaʿa,* he contends, is "perhaps the most crucial work on *ʿerfān*."* In this popular perspective, *ʿirfan* is a broad and amorphous term used to describe attempts by Shiʿi scholars to synthesize several intellectual traditions they inherited, including the Illuminationist tradition of Islamic philosophy, the Sufi tradition exemplified by Ibn ʿArabi, and the Shiʿi hadith tradition. Contributions of figures such as Sayyid Haydar Amuli and Ibn Abi Jumhur are considered significant turning points in the formation of this "Shiʿi gnosis," to use Corbin's terminology, which reached full expression in the writings of Mulla Sadra.† Sayyid Haydar's *Jamiʿ al-asrar* (*The Sum of [Divine] Secrets*) is cited as a pivotal text,‡ and Ibn Abi Jumhur's *Kitab al-mujli* is said to have created "the perfect cohesion between the theosophy of al-Suhravardi's *Ishraq,* the theosophy of Ibn al-ʿArabi and the Shiite tradition."§

Not everyone agrees with this account of Twelver intellectual history, though. Nasr, for example, argues that Sadra's thought, in spite of being deeply influenced by Ibn ʿArabi, should be categorized as a form of philosophy (*hikma*) rather than ʿirfan. For Nasr, the latter term refers to doctrinal or speculative aspects of the Sufi tradition that culminate with Ibn ʿArabi's school of thought, and he argues that it is highly significant that neither Sadra nor his students wrote "major works devoted purely to theoretical gnosis or ʿ*irfan-i nazari*." The major intellectual thrust of the Safavid period, says Nasr, "lay in creating the School of Transcendent Theosophy, which had incorporated major theses of ʿ*irfan* such as the transcendent oneness of being

* Böwering, "ʿErfān (1)."

† Corbin, *History of Islamic Philosophy,* 342.

‡ Although he criticizes Ibn ʿArabi in a number of places on the doctrine of sainthood, the fundamental structure of Sayyid Haydar's understanding of *valaya* as it applies to the infallible imams is shaped by Ibn ʿArabi's school of thought.

§ Corbin, *History of Islamic Philosophy,* 335.

[*wahdat al-wujud*] into its philosophical system, but which was distinct in the structure of its doctrines, manner of presentation, and method of demonstration from *ʿirfan*."*

There is nothing wrong with such attempts by scholars to organize the past—any meaningful understanding of the present involves a coherent narrative of the past. Sometimes as scholars, however, we can forget our role in constructing the concepts and categories through which we organize and understand the past. This lack of self-reflection and historical awareness can lead to a teleological mode of interpretation that leaves out or downplays otherwise significant historical developments in favor of the ones that serve our teleology well. In the case of the issue at hand, this plays out in scholars who confuse contemporary etic constructions of ʿirfan with historical emic ones. One may have reasons for considering Ibn ʿArabi, Mulla Sadra, or Khomeini, for that matter, the founder or the culmination of the tradition of ʿirfan, but such projections tell us more about the intellectual priorities and preferences of contemporary scholars than they do about how ʿirfan came into being as a category and how its meaning evolved through history.

The truth is that when we examine the writings of these so-called champions of Shiʿi gnosis, we witness no significant departure in the semantics of the term *ʿirfan* or its cognates from the work of their predecessors. The term *ʿarif,* for example, is used in Mulla Sadra's works in accordance with its traditional meaning, that is, to denote the advanced among the saints (*awliya*). What is noteworthy about Sadra's usage, however, is his coupling of ʿarifs with those whom he calls divine philosophers (*hukama al-mutaʾallihin*).† This is a clear indication of the Sadraian synthesis in which the ideal ʿarif and the ideal hakim are one and the same. In contrast to Sadra's frequent use of the term *ʿarif,* the term *Sufi* rarely appears. The term *ʿirfan* is likewise infrequently used, but when it does appear it follows this paradigm and is used in conjunction with terms and phrases like *philosophic argument* (*burhan*), *certitude* (*yaqin*), and *divine philosophy* (*al-hikma al-ilahiyya*). The paucity of instances in which Sadra uses the term makes it clear that it had not yet become the semantic locus of an established set of beliefs or practices. In other words, its scattered and casual use indicates that it does not refer to a particular concept with clear boundaries classified under an -ism like Sufism. Instead, ʿirfan refers to an ideal—the highest and ultimate goal of the seeker of maʿrifa.

The same seems to be true in the writings of Sadra's prominent students, who increasingly emphasized the category of ʿarif but not in a way that refers

* Nasr, *Garden of Truth,* 225.

† See, for example, Shirazi (Mulla Sadra), *al-Hikma al-mutaʿaliya,* 1:6.

to a member of a coherent and distinct group with a defined set of beliefs and practices. *Gawhar-i murad,* an important work by ʿAbd al-Razzaq Lahiji, a prominent student of Sadra, provides us with an illuminating statement in this regard. In his classification of the rational sciences, he emphasizes that, unlike kalam and Peripatetic philosophy (*hikmat-i mashshaʾi*), Illuminationist philosophy and Sufism cannot be categorized as branches of knowledge. The former two are, according to Lahiji, concerned with exoteric ways of acquiring knowledge, but Sufism and Illuminationist philosophy are concerned with practicalities of the mystical/esoteric path.* Lahiji notes, however, that philosopher and Sufi come closer to each other in another school of philosophy. "The most urgent kind of knowledge," he says, "is knowing yourself and returning to it, and knowing your God and recognizing your God's command. It is the totality of this kind of knowledge that theologians call the principles of religion [*usul al-din*], philosophers call divine philosophy [*hikmat-i ilahi*], and Sufis call maʿrifat."†

A similar trend is observable in the writings of Mulla Sadra's other prominent student, Mulla Muhsin Fayz Kashani. In *Kalimat maknuna* and *Usul al-maʿarif,* the two works in which his indebtedness to his teacher is most obvious, the category of maʿrifa is at the fore. The very title of the former work, *Kalimat maknuna min ʿulum ahl al-hikma va-l-maʿrifa,* is telling in this regard. Again, we see the pairing of hikma and maʿrifa, which indicates their increasing synonymity in Transcendent philosophy. A quick look at the contents of the book reveals that Fayz draws heavily upon the school of Ibn ʿArabi to explain fundamental questions regarding the reality of being and the position of human beings. He begins most of the chapters by laying out what the "folk of maʿrifa" (*ahl al-maʿrifa*) say regarding the topic of the chapter.‡ In most cases, what they say is saturated with the vocabulary of the school of Ibn ʿArabi. Fayz mentions Rumi, calling him *al-ʿarif al-rumi,*§ and he mentions Mulla Sadra in his autobiography, calling him the "chief of the folk of ʿirfan" (*sadr-i ahl-i ʿirfan*).**

In associating hikma with maʿrifa, Fayz is careful to distinguish between the mainstream discursive philosophy known as Peripatetic philosophy and the type of philosophy that to him epitomizes true hikma.†† The difference can be gleaned from a brief comparison of two of his important

* Lahiji, *Gawhar-i murad,* 38–41.
† Lahiji, *Gawhar-i murad,* 19.
‡ See Fayz Kashani, *Kalimat maknuna,* 5, 24, 25, 28, 36, 42, 45, 48, 54, 55, and 74, among other pages.
§ Fayz Kashani, *Kalimat maknuna,* 16.
** Fayz Kashani, *Risala-yi sharh-i sadr,* quoted in Jaʿfariyan, *Safaviyya,* 2:545.
†† Fayz Kashani, *Kalimat maknuna,* 341.

works *Usul al-maʿarif* and *Kalima*. In the former, Fayz rarely talks about *ahl al-maʿrifa*. In fact, the book is an standard exercise in discursive philosophy, although, like his master, he deviates somewhat from the accepted norms of Peripatetic philosophy and argues for the alternative principles, including the primacy of existence (*asalat al-vujud*) and substantial motion (*al-haraka al-jawhariyya*), that distinguish Sadra's Transcendent philosophy from other schools of philosophy. On the rare occasions that he speaks of *ahl al-maʿrifa*, it is in reference to his master teacher, to other figures in the school of Ibn ʿArabi, or to Ibn ʿArabi himself.*

We get a better sense of what true hikma or maʿrifa means for Fayz in *Kalimat*, which, in the vein of Mulla Sadra's work, synthesizes the metaphysical principles of Ibn ʿArabi with the traditions of the twelve imams.† Copious quotations from canonical and noncanonical hadith sources are followed by comments and explanations in accordance with the principles of *ahl al-maʿrifa*. The author's primary concern is to reconcile philosophical and mystical principles with the statements of the imams found in hadith literature, thereby demonstrating that the way of true hikma and the way of prophecy do not contradict each other.‡ Fayz shared this concern not only with his teacher Mulla Sadra but with many other members of the ulama, whether philosophically inclined or of Akhbari leanings. As the new Shiʿite orthodoxy expanded its reach across various disciplines, the most urgent need of proponents of those disciplines was to authenticate their hermeneutic by drawing upon authoritative hadith sources. Fayz's *Kalimat* is so steeped in the vocabulary of Sufi metaphysical thought that it is tempting to categorize it as a work of Sufism. As Lawson indicates in his excellent study of the book, however, conceptualizing and categorizing *Kalimat* in this manner would be incorrect.§ Instead, it is better understood as a representative of an emerging, independent Twelver spiritual discourse that was later called by the term *ʿirfan*.

It is precisely this understanding of maʿrifa and hikma that Qummi opposes in his own *Hikmat al-ʿarifin*, which was discussed briefly earlier. For him, maʿrifa is not the self-knowledge that Lahiji emphasizes but the knowledge of the imam, without which the person will die a jahili death. Sadra's and Fayz's attempts to bring the Shiʿi hadith literature into conversation

* Fayz Kashani, *Usul al-maʿarif*, 56, 94, 176, and 178.

† Having said this, the role of his other teacher in Shiraz, the prominent Akhbari scholar Sayyid Majid Bahrani (d. 1629) cannot be underestimated. A cursory look at the Fayzian oeuvre makes clear that his concern and engagement with the hadith literature are much more serious and extensive than Sadra's.

‡ Fayz Kashani, *Usul al-maʿarif*, 4.

§ Lawson, "Hidden Words," 428–32.

with some entity called divine philosophy or hikmat-i ilahi is alarming because, for him, "Hikma is the knowledge [maʿrifa] of the imam; and the hakim is the one who knows the true imam and learns religious knowledge from him. There is no question that the purified imams from the Family [of the Prophet] are the leaders of truth and the mines of hikma who learned it from the Prophet himself, Peace be upon him. . . . who said 'I am the house of hikma and ʿAli is its door, whomever desires hikma has to approach the door.' Therefore, hikma is what is understood from the sayings of the pure imams, the companions of infallibility, and the interpreters of God's Book . . . not the problems of philosophy, which are in contradiction with the Book and the tradition [*sunna*]."*

In spite of this important disagreement over the proper definition of maʿrifa and hikma, Fayz agreed with Qummi in a fundamantal level: that it was imperative for him and for like-minded people to demonstrate how the foundations of knowledge traditions such as philosophy and Sufism were based on the teachings of imams. The newly established Twelver sacred nomos not only gave Qummi a vital edge in this debate but also gradually moved the Sufi-minded scholars of time, including Fayz, toward a more reserved position when it came to Sufi vocabulary and worldview.

Fayz's writings, covering the span of almost a half-century, beautifully reflect how, under the influence of the changing religious milieu, he increasingly distanced himself from the traditional Sufi and philosophical vocabulary, opting instead to put more emphasis on hadith reports. In the case of his *Kalimat*, Zargar has demonstrated how his evolving attitudes toward philosophy and Sufism led him to produce a new version of that work, *Qurrat al-ʿuyun*, in which he relied more heavily on scripture to argue for the same points.† Another treatise written by Fayz toward the end of his life and at the height of the anti-Sufi campaign is *al-Insaf*, which was completed in 1672 and which expresses his disenchantment with theology, philosophy, and Sufism. He declares, "I am not a theologian, a philosopher, or a Sufi . . . rather, I am an imitator of the Qur'an, hadith, and the Prophet, and a follower of the household of the Prophet."‡

Although the debate between anti-Sufi and pro-Sufi ulama was mostly over the proper definition of already established terms such as hikma and maʿrifa, it prepared the grounds for the emergence of the category of ʿirfan. By the middle of the seventeenth century, neither Sadra's school of thought

* Qummi, *Hikmat al-arifin* MS, 5

† Zargar, "Revealing Revisions," 20

‡ For this quotation and an extensive analysis of Fayz's late-life disenchantment with philosophy and Sufism, see Jaʿfariyan, *Safaviyya*, 2:537–55.

nor the Sufi metaphysical thought was referred to by the term *ʿirfan*. A century later, however, the situation had changed, and religious scholars such as Mulla Mahdi Niraqi (d. 1794) and his son Mulla Ahmad (d. 1829), who were trained in Sadra's mystical philosophy, would refer to this tradition explicitly as ʿirfan.*

This brief excursion into the semantics of ʿirfan and its cognates in the writings of adherents to the school of Mulla Sadra reveals some of the ways Sadra and especially his students, as well as their opponents, such as Qummi, contributed to the formation of this discourse. They did not, however, coin the term *ʿirfan*. Rather, in our search for the origins of the category of ʿirfan, I argue the focus should move away from the School of Isfahan and toward the life and works of two influential, yet little known scholars hailing from the ancient province of Fars: Shah Muhammad Darabi and Qutb al-Din Nayrizi.

Shah Muhammad Darabi, Sufism, and ʿIrfan

Information about Darabi's (d. 1718) life and works is scattered across a wide variety of primary sources. Bibliographers of poets and members of the ulama have used these sources to construct a picture of his career and life that can be quite puzzling at times.† Because of his extended lifespan (his students insist that he lived more than a hundred years)‡ and the probability that he, like many poets and writers of his period, spent many years in India in pursuit of royal sponsorship, his life and work are discussed under two, and sometimes three, different names.§

Miraculous length of life is often attributed to saintly figures, but in Darabi's case, the number of reports of longevity by his contemporaries lead one to believe that he indeed lived close to, if not slightly more than, one hundred years. The earliest known literary trace left by him is an extant copy of ʿUrfi

* More on the two Niraqis in chapter 5.

† The best attempt to reconstruct the basic chronology of Darabi's life was accomplished recently in Ashkevari, "Introduction." A comprehensive list of Darabi's writings is included in Ashkevari's informative overview.

‡ For example, Hazin claims that he lived to be nearly 130 years old. Hazin, *Tarikh*, 178.

§ For example, Adamiyyat has divided Darabi's works under three different entries. See Ruknzade Adamiyyat, *Danishmandan*, 3:229, 230, and 544). Similarly, Aqa Bozorg contends that there are two Darabis in this period whose identity and work should not be mixed. See Tehrani, *al-Zariʿa*, 9:665–66. Other examples of this confusion, most of which are based on Aqa Bozorg's misleading comments, include Karbasi-zade, *Hakim-i mutaʾallih bidabadi*, 68.

Shirazi's *Divan,* copied by Darabi himself in India in 1636.* The maturity of the handwriting suggests that Darabi was at least in his early twenties by that time, which puts his birth date somewhere around the middle of the second decade of the seventeenth century. Other concrete dates related to his literary activities belong to a much later period of his life. He mentions the year 1692 in two treatises, *Miʿraj al-kamal* and *Maqamat al-salikin.*† The latest date mentioned in his writings can be found in his commentary on the fourth imam's *al-Sahifa,* which Darabi penned in Isfahan in 1702.‡ Another important piece of information about the chronology of his life comes from his student Hazin, who mentions that Darabi passed away while the former was studying in Shiraz. Although we know Hazin stayed in Iran until 1733, we do not know the exact dates of his study in Shiraz. He was likely in his late twenties and early thirties while there, and his stay must have occurred during the last decade of Safavid rule, some years before the fall of Isfahan in 1722. This gives us a general range, but another piece of evidence helps narrow the time frame further. ʿAli-Naqi Istahbanati, in his *Burhan al-murtazin,* the content of which are discussed later, mentions Darabi's name and follows it with the phrase "*rahmatullah ʿalayhi,*" which means the latter was already dead at the time *Burhan* was being penned.§ We don't have a firm date for the writing of *Burhan,* but the sources are unanimous that Istahbanati died in 1714. This means Darabi's death must have happened prior to that time. This puts his death date sometime in the early 1710s, when he was around a hundred years old.** If we rely on this timeline, his claim to have been a student of Shaykh Bahaʾi might not be that farfetched.††

Darabi also appears to have lived in India for multiple extended periods of time. The use of the title *shah* before his name indicates a strong connection to India, where it was customary for Sufi saints to be honored with this title.‡‡ All three of Darabi's prominent students who left behind biographical information about him noted that he was their primary teacher in hadith

* This beautiful manuscript was brought to my attention by Sadeq Ashkevari. I later found out that it was the property of the late Stuart Cary Welch. His descendants put it up for sale, and it was auctioned off by Sotheby's for £73,250 on April 6, 2011.

† See Darabi, *Miʿraj* MS, 464.

‡ Darabi, *Riyaz al-ʿarifin,* 10.

§ Istahbanati, *Burhan al-murtazin,* 194.

** For a list of different death dates mentioned in primary sources see Darabi, *Tazkira,* xx. I am inclined toward Aqa Bozorg's conclusion in this regard. See Tehrani, *al-Zariʿa,* 9:666.

†† Khuyi, *Mizan al-savab,* 2:1212. See also Golchin Maʿani, *Tarikh-i tazkira-ha-yi farsi,* 2:101. Golchin refers to *Lataʾif al-khayal* as his source.

‡‡ For a summary of his trips see Darabi, *Tazkira,* xviii-xix.

and mention that he taught classical philosophy textbooks as well as other sciences.*

Darabi's mastery of hadith is best exemplified in his commentary on *al-Sahifa al-sajjadiyya,* which he titled *Riyaz al-ʿarifin.* This work was written during the reign of and was dedicated to Shah Sultan Husayn. It is no surprise, then, that Nayrizi cited Darabi as teacher on whose authority he narrated the traditions of the family of the Prophet (his *shaykh al-ijaza,* in other words). In Nayrizi's words, "First among the learned with whom I have associated was . . . my teacher, the one whom I reference in narrating from the infallible imams. . . . [He was] a master of the rational and narrative disciplines [*jamiʿ al-maʿqul va al-manqul*] and a repository of the principles and the branches [of religion]. [He was] the most knowledgeable and intelligent Mawla Shah Muhammad Darabi, peace be upon him. He was the teacher of all the learned of Shiraz in his age, and I am in possession of a treatise by him in his own handwriting titled *Miʿraj al-kamal,* which is an inquiry about the meaning of shaykh and guidance, and disciple and seeking guidance."†

This emphasis on hadith by Darabi and his students is another testament to how hadith study was a centerpiece of the madrasa curriculum in this period, whether one was interested in hadith and jurisprudence or in philosophy and mysticism. Other students of Darabi used equally laudatory language and recounted the classes they took from him on a wide variety of topics ranging from *Usul al-kafi* and *Hikmat al-ʿayn* to music, mathematics, and kalam. Here is what Hazin had to say:

> The teacher of the ulama, our great master Maulana Shah Muhammad Shirazi was in that town [Shiraz]. I began to hear *Usul al-kafi* in his class, and I benefited from him all the time, day and night. . . .That knowledgeable man was one of a kind across all ages . . . he enjoyed the company of many scholars and great ʿurafa, he saw many countries of the world, and in order to reach the highest stations and perfect his soul, he experienced mortification. He had a deep respect for the masters and saints . . . and he lived close to a hundred and thirty years, all spent in the service of disseminating knowledge, pursuing truth, and caring for the servants [of God]. He is the author of several treatises on hadith, philosophy and Sufism. He died sometime after I migrated to that town.‡

Another interesting fact about Darabi is that, despite his strong penchant for mysticism and the fact that his vocabulary was borrowed heavily from

* For a comprehensive list of his students, see Ashkevari's notes in Darabi, *Tazkira,* xxii-xxiv.

† Khuyi, *Mizan al-savab,* 2:1201.

‡ Hazin, *Tarikh,* 177–78.

Sufi literature, none of his contemporaries associated him with organized Sufi orders in either Iran or India. The fact that Nayrizi refers to Istahbanati, and not Darabi, as his *shaykh al-tariqa* (master of the [Sufi] path) also reflects Darabi's hesitation to operate within the framework of traditional Sufi institutions.

Darabi is important to our inquiry because the earliest attempts to replace and contrast terms such as *Sufi* and *Sufism* with *ʿarif* and *ʿirfan* occur in his writings. Later figures such as Nayrizi operated under his direct influence as they unburdened themselves of words weighted with negative connotations in the aftermath of the anti-Sufi campaign. In fact, an examination of the numerous extant works by Darabi demonstrates that he, along with Mu'azzin and Nayrizi, was at the front line of the Sufi response to this campaign. He wrote works dedicated to three hotly debated issues of the time related to Sufism: *Maqamat al-salikin* on the issue of music (*ghina*) and its legitimate and illegitimate forms,* *Miʿraj al-kamal* on the master/disciple relationship in Sufism,† *Farah al-salikin* in defense of the Sufi practices of samaʿ and ecstasy,‡ and *Latifa-yi ghaybi,* which contains his take on the debate over terms like *Sufi* and *Sufism.* It is worthwhile to focus on him not only because of his influence on Nayrizi and the latter's choice to distance himself from the term *Sufi* but also because of his larger influence on the intellectual circles of Shiraz. As a long-lived and universally respected teacher in the city who influenced a great number of students, he made unparalleled contributions to the nascent stages of the formation of the paradigm of ʿirfan. Two of his most influential contributions to the debate on Sufism during the seventeenth century were *Miʿraj al-kamal* and *Latifa-yi ghaybi,* and thus I proceed to an examination of their contents.

Miʿraj al-kamal

Miʿraj al-kamal is focused on what was perhaps the most volatile issue debate over Sufism: the master/disciple relationship. Sufi-minded and anti-Sufi camps disagreed over whether it could be construed as analogous to the relationship between the imams and their followers and the related questions of whether it constituted bidʿa or "innovation." In discussing the master/

* This was recently published. See Darabi, *Maqamat al-salikin,* 283–496.

† Unpublished. There are two known copies of this work available; one is held in Mashhad, at Astan-i Quds, which I consulted for this analysis. This is a clean yet late manuscript, copied in 1351 hijri, and I would like to thank Mr. Ashkevari for providing me with a digital copy. There is another manuscript of *Miʿraj* held in Najaf at the archives of Amir al-Mu'minin Public Library.

‡ Unpublished; one known manuscript. See Darabi, *Farah* MS. To judge from internal evidence, it was written after *Maqamat al-salikin.* See Darabi, *Farah* MS, f. 27b.

disciple relationship, I am not interested in the individual and personal aspects of the relationship and its connection to spiritual matters. Instead, I am concerned with the relationship as a significant social phenomenon that developed across centuries and formed the bedrock of an elaborate ethos and an array of social rituals. Rituals and codes of conduct shaped by this relationship played an important role in regulating not only the social hierarchy of the khanaqah but also the larger network of social groups that were connected in different ways to Sufi institutions. The social implications of this relationship were what the emerging hierocracy found most threatening to its authority and power in religious matters and beyond. This sense of threat led the Sufis to come under verbal attacks and, sometimes, to face actual persecution. The ulama were a highly complex and amorphous group, however, and their activities went far beyond attempts to silence Sufis and dervishes. As mentioned at earlier, a highly innovative and syncretistic attempt was also being made within clerical circles to offer an alternative model of guidance with the imams at its center, a sacred nomos to ground the populace. In other words, the ulama did not simply express what they believed was wrong with Sufism. They also offered an alternative vision of how one could pursue spirituality the "right" way. I believe that this, in addition to the unwavering support of the political establishment for the ulama, contributed significantly to their ultimate success. At a popular level, the development of cults of veneration and worship around the tombs of imams and their descendants and the widespread retellings of miraculous stories about the infallible imams by passionate mullas, wandering dervishes, and maddahs was instrumental in focusing public attention on the imams instead of on Sufi saints. At the same time, similar stories took shape around charismatic and high-ranking members of the hierocracy, whose status as deputies (*nuvvab*) of the Hidden Imam lent itself to the formation of cults of worship. For the learned ulama, dreams and visions of the imams and the enormous literary legacy preserved in hadith literature functioned as primary sources of spiritual guidance. A new spiritual hierarchy developed in which the gates of heaven opened at the behest not of the saintly Sufi shaykh of the khanaqah or local shrine but of the charismatic clergy and the local imam-zada.

In the midst of these negotiations over authentic channels of connection between heaven and earth, Darabi dedicated an entire treatise to explaining the meaning of guidance. That he felt the need to do so indicates a certain level of confusion and uncertainty about the boundaries and definition of the notion. The stakes were high: those who successfully defined such boundaries would be the new guardians of the gates of heaven.

As one of the Sufi-minded ulama, Darabi straddled the worlds of traditional Sufism and the new Twelver orthodoxy, much as Muʾazzin had done before him in *Tuhfa*. There are differences, however, between the two authors' approaches. As someone solidly grounded in the world of organized Sufism, Mu'azzin was a transitional figure who approached the area where the two worlds intermingled while still privileging traditional Sufi discourse. For his part, Darabi was solidly grounded in the madrasa tradition and lived fully beneath the new Twelver sacred canopy, and his primary commitment was to orthodox Twelver discourse. His arguments in *Mi'raj,* although informed by traditional Sufi discourse and employed in defense of its fundamental ideas, can be seen as an attempt to domesticate the Sufi tradition by revisiting key concepts and adjusting their premises and definitions.

Like Mu'azzin in *Tuhfa,* Darabi opens his remarks in *Miʿraj* with a discussion of the nature of religious knowledge and a basic classification of the scholars of religion, the ulama. This is another affirmation that the crucial point of disagreement between the Sufis and the emerging clerical class was the proper relationship between disciplinary/rational knowledge, which is acquired in the madrasa, and inspirational/intuitive knowledge, which is gained through training in the khanaqah. *Miʿraj* contains the same tripartite division seen in *Tuhfa;* the ulama are divided between those who are experts in the exoteric disciplines (*ulama al-zahir*) and those who are experts in the esoteric disciplines (*ulama al-batin*). Ideal spiritual guides, the ulama who are competent in both the esoteric and exoteric sciences, occupy the third category.* Representatives of this third group are called divine religious scholars (*al-ulama al-rabbaniyyin*), and, according to Darabi, terms like *pir* and *murshid* are references to these men.† He maintains that these ulama are one and the same with those the Second Martyr called the *ulama al-haqiqa,* those who embark on the path of asceticism and spiritual advancement after finishing formal training in the religious disciplines. In other words, they combine the knowledge of Shariʿa with accomplishments in tariqa and the realization of *haqiqa.*‡ Another phrase, *ʿalim rabbani,* was used in later Shiʿi mystical literature as an important alternative to the original Sufi concept of pir. Thus a new set of terms appeared, suited to a context where organized Sufism and important elements of its technical language were being purged in favor of a new, Shiʿi-inspired lexicon.

This is only one of many instances in this treatise where the author makes a pointed effort to reframe traditional Sufi concepts. The reinterpretation of Sufi concepts in a way that weakens their connection to the technical vocabulary of traditional Sufism is a striking feature of *Miʿraj.* Darabi's

* Darabi, *Miʿraj* MS, 97.
† Darabi, *Miʿraj* MS, 129 and 134–35.
‡ *Darabi, Miʿraj MS, 66.*

willingness to discard long-standing Sufi terminology in favor of less problematic and more authentic-looking alternative terms can be seen throughout, and he reminds us often that one's choice of technical terms does not matter. "*La mushahhata fi al-istilah*" (there is no dispute in terminology), he says.* What truly matters, he remarks, is the realities to which such terms point.† This conscious attempt to deemphasize traditional Sufi terminology can be understood as a response to the criticism that Sufi vocabulary is, for the most part, alien to that found in authoritative hadith collections. Darabi pursued a dual strategy of deemphasizing the technical meanings of such terms and citing examples from other disciplines in which extracanonical terminology are used without being subject to charges of innovation.‡ Despite Darabi's claim otherwise, his willingness to compromise on terminology was not simply a superficial exchange of different words referring to the same truth. On to the contrary, he took terms deeply rooted in a Sunni–Sufi heritage out of their original register and reintroduced them into a new web of meaning and signification that revolves around Twelver teaching. Here we see the beginning of a cluster of terms that form the basis of a new discourse on spirituality, one that is grounded in a new social reality, that of the Shiʿi hierocracy.

Darabi's literary strategy was innovative and synthetic; it reduces and effaces difference. It stands in contrast to Qummi's semantics, where difference is essentialized and emphasized.§ In fact, Darabi's might have chosen his strategy of deemphasizing semantic difference in a direct response to Qummi and his emphasis that essential terms and their traditional fields of meaning can be seen as easy and straightforward indicators of "foreign" elements in Islamic thought. For example, one of his primary methods of defending the orthodoxy of terms like *pir* or *qutb,* which are found in abundance in Sufi literature, was to downplay their technical meanings and treat them as synonyms of less loaded terms like teacher (*ustad*), guide (*rahnama*), student (*shagird*), wayfarer (*rahru*), scholar (*ʿalim*), and learner (*mutaʿallim*).

* For example, see Darabi, *Miʿraj* MS, 106–7 and 160. Darabi's tendency to deemphasize and decontextualize the technical meanings of Sufi terms is also clearly seen in *Latifa.* As long as one submits to the path laid out by the infallible imams, in matters both exoteric and esoteric, Darabi says, it is of no importance whether one is called Sufi or jurist (faqih). *Sufism* is not just a word; "it is its meaning that is the criteria . . . the letters fa, qaf, and ha [which spell fiqh] are not [in and of themselves] luminous (*nurani*), neither are the letters ta, sad, vav, and fa [which spell tasavvuf] dark ones (*zulumani*) that belong to hell (*jahannami*)." Darabi, *Latifa,* 110.

† Darabi, *Latifa,* 100.

‡ Darabi, *Miraj* MS, 105–6.

§ See our discussion of Qummi's strategy in chapter 2.

All of these terms, according to him, refer simply to an educational relationship in which knowledge flows from the more to the less informed.*

Nonetheless, Darabi stood firm in his belief that embarking upon the spiritual path is impossible without the proper training of a master, a murshid or pir.† He qualified this, however, by saying that no one can be the ultimate spiritual guide but the imam. It is only in the period of occultation, when the ultimate qutb of the universe is not accessible, that any degree of authority can be attributed to the ʿarifin, the divine religious scholars who are masters of both exoteric and esoteric aspects of religion.

> So, if you say [terms like] murshid refer to no one other than the infallible [imams], I say yes, but when they are present. When they are in occultation, however, the ʿarifin among the religious scholars who know the esoteric sciences are, with the help of their hadiths, their deputies [*nuvvab*]. Then, if it is said that their hadith is sufficient for us, I would say, if their hadith is sufficient, then why do exoteric religious scholars [go to their teachers in hadith] and take the hadith and hear it from their *mashayikh al-ijaza?* Therefore, [one] learns the way of practice [*tariqat al-ʿamal*] from the murshid just as one learns his way in the discipline of hadith from the masters of hadith [*mashayikh al-hadith*].‡

The language of deputyship (*niyaba*) here is highly significant. Beginning with ʿAli Karaki in the early sixteenth century, Twelver mujtahids began, with the support of Safavid monarchs, to employ the language of niyaba to solidify their authority as true representatives of the Hidden Imam.§ The Safavid monarchs benefited from this state of affairs, since, they claimed, the mujtahids graciously relegated the burden of governance to them. The shah, in other words, was approved by the learned mujtahid to act as a deputy of the Hidden Imam and to rule over the masses. While Darabi did not directly challenge the deputyship claims of the exoteric mujtahid whose expertise was solely in the matter of Shariʿa, he stated emphatically that it was the third group, those who combined exotericism and esotericism, who were the true deputies of the Hidden Imam. Darabi quoted a number of hadith to substantiate his claim, concluding they were "explicit that the perfect master who is a 'believer' [*mu'min*] stands as the representative of the infallible imam, and there is no doubt that [this believer] has partial [*naqisa*] *valaya.* This is the status of the murshid. It should be clear that [such] a master of the

* Darabi, *Latifa,* 95.

† Darabi, *Latifa,* 94.

‡ Darabi, *Latifa,* 105 (marginalia),

§ Jaʿfariyan, *Safaviyya,* 1:122, 212, and 215.

esoteric disciplines should also have mastery of the exoteric disciplines. Otherwise, he would not be qualified for the position."*

The concept of *valaya,* which appears in this quotation in conjunction with the concept of pir, deserves attention here. In his attempt to decontextualize and then redefine central Sufi notions connected to the concept of pir, Darabi addressed the notions of sainthood (valaya) and the saint (*vali*). Few terms are more important in classical Sufi literature. Accomplished Sufis, by virtue of their advanced spiritual station and closeness to God, become God's favorite servants, the pinnacle of his creation, and the raison d'être for its sustenance. This traditional semantic field, however, is not what Darabi wished to discuss. Instead, he pointed out that valaya has multiple meanings, including *helper* (*nasir*) and *lover* (*muhibb,* in an affectionate rather than a sexual relationship).† The meaning on which he spent the most time, however, was valaya as it occurs in Islamic legal texts, where it is connected to the notion of the "*awla bi al-tasarruf,*" someone who has precedence in managing the affairs of someone else. Darabi extended this notion beyond matters of the Shariʿa to the sphere of spiritual guidance. A true vali, for him, was a person to whom God has given material and spiritual authority over someone else.

Darabi made it clear that absolute authority of this kind can be conferred by God only on his most perfect servants, the imams. Therefore, he argued, the only case in which an adept is truly "a corpse in the hands of a washer" is one in which it comes to acquiescing to the infallibles and their commands.‡ In light of the occultation, however, he advanced the notion that a weaker (*naqis*) or partial sense of *tasarruf* or valaya applies to the perfect spiritual master (*al-ʿalim al-rabbani*), who is present and accessible while the last imam remains in hiding.

The political implications of this model of authority were not explored by Darabi, but they loomed large in the background. The fact that such a politically potent notion of valaya emerged in the Safavid milieu reveals an immense power struggle within the hierocracy. This was not merely a debate between Sufi shaykh and jurist. It was a contest over who had the right to claim the deputyship of the Hidden Imam, a battle that has had profound ramifications for the social and political landscape of contemporary Iran. The debates in which Darabi was engaged foreshadowed the later concept of *valayat al-faqih,* a political system at whose head stood *al-vali al-faqih,* someone like Khomeini, who was not only a mujtahid but also an accomplished and

* Darabi, *Miʿraj MS,* 172.

† Darabi, *Latifa,* 97–98.

‡ Darabi, *Latifa,* 149.

highly knowledgeable ʿarif. Noticeable in this regard is the fact that Mulla Ahmad Niraqi, himself a polymath, a reputable ʿalim, and a renowned ʿarif and who is usually credited as one of the earliest figures who argued for the idea of *valayat al-faqih* in its earliest form, was influenced by the Nurbakhshi Sufi network in general and by the work of Shah Muhammad in particular. In other words, the attempts to depoliticize Sufism by stripping it of its extensive social network and institutions and to assimilate what remained into the madrasa system under the heading of ʿirfan created space for a new kind of politics. In Qajar times and beyond, it was no longer the Sufi shaykh but rather the mujtahid-ʿarif who had the social capital to influence the trajectory of political life.

Another striking similarity between *Miʿraj* and *Tuhfa* becomes clear in the final pages of the former, where Darabi begins a discussion of qualities necessary for master and disciple. The list is almost identical to that in *Tuhfa.** A few points of divergence, however, indicate that Darabi's vision of the master/disciple relationship was different from that of a member of organized Sufism such as Mu'azzin. First, though Darabi mentions the necessity of the disciple submitting to the master, he qualifies this assertion by saying that an adept does not need to obey the shaykh if the latter's demands are contrary to the Shariʿa.† Darabi has set up an image of the pir that makes it inconceivable that he would require the adept to do something contrary to the law, but the fact that he entertains this as a hypothetical is a significant departure from the traditional Sufi understanding in which, on the basis of the famous story of Moses and a companion traditionally understood to be Khizr, the disciple is required to submit to the will of the master even when doing so violates common sense and the basic tenets of the Shariʿa.‡ This is exactly the point where Darabi departs from long-standing Sufi tradition. In his elaboration of the twentieth qualification for the disciple, which is taken almost word for word from *Tuhfa,* he drops all reference to the traditional corpse/washer analogy, even though he retains the Qur'anic story to emphasize the importance of disciple's submission.

To return to Darabi's willingness to compromise on terminology, it is revealing to see his treatment of the term *hikma.* As a prominent teacher of Peripatetic philosophy and in response to criticism from the anti-Sufi and anti-philosopher camp that Qur'anic hikma had nothing in common with

* *Darabi, Latifa, 174.*

† Darabi, *Latifa,* 178.

‡ In fact, Najm al-Din Razi, in his classic *Mirsad al-ʿibad,* says explicitly that, on the basis of the logic of the Qur'anic story mentioned, the disciple is to submit to the will of the master like a corpse in the hands of the washer, even when he thinks doing so contradicts the law. See Razi, *Mirsad al-ʿibad,* 147.

the field of knowledge known as philosophy, he redefined the term in the following manner:

> So, if you say that the hikma praised in the discipline of Shariʿa is different from the hikma that is customary among the students, I would say that hikma is knowing the reality of things as they are according to the capacity of human understanding . . . the result is that the philosopher [hakim] is one who knows things as they are and acts accordingly. That is why in *Hikmat-i ʿalaʾi* it is said—in Persian—that the hakim is truthful [*rast-guftar*] and righteous [*durust-kirdar*]. Therefore, hikma is something that includes the discipline of Shariʿa, . . . and the discipline of tafsir, hadith, and fiqh are all included in hikma. . . . Our master, Shaykh Bahaʾi, has pointed out in some of his writings that hikma is derived from the fountain of prophethood [*nubuvva*], and because the names of some prophets were recorded in Greek, people were confused [and thought] that those names referred to philosophers rather than prophets, and then he explained that Hermes Trismagestus is the [Greek] name of prophet Idris, and Pythagoras the name of prophet Shis [Seth, son of Adam].*

Another term with which Darabi grappled is the word *tasavvuf* itself. Darabi experimented with several alternative terms for this concept, *ʿirfan* among them. For Darabi, ʿirfan served as an authentic Shiʿi word for spirituality, in contrast to the problematic, Sunni-related aspects of tasavvuf. He wrote, "If the fact that Sunni scholars are numbered among jurists is not considered a stain on the face of the glorious science of fiqh, then similarly, the fact that there are rare Sunni Sufis among the ʿurafa is not a blemish for ʿirfan.†

An ʿarif, ideally, cannot be a Sunni. Darabi made this clear in a number of places in *Miʿraj* by emphasizing that the spiritual lineages originating from problematic Sunni figures like Hasan Basri and Sufiyan Sawri are illegitimate.

> If you were to say that some orders trace their lineage back to Hasan Basri or Sufiyan Sawri and that those two are condemned [by the imams], I would say that only a few among the orders end in those two, and that does not cast a negative light upon the discipline of Sufism and ʿirfan.‡ . . . [T]he disparagement of Sufism that is found in some hadiths refers to the group who were opposed to Their Excellencies, who disputed them, and who actively pursued a way contrary to the true way of

* Darabi, *Miʿraj* MS, 155–56.

† Darabi, *Miʿraj* MS, 113.

‡ Darabi, *Miʿraj* MS, 125 and 113.

> Twelverism. It does not refer to the group whose spoken words, deeds, and religious observances most closely followed Their Highnesses, the pure imams. How it is fair to call this latter group Sufis [that is, to denigrate them by calling them Sufis] simply because they persisted in zikr, purified their food and their soul, and refined their ethical qualities, and then to fight them, express hostility toward them, and reject them? As soon as we have learned a few [jurisprudential] issues [*mas'ala*] from the books of transactions and trade [*muʿamalat va tijarat*], we consider ourselves better than the group we have called Sufis, even if we observe them doing their best to follow Their Highnesses, the imams, and even if we have done thousands of blameworthy deeds opposed to the exalted tradition of Their Excellencies. [And we do this] only on the grounds that we are jurists and they are Sufis. What kind of logic is this, and according to what notion of fairness, judgment, and law?*

Though Darabi set up a clear Shiʿi–Sunni dichotomy, he used the words *ʿirfan* and *Sufism* in conjunction with each other in this passage and in many other. Presenting these two words as synonyms helped give his readers a sense of what the newly introduced category of ʿirfan meant. As far as I have been able to determine, Darabi was the first author to use ʿirfan as an equivalent term for Sufism, transcribing many of the semantic denotations and connotations of latter onto the former. In his writing, *ʿirfan* became a substantive term signifying a particular discipline (*fann*) instead of a word for the advanced spiritual station marked by ʿarif realization of the unity beneath apparent multiplicity. Darabi also called it a *mazhab*, which implies a defined set of beliefs and practices or a particular school of thought.†

As mentioned, the most literal meaning of the term *tasavvuf* is the process by which one becomes a Sufi. This procedural denotation was also transcribed onto ʿirfan by Darabi. In a brief but important passage, he provided a rough definition of these terms, saying, "tasavvuf and ʿirfan mean being free of all vices [*raza'il*], adorned with all virtues [*faza'il*], and observing the exoteric and the esoteric [aspects] of the Shariʿa.‡ This definition clearly draws on that of Ibn Sina in his *al-Isharat* and Dasktaki's treatise *Maqamat al-ʿarifin*, discussed earlier. Darabi, a teacher of philosophy in Shiraz, was fully aware of the Avicennan tradition of ʿirfan. As a member of the Shirazi intellectual elite, he likely knew Sadra personally during the later stages of the Sadra's teaching career, and Darabi actually mentions the latter's name with approval in *Maqamat al-salikin* and in a small treatise called *Maslak-i ahl-i*

* Darabi, *Latifa*, 108–9.
† Darabi, *Miʿraj* MS, 150.
‡ Darabi, *Miʿraj* MS, 148.

*ʿirfan.** Sadra's mystical philosophy, however, does not seem to have informed Darabi's notion of ʿirfan. The latter's philosophical approach, especially to fundamental questions of the metaphysics of being, was similar to that of many of his contemporaries in that it remained largely Avicennan.† The primary medium through which he interpreted the Avicennan tradition is the work of Nasir al-Din Tusi, whose name appears more frequently in Darabi's writings than that of any other scholar. Darabi cited passages from Tusi's works frequently, with many of the quotations taken from *Sharh al-tajrid* and *Awsaf al-ashraf*.‡

Yet, Darabi's notion of ʿirfan, as explained in *Miʿraj,* was far from just being derived from this Avicennan tradition. Rather, he built his notion of ʿirfan on his innovative synthesis of multiple traditions of learning, from philosophy and Sufism to the rich tradition of Persian poetry in Shiraz. Thus far my discussion of Darabi has focused on his status as a religious scholar and the way his scholarly background and commitments informed his conception of ʿirfan. Yet Darabi was also a poet from the city that was home to two of the most celebrated and popular Persian poets, Hafez and Saʿdi. Centuries after these poets' deaths, the cultural environment of Shiraz was still indelibly marked by the legacy of these two towering figures in the history of Persian literature. Interestingly for this study, Darabi composed poetry under the pen name ʿArif, an indication of the significance of this notion in Darabi's overall mystical-poetic thought. Furthermore, Darabi is the author of what can be considered the first commentary on the ghazals of Hafez.§ His *Latifa-yi ghaybi,* a brief commentary on a limited number of Hafez's odes, is

* Darabi, *Maqamat al-salikin,* 323–24, as well as *Maslak* MS, 190.

† See, for example, in his comments on the issue of *vahdat al-vujud va al-mawjud,* which appear on the margins. Darabi, *Miʿraj* MS, 151. The lack of attention to Sadra's philosophy is not surprising, even for a denizen of Shiraz. We know that despite Muhammad-Tahir Qummi's early attacks on Sadra for his synthesis of Sufism with philosophy, Sadra's philosophy remained marginal in philosophical circles until the end of the eighteenth century and the emergence of Mulla ʿAli Nuri (d. 1830). See Ashtiyani's remarks in this regard in "Introduction III," cvi–cviii. It is also worth mentioning that Darabi wrote a work called *A Treatise on the Existence of the Imaginal World* (*Risala fi tahqiq ʿalam al-misal*), which indicates the extent to which Sufi-Illuminationist trends influenced his thought. In this treatise Darabi contends that, although the existence of such a realm cannot be proved by reasoning, it has been confirmed by mystical visions and also by implication in hadith literature. See Darabi, *Risala* MS. See also Ashkevari's brief report of this treatise in Ashkevari, "ʿAlam al-misal," 34–35.

‡ Darabi also frequently quotes from Tusi's foundational theological work, *Tajrid al-iʿtiqad.* See, for example, Darabi, *Miʿraj* MS, 137–38.

§ The only work preceding *Latifa* in this genre is Davani's commentary on a single ghazal and two lines of poetry from Hafiz. See Davani, *Naqd-i niyazi.*

arguably the most widely read of his works, certainly among Persian belles-lettrists. It is also the work in which he used the category of ʿirfan most frequently and consistently. Given the popularity of *Latifa* among a wide range of learned Iranians who were interested in reading about Hafez's poetry, this work may have played a more important role than *Miʿraj* in the establishment and spread of the notion of ʿirfan.*

As Darabi mentions in his introduction of the work, the major impetus for the writing of *Latifa* was to defend Hafez against increasing attacks by critics who accused the poet of being a Sunni and a heretic based upon their reading of his odes.† I have not been able to find any literary evidence of Hafez being attacked in anti-Sufi literature, but it is quite obvious from the text of *Latifa* as well as from the reason stated by its author for its writing that Hafez was targeted by the puritan defenders of orthodoxy who attacked Sufism. In fact, it would be surprising if this were not the case, given Hafez's subversive and erotic imagery, his syncretistic and pluralist tendencies, and his anti-establishment tone and indulgent manners.

Darabi's commentary, the earliest substantial one in which Hafez's poems are interpreted in a symbolic and otherworldly manner that goes against the grain of their literal meaning, should be understood in the context of such attacks. The long tradition of treating Hafez's language symbolically, as representative of a purely metaphysical eros, might best be attributed to the desire among religious readers to make this beloved Persian poet acceptable to the guardians of orthodoxy. Doing this required the domestication of the explicitly sexual, pluralistic, and sometimes antinomian nature of Hafez's language. The subversive potential of his poetry had to be neutralized by transferring its referents to the afterworld and a heavenly beloved.

In his attempt to avoid the stigma of Sufism and associate himself with the new paradigm of ʿirfan as an alternative, Darabi found in Hafez, with his anti-establishment tone and aversion to religious formality and hypocrisy, an important ally. His imagined community of *ahl-i ʿirfan* was not entangled in a convoluted and corrupt web of social hierarchies, and it found a natural home in the world of Hafez. I say "imagined community," because the notion of ʿirfan was still in its infancy, and no set of beliefs yet bound together a like-minded group of elite ʿarifin. Religious communities need founding myths, and Darabi was engaged in myth-making. By referring frequently to

* The popularity of *Latifa* is evident from the number of extant manuscripts; more than one hundred survive around the world. Since the emergence of print in Persia, it has been published several times. Most notably, it was among the first publications printed at Dar al-Funun, the first modern-style university established in Iran, where it was published in 1886.

† Darabi, *Latifa*, 7.

prominent Sufis and Sufi-minded poets such as Ibn ʿArabi, Najm al-Din Kubra, ʿAla al-Dawla Hamadani, Shams al-Din Maghribi, Baba Afzal Kashani, Fakhr al-Din ʿIraqi, and others and by positioning them as part and parcel of a tradition of ʿirfan that could be traced back to the first imam, who was the "the head of the chain of the lords of ʿirfan" (*sar halqa-yi arbab-i ʿirfan*),* he created an imagined community of ʿirfan-minded people that had existed throughout the ages. In doing so, he took a first step toward building an actual present community.

Darabi's attempt to build an imagined community of ʿirfan-minded people manifested itself in another way in a short treatise that has no title but is catalogued under the heading *Risala dar maslak-i ahl al-ʿirfan* and appears at the end of *Miʿraj*. In it he lists a number of prominent Shiʿi jurists who were also theologians, philosophers, scholars of hadith, and so on and who, according to Darabi, supported the path of the folk of ʿirfan (*mashrab-i ahl-i ʿirfan*). In addition to these names, he lists some of the works authored by these figures that he said demonstrate their inclination toward ʿirfan. Many of these are the figures and writings studied earlier. It is helpful, however, to list them here in the order in which Darabi presents them:†

Nasir al-Din Tusi, *Awsaf al-ashraf, Aghaz va anjam*
Muhammad b. ʿAli b. Abi Jumhur Ahsaʾi, *ʿAvali al-laʾali, Mujli mirʾat al-yaqin*
Shaykh Jamal al-Din Hilli (ʿAllama), *Minhaj al-karama*
Shaykh Safi al-Din Ardabili, his son Sadr al-Din, and his brother Salah al-Din
Baba Afzal Kashani (d. 1213), *Zajr al-nafs, Madarij al-kamal,* and others
Sayyid Haydar Amuli, *Jamiʿ al-asrar*
Sayyid Murtaza ʿAlam al-Huda (d. 1044), *Durar al-favaʾid*
Sayyid Razi (d. 1015), *Nahj al-balaqa, Misbah al-shariʿa*‡
Shaykh Zayn al-Din Ahmad Jubbaʿi ʿAmili (Shahid Sani), *Munyat al-murid*
Shaykh Shams al-Din Jizzini ʿAmili (Shahid Avval [d. 1386])
Shaykh Rajab Bursi (d. 1410)
Shaykh ʿAli b. Hilal Jazaʾiri (d. 1530)
Sayyid b. Tavus, *Iqbal al-aʿmal,* and others
Shaykh Ibn Fahd Hilli (d. 1437), *al-Tahsin, ʿUdda al-daʿi*
Shaykh Bahaʾi
Mir Damad, *al-Khalʿatiyya, al-Khalsa al-malakutiyya,* and others

* For example, Darabi, *Latifa,* 8.

† Darabi, *Maslak* MS, 188–91.

‡ Esoteric sermons and sayings attributed to Imam ʿAli, some included in *Nahj al-balagha,* were the subjects of extensive commentaries by mystically minded ulama, especially beginning in the seventeenth century. Darabi was aware of the shakiness of *Misbah*'s attribution to ʿAli.

Muhammad Baqir Khurasani (Muhaqqiq Sabzavari, d. 1679), *al-Kifaya**
Majlisi Sr., because of his responses to Mulla Tahir Qummi
ʿAbd al-Razzaq Kashani (Fayyaz)
Mirza Hasan Gilani Qummi (d. 1709)†
Mulla Muhsin Kashani (Fayz)
Mulla Sadra, *al-Asfar, al-Shavahid, al-ʿArshiyya,* and others
Shaykh Husayn Tunikabuni‡

Such lists are a regular feature of early ʿirfani writings of the late seventeenth and early eighteenth centuries. They are an indication of the urgent need to legitimize the nascent ʿirfanian discourse by portraying uncontroversial and prominent figures among the ulama as sympathetic to the folk of ʿirfan.

Another important aspect of Darabi's effort is his portrayal of ahl-i ʿirfan as a group with a distinct vocabulary. At the end of *Latifa,* under the heading "The Terminology of the Folk of ʿIrfan" (*istilahat-i ahl-i ʿirfan*), he includes a concise lexicon of technical terms used mainly by Hafez and other Sufi poets. The lexicon is somewhat similar to that offered by Dashtaki in *Maqamat,* but a key difference is that Darabi's list uses Hafez as the source of the terminology rather than an elitist philosopher-Sufi like Suhravardi.§

Darabi's efforts to establish a distinct ʿirfanian discourse by imagining a community, developing a vocabulary, and defending it as an authentically Shiʿi tradition were continued by his disciples and Sufi contemporaries. This was most notably the case in the Zahabi lineage, where Shaykh ʿAli-Naqi Istahbanati and Sayyid Qutb al-Din Nayrizi followed in Darabi's footsteps.

* He was included here solely on the basis of his perceived views on the permissibility of ghina in *al-Kifaya* (which would allow zikr and samaʿ sessions to be permissible as well).

† The son of ʿAbd al-Razzaq. He lived most of his life in Qum, where he died in 1709. Zanuzi says that he was persecuted by the people of Qum, at the instigation of Muhammad-Tahir Qummi, for his Sufi proclivities. See Zanuzi, *Riyaz al-janna,* 4:438–40.

‡ He was, along with Fayz and Fayyaz, a prominent student of Mulla Sadra. Afandi describes him as "a Sufi, and a philosopher of the Illuminationist School." See Afandi, *Riyaz,* 2:34.

§ *Istilahat* does not seem to be included as part of some of the earlier manuscripts of *Latifa* that I was able to check and therefore it is possible that it is a later addition to the text of *Latifa.* As such, it needs to be taken with a grain of salt, so to speak. Another difference is that Darabi drew on classical works like Shabistari's *Gulshan-i raz* instead of a treatise like *Kalimat al-tasavvuf* (see Darabi, *Latifa,* 19–20 and 38).

ʿAli-Naqi Istahbanati and *Burhan al-murtazin*

Because of the extremely hostile environment in Isfahan, ʿAli-Naqi Istahbanati, a disciple of Najib who was later recognized as the next pole of the Zahabi network, moved to the vicinity of Shiraz, a place more welcoming and tolerant of unorthodox figures. According to his disciple, Istahbanati died in anonymity in 1714.* The only piece of his work that survives today is a treatise titled *Burhan al-murtazin,* which was published recently in Iran.†

This monograph is not very original, but it contains themes that substantiate my claim about the influence of Darabi and Mu'azzin on later developments in ʿirfanian discourse. *Burhan* contains an introduction, five chapters, and an epilogue. The lengthy introduction addresses the definition of Sufism and attempts to prove that the Sufi path is "the same as the path of the Prophet and his legatees,peace be upon them, and the purified among their partisans."‡ It is clearly inspired by and sometimes copied verbatim from Mu'azzin's *Tuhfa.*

The first chapter is dedicated to the question of the "pleasant voice" (*sawt-i hasan*), its permissibility, and how it differs from illicit music (ghina). The Sufi practice of samaʿ is clearly at stake. Istahbanati's contribution is hardly original; most of the content of this chapter is either a paraphrase or a verbatim copy of Darabi's *Maqamat al-salikin,* a monograph on the permissibility of music. The next chapter of *Burhan* focuses on the question of ecstasy during zikr gatherings, another controversial topic previously covered in both Mu'azzin's *Tuhfa* and Darabi's *Farah al-salikin.* Chapter 3 is about yet another controversial issue, that of some involuntary, and sometimes violent, physical manifestations of Sufi meditative practices. The final two chapters of *Burhan* deal with two other salient debates for Sufis of the time, and both are aimed at establishing a strong connection between Sufi lineages and the infallible imams. Istahbanati begins his third chapter by mentioning Mu'azzin and his seminal work, *Tuhfa,* continuing with an extensive quotation from the work about how all Sufi lineages go back to one of the imams and how the Sufi networks of his time, especially the Zahabis, trace their

* Khuyi, *Mizan al-savab,* 3:1199. On his date of death, see Khavari, *Zahabiyya,* 296.

† We do not know when this treatise was finished. Internal evidence tells us, however, that Darabi was not alive at the time of *Burhan*'s writing. However, as our discussion of Darabi's longevity indicates, we know that he was definitely alive until the year 1702 or 1703, which means *Burhan* must have been written between 1702 and 1714, when Istahbanati died.

‡ Istahbanati, *Burhan al-murtazin,* 6.

spiritual lineage to the eighth imam.* Finally, in the epilogue of *Burhan,* Istahbanati follows the example of Darabi as he outlines the myth of an uninterrupted tradition of ʿirfan by identifying prominent Twelver figures who, according to him, "followed the path of Sufism and ʿirfan."† The use of the term *ʿirfan* in conjunction with Sufism is significant, because it is one of the first cases of such use after Darabi. Istahbanati was aware of Darabi's writings and seems to have adopted this new use of *ʿirfan* from him. Moreover, Istahbanati's list of ʿirfan-minded ulama is an almost verbatim translation into Persian of Darabi's list in *Maslak.*‡

A noteworthy feature of Darabi's and Istahbanati's list is the inclusion of a considerable number of philosophers. Mir Damad is included in the list despite the disdain he sometimes expressed for popular and organized Sufism, and his mystically oriented works are emphasized, including *al-Khalsa al-malakutiyya,* which contains an extraordinary autobiographical narrative of two of his ecstatic visions. Mulla Sadra and his students Fayz, Fayyaz, and Tunikabuni are particularly prominent on the list, and the inclusion of such philosophers among the ʿirfan-minded religious scholars is significant. As we saw in the discussion of *Hikmat al-ʿarifin,* the earliest attack from outside philosophical circles claiming that Sadra's philosophy was an innovation came from Muhammad-Tahir Qummi toward the end of the seventeenth century, when he attacked Sadra for what he considered the double heresy of positioning Sufi ideas within a philosophical framework. In fact, such attacks from the most prominent anti-Sufi figure of the era may have been part of what brought Sadra and his philosophy to the attention of Sufi-minded people such as Darabi. The fact that Sadra and his students had mystical inclinations helped Istahbanati and others overlook their occasional criticism of Sufism and emphasize their pro-Sufi ideas and ideals. Moreover, given how the Zahabis themselves emerged as a reformed Twelver Sufi network precisely at this time, it is likely that Istahbanati, similar to Muʿazzin

* Istahbanati, *Burhan al-murtazin,* 173–82.

† Istahbanati, *Burhan al-murtazin,* 189.

‡ There are only two differences in Istahbanati's list. First, he begins the list of later Shiʿi figures with Mulla Ahmad Ardabili, otherwise known as Muqaddas Ardabili, to whom the notoriously anti-Sufi work *Hadiqat al-shiʿa* is attributed. Istahbanati not only quotes seemingly pro-Sufi lines from Ardabili's works to prove his Sufi proclivities but also rejects the attribution of *Hadiqa* to him, referring the reader to Darabi's writing on the issue. Darabi addresses this controversy in several places in his writings (see Darabi, *Maslak* MS, 190, and, more extensively, Darabi, *Maqamat al-salikin,* 463–65). Second, Istahbanati adds to his list the name of Sayyid Ahmad ʿAlavi, Mir Damad's student, on the basis of treatises like *Maʿarif ilahiyya,* his commentary on *al-Shifa,* and other works. This despite Sayyid Ammad's attacks on storytellers and Abu Muslim, mentioned in chapter 2.

in *Tuhfa,* sympathized with Sadra's critique of organized Sufism, associating it with the previous "inauthentic" and "vulgar" form of Sufism that did not comply with the way of the twelve imams. Here we see the initial stages of a process in which Sadra's philosophical system was gradually incorporated into the newly emerging framework of ʿirfan. Later, in the Qajar period, Sadra's thought became a hallmark of ʿirfanian discourse, but during this initial stage, Sadra and his students were not the central players in the formation of this discourse. Instead, they were appropriated because their overall intellectual outlook lent itself to the purposes of Sufis such as Darabi, Istahbanati, and, later, Nayrizi, who did the work of building an authentically Twelver ʿirfanian discourse.

Sayyid Qutb al-Din Nayrizi, *Fasl al-khitab*, and the Zahabi Network

Sayyid Muhammad Qutb al-Din Nayrizi (d. 1760) was born around 1688 in Nayriz, a small town in the ancient province of Fars.* He is considered by Zahabi Sufis to be the successor to ʿAli-Naqi Istahbanati and the thirty-second qutb of the network.† The network underwent a revival under the leadership of Nayrizi, who was a prolific writer and respected teacher for nearly a half-century.‡ In Zahabi sources, he is frequently called the Reviver (mujaddid).§

Nayrizi has been at the center of Zahabi hagiographical accounts since the nineteenth century, when the first detailed account of his life was written by the influential Zahabi master Abu al-Qasim Sharifi Shirazi (d. 1869), otherwise known as Mirza Baba. Shirazi was Nayrizi's grandson, a poet with the pen-name Raz, and the thirty-fifth pole of the network, and his account does not lend itself well to the purposes of historians. It is peppered with miraculous events (*karamat*), fantastical narratives, and anachronistic accounts of meetings between Nayrizi and prominent religious scholars. For example, we are told that Mirza Muhammad Nishaburi (b. 1764, d. 1817) met Nayrizi on Khark Island near the Persian Gulf, where the latter had taken refuge to dedicate his time to prayers and ascetic practices in seclusion.** However, Mirza Muhammad, who is also known as the Akhbari, was not even born when Nayrizi died, in 1760. Similarly, Nayrizi is said to have traveled to Ahsa and to have met and impressed Shaykh Ahmad Ahsaʾi (b. 1752, d. 1826) with his recipe for spiritual exercise, which the Hidden Imam affirmed in a dream the

* Khuyi, *Mizan al-savab,* 1:v. See Sharifi Shirazi, "Tarikh-i hayat," 4. For his date of birth, see Khavari, *Zahabiyya,* 299–300.

† Khuyi, *Mizan al-savab,* 3:1199.

‡ For an account of later developments in Zahabi leadership, see Lewisohn, "Modern Persian Sufism, Part II."

§ Khuyi, *Mizan al-savab,* 1:xviii.

** Parvizi, *Tazkira,* 24–25.

latter had while in seclusion.* Again, this is a historical impossibility, since Ahsa'i would have been a small child when Nayrizi died.

The story of Nayrizi's initiation into Sufism as told by Raz Shirazi follows a trajectory familiar in Sufi hagiography. He is said to have spent years mastering and then teaching the official fields of discursive knowledge, especially the rational sciences of philosophy and theology, with the purpose of finding satisfaction and salvation.† Disillusioned, he gave up the madrasa and left Shiraz in search of someone who could teach him true knowledge. Finally, he found an accomplished Sufi master, ʿAli-Naqi Istahbanati, and became his disciple.‡ After he spent many years in seclusion, meditation, and self-mortification, his master was impressed with his spiritual progress and promised to give his daughter to him in marriage in the future, a move that became standard for Zahabi masters and served as confirmation of their choice of successor.§

Given the layers of hagiographical embellishment, it is difficult to construct a historically reliable narrative of Nayrizi's life. It is clear that he spent most of the first couple of decades of his life in or near Shiraz. He then moved to Isfahan, probably during the last decade of Safavid rule, and he witnessed the fall of the Safavid capital.** In the aftermath of this catastrophic event, he stayed in Iran for a time, trying to convince the ulama and other influential figures to take the steps he believed were necessary to restore order to the land of Iran. Later hagiographers even claimed that he gave the last Safavid king prior warning of the catastrophe,†† and Nayrizi himself claimed that his master had foretold the fall of the Safavids.‡‡ Whether or not we accept such accounts, there is no question that Nayrizi wrote extensively about his view and his diagnosis of the fall of the Safavid dynasty in several of his

* Parvizi, *Tazkira,* 33–34.

† Parvizi, *Tazkira,* 4–6.

‡ Jaʿfariyan asserts that Nayrizi met his master in Isfahan, but this is based on a misreading of the relevant verses in *Fasl al-khitab* (see Jaʿfariyan, *Safaviyya,* 3:1310). Early Zahabi hagiographies claim this meeting happened in Istahban, the hometown of Nayrizi's master (see Parvizi, *Tazkira,* 7). This seems a more reasonable claim, because, as mentioned earlier, the seat of the Zahabi masters was moved to the province of Fars during the last decade of Najib's life.

§ Parvizi, *Tazkira,* 7, and Khuyi, *Mizan al-Savab,* 3:1317.

** In *Fasl al-khitab,* he mentions that he spent seven years in the companionship of Mulla Sadiq Ardistani (d. 1721) in Isfahan.

†† Khuyi, *Mizan al-savab,* 3:1249–54 (see the long footnote by Jalal al-Din Muhammad Husayni, better known as Majd al-Ashraf, the great-grandson of Nayrizi). The same story, with minor differences, is also told by Raz Shirazi in Parvizi, *Tazkira,* 29–31.

‡‡ Khuyi, *Mizan al-savab,* 1:104.

works, including an independent treatise titled *Tibb al-mamalik.** In the immediate aftermath of the fall, Nayrizi stayed in Iran, hoping that the situation would change.† Eventually, though, he gave up hope and followed many of the learned of Isfahan in their exodus to the ʿAtabat.‡ There, according to Raz Shirazi, Nayrizi became a prominent teacher to both Shiʿi and Sunni students in Najaf.§ He may have returned to Shiraz for a brief period, only to return to Najaf in 1750, where he spent the final decade of his life. He died there on April 5, 1760.** Raz Shirazi portrays Nayrizi during his years in Najaf as a well-connected religious scholar who was given land grants by the Ottoman Pasha in recognition of his prominence. A unique manuscript dating to six or seven years into Nayrizi's stay in Najaf (1756–1757), however, contains a letter in which he writes that he had been unable to find patrons or sponsors to support his family and had thus incurred substantial debt.††

* Khuyi, *Mizan al-savab,* 1266. For a detailed analysis of this important political treatise and its full transcript in Arabic, see Jaʿfariyan, *Safaviyya,* 3:1309–83. While no manuscript under this title has survived, Jaʿfariyan has reported extensively on a unique manuscript preserved without a title in the library of the Shrine of Maʿsuma in Qum, which he argues is *Tibb al-mamalik.*

† See Khuyi, *Mizan al-savab,* 3:1266, where he mentions the return of Shah Tahmasp II to Isfahan. He initially takes this as a sign of things moving in the right direction, but later he is disappointed by the apathy of the religious and political elite and leaves Iran for Najaf.

‡ He chooses the word "escape" to refer to his departure from Iran, an indication of his mounting frustration with his failure to convince the elite of his time of his remedies for restoring Iran as a Shiʿite nation. It was in Najaf, he says, that he was able to put together the verses that constitute *Fasl al-khitab* as it exists today. Khuyi, *Mizan al-savab,* 3:1266, 1267.

§ Parvizi, *Tazkira,* 34. He is even said to have taught Ibn ʿArabi's *al-Futuhat* there, educating prominent mystically minded students such as Sayyid Mahdi Tabatabaʾi Bahr al-ʿUlum (d. 1797) and Mawla Mihrab Gilani (d. 1802), among others. See Maʿsum-ʿAli Shah, *Taraʾiq al-haqaʾiq,* 3:217, where he paraphrases Raz Shirazi's *Sharayit al-tariqa.*

** Umm-Salama Nayrizi, *Jamiʿ al-kulliyat,* 19.

†† See Nayrizi, *Risala-yi juzʾ va kull* MS, f. 16–17, where he complains to his disciple Hashim Darvish (who succeeded Nayrizi as pole of the Zahabi network) about his financial situation. He blames his difficult situation on the negligence of people to pay their dues to the descendants of the Prophet (he was a sayyid). Despairing of finding any sources of help in Iraq, he asks Hashim to remind his countrymen while he is traveling in Fars of their duty to take care of the family of the Prophet. This stands in contrast to Raz Shirazi's embellished account of how the Ottoman authorities, impressed with Nayrizi's knowledge and erudition, gave him a generous stipend from Baghdad as well as a land grant (*tuyul*) in Basra. See Parvizi, *Tazkira,* 35.

Nayrizi was a prolific author.* He wrote works of Arabic grammar and treatises eulogizing the infallible imams. Most of his writings, however, are dedicated to the explication of his mystical thought. His most celebrated and extensive work is *Fasl al-khitab,* also known as *al-Hikmat al-ʿalaviyya.*† This lengthy work of poetry is written in Arabic, and in it Nayrizi laid out his mystical worldview in detail. Although most of *Fasl al-khitab* was written at the height of Nayrizi's career as a Sufi master in Isfahan as Safavid rule crumbled, he assembled the scattered pieces and edited them as a single work only after the fall of the city. It was in the relatively safe and tranquil environment of Najaf that he was able to gather the disparate parts between the two covers of *Fasl al-khitab.*‡

The picture of Nayrizi reflected in *Fasl al-khitab* is that of a maverick, a mystically minded, erudite, Akhbari-leaning scholar who has been marginalized. He is angry both at the pseudo-ulama (his name for members of the religious establishment) and at pseudo-faqirs (his name for Sufis) for neglecting the teachings of the imams and corrupting God's religion. He considers himself a servant of the lineage of learned and great Shiʿi ʿarifin, "the kings of spiritual poverty" (*muluk al-faqr*). "I have served the ʿarifin," he says, "the leaders of the ʿAlid Shiʿa party . . . who were the kings of poverty in their age, and the tariqa with which they associated is the holy razavi order known as the Zahabiyya."§ He highlights the name of his pir, ʿAli-Naqi Istahbanati, saying the latter was the "pride of the greatest divine men [*ilahiyyin*] in asceticism and the king of kings of poverty, my shaykh and master, and my reference for divinely-endowed philosophy [*al-hikma al-mawhibiyya*]. . . . [He] was unique among the dervishes of his age, and I met no one who could match his glory."** Unfortunately, he laments, the people of his master's time did not recognize the man's great spiritual gifts.†† He mentions only one other figure as his teacher, Shah Muhammad Darabi, under whom he studied hadith and who was, according to Nayrizi, "the teacher of all of the learned

* To my knowledge, the most accurate enumeration of Nayrizi's works is that of Khajavi. See Khajavi, "Introduction," 15–33. Most of Nayrizi's writings have been published in recent decades thanks to the active Zahabi publication house in Shiraz (Intisharat-i Khanaqah-i Ahmadi). For another detailed bibliography of Nayrizi's works, see Khavari, *Zahabiyya,* 526–65. The earliest report we have regarding Nayrizi's writings is by his daughter, Umm-Salama, in her *Jamiʿ al-kulliyat.* She mentions that her father penned fourteen works, though she names only a few. See Umm-Salama Nayrizi, *Jamiʿ al-kulliyat,* 18.

† *Khuyi, Mizan al-savab, 1:28.*

‡ *Khuyi, Mizan al-savab,* 3:1309 and 1267.

§ Khuyi, *Mizan al-savab,* 3:1198 and 1318.

** Khuyi, *Mizan al-savab,* 1199.

†† Khuyi, *Mizan al-savab,* 1199.

in Shiraz in his time."* Both this statement and a close examination of Nayrizi's writings make it clear that Darabi was a major influence in the formation of Nayrizi's intellectual outlook. This influence played itself out in more than one way.

Nayrizi's *Fasl,* like Istahbanati's *Burhan* and the writings of Darabi, evokes a sense of deeply rooted tradition, of a community of like-minded people made up of "the knowledgeable people of the past and the pioneering ulama whose writings demonstrate that they were sincere friends of the impoverished ʿarifin [*al-fuqara al-ʿarifin*]. Some were even their disciples in their mystical quest [*sayri-him va suluki-him*]."† Nayrizi's avoidance of the term *Sufi* is noticeable here. His list of such people contains familiar names, including many we have already encountered in Mu'azzin's *Tuhfa* and in the epilogue of *Burhan.* But his canon of ahl-i ʿirfan departs from that of his predecessors in that he creates a more elaborate hagiography that assimilates the most important Sufi-minded figures of the recent past into the Zahabi narrative of sacred history.

The first major difference is that the names of two foundational figures in the official Safavid spiritual lineage, Shaykh Safi al-Din Ardabili and his son, who are mentioned without fail in almost all seventeenth century Sufi writings, are dropped in Nayrizi's list. The fact that Nayrizi felt no need to include the legendary founder of the Safavid order in his list is a clear reflection of the dramatic fall of the dynasty.

The second major difference, which reflects Nayrizi's agenda as the master of the Zahabi network, is the way biographies of figures such as Shaykh Baha'i and Fayz Kashani are embellished and expanded in an effort to prove that these men belong to the Zahabi spiritual lineage. His statement about Shaykh Baha'i deserves to be quoted in full, as it introduces a new hagiographical layer to the mythical past that is constructed for ʿirfan:

> And among them [the friends of the folk of poverty] is the teacher of my abovementioned teacher Maula Shah Muhammad Darabi, namely . . . Shaykh Baha al-Din Muhammad ʿAmili . . . he entered the divine order of the folk of poverty, and his allegiance [*iradat*] is attributed to . . . Shaykh Mu'min Mashhadi, and the latter is one of the most important disciples of Shaykh Muhammad ʿArif, to whom is linked the allegiance of my *shaykh al-irshad,* the one to whom I refer in walking the path of poverty, Shaykh ʿAli-Naqi Istahbanati. God willing, I will mention his spiritual lineage [*mashikha*] in this book . . . as it is reflected in the scroll

* Khuyi, *Mizan al-savab,* 1201.
† Khuyi, *Mizan al-savab,* 1204.

> of the Zahabi, Kubravi, Razavi order. This scroll was bequeathed to the noble shaykh, Shaykh Hatam, by Shaykh Muhammad ʿArif, whose cloister [*sawmiʿa*] is in the holy city of Mashhad and he [Shaykh Hatam] to Shaykh Muhammad-ʿAli Mu'azzin, and he to Shaykh Najib al-Din Riza Tabrizi, and he to my above-mentioned master, ʿAli-Naqi, and the scroll is in my possession today.*

This passage contains a number of significant pieces of information. First, this is the first time we see Shaykh Baha'i explicitly portrayed as an initiate to a specific Sufi network, the Zahabiyya. A couple of pages later, in a similar description, Fayz Kashani is also said to have been initiated to the order via Shaykh Muhammad Mashhadi.† The anachronistic connection of these figures to the Zahabi network is an attempt to construct a hagiographical narrative that emphasizes the network's ties to celebrated figures in the ulama. Conversely, such attempts can be understood as the earliest stages of the development of ʿirfanian genealogies for Shiʿi ulama modeled after Sufi spiritual genealogies. Nayrizi mentions these connections in the passive voice, an indication that he had no concrete evidence for them; whether he concocted such links himself or was repeating recently developed rumors is impossible to ascertain.‡ Nayrizi's task of connecting the Zahabi network to prominent figures among the ulama was furthered by his practice of assimilating figures such as Shaykh Mu'min Mashhadi and Shaykh Muhammad ʿArif (Pir Palanduz), who were probably prominent Nurbakhshi masters in the early to mid-seventeenth century, into the lineage.§ These revisionist attempts have personal ramifications as well: the lineage Nayrizi constructs positioned him as the exclusive representative not only of the Nurbakshi line but also of the legacy of Sufi-minded luminaries such as Shaykh Baha'i, Mulla Sadra, and Fayz Kashani. His status as the spiritual successor of such towering figures was given concrete form in the scroll that he claimed to have inherited from his masters.**

The third noticeable change has to do with the way some philosophers in Nayrizi's narrative are presented. Because of his strong opposition to traditional philosophical discourse (which will be discussed shortly), Nayrizi

* Khuyi, *Mizan al-savab,* 1212.
† Khuyi, *Mizan al-savab,* 1222.
‡ This attribution is not mentioned in Istahbanati's work.
§ For more on these figures, see Anzali, "Emergence."
** As demonstrated elsewhere, the scroll that contained the purported spiritual lineage of the Zahabi network was produced by a close collaboration between Najib and Mu'azzin. See Anzali, "Emergence."

was careful to explain that philosophers he endorsed in *Fasl,* including Tusi, Davani, and Mir Damad, had conversion-like experiences at relatively late stages of their careers and were rescued from "the abyss of philosophical illusions."* Mulla Sadra, however, is an exception. Nayrizi maintained that he was a friend of "the folk of poverty" from the very beginning of his career and that his philosophical writings were merely an acquiescence to the spirit of his age. He wrote, "[B]ecause in his age the philosophers were dominant, he had no choice but to speak in their language, and [that is why] he explained the divine knowledge in possession of the folk of poverty [*al-fuqara al-ilahiyyin*] according to the logic of the philosopher and the language of theologians [*mutakallimun*], and there is no dispute in terminology."†

Nayrizi added that he had in his possession many of Sadra's writings, some of which were original copies written by Sadra himself. This is significant, I believe, because it indicates the kind of people for whom Sadra was a defining influence. Nayrizi treats *vahdat al-vujud* (oneness of being) extensively in *Fasl.* His thoughts on the subject reflect a noticeable engagement with Sadra's writings, and it is probably fair to say that it played an important role in introducing and assimilating Sadra's philosophical framework into ʿirfanian discourse at its earliest stages of development.

A curious and puzzling addition to Nayrizi's list of ʿirfan-friendly Shiʿi scholars is Shaykh Hurr ʿAmili! Nayrizi justifies his choice on the basis of a monograph written by ʿAmili and titled *Jawahir al-saniyya fi al-ahadis al-qudsiyya,* a fairly comprehensive collection of Qudsi hadith reports (hadiths in which God himself is the speaker). Given ʿAmili's strong opposition to Sufism and his important role in the anti-Sufi campaign of the late seventeenth century, one wonders how to make sense of his inclusion. I argue that Nayrizi's strong aversion to being called a Sufi, his strong rejection of philosophy, and his Akhbari leanings, which are discussed later, can help us understand this inclusion as a sign of the ultimate success of the process of domestication of Sufism in his case. In other words, by the early eighteenth century the landscape had changed so much that, for a religious scholar like Nayrizi, many elements of Qummi and ʿAmili's attacks on Sufism and philosophy were understood as legitimate critiques leveled against the Sunni pretend-Sufis, or philosophers, of the past. In other words, hermeneutically a possibility had been opened up for Nayrizi not to understand them as his enemies or the enemies of ʿirfanian discourse as he understood it. A focus on

* Khuyi, *Mizan al-savab,* 3:1204 and 1211.

† Khuyi, *Mizan al-savab,*1220. Note the similarity of this expression to that used by Darabi.

their advocacy for a spiritual life thoroughly informed by the teachings of the imams, as we saw in the case of Qummi, might have opened the way to consider them as ʿirfan-friendly scholars in Nayrizi's mind.*

A final distinctive feature of Nayrizi's list is his unusual decision to introduce his readers to prominent ʿirfan-friendly scholars and mystics he had met *in his own lifetime.*† This list is important, because it gives us information about the members of the learned elite with whom Nayrizi associated. Nayrizi claims a close relationship with six figures: (1) Shah Muhammad Darabi, whom he praises as the teacher of all the knowledgeable people in Shiraz;‡ (2) Muhammad-ʿAli Sakaki Shirazi (d. 1722);§ (3) Muhammad-Sadiq Ardistani (d. 1721), with whom, he says, he had a close relationship for seven years;** (4) Aqa Khalil Isfahani [Qazvini] (d. 1136), whom he says he met in

* Therefore, Nayrizi seems to be deeply influenced by the intellectual movement that was spearheaded by Qummi in many ways. His opposition to philosophy, his understanding of Shiʿi spirituality encapsulated in ʿirfan, and his attempt to offer an alternative framework of understanding for the notion of the Oneness of Being can all be seen as deeply influenced by Qummi's arguments. In fact, his *Fasl al-khitab,* discussed later, can be read as a response to Qummi's *Hikmat al-ʿarifin.*

† *Khuyi, Mizan al-savab, 3:1203.*

‡ Khuyi, *Mizan al-savab,* 1201.

§ His name appears as Muhammad-ʿAli Kali rather than Sakaki in the print version of *Fasl al-khitab* (see Khuyi, *Mizan al-savab,* 3:1201–2). This is most probably an editorial mistake, especially given orthographic similarities that can mislead the reader if the strokes of the letter kaf are not written carefully (a frequent occurrence in Persian manuscripts). Furthermore, the biographical dictionaries do not contain any information on a Muhammad-ʿAli Kali. Muhammad-ʿAli Sakaki, however, is known from several sources. I have not yet had access to manuscripts of *Fasl* to confirm my sense that this is an error, however. For more on Sakaki see Hazin, *Tarikh,* 179. Unfortunately, contemporaneous sources are silent about the exact network to which Sakaki paid allegiance. A later source, *Farsnama-yi nasiri,* associates Sakaki with the Zahabi network. See Fasa'i, *Farsnama-yi nasiri,* 2:1171. This seems to be conjecture based on the prominence of the Zahabi network in Shiraz in Sakaki's lifetime rather than a reflection of an earlier source. Sakaki's affiliation with organized Sufism is clearly mentioned in Hazin's remarks as well, but it is highly unlikely that the former was a Zahabi. If that were the case, why would Nayrizi have failed to mention it? In fact, given Nayrizi's effacement of the Nurbakhshi identity of contemporaneous Sufi masters he mentions earlier and given Nayrizi's own statement about the reservations some of the figures had about one another (see Khuyi, *Mizan al-savab,* 1203), it is plausible to believe that Sakaki was a Nurbakhshi.

** We are told that Ardistani was expelled from Isfahan because of his Sufi proclivities. Although we cannot be sure of the historicity of this incident (see Jaʿfariyan, *Savafiyya,* 2:587), there is no doubt about his Sufi inclinations. Zanuzi describes him as someone with "a strong passion for Sufism." See Zanuzi, *Riyaz al-janna,* 3:316. It is not difficult to see how this could have been a link that connected him

Isfahan;* (5) Amir Ibrahim Qazvini (d. 1736);† and (6) Mir Muhammad-Taqi Khurasani (d. circa. 1737), whom he praises as "the knowledgeable sayyid renowned in every quarter of the earth, [who is numbered] among the guides of those who seek guidance on the spiritual path . . . and I accompanied him frequently when I entered the holy city of Mashhad."‡ Research on the background of these figures reveals that of the six, three (numbers 2, 5, and 6) were most likely affiliated with the Nurbakhshi Sufi network, and two others (numbers 1 and 3) had strong mystical proclivities.

Reading Nayrizi's list of ʿirfan-minded people also gives us information about his library. He points out with satisfaction that he possesses some of the works of Sayyid Haydar, Mulla Sadra, Darabi, and Fayz, among others. He makes specific reference to Sayyid Haydar's *Jamiʿ al-asrar* and *al-Muhit al-aʿzam,* saying that he "adored" these two books.§ He also mentions many of Mulla Sadra's monographs, such as the latter's commentaries on the Qurʾan and *Usul al-kafi,* as well as his *al-Asfar al-arbaʿa* and *al-Shavahid al-rububiyya.* As for Darabi, Nayrizi mentions with pride that he is in possession of the original copy of *Miʿraj al-kamal,* the treatise discussed at length earlier in this chapter. Finally, he mentions two works of commentary by Fayz, *al-Vafi* and *al-Safi,* saying that he also has the latter's *Divan* in his library. These works give us a clear indication of the intellectual and spiritual traditions to

with students including Nayrizi, ʿAbd al-Rahim Damavandi (discussed in the next chapter), and Hazin Lahiji.

* Tehrani, *Tabaqat,* 6:15–16, and also in Qazvini, *Tatmim,* 142–46.

† See ʿAmili, *Aʿyan al-shiʿa,* 2:227–8. On his Sufi proclivities and his close relationship to Mir Muhammad-Taqi, see Qazvini, *Tatmim,* 85.

‡ Khuyi, *Mizan al-savab,* 1202. Khurasani is known in many sources as Shahi. For more on him, see Qazvini, *Tatmim,* 84–87. A note of caution about the author of *Tatmim* is necessary here. He inherited strong anti-Sufi sentiments from his teacher Mulla Khalil Qazvini, and, after giving a quite detailed account of Khurasani's miracles and his exemplary piety and asceticism, he feels it necessary to establish that "all the people of knowledge and nobility who met him and with whom I met mentioned that he never spoke as Sufis speak about their superstition, their technical vocabulary, their pretentions, and beliefs" (Qazvini, *Tatmim,* 86). Curiously, the name of the Sufi network with which Khurasani associated is not mentioned either by Nayrizi or in other biographical sources that mention him. A unique manuscript, however, mentions him as a master of the Nurbakhshi Sufi network. His name appears in the lineage, where he is said to have been a student of Muhammad Muʾmin Sidiri of the khanaqah in Sidir. See Shirvani, *Riyaz al-siyaha,* 336. Most probably his source is Anonymous, *Silsila-yi sidiriyya-yi nurbakhshiyya-yi hamadaniyya* MS, f. 2. For more on this specific khanaqah, see my recent article in Persian: Anzali, "Khanaqah-i nurbakhshiyya dar sidir."

§ Khuyi, *Mizan al-savab,* 3:1207.

which Nayrizi saw himself as heir. The same cluster would become the lineage and heritage claimed by later ʿirfan-minded people.

In addition to the information we glean from Nayrizi's accounts of the ʿirfan-minded people of his time, the topics he deals with in *Fasl* give us a wealth of information about the intellectual and social forces of the period. Nayrizi's heroes are a group he calls the folk of poverty (*ahl al-faqr*), a chosen group of the learned (*ahl al-ʿilm*) also known as the ʿurafa.* They stand as the pinnacle of creation in opposition to three groups that form what I call a "triangle of evil" in his thought.

One corner of this triangle is composed of many of the mainstream philosophers and the scholars of kalam who borrow heavily from them. These are Nayrizi's primary targets, and he bashes them for having hijacked the path of God by introducing their innovations, the "foreign disciplines" they have borrowed from the Greeks. Nayrizi's intense rhetoric against philosophy should be understood in the context of the final three decades of Safavid rule, when philosophy came under increased attack.†

The second corner of the triangle of evil is occupied by those whom Nayrizi calls *pseudo-ulama* (*ashbah ahl al-ʿilm*). These are closely associated with the philosophers, and Nayrizi argues that the catastrophe visited by God on the people of Iran was primarily in retribution for their failings.‡ The obsession of the political elite with wealth and the resulting corruption of the system in favor of the privileged were matched by an obsession among the pseudo-ulama with social status and closeness to the political elite. These so-called ulama were meant to be the guardians of the teachings of the imams, the ones who commanded good, forbade evil, and advised kings and amirs to rule with justice. Instead, Nayrizi laments, they cared only for status,

* See, for example, Khuyi, *Mizan al-savab*, 546.

† For example, he attacks basic principles of traditional philosophy such as the exclusive division of concepts into either universal (*kulli*) or specific (*juzʾi*) as inapplicable when it comes to the Divine Being. From his perspective, lack of attention to this simple but important shortcoming of traditional logic/philosophy is the major reason that philosophers, theologians, and jurists alike went astray in building their understanding of God's unity on the assumption of either the univocality of being (*ishtirak maʿnavi vujud*) or its multivocality (*ishtirak lafzi vujud*). Both positions, Nayrizi holds, fall extremely short of offering a proper understanding of God's unity and caused a feud between different factions of the learned over the real meaning of tawhid. According to Nayrizi, all of them fundamentally misunderstand the unity of God in terms of numerical unity rather than what he considers "the true and essential unity of God" beyond concepts, allusions, and personifications. See Khuyi, *Mizan al-savab*, 1:127–28, 269–301, and 557–62. See also Nayrizi, "Risala-yi vahdat-i ʿadadi," 98–101.

‡ See, for example, Khuyi, *Mizan al-savab*, 3:1302.

position, and proximity to the political establishment that allowed them to enjoy worldly pleasures. They failed to distinguish between the true folk of poverty and pseudo-dervishes (*ashbah ahl al-faqr*), and their reaction against the latter created an environment of persecution and hostility toward the former. The actions of this group of pseudo-ulama, says Nayrizi, weakened the legitimacy of the Safavid rule and towering figures among the folk of poverty such as Shaykh Safi al-Din Ardabili. In his own words,

> They blocked the way of poverty because of their love of status, their worldly standing, and their love of leadership . . . they were hostile toward the saints in all gatherings . . . and the knowledgeable people in their era cursed the exalted saints from their pulpits . . . alas, alas, for the illustrious ulama who live in luxury in our times . . . they are amazed by their non-existent erudition, and they have destroyed their towns with this erudition. Their erudition is the hairsplitting of nonsensical statements with philosophical method; their erudition is in imitating people whom they favor based on illusion [*khayal*] without apprehending the meaning of reality. Their erudition is their thoughts on the nuances they have concocted in old marginalia, their erudition is the rejection of His unity, *vahdat al-vujud,* as [explained] in ʿAlid philosophy, their erudition is [sticking to] the letter of hadiths outwardly without understanding their meaning with the light of discernment. Their erudition is their illusionary metaphorical interpretations [*taʾvil*] of hadiths without their feeble minds understanding them. Their erudition is their legitimacy and position among the ignorant and haughty amirs. Their erudition is flattering kings for the sake of worldly decorum. Their erudition is abandoning [the practice of] forbidding evil because of their obeisance to kings [and failure to] honor the commands of the Shariʿa. Their erudition is blocking the path of all who live in poverty [according to] His Eminence, Prophet Muhammad. Their erudition is hurting the folk whose path is the path of the People of the Bench [*ahl al-suffa*] [of the times of] the Messenger. . . .Their erudition is their hate when they curse the saints, exalted they are, in their enmity. Their erudition is blocking the sacred Safavid state from the source of grace.*

The last corner of the triangle—the final group to attract Nayrizi's ire—is a group of people he calls pseudo-faqirs (*ashbah ahl al-faqr*) to distinguish them from the real saints, the true faqirs, the folk of poverty. There is, of course, a long and strong tradition of prominent Sufis levying harsh criticism against pseudo-Sufis. This self-critical tradition, however, usually reserves space for

* Khuyi, *Mizan al-savab,* 3:1254–55.

the few who embody the ideals of true Sufism. We do not find this, however, in Nayrizi's approach. He rejects the notion of Sufism altogether, placing it in diametric opposition to *faqr*. It seems that for Nayrizi, terms like Sufi and Sufism are stigmatized beyond hope of redemption. They are so tainted in the public eye that Nayrizi finds the old strategy of differentiating between good and bad Sufis useless. In a strategic semantic retreat, he gives up on the term *sufi* and uses it exactly as opponents of Sufism would. The term *sufi* in Nayrizi's lexicon is a synonym for *mutasavvif*, the psuedo-Sufi of his predecessor.* Those who previously would have been called true Sufis are now called faqirs, dervishes, or, more frequently, ʿarifs.

In what seems an ironic turn for a Sufi master, Nayrizi vehemently admonishes those who accuse him of being a Sufi. "Those liars have called us infidels," he says. "We will truthfully call them stupid."† He also says, "In their foolish understanding, and because of their excessive ignorance, they called all the ʿarifin Sufis."‡ In a statement that reveals the continuation of such accusations even after the fall of Isfahan, he says, "I heard the lowly liars accuse me of Sufism, without any knowledge and solely on the basis of their stupidity . . . people like them destroyed the Iranian territories with similar stupid accusations. Those among them who have survived in different corners of your land are [once again] expressing their animosity toward the folk of God [*ahl Allah*] with the same accusation by which they destroyed cities and opposed the great noble Shiʿa of ʿAli.§

Nayrizi also laments that, in spite of his master's outstanding accomplishments in asceticism and unique mastery of divine secrets, the people around him not only failed learn from him but also looked down on him. "The arrogant people of Isfahan," he says, "belittled the saints in every land. Because of their deficient insight, they called they who were greatest among the pious 'Sufis,' simply because of their asceticism."**

At the same time, he takes pride in the history of organized Sufism, though he eschews that term and makes use of alternative titles such as *faqr*

* For some examples, see Khuyi, *Mizan al-savab*, 2:551, 612 and 3:1182, 1199, 1241, 1243, 1249, and 1302. Interestingly, in most of these cases, Khuyi tries to explain Nayrizi's blanket rejection of the term *Sufi* by resorting to the strategy of differentiating between bad and good Sufis, using the term *sufiyya-yi radiʾa* (literally, "bad Sufis") in each instance where Nayrizi uses only the term *Sufi*. Additionally, Khuyi explains Nayrizi's explicit effort to disassociate himself from Sufism in terms of its popular semantic association with heretical and antinomian beliefs (Khuyi, *Mizan al-savab*, 2:552).

† Khuyi, *Mizan al-savab*, 3:1241.

‡ Khuyi, *Mizan al-savab*, 3: 1182.

§ Khuyi, *Mizan al-savab*, 3:1302.

** Khuyi, *Mizan al-savab*, 3:1199.

(poverty). For example, he tells us that there are four important "orders of the folk of poverty" (*salasil ahl al-faqr*) in the Muslim community.* Here, Nayrizi is referencing the fourfold classification of Sufi orders listed by the Zahabi master Najib in *Nur al-hidaya* and by Istahbanati in *Burhan al-murtazin*.† These four orders are the Naqshbandiyya, the Shattariyya, the Rifaʿiyya, and the Zahabiyya. Only the last one, Nayrizi notes, is active in Iran and holds the honored status of being associated with the eighth imam.‡ This is the order whose guardian Nayrizi considers himself to be.

While space does not allow to have a more extensive discussion, it is important to note that *Fasl* extends well beyond Nayrizi's self-identification and condemnation of his enemies in the late Safavid and early interregnum period. It is a massive work that, like Mu'azzin's *Tuhfa*, is concerned primarily with establishing an authentic discourse of what Nayrizi calls poverty by rooting Sufi doctrines in the teachings of the imams. Quotations of hadith and references to the imams and their teachings are myriad, and it is clear that Nayrizi was tremendously influenced by the hadith movement.§

The works covered above represent the earliest attempts to carve out a semantic and discursive space marked by the term *ʿirfan* as the authentic and original Twelver mystical tradition. Darabi and Nayrizi deserve credit for

* Khuyi, *Mizan al-savab*, 3:1185.

† *Istahbanati, Burhan*, 183–84. See also Tabrizi Isfahani, *Nur al-hidaya* MS, f. 186a–186b.

‡ Khuyi, *Mizan al-savab*, 3:1187.

§ One issue treated most conspicuously in *Fasl* (and in many other treatises by Nayrizi) is that of the unity of God (*vahdat al-haqq*). Acutely aware of the heavy criticisms levied against the Sufi tradition for its adherance to the doctrine of oneness of being, Nayrizi takes great pains to prove how all philosophers and scholars of kalam as well as the jurists who follow them have a fundamentally flawed understanding of tawhid. He argues then that the real folk of poverty, the true ʿarifin, invented the phrase *vahdat al-vujud* in order to steer clear of a widespread and flawed understanding of tawhid that is nothing less than polytheism. Unfortunately, says Nayrizi, the pseudo-faqirs (that is, the Sufis) interpreted the idea of oneness of being according to their own whims and fantasies, preparing the grounds for the pseudo-ulama to attack and slander the true ʿarifin, the only ones who knew the true meaning of the unity of God. Ibn ʿArabi's influence on Nayrizi's thought, at least at the level of vocabulary, is unmistakable; the latter uses terms like *tajalli* as well as more technical phrases like *al-fayz al-aqdas* (the most holy emanation) and *al-fayz al-muqaddas* (the holy emanation) to explain some of his views. See, for example, Khuyi, *Mizan al-Savab*, 1:213–14, 252, and 2:509. At the same time, Nayrizi meticulously avoids any mention of Ibn ʿArabi's name, probably because of the highly charged environment in which he operated. As for Mulla Sadra, some passages from his writings find their way verbatim into Nayrizi's *Fasl*. See, for example, Khuyi, *Mizan al-Savab*, 1:287.

transforming this term into a concept that stood in contrast to (or in place of) the traditional concept of Sufism, but that is only the beginning of the long story of ʿirfan. The next section of the story is about the development of what I call an "ʿirfanian discourse" in the eighteenth and nineteenth century, when the abstract idea of ʿirfan found an institutional home within the intellectual and spiritual circles of a group of mystically minded Twelver religious scholars at the margins of the madrasas of Iran and Iraq.

5 The Institutionalization of ʿIrfan

The sudden collapse of the Safavid dynasty was a catastrophe of monumental proportions for the elite, especially residents of the capital whose livelihood depended on royal patronage or the endowment revenues that flowed into madrasas with the support of the Safavid court. Some scholars were killed, and others fled the devastation for Indian courts or the shrine cities of Najaf and Karbala, which fell within the territory of the Ottoman Empire. The process of emigration did not happen overnight or even within the first year after the fall. The extensive religious endowment system that supported the madrasas and the mosques was weakened, but it outlived Safavid rule. Some scholars stayed in the "Shiʿite Realm" for a decade before exhausting all alternatives, while others were able to remain in Isfahan despite the decline in revenues resulting from the dramatic decrease in the city's population.

Ultimately, the Twelver-Safavid nomos built across two hundred years proved resilient. After the initial takeover by the Sunni Afghan invaders, Nadir Shah conquered most Safavid territory. He instituted many new religious policies aimed at legitimizing his rule and distinguishing it from the Safavid model he had helped destroy.* His move to normalize relations with the Ottomans, his ban on the practice of public cursing, and his declaration that Twelver Shiʿism was a fifth school of law alongside the four Sunni ones can all be seen as attempts to roll back the transformation of Safavid Shiʿism and to reduce it from a world religion to a denomination within the world religion of Islam. Nadir Shah's rule, however, was short, and these policies were abandoned by Karim Khan (r. 1751–1779). With the rise of Qajars, the status of Shiʿism as world religion was assured, and the Twelver ulama emerged more powerful than ever.

ʿIrfan after the Safavids

In the immediate aftermath of the fall of Isfahan, most of the exiled ulama made their way to the Sacred Thresholds of Karbala and Najaf. This is not

* For more on this see Tucker, *Nadir Shah's Quest.*

surprising given that religious scholars had long flowed back and forth on pilgrimages between Iranian urban centers and the ʿAtabat, which meant that a network of social and economic supports existed prior to the fall of the Safavids. Among those who eventually left for the ʿAtabat was Qutb al-Din Nayrizi, who, after spending some years in Iran after the collapse hoping in vain for events to take a more positive turn, finally decided to move to Najaf and begin teaching there.

Important ʿirfan-minded scholars were active in the ʿAtabat after the fall of the Safavids. It was there, evidence suggests, that a significant and under-studied part of the story of ʿirfan and its development unfolded. I focus on a handful of religious scholars in the interregnum period (that is, the time between the fall of Isfahan and the establishment of Qajar dynasty) to further illuminate how the Safavid transformation was reflected in interesting and unexpected ways in the worldview of some of the ulama, how a process of institutionalization gradually began for ʿirfan in Shiʿi madrasas, and finally how this process resulted in a the emergence of a relatively loose corporatized identity for the ʿirfan-minded ulama. It should be noted that this period is among the least studied and least understood parts of Iranian history. As such, this is a not a definitive account but a preliminary exploration offering glimpses of where future research might lead us.

ʿAbd al-Rahim Damavandi, Sufism, and ʿIrfan

One mystically minded religious scholars who left Isfahan for the ʿAtabat and whose career and work are pertinent to my goal of outlining the development of the ʿirfanian discourse in the post-Safavid era is ʿAbd al-Rahim Damavandi (d. after 1747). Although a number of his writings are available (mostly in manuscript form, though some have been printed recently), we know little about his life. His early education and potential travels are a mystery, though we know that, like Nayrizi, he was a student of Muhammad Sadiq Ardistani.* The fact that he is called ʿAbd al-Rahim "Isfahani" by one of his students indicates that he resided in the Safavid capital for an extended period of time.† In keeping with the intellectual climate of the early eighteenth century, Damavandi's intellectual and literary activities were focused on the traditions of the infallible imams.‡ In addition to Ardistani, his scholarly pedigree includes the names of prominent members of the Shirazi elite,

* Damavandi, "Miftah," 589–90 and 736.

† Tustari, *al-Ijaza al-kabira,* 144. The author mistakenly claims that Damavandi died in 1737, but we know that he was alive until at least 1747. See note 9 below.

‡ This is obvious even in the titles of his writings, most of which include an imam's name.

including Mulla Sadra,* the latter's student Fayz Kashani,† and Shah Muhammad Darabi,‡ all of whom he frequently cited. Additionally, it is clear that Ibn ʿArabi and his school of thought influenced Damavandi significantly. He called Ibn ʿArabi "the master of visionaries" (*raʾis al-mukashifin*) and drew heavily on the latter's *Fusus* and *al-Futuhat* in discussions of the seal of the saints (*khatam al-awliya*). Damavandi also demonstrated familiarity with the commentarial tradition on Ibn ʿArabi's works exemplified by figures such as Qaysari and Qashani.§

Miftah asrar al-Husayni

The most extensive of Damavandi's surviving works and the one that illustrates the mentioned influences most clearly is *Miftah asrar al-Husayni,* which was completed in 1747 and which deals with topics related to philosophy and ʿirfan.** According to the author, this work was written to communicate secret teachings not found in the writings of other divine philosophers and ʿarifin. Additionally, said Damavandi, its writing gave him the opportunity to share some of his own visions and mystical experiences.†† Damavandi begins *Miftah* with a note on how paths toward God can be divided into two broad categories: exoteric ways that lead to knowledge of Him and esoteric ways that lead to realization of Him. For the author, this dichotomy is ultimately about the contrast between discursive knowledge (ʿilm) and maʿrifa. The former is to know God via reasoning and exoteric disciplines of knowledge, and

* See, for example, his discussion of the concept of vujud, in which he quotes Sadra's *al-Asfar* at some length (Damavandi, *Hall-i rumuz* MS, f. 60a). See also his extensive quotations of Sadra's discussions on the nature of knowledge in abstract beings, or *mujarradat* (Damavandi, *Sharh-i kalam* MS, f. 72a–73a).

† See, for example, his references to *al-Vafi* and *ʿAyn al-yaqin,* both by Fayz, in Damavandi, *Fuyuzat* MS, f. 63b–64a; *al-Tawhid* MS, f. 68b; and *Sharh-i kalam* MS, f. 74a. His special attention to Kashani's works is also evident from the fact that he wrote a marginalia on the latter's Qur'anic commentary, *al-Safi.* See Damavandi, *Fuyuzat* MS, f. 65b, and Tehrani, *al-Zariʿa,* 4:281.

‡ For example, see Damavandi, *Fuyuzat* MS, f. 64b. See also Damavandi, *al-Tawhid* MS, f. 67a–68a. A major portion of the content of these pages is taken verbatim from Darabi's *Miʿraj.* See Darabi, *Miʿraj* MS, 151.

§ See, for example, Damavandi, *Sharh-i kalam* MS, f. 79a, and "Miftah," 723–47.

** On the book's completion date, see Damavandi, "Miftah," 578. See also Tehrani, *al-Zariʿa,* 21:316–17. Aqa Bozorg seems to have committed a minor calculation error when figuring the date "Miftah" was finished. Damavandi explicitly mentions that the date corresponds to the abjad value of the title of the book, which is 1160 hijri (1747) and not 1149 hijri, as Aqa Bozorg asserts. Furthermore, as we will see, Damavandi mentions the years 1741 and 1746 in the text, which means the work was finished after the latter date at the earliest.

†† Damavandi, "Miftah," 577–78.

the latter is to reach God via mystical visions and esoteric knowledge. A religious scholar is one who has discursive knowledge of God, and a ʿarif is one who has reached perfect union with God.* It is the latter who ultimately interests him in this book, which he begins with introductory chapters dedicated to rational proofs of God's existence and His unity. The proofs have no inherent value for Damavandi, who sees them as helpful only insofar as they protect the seeker against doubts put into the mind by God's enemies.† *Miftah* continues with the discussion of God's unity "according to the way of ʿarifin." Damavandi states explicitly that a ʿarif understanding of the unity of God can be attained only through mystical visions, not through rational argumentations. In other words, apprehending what the ʿarif means by oneness of being is outside the purview of reason.‡ It is important to note that the group of divine philosophers Damavandi identifies using adjectives like *ilahi* or *muta'allih* is distinguished from traditional discursive philosophers by the former's acceptance of mystical visions as legitimate venues for ascertaining the truth upon which their philosophy is based.

Throughout *Miftah* and in the rest of his oeuvre, Damavandi rarely used the stigmatized terms *Sufism* and *Sufi.* Following the example of his predecessors, he replaced them with words like *ʿarif* and *ʿirfan.* He frequently used the label *ahl-i ʿirfan* to designate ʿarifin who adhere to a distinctive spiritual ideal—one that is reflected in their spiritual lives, their metaphysical beliefs, and their writings.§ A major difference between Damavandi's writings and those of Darabi and Nayrizi is that he seems to have been much more at home with terms like *ʿarif* and *ʿirfan.* He was not as conscious and defensive about using them or avoiding the term *Sufism* as his predecessors were.

Moreover, Damavandi's conception of ahl-i ʿirfan is more coherent and systematic. The people of ʿirfan do not merely have in common a reliance on mystical unveilings. Damavandi also attributed to them a set of specific metaphysical and epistemological beliefs. They are united as a group by their belief in oneness of being and their acceptance of an intermediary metaphysical realm called the imaginal world (alam al-misal), which exists between the material world and the divine world. The latter issue, as mentioned previously, had long separated Peripatetic philosophers, who rejected the existence of such a realm, and Sufis, who emphasized its existence. Suhravardi, the founder of the Illuminationist school of philosophy, was the first to assimilate conceptions of this realm into a philosophical tradition based on his

* Damavandi, "Miftah," 607.
† Damavandi, "Miftah," 584.
‡ Damavandi, "Miftah," 604–8.
§ Damavandi, "Miftah," 648, 681, and others.

own mystical visions rather than a particular discursive argument.* As mentioned earlier, Darabi followed in Suhravardi's footsteps, dedicating a treatise to proving the existence of this realm on the basis of his visions and on his reading of traditions from the imams. Damavandi in turn claimed that many traditions of the imams that are not sensible otherwise can be understood perfectly when interpreted as events taking place in the intermediary realm, rather than in the material world.†

This common core of metaphysical and epistemological commitments constitute the basis of the fann of the ʿarifin, their unique discipline, which stands alongside theology, jurisprudence, and philosophy. Revealing the influence of Ibn ʿArabi's school of thought, Damavandi called this discipline not ʿirfan but "true divine knowledge" (*ʿilm-i ilahi-yi haqiqi*). ʿArifin had mastery of it, as did some of the "realizers among the divine philosophers" (*muhaqqiqin min al-hukama* or *muta'allihin min al-hukama*), he claimed.‡ All of these terms also appear repeatedly in Sadra's oeuvre. Several decades passed before the term *ʿirfan* became the official title of this "divine discipline" of knowledge. This happened in the time of Mulla Mahdi Niraqi.

Damavandi and the Master/Disciple Relationship

I have used the master/disciple relationship and perceptions of the identity, authority, and functions of the spiritual master as a litmus test for the extent to which Sufism had been brought into the Twelver Shiʿi fold. Damavandi's views on this issue reveal some fascinating developments. Like Darabi and many other mystically minded authors, Damavandi insisted on the necessity of pursuing the spiritual path under the guidance of a master.§ When it came to identifying his own master, however, we see a phenomenon that, as far as I have been able to tell, was recorded for the first time in Damavandi's writings. Refusing to name any ordinary human being as his mentor, Damavandi instead insisted that the third imam, Husayn b. ʿAli, was his murshid.** This is an important turning point in the domestication of Sufism. The transition from the traditional Sufi register into the newly developed Twelver-Safavid framework was nearly complete. In this new framework, it was the imam

* Damavandi is well aware of this tradition and explicitly mentions that the existence of this realm, which is implied in the hadith literature, is confirmed by the Illuminationist philosophers and the folk of ʿirfan ("Miftah," 699).

† For an extensive discussion of the issue of the imaginal world, see Ashtiyani, "Introduction I," 5–165.

‡ Damavandi, "Miftah," 661–65.

§ Damavandi, "Miftah," 672.

** Damavandi, "Miftah," 622, 728.

who dominated the spiritual realm, acting as the murshid-i kamil of spiritual seekers.

The imams, however, were not physically present. This brings us to the issue of dreams and visions, through which Damavandi claimed immediate access to the infallibles and by which he received spiritual initiation and guidance from them. *Miftah* contains detailed, vivid accounts of multiple encounters between Damavandi and the imams and Muhammad. Not surprisingly, the Hidden Imam looms large in these reports. Damavandi, unlike ordinary people, seems to have had frequent access to the Mahdi:

> In the year 1154 [1741 C.E.] I was at the station of thirst (*maqam-i ʿatash*) . . . and in that year this poor [servant] was blessed with a spiritual ascent to the fourth heaven.* I ascended to the top of the fourth heaven seeking what I was seeking like a crazy man. I could not find it, and so I returned to my body . . . until, on the night of the fifteenth of the sacred month of Shaʿban, which is the auspicious night of the birth of the seal of the saints, the Mahdi, I was in the presence of my master, peace be upon him [that is, at the shrine of Husayn]. I returned home after I finished my supplications and prayers, and I was in good spirits. It was a bit after midnight, and I thought I would go to sleep for a while and then wake up to do the night prayers. When I went to sleep, I saw the seal of the saints, the Mahdi, come and give this one who is thirsty for love [that is, Damavandi] a glass of wine [*sharab*]. I woke up after I drank it, and I could still feel the moisture of that wine on my upper lip, and this poor [servant] had tremendous [spiritual] revelations after that blessing from His Excellency.†
>
> . . . [A]nd in the year 1159 [1746 C.E.], it was the end of the month of Safar or early Rabiʿ al-Awwal, I can't remember exactly, and I was done with my morning prayers and doing the supplications in a meditative state. . . . [Suddenly], in that state I saw the Seal of the Saints appear on my right along with two of his sons. The sons do not belong to this world, but are among the ones who reside in His Excellency's own town, to which people cannot go. His Excellency pointed to those two. One of them came and took my right arm and the other my left, and His Excellency went in the direction of *qibla* and disappeared. Immediately the Seal of the Prophets (peace be upon him) appeared from the direction of qibla and came toward his weak servant and poured a finger-tip amount of his blessed saliva, whiter than snow, into my mouth and left.‡

* He makes his way to the seventh heaven and beyond in later visions.

† Damavandi, "Miftah," 749–50.

‡ Damavandi, "Miftah," 753–54.

The latter vision has all the features of an initiatory rite. Damavandi is initiated by Muhammad, who guides him toward the same divine destination (symbolized by qibla) as the Mahdi. There is no difference between the Prophet and the imams; all are members of the celestial constellation of fourteen infallibles.

Interestingly, Damavandi dedicates an entire chapter of his *Miftah* to the crucial issue of "masterology" (*murshid-shanasi*). He speaks of the increasingly difficulty of finding a legitimate master. There are no pirs to follow, or so it appears. However, he says, the world cannot be empty of the saints, though they may be hidden. In order to help the seeker find a spiritual mentor, he proposes a combination of prayers and daily meditational and devotional practices, almost all of which are focused on the intercessory power of the imams.* Though Damavandi may not have conceptualized it in this manner, it is clear that the eclipse of the khanaqah as a social space had resulted in a lack of socially visible and accessible spiritual mentors. Gone was the charismatic Sufi shaykh; his social function and place of residence had disappeared. Mulla Sadra's elitist and self-fulfilling dream had come true: all those who might have taken refuge in khanaqah had indeed been declared "deficient, damned fools, imprisoned by the fetters of lust." The exalted and elite servants of God who possessed ma'rifa, the "fruits of creation" and "purpose of the universe," are hidden by God himself from "ignorant" people with their "lowly natures."† This is an apt description of the Hidden Imam, the Mahdi, who is the perfect master. His occultation impedes direct access, but God chooses select Shi'a to meet him in person and receive spiritual guidance from him directly. Why, then, is there a need for for the less-than-perfect spiritual masters? This was the question Darabi sought to answer in *Mi'raj.* Damavandi also provides an answer, though he does not speak in the language of the deputyship of the 'arifin as Darabi had done. Instead, his answer comes as part of a defense of the controversial Sufi practice of visualizing and contemplating the face of the master: "Some people, lacking in insight, might ask, 'If we have the universal master [*murshid-i kull*], what is the need to visualize the face of the [ordinary] master?' The answer is that this visible master [*murshid-i zahir*] is the image of universal one. The [spiritually] weak cannot be helped by [the latter's] strong light. The soul of the seeker needs to be strengthened with the help of the visible master until [it is ready] to benefit from the universal master to the extent that its potential allows."‡

* Damavandi, "Miftah," 676–77.
† Shirazi (Mulla Sadra), *Kasr,* 177–78.
‡ Damavandi, "Miftah," 679.

In what sense is the ordinary master the image of the perfect one? Damavandi addresses this question, among others, in extensive chapters dedicated to the concept of the seal of the saints and to the concept of the Mahdi. The unusual nature of Damavandi's teachings is clearest in these two chapters. The dominant theological understanding of the Mahdi in Twelver tradition is that he is one and the same as the twelfth imam, who has long been in occultation and who will return at the end of time to restore justice to the world. Damavandi's understanding, heavily influenced by messianic Sufi traditions, is not exactly the same. He makes a distinction between two types of sainthood, which he says can be either "solar" (*shamsi*) or "lunar" (*qamari*). The perfect man, the seal of the saints, is a flawless mirror in which all divine attributes are comprehensively reflected, and Damavandi likens him to the sun and portrays him as the original source of the light of sainthood. He likens all other saints to the moon, for they are dependent on that original light. In other words, their sainthood is a reflection of that of the perfect man. The more spiritually accomplished they are, the more perfectly their mirror reflects, until at last they full moons that perfectly mirror the sun.*

Damavandi does not stop here. According to him, saints whose advanced level of mystical realization allows them to stand face to face with the sun and reflect it fully *often* make claims of mahdihood, a claim that would be rigorously denied by the ulama and ignorant disciples. In such cases, he says, the disciple should accept the claim, understanding the difference between the eschatological Mahdi who will come at the end of time and those who claim "lunar" mahdihood as a result of a perfect union, a merger of identity, between the ʿarif and the seal of the saints.† Damavandi explains this idea further by introducing the concept of the perfect projection (*buruz-i kamil*), which means "the flow [*sarayan*] of the perfect saint [the Mahdi] in others."

Projection is among the original ideas of the founder of the Nurbakhshi Sufi network and relates to his understanding of the role of the perfect man. Although it still is not clear exactly what Nurbakhsh himself meant by the idea, his most prominent student, Shams al-Din Muhammad Lahiji (d. circa. 1506), offered his own interpretation in *Mafatih al-iʿjaz,* his famous commentary on Shabistari's *Gulshan-i raz.* According to Shahzad Bashir's analysis, Lahiji held that "the Muhammadan Reality manifests itself in the bodies of living human beings through the process of projection [*buruz*]. This occurs at varying levels, so that the perfect humans in a given historical period are receptacles of the projection available in that age." Bashir's study of Lahiji's worldview leads him to believe that "Lahiji most likely regarded Nurbakhsh

* Damavandi, "Miftah," 730–33.
† Damavandi, "Miftah," 734.

as the physical manifestation of Muhammadan Reality in his lifetime in this sense [thus the term *mahdi-yi dawran*], and not as the eschatological savior who is to be the only other complete manifestation of the Muhammadan Reality besides Muhammad the Prophet"*—an analysis that is confirmed by Damavandi's understanding, which draws heavily upon *Mafatih*. Damavandi warns his readers in *Miftah* that ignorant people sometimes confuse the idea of projection with the (heretical) idea of the transmigration of the soul (*tanasukh*). The two concepts are completely different, he says, for several reasons. One reason is that the latter entails the soul migrating to another body only after the original body stops functioning, while in the former, the perfect saint is embodied in a single body but can project himself in multiple manifestations "like a person who steps in a house of mirrors [*ayina-khana*] where multiple mirrors are installed."† Damavandi continues this fascinating discussion with a personal account of how a friend of his met such a mahdi in person:

> A knowledgeable man and a perfect ʿarif named Shaykh Husayn of the people of Qatif came to this sacred ground [Karbala]. Once, in the middle of a conversation, he told us a story from his teacher, whose name was Mulla Muhammad- ʿAli. I knew this dear friend, and he was among the students of my teacher, the master of divine philosophers, Mulla Muhammad Sadiq Ardistani. Mulla Muhammad-ʿAli (God bless his soul) had travelled to India. "My teacher told me," Shaykh Husayn said, "that I travelled from India to Mecca. One day, within the boundaries of the Sacred Threshhold [*haram*], I met a knowledgeable man whom I knew from Isfahan. I heard some things from him concerning the other world that surprised me. I told him, "My dear friend, I knew you in Isfahan as a man of knowledge; what has happened to you, and how long have you been in this condition?" . . . He said, "What happened, happened here." I said to him, "Tell me about it." He said, "There is a shoekeeper [*kafshdar*] where I remove my shoes [upon entering the haram]. Whenever it came time to leave, it would be impressed on my heart to give him more than is customary for a tip, and so I would do it. Time passed in this manner until one day he asked me, "Why do you give me extra money?" I told him, "It is something impressed on my heart." He asked me to sit down, and I did. Then he asked, "Do you know your God?" I laid everything I knew of God's *maʿrifa* on the table. He said, "Do you think this

* Bashir, *Messianic Hopes*, 174–75.

† Damavandi, "Miftah," 735. The idea of projection is also used by Damavandi to reconcile Ibn ʿArabi's views on the identity of the Seal of Muhammadan Sainthood and his occasional claims of that position for himself.

> is enough?" That prompted me to think, and then I asked him, "What do you say?" He said, "I am the Mahdi; whatever he [God?] said I accepted and acted upon it." Mulla Muhammad-ʿAli asked that dear man, "Did you not achieve certitude?" His eyes filled with tears, and he said yes. Mulla Muhammad-ʿAli wanted to say good-bye and go toward Jeddah to catch a ship that was headed for India, but that dear friend begged him to stay a few more days, saying, "I am going to die on such and such a day, and I would like you to pray over my corpse, prepare and bury it, and then leave." Mulla Muhammad-ʿAli agreed, and the man died exactly as he predicted.*

Damavandi quotes extensively from Ibn ʿArabi and his students on the idea of the seal of sainthood, shrugging off charges of heresy and heterodoxy. "The bottom line," he says "is that Ibn ʿArabi has been explicit [about this topic] while other great [scholars] have chosen some level of secrecy. That is why the exoteric ulama condemn Ibn ʿArabi and charge him with heresy. Some of the ulama who have never tasted ʿirfan and are not drunk with the wine of sainthood have decided to interpret the sayings of the Shaykh [Ibn ʿArabi] so as to pave the way for refutation and charges of heresy, although their tasteless interpretations have failed. It occurred to this poor [servant], with the blessing of my master, Imam Husayn, to explain the statements of the Shaykh according to ʿirfan and divine philosophy so that [the reader will glean] the most benefit."†

Damavandi's discussions in *Miftah* provide us with an excellent and fascinating example of how mystically minded ulama of his era grappled with traditional and nontraditional Sufi ideas such as the necessity of a spiritual guide, projection, the perfect man, and the seal of sainthood and how they integrated those ideas into the newly forged Twelver- Safavid worldview, which judged legitimacy on the basis of the imams and their hadiths. Although the appearance of uniquely Nurbakhshi ideas such as projection indicate extensive exposure to the Nurbakhshi Sufi worldview, neither Damavandi nor his contemporary sources mention an official affiliation. The author of a much later source, *Tara'iq al-haqa'iq,* classifies him "among the greatest shaykhs of the Nurbakhshi order," but without any reference.‡ Whether or not he identified as a Nurbakhshi Sufi is not particularly important, because such an

* "Miftah," 736–37.

† "Miftah," 739.

‡ Maʿsum-ʿAli Shah, *Tara'iq al-haqa'iq,* 3:163. Ashtiyani, in his short introduction to *Miftah*, contends that the author was among the Zahabi Sufis of his time (see Damavandi, "Miftah," 576). He does not, however, share with us the source upon which he has relied.

affiliation counted for little in the new sacred nomos of Twelver Shiʿism. The domesticated version of Sufism to which Damavandi subscribed lacked the social institutions and networks of traditional Sufism, and it was no longer a significant source for the production of social identity. Damavandi's idiosyncratic views, however, were not totally amenable to the centrifugal forces of orthodoxy, at the heart of which now lay the madrasas of the ʿAtabat. It was left to a group of less heterodox ulama to promote ʿirfan in the dominant Twelver institution: the madrasa.

The second half of the eighteenth century witnessed the activity of a number of mystically minded religious scholars who later came to be regarded as foundational figures in the Shiʿi tradition of ʿirfan. As trainees of the madrasa system, these ulama were highly educated in the exoteric disciplines of knowledge taught in the madrasas. At the same time, they were deeply inspired by the teachings of the imams, strictly observant of both the obligatory injunctions and supererogatory recommendations of divine law, and highly revered as exemplars of piety and morality. They operated within the sphere of the established Twelver hierocracy and orthodoxy, and in that context they served as guides for students of religious knowledge who sought instruction in matters pertaining to the spiritual quest (sayr va suluk). In spite of the glaring similarities between all aspects of sayr va suluk and the traditional Sufi path, the mystically minded ulama of this period were reluctant—afraid, even—to be associated with the worldview or lived reality of Sufism. Prominent figures who forwarded the cause of ʿirfan in this era include Aqa Muhammad Bidabadi, Mulla Muhammad-Mahdi Niraqi, Sayyid Mahdi b. Murtaza Najafi, better known as Bahr al-ʿUlum (d. 1797), Mulla ʿAbd al-Samad Hamadani (d. 1801), and Mulla Ahmad Niraqi.

The intellectual and spiritual outlooks of these men had meaningful differences. Bahr al-ʿUlum, for example, was a prominent Arab mujtahid with an intellectual background very different from those of the other scholars mentioned. Unlike them, he did not incorporate the philosophical mysticism of Mulla Sadra into his thought, nor does he appear to have been particularly enchanted with Ibn ʿArabi and the doctrine of oneness of being.* Bahr

* Sources leave many questions regarding his mystical tendencies unanswered. The life events most frequently highlighted in hagiographical narratives written by other religious scholars are the meetings we are told he had with the Hidden Imam, in which he was greeted with a warm hug (for some narratives see Zanuzi, *Riayz al-janna*, 4:592–96). In Sufi literature, however, he is remembered for seeking spiritual advice in secret meetings with the Niʿmatullahi master Nur-ʿAli Shah (see Maʿsum-ʿAli Shah, *Tara'iq al-haqa'iq*, 3:199–200). More important, a brief treatise entitled *Sayr va suluk*, which has been ascribed to Bahr al-ʿUlum, is filled with technical Sufi vocabulary, especially in the second half. Aqa Bozorg has suggested that

al-ʿUlum and other scholars also differed in their relationships to organized Sufism. Hamadani was quite close to and most probably an initiate of the Niʿmatullahi Sufi network, but the others consciously avoided such associations. Nonetheless, they all had mystical proclivities, were less hostile to the Sufi tradition than were many in the clerical establishment, and made significant contributions to the formation of ʿirfanian discourse. Some of them seem to have taught jurisprudence as a means of establishing their authority and/or adhering to the dominant madrasa paradigm. While doing so, they had smaller circles of students with whom they studied texts of divine philosophy and mysticism. The details of important changes in the Twelver Shiʿi intellectual tradition, especially the rapid decline of the Akhbari school in Karbala in the second half of the eighteenth century, are beyond the scope of this book, but I do want to discuss continuity and change in the writings on ʿirfan by Bidabadi, the Niraqis, and Hamadani.

Aqa Muhammad Bidabadi

Aqa Muhammad Bidabadi (d. December 12, 1783) was trained mainly in post-Safavid Isfahan, in an intellectual environment in disarray.* Unlike many of his contemporaries, he is not recorded as having spent extensive time in Najaf or Kabala. In the early years of his training, he studied hadith and tafsir with Muhammad-Taqi Almasi (d. 1746), a prominent Akhbari scholar of his time† and a great-grandson of Majlisi Sr.‡ The teachings of Almasi and others like him and the dominance of the Akhbari school in major centers of learning in Iraq and Iran at that time ensured that Bidabadi was heavily influenced

the whole treatise or at least the latter parts of it are not by Bahr al-ʿUlum (Tehrani, *al-Zariʿa,* 12:284). The ʿirfan-minded editor of the treatise, the famous Allame Mohammad-Hoseyn Tehrani (d. 1995), is convinced otherwise, however (see his introduction to Bahr al-ʿUlum, *Risalat al-sayr va al-suluk,* 10–13). A critical analysis of this important and influential treatise is long overdue.

* Unlike figures such as Muʾazzin and Darabi, Bidabadi has been the subject of attention by Iranian scholars, especially recently. ʿAli Sadraʾi Khuyi and ʿAli Karbasizade Esfahani have made two major attempts to write a comprehensive biography of his life and a bibliography of his works. My analysis here draws heavily on their studies and on the primary source material on Bidabadi gathered by Sadraʾi Khuyi in his *Tazkirat al-zakirin.* Some of his writings are also reproduced by Zanuzi in Zanuzi, *Riyaz al-janna,* 4:423–38.

† Khansari, *Rawzat al-jannat,* 7:118. Almasi is also said to have been one of the first scholars to take Sadra's mystical philosophy seriously into consideration for teaching, and thus he played an instrumental role in promoting the latter's works. See Ashtiyani's assessment in Ashtiyani, "Introduction II," 17. I have been unable to substantiate this claim in the primary sources, and thus it should perhaps be taken with a grain of salt.

‡ Sadraʾi Khuyi, *Ashna-yi haqq,* 21–22.

by Akhbarism. In addition to studying under Almasi, Bidabadi is said to have studied rational disciplines with the prominent post-Safavid philosopher of Isfahan Mulla Ismaʿil Khajuʾi (d. 1760).* Bidabadi was also the teacher of Mulla ʿAli Nuri (d. 1830), who has been credited with bringing Sadra's philosophy into the mainstream and causing his writings to become standard textbooks for students of philosophy.† Bidabadi's own writings clearly demonstrate his deep engagement with Mulla Sadra's philosophy. While the former did not leave behind any substantial work on philosophy (or any other topic for that matter), we get a clear sense of his intellectual proclivities from reading his glosses (*hashiya*) of philosophical and hadith works. Virtually all his glosses are of works by Mulla Sadra, including *al-Asfar al-arbaʿa*, *al-ʿArshiyya*, and *al-Mashaʿir*.‡ To judge from this, and given the fact that such commentaries were usually produced as a result of a particular text having been chosen for teaching purposes, it is probable that Bidabadi taught Mulla Sadra's works in Isfahan. He is thus an important link in the crystallization of a tradition of mystical philosophy that began to gain traction in the late Safavid period, continued to develop and crystallize through the interregnum, and, by the early Qajar period, became the predominant philosophical tradition in Iran. This tradition was, of course, Mulla Sadra's school of Tran-

* For a succinct but rich biography of Khajuʾi, see Karbasi-zade, *Hakim-i mutaʾallih*, 65–68. Some may have questions regarding the relationship between Khajuʾi and Bidabadi because of the purportedly anti-Sufi sentiments of the former, who is said to have written a treatise refuting the notion of unity of being (see Khajuʾi, *Vahdat-i vujud* MS) and another on the vices of Sufis general (see Khajuʾi, *Radd-i sufiyan* MS). How can this be reconciled with the mystical proclivities we see in Bidabadi? The question could be dismissed as another example of how students may differ significantly from their teachers, but, upon closer examination, Khajuʾi's position on Sufism appears to have been more nuanced than the titles of the treatises just mentioned suggest. For example, he ends his piece on the refutation of oneness of being with an epilogue in which he enumerates twelve groups of Sufis. All the groups but one are misguided, he tells us. The only Sufis of whom he approves are those who adhere to the orthodoxy of Twelver Shiʿism. That is to say, they avoid antinomian behavior, including singing, dancing, drinking, and looking at beautiful visages, devoting themselves instead to a life of asceticism modeled after the imams (see Khajuʾi, *Vahdat-i vujud* MS, f. 11b). While Khajuʾi's description of the eleven deviant groups of Sufis seems to be informed by *Hadiqat al-shiʿa*, his decision to allow for a group of true Sufis stands in contrast to all other anti-Sufi treatises of the period, which categorically condemn Sufism in all its forms. This decision is probably rooted in his personal familiarity with types of Sufism compliant with Safavid Shiʿism, adherents to which had amenable relationships with his teacher, Mulla Sadiq Ardistani, and students of his, including Qutb al-Din Nayrizi.

† For more on Nuri's influence in reviving Sadra's philosophy, see Ashtiyani's remarks in his Ashtiyani, "Introduction III," cvi-cxvi.

‡ Sadraʾi Khuyi, *Ashna-yi haqq*, 102–5.

scendent philosophy. In bibliographical sources, representatives of this philosophical tradition are usually referred to as ʿarif and hakim in reference to their mastery of discursive philosophy and openness to mystical visions.* Some of these men were on good terms and sometimes in intimate conversation with elite representatives of Shiʿi Sufism.†

We know few details of Bidabadi's spiritual life and journey. The most substantial description comes from Bidabadi himself, in a letter that he wrote in response to a request by a certain Haji ʿAbdullah Bidguli. It follows a familiar pattern in the genre of spiritual autobiography. Bidabadi describes an early period of extensive exposure to discursive Islamic disciplines ranging from Arabic grammar and linguistics to the study of hadith, jurisprudence, theology, and philosophy. This was followed by a phase of deep disenchantment, where Bidabadi found that all the knowledge he had gained did nothing to bring him closer to God. "Whatever I have learned in the madrasa," he lamented, "will not help but harm me when I am put in the grave."‡ This realization led to an awakening and a strong desire to remedy the situation by committing himself to religious observance, purification, and a battle against the demands and trickery of the carnal soul.§ It is interesting that Bidabadi's letter, unlike many other such accounts, does not include any details of the actual conversion experience, though it began a process of "burning, melting, and living with it like a candle until today."** The letter also contains no mention of a spiritual master in charge of his spiritual growth.

Nonetheless, we know that he studied with mystically minded scholars of his time. During his years of learning in Isfahan, he is said to have been a student of Qutb al-Din Nayrizi.†† This is the major factor that has prompted Zahabi authors to include Bidabadi in their lineage as a disciple of Nayrizi.‡‡

* See, for example Maʿsum-ʿAli Shah, *Taraʾiq al-haqaʾiq,* 3:214.

† This, of course, is not true of all of them. Mulla ʿAli Nuri, for example, despised and was despised by Sufis. See Maʿsum-ʿAli Shah, *Taraʾiq al-haqaʾiq,* 3:223–24. By contrast, Mulla Hadi Sabzavari (d. 1873) is famous for his friendly relationship with dervishes and Sufis. See Saduqi Soha, *Tarikh-i hukama,* 166–67.

‡ Sadraʾi Khuyi, *Tazkirat al-salikin,* 57.

§ Sadraʾi Khuyi, *Tazkirat al-salikin,* 54–59.

** Sadraʾi Khuyi, *Tazkirat al-salikin,* 58.

†† Ashtiyani has disputed this claim (see Karbasi-zade, *Hakim-i mutaʾallih,* 203). His objection seems to be based on his disdain for Sufis, and though we do not have any historical evidence, it is probable, as Karbasi-zade says, that he did in fact learn from Nayrizi during his stay in Isfahan as the latter's student.

‡‡ Sharifi Shirazi, "Tarikh-i hayat," 37. From there, Niʿmatullahi authors have assumed the same. See Maʿsum-ʿAli Shah, *Taraʾiq al-haqaʾiq,* 3:215 and Shirvani, *Riyaz al-siyaha,* 336. Neither his own writings nor the biographical information we have from non-Sufi-affiliated authors confirm this claim.

Bidabadi's affiliation with the Zahabiyya is most probably a fiction, but his penchant for esotericism and mysticism is beyond doubt. He was best known as a master of esoteric disciplines (*al-ʿulum al-ghariba*), and several of his treatises on the subject have survived.* Additionally, much of what survives of his writing is composed of pieces of correspondence detailing various aspects of the spiritual path in response to questions directed at him as an expert in such issues.†

One of the most noteworthy surviving pieces of correspondence is a letter Bidabadi wrote in response to a request from one of the most famous and influential jurists of his time, Mirza Abu al-Qasim Qummi (d. 1815). The latter was a respected and popular mujtahid who was also famous for his anti-Sufi views. Toward the turn of the century, in response to questions he received about the validity of certain Sufi beliefs and practices, he wrote several treatises and letters refuting beliefs such as oneness of being and practices such as Sufi zikr.‡ It is significant that a well-established and well-connected mujtahid§ who explicitly opposed many Sufi ideas requested spiritual advice from a mystically minded scholar such as Bidabadi.

In his advice to Mirza Qummi, Bidabadi pointed out some of the obstacles faced by a prominent jurist such as Qummi on the path to salvation. He warned the latter against "spending all your time teaching the conventional disciplines of knowledge" at the expense of the purification of the soul. He recommended learning only the best of such disciplines, to the extent that was absolutely necessary, and spending the remaining time on purification. While Bidabadi did not attack jurisprudence explicitly, he warned Qummi against limiting his understanding to the outward meaning of the verses of the Qur'an and urged him to embrace the hidden aspects as well. He even went so far as to advise Qummi to "hold fast to the essence and leave the shell in all matters."** This response reveals an interesting power dynamic.

* For a brief discussion of the treatise he wrote on alchemy, see Karbasi-zade, *Hakim-i muta'allih*, 40–44 and 178–79. For excerpts from these treatises and a comprehensive bibliography of the manuscripts, see Sadra'i Khuyi, *Ashina-yi haqq*, 105–9 and 230–44.

† Many of these letters and treatises have been published multiple times in different venues. For a fairly comprehensive attempt to gather them all in one place with helpful bibliographical information about the manuscripts and previous venues of publication, see Sadra'i Khuyi, *Tazkirat al-salikin*.

‡ These treatises and letters have been published in different venues. See, for example, Qummi, *Jamiʿ al-shattat*, 786–804, and, more recently, Qummi, *Si risala dar naqd-i ʿirfan*.

§ Fath-ʿAli Shah had tremendous respect for Mirza Qummi, correspondence between them shows. See Modarressi, "Panj nama."

** Sadra'i Khuyi, *Takirat al-salikin*, 72.

In matters of spirituality, Bidabadi was a more authoritative figure than the mujtahid.*

I argue that this letter encapsulates an important moment in the history of ʿirfan in Shiʿi Iran. By the end of the nineteenth century, a division of labor had emerged in which certain members of the ulama, such as Bidabadi, were recognized not only by the populace but by the highest members of the hierocracy as authorities in matters of the spiritual quest. This was a complementary relationship of sorts, in which men such as Qummi claimed authority in the worldly domain and, as deputies of the Hidden Imam, relegated the otherworldly domain of spiritual guidance to figures like Bidabadi. The process of institutionalization was still at its earliest stages, but later, as it progressed and the followers of ʿirfan began to construct spiritual lineages, Bidabadi was a crucial link in their chains. The legendary ʿarif Sayyid Ahmad Karbalaʾi (d. 1914) reportedly said that "the true ʿurafa of the holy city of Najaf validate their lineage with Aqa Muhammad Bidabadi, the universal ʿarif and the source of the masters of certitude."† In other words, as twentieth-century hagiographies began to conceptualize the madrasa-trained ʿarifin of the late eighteenth and early nineteenth centuries as a group resembling a Sufi network, with clearly defined spiritual chains of transmission, Bidabadi became a paradigmatic figure to whom the specific teachings of later ʿarifin could be traced.‡

Bidabadi's surviving letters, written mainly in response to requests for spiritual guidance from students and acquaintances, stand in sharp contrast to later perceptions of him as a spiritual master with a lineage. In his correspondence, he never came close to identifying himself as a *murshid-i kamil,* let alone envisioning himself as part of a well-defined spiritual lineage. In fact, Bidabadi differed sharply from authors discussed earlier in how rarely he used terms such as *murshid* and *pir* in his writings. In the few places he

* In the same letter, Bidabadi clarifies his position against other disciplines of Islamic learning. He praises God for bestowing upon him "the Qurʾanic, divine, and faith-based hikma" that allowed him to dispense with natural and mathematical arguments and the invented principles of the Muʿtazilite and the Ashʿarite theologians and that healed him of "the chronic illnesses that are caused by considering the works of Greek philosophy." The Peripatetic and Illuminationist schools of philosophy are singled out in his condemnation, and he also mentions condescendingly the names of a number of prominent and/or widely used textbooks of philosophy and mysticism. These include Ibn Sina's *al-Najat* and *al-Shifa* and Ibn ʿArabi's *al-Futuhat* (see Sadraʾi Khuyi, *Takirat al-salikin,* 70–71).

† See Saduqi Soha, *Tarikh-i hukama,* 211.

‡ For an informative summary of all the ways in which Bidabadi appeared in these later genealogies, see Karbasi-zade, *Hakim-i mutaʾallih,* 208–18, and Saduqi Soha, *Tarikh-i hukama,* 85–123.

did use them, he was referring explicitly to the infallible imams and the necessity of seeking help from them in their status as perfect or universal masters.* Bidabadi seems to have taken the implication of Darabi's and Damavandi's thinking to its logical conclusion: no one other than the infallibles themselves should be recognized with such a title.

Regardless of how he perceived himself, it is clear from the letters addressed to him that some of his contemporaries and would-be disciples considered him a perfect spiritual master. In an interesting written exchange, Sadr al-Din Kashif Dizfuli (d. 1842) calls himself Bidabadi's murid despite the fact that the two never actually met, and he asks the latter for a zikr formula that he can use as a novice on his spiritual quest.† Bidabadi, in a brief and evasive response, merely says, "According to the reports [from the imams], there is no better zikr than *la ilaha illa allah* (There is no god but God). Be persistent [in reciting it while] remembering the meaning."‡ Dizfuli, in a response that reflects his disappointment, writes, "Oh my master and my lord, this zikr is brief. It has neither a number, nor a set time. [May I further ask,] should it be [recited as] a vocal zikr or a zikr of the heart [*zikr-i qalbi*] as the folk of visions and ʿirfan have written about it? Is it supposed to be [performed] after mortification [*riyazat*] or not? Please kindly explain its requirements and its etiquette [*adab*] in detail for this humble servant."§

Bidabadi's response to Dizfuli gives us a glimpse of a salient feature of all his treatises and correspondence: the general and abstract nature of his guidance. He refused to play the role that Sufi masters had played for centuries in offering detailed instructions for their followers.** He rarely went beyond

* See, for example, Sadraʾi Khuyi, *Ashna-yi haqq*, 60, 74, 94, and 155.

† Kashif Dizfuli, *Mirʾat al-ghayb*, 83–85.

‡ Sadraʾi Khuyi, *Tazkirat al-salikin*, 151.

§ Kashif Dizfuli, *Mirʾat al-ghayb*, 87. Dizfuli's eagerness to consider Bidabadi his spiritual master and to receive a personally tailored formula of zikr from him clearly demonstrates how open he was (in contrast to what we know of Bidabadi) to Sufi beliefs and practices that some ulama considered bidʿa. This enthusiasm earns him an important place in both Sufi and ʿirfanian spiritual lineages. He is considered the crucial link through which, as mentioned, the ʿarifin of Najaf are connected to Bidabadi. See Saduqi Soha, *Tarikh-i hukama*, 211ff. Additionally, the Zahabis have claimed Dizfuli and, because of him, Bidabadi in their own lineage.

** This important feature of Bidabadi's thought confirms the doubts scholars have had about the validity of the attribution of a very popular sayr va suluk treatise to Bidabadi (see Sadraʾi Khuyi, *Ashna-yi haqq*, 197–223). This treatise, unlike Bidabadi's other writings, strongly emphasizes the role of the spiritual master, his initiation, and his guidance in the process of suluk. The extreme level of detail in the recommended zikr regimen included in this treatise is also unparalleled in other letters by Bidabadi. It is quite possible that this letter is authored by one of the early Niʿmatullahi masters of the late nineteenth century (see Sadraʾi Khuyi, *Ashna-yi*

reminding his audience of the dangers and temptations of being attached to this world and inviting them to do everything they could to control their carnal souls. One can succeed in this essential task, he said, only by asking for help from the imams and following all the divine injunctions as laid out in the Shariʿa. Additionally, he underlined the importance of performing the supererogatory prayers and supplications (*mustahabbat*) to the best of one's ability and avoiding practices that, while not illicit, are considered reprehensible (*makruhat*). This strict adherence to Shariʿa, for him, defined the contours of "lawful mortification" (*riyazat-i sharʿi*), such as fasting for forty days, performing supererogatory rituals, avoiding lawful indulgences that satisfy the carnal soul in addition to those that are prohibited and reprehensible, and avoiding intimate relationships with people of power and the acceptance of such positions. Here, "lawful" is an important qualifier of a key term (riyazat) that draws a clear line between his ʿirfan and Sufism.*

Finally, I would like note that Bidabadi joins Sayyid Mahdi Bahr al-ʿUlum in having attributed to him the writing of a treatise titled *Sayr va suluk*. Neither attribution has any basis in reality, but the fact that two figures who played a foundational role in formulating ʿirfanian discourse are said to have written this work tells us something about the intellectual history of ʿirfan. Such attributions, I believe, are products of a later phase of the development of this discourse.† As ʿirfan moved further toward a corporate and institutionalized identity during the nineteenth and early twentieth centuries, ex

haqq, 199–200). I would also argue that another letter considered authentic by both Modarressi (see "Du risala") and Sadra'i Khuyi (see *Tazkirat al-salikin*, 42–49) diverges significantly from other writings of Bidabadi in style and in the details of its instructions and therefore is probably not his.

* It is instructive to contrast Bidabadi's attitude in his correspondence with Dizfuli to Fayz Kashani attitude in similar correspondence from almost a century earlier between him and a prominent student of his, Qazi Saʿid Qummi. The latter, apparently stuck in a "dark night of the soul" mood with no guide to ask for help, wrote to Fayz to ask for spiritual advice. In response, Fayz reminded him that, ultimately, it is too difficult to embark successfully on the treacherous spiritual journey toward God without a master. Throughout the letter, Fayz refused to play the role of such a master, giving only broad and general advice and adding that "whoever among the seekers for whom God wills abundant good, He facilitates for him to find a shaykh among the folks of this Path to take the responsibility of training him in the path of truth. Otherwise, the Path will be prolonged for him, achieving [the goal] will be delayed, and his steps will tremble" (Modarressi, "Mukatabat," 675–76).

† In addition to Bidabadi and Bahr al-ʿUlum, Sayyid Kazim Rashti and Nur-ʿAli Shah are credited with writing such treatises. A critical side-by-side analysis of these treatises could dramatically improve our understanding of this early stage of the developments of ʿirfanian discourse.

post facto attributions such as this provided much-needed legitimacy for some of the meditative practices, codes of conduct, and ethical values that have become part of the mystical regime of ʿirfan.*

Mulla Muhammad-Mahdi Niraqi

Another prominent religious scholar of the second half of the eighteenth century who made significant contributions to the development of the ʿirfanian discourse was Mulla Mahdi Niraqi. He was a polymath of profound erudition, and his magnificent portfolio of written works, broad intellectual interests, literary gifts, and deep spirituality are reminiscent of the legendary Shaykh Baha'i.† Born in Niraq around 1734, Mulla Mahdi had a long career that began with a short period of study in Kashan, followed by a couple of decades of study and teaching in Isfahan. From there he emigrated to the ʿAtabat, where he spent a decade before returning to Kashan for the last twenty-five years of his life.‡ In Kashan he was respected as the town's most prominent scholar, and after his death, on February 28, 1795, he was buried in Najaf.§ Niraqi studied with many prominent scholars of the time in both Iran and Iraq. In the study of jurisprudence and hadith, he learned from scholars with widely opposing views, including Mirza Muhammad Akhbari (d. 1818) and Vahid Bihbahani (d. 1791). Like Bidabadi, he studied philosophy at length under Khajuʿi in Isfahan, as well as other teachers.

Niraqi's written works span a variety of genres.** *Qurrat al-ʿuyun,* a major philosophical treatise on the metaphysics of being completed in 1772, is a testimony to his mastery of philosophical discourse. It is heavily influenced by Sadra as well by the high Sufi tradition as expressed in the school of Ibn ʿArabi, and Niraqi cites both of these names frequently throughout the work, conceptualizing them as ʿarifs rather than Sufis. Sadra is referred to as the *ʿarif-i shirazi,* and overall, *Qurrat al-ʿuyun* illustrates the fact that the received philosophical paradigm had shifted from traditional Peripatetic philosophy Sadra's synthesis.††

* As such, and as part of the process of domestication of Sufism mentioned earlier, *sayr va suluk* can perhaps be understood as a new genre that replaced the traditional Sufi genre of *adab al-muridin.*

† For a brief biography and an extensive bibliography, see Zanuzi, *Riyaz al-janna,* 4:567–74.

‡ For a detailed and wonderful analysis of the intellectual outlook of Mahdi Niraqi in the context of the eighteenth-century religious and cultural trends in Iran and Iraq, see Cole, "Ideology."

§ Fatimi, "Kuhan-tarin sharh," 26–30.

** For a fairly detailed biography and a comprehensive bibliography, see Niraqi, *al-Lumʿa al-ilahiyya,* 1–47.

†† See, for example, Niraqi, "Qurrat al-ʿuyun," 483–86, 495–507, 514ff.

Jamiʿ al-saʿadat is another important work by Niraqi. The popularity of this treatise on ethics increased after Niraqi's son, at the request of Fath-ʿAli Shah (r. 1797–1834), translated it (with some additions) into Persian and gave it the title *Miʿraj al-saʿada*. Niraqi's discussion of the vices and virtues of the soul and the steps one should take to purify it is deeply influenced by Aristotelian virtue ethics, in which virtue is understood primarily in terms of moderation and vice in terms of excess. Niraqi infused this Aristotelian framework with religious language and frequent quotations from the imams. He included many verbatim quotations from Ghazali's *Ihya ʿulum al-din* as well as from Fayz Kashani's *al-Mahajja al-bayza* (which is essentially a Twelver adaptation of Ghazali's work). This is especially true toward the end of the book, where he discussed the etiquette of worship.

Jamiʿ relates to our discussion of ʿirfan in two basic ways. First, it is an excellent example of ʿirfan being invoked as a category. Niraqi used it as such, conceptualizing it as a discipline that stands alongside philosophy and theology and is distinct from Sufism. In the introduction to *Jamiʿ*, he explains that the book is a compendium on ethics, composed of traditions from the Prophet and the imams and a summary of what the pillars of hikma and ʿirfan have said on the subject.* He continues with advice for the pupil embarking on the laborious path of knowledge and learning. In keeping with the overall tenor of the book, he suggests that students avoid obsession with one discipline of knowledge at the expense of the others and that they take a balanced approach, learning from all disciplines in moderation:

> [T]hen, when it comes to the disciplines of knowledge, have a moderate position between the rational esoteric disciplines [*al-ʿulum al-batiniyya al-ʿaqliyya*] and the sharʿi exoteric ones. Don't be among those who limit their perspective to the apparent meaning of the verses and do not learn from the realities they express, those who censure "the ulama of reality" [*ulama al-haqiqa*] and accuse them of unbelief [*zandaqa*] and apostasy [*ilhad*]. Neither be among those who spend their lives on the superfluities of the people of Greece and neglect what the bearer of revelation brought down, censuring "the ulama of the Shariʿa" and characterizing them as people who lack talent but claim for themselves the qualities of astuteness and ingenuity. . . . When it comes to the rational disciplines, take a balanced stance between the many ways of rationalists without rigidly adhering to one particular way out of bias and [blind] imitation. That is to say, retain a balance between hikma, kalam, ishraq, and ʿirfan. Combine arguments with purification of the soul through worship and

* Niraqi, *Jamiʿ al-saʿadat*, 1:34.

> mortification. Do not be a pure theologian who knows nothing except disputations, nor a Peripatetic philosopher who neglected and ruined religion, nor a pseudo-Sufi who grew complacent with claims of visions and realization without arguments or evidence.*

In this passage Niraqi classifies ʿirfan alongside theology and the Peripatetic and Illuminationist schools of philosophy as a discipline concerned with rational inquiry (*ʿaqliyyat*). When we compare Niraqi's classifications to Lahiji's, we observe two important developments. First, the term *ʿirfan* has completely replaced Sufism. Second, Lahiji's view that Sufism cannot be classified alongside other disciplines of knowledge because it is concerned with realization, not discursive knowledge,† is not shared by Niraqi. In fact, we have suggested that, in Niraqi's classification, ʿirfan can be understood as an "esoteric rational" discipline. This difference in conceptualization is best understood in light of the mainstream status Mulla Sadra's thought had achieved among ʿirfan-minded ulama in the time between Lahiji's and Niraqi's lives. The straightforward condemnation of the Peripatetic tradition is an additional testimony to the significant paradigm shift in philosophy compared to the seventeenth century.

Later in the twentieth century, as the category of ʿirfan as a discipline of knowledge expanded and subsumed the traditional category of hikma,‡ the genres that came to be most closely associated with it were ethics and sayr va suluk mentioned earlier. These two genres are usually categorized under the "practical" branch of ʿirfan, known as *ʿirfan-i ʿamali* in contrast to the speculative branch, or *ʿirfan-i nazari*. This division, of course, replicates and sometimes replaces the division of philosophy into practical and speculative (*al-hikma al-ʿamaliyya* versus *al-hikma al-nazariyyra*), which can be traced back to the Greek philosophers themselves. Many of the teachers of ʿirfan in Shiʿi madrasas in the twentieth century are famous for teaching public lessons on ethics, or *dars-i akhlaq*, drawing their audience both from their students and from members of the general public interested in issues related to the spiritual quest (sayr va suluk) and the purification of the soul (*tahzib-i nafs*). Niraqi's *Jamiʿ* and its translation, *Miʿraj*, became textbooks of sorts, providing further guidance to interested parties. Gone were the Sufi pirs that had dotted the landscape of the medieval Islamic world and the Sufi ethos that, as Hodgson eloquently argues,§ stood alongside the Shariʿa as a moral backbone

* Niraqi, *Jamiʿ al-saʿadat*, 1:119.

† Lahiji, *Gawhar-i murad*, 38–40.

‡ Hikma itself is used as a more acceptable and less stigmatized replacement for the term *falsafa* (philosophy).

§ Hodgson, *Venture of Islam*, 2:204.

to the social order. In post-Safavid Twelver Iran, akhlaq emerged as a substitute moral framework that complemented the Shariʿa and helped the average Shiʿi Muslim understand what it means to live a good life.

Another fascinating indication of how much ʿirfan had replaced Sufism in the language of mystically minded Twelver ulama by the end of the eighteenth century is found toward the end of *Jamiʿ*, where the author lists six groups of people most susceptible to the vice of conceit (*ghurur*). Among them are pseudo-Sufis, preachers, and the folk of knowledge (that is, the ulama). Naraqi's criticisms of pseudo-Sufis, though similar in content to those discussed previously, are unique in one aspect: he uses the designations *Sufi* and *ʿarif* interchangeably, even in his condemnations. For the first time, we witness the phrase *pseudo-ʿarifin* (*mutashabbihun bi al-ʿurafa*) used as a counterpart to the phrase *pseudo-Sufis* to condemn those who portray themselves as ʿarifin despite lacking proper knowledge of or experience on the spiritual path. Such people, he says, think if they resemble the "true ʿarifin in their lifestyle (*ziyy*), appearance, etiquette (*adab*), customs (*marasim*), and vocabulary," they have succeeded in reaching advanced stages of "ʿirfan and Sufism."* The use of the term *pseudo-ʿarif* is significant for two reasons. First, like Nayrizi's use of the term *pseudo-faqir*, it demonstrates how the term *Sufi* no longer carries the positive semantic associations that made the contrast with the term *pseudo-Sufi* meaningful. In its stead are the terms *ʿarif* and *ʿirfan*, which had come to be associated with a desirable model of spirituality, against which the pseudo-ʿarif stands in contrast. Second, putting true ʿarifin in apposition to pseudo-ʿarifin may be a reflection of conflicts within the early community of madras-trained ʿarifin or a reflection of the power dynamics involved in the early phases of the institutionalization of ʿirfan.† Further research is needed, however, to determine whether there is evidence to support this hypothesis.

Niraqi's reference to the lifestyle, appearance, code of conduct, customs, and vocabulary of the true ʿarifin makes it clear that his idea of true ʿarifin

* Niraqi, *Jamiʿ al-saʿadat*, 3:29–30. Much later, Muhammad Bahari Hamadani (d. 1907), a well-known student of Mulla Husayn-Quli Hamadani, a sought-after ʿarif and teacher of ethics, eschewed any mention of the terms *Sufi* or *pseudo-Sufi* in a section of his *Tazkirat al-muttaqin*, which is clearly inspired by Niraqi. Hamadani used only the terms *ʿirfan* and *ʿarif* when he discussed how some people are deluded to think of themselves as such. See Hamadani, *Tazkirat al-muttaqin*, 116.

† The term *Sufism* went through a similar process in the early Islamic centuries. As Sufism gained more popularity and a Sufi lifestyle developed that visibly distinguished its adherents from other groups, the term *pseudo-Sufi* emerged in reference to those who were not sincere in following the lifestyle but were interested only in the social capital that such a title provided. See Bahari Karamustafa, *Sufism: The Formative Period*, 99–100.

was not limited to elitist members of the ulama well versed in Mulla Sadra's school of philosophy and Ibn ʿArabi's mysticism. His remarks about Sufis and their beliefs and practices make it clear that he was willing to include some of the signature practices of Sufism in the portfolio of ʿirfan as long as the issue of spiritual authority was squarely understood within the Twelver Shiʿi framework laid out by the ulama.

An interesting example of this can be found at the end of a fascinating monograph titled *Mushkilat al-ʿulum,* which was inspired by the *kashkul* genre and which brings together a variety of unrelated topics. In it, Niraqi tackled the tricky issue of how to distinguish between authentic tradition (sunna) and heretical innovation (bidʿa). The question had been discussed in a variety of contexts long before Niraqi's time, but he appears to have been interested in applying it to the etiquette of spiritual quest as developed by the folk of mortification (*ahl al-riyazat*).* The stakes were high for the mystically minded. Sufi practices of zikr often involve detailed observances related to number, occasion, place, and manner, and these specifications are often not supported by hadith. As such, are they misguided innovations or beneficial traditions? Niraqi was quite aware of the controversy surrounding this issue, and in his introductory remarks he notes that the "opinions of the learned" are often confused, to say the least, when it comes to this matter.† As a highly educated religious scholar, he approached the issue in a systematic way reminiscent of arguments in usul al-fiqh (and he was, in fact, more inclined to the Usuli camp). The details of his argument involve technical vocabulary and are not always directly related to the topic under examination here, but I find it imperative to offer a synopsis because of the ramifications I believe his arguments had on subsequent developments of ʿirfan.

Niraqi begins his argument with a broad classification of religious matters, which, he says, can be divided into two categories: the prescribed (*taʿabuddi*) and the preparatory (*tavassuli*). The former refers to matters prescribed by divine law because of their inherent religious value and direct relevance to one's eternal salvation (for example, the Hajj). The latter describes any matter that, while not of inherent religious value, prepares the conditions necessary for a prescribed act to be performed. An example of this is the journey to Mecca one must take in order to perform the Hajj. Niraqi makes further divisions to the category of prescribed matters, separating them into matters of choice (*taʿabbudi-takhiyri*) and matters of stipulation (*taʿabbudi-taʿyini*). The former refers to religious matters in which only the essence or spirit of a specific duty is required. Examples of this are almsgiving

* Niraqi, *Mushkilat al-ʿulum,* 366.
† Niraqi, *Mushkilat al-ʿulum,* 366.

(*sadaqa*), remembering God, and performing general supplications (*mutlaq al-zikr va al-duʿa*), which are required but the forms of which are left up to the worshipper. The latter, by contrast, refers to religious matters in which the worshiper is required to perform a duty in a specific manner stipulated by divine law. This includes matters such as daily prayers and the Hajj rituals.

The upshot of Niraqi's argument is that change leads to innovation only in matters of stipulation. When it comes to matters of choice (*taʿabbudi-takhyiri*), innovation results only if a change in practice interferes with the *essence* of what is prescribed. For example, Niraqi says, if one decides to commit oneself to a certain number of recitations of a specific name of God in a particular place or posture, this does not count as innovation as long as (1) such details are not in violation of any divine injunctions as explained in the Shariʿa and, more important, (2) the worshipper does not present such details as matters of divine prescription or consider them to be such. Similarly, if a worshipper commits herself to a particular preparatory routine (*tavassuli*) to achieve the conditions necessary to accomplish a prescribed religious duty, her actions could not be categorized as innovation as long as the two caveats are avoided. Both caveats are of the utmost relevance to the issue at hand. First, Sufis have routinely been accused of violating the Shariʿa because of their adherence to practices of bodily mortification not usually found in the sacred canon. Second, Sufis have historically held that their practices, such as unique formulas for zikr, have inherent religious value (*al-mashruʿiyya va al-matlubiyya al-zatiyya*) and have believed that deviation from such formulas renders the practice inefficacious.

Niraqi has an interesting solution, however. After a bit of back and forth, he ultimately agrees that technical and elaborate Sufi practices like the hidden zikr (*zikr-i khafi*) fall under the purview of the principle of *al-tasamuh fi adilla al-sunan* in jurisprudence. This principle is derived from reports of the imams that state that if someone hears a report that God has designated specific rewards for a specific action and, on the basis of that report, performs that action, that person will get the expected reward even if the report has no basis in reality.* Because of such hadith, jurists have been more relaxed in their approach to verifying reports that deal with supererogatory acts of worship. The only caveat, says Niraqi, is that this principle applies only when the trustworthiness of the person reporting the hadith is not seriously doubted—that is, if there is no grounds to believe that there was an evil agenda behind the concocting of that hadith. For Niraqi, this means that the report must have come from a sincere Shiʿi person numbered among either

* Niraqi, *Mushkilat al-ʿulum*, 367–68. Such reports are known as *man balagha-hu al-savab* (lit. to whomever it reaches, the reward).

the orthodox ulama or righteous people renowned for their piety. The reason so many practices passed down to us by Sufis have been classified as innovation, Niraqi says, is that their "Shiʿism is not clear, and more, they are often known as liars and for their corruption of beliefs."* Conversely, if a respected religious scholar or a sincere Shiʿa reports a similar practice, it should be accepted as a legitimate tradition with inherent religious value. The bottom line is that the legitimacy of practices such as the hidden zikr depends on who reports or practices them. Niraqi goes even farther, saying that as long as we follow the right people, whether or not what they do or report originated with the imams is not a deal breaker. In other words, practices that trustworthy people have found in their own personal experience (*tajribat nafsahu*) to be efficacious can be considered legitimate, and the term *innovation* does not apply to them. "It is not unlikely," he says, "that it is permitted to act on its basis."† Given the long list of ʿirfan-friendly ulama established by men such as Muʾazzin, Darabi, and Nayrizi, Niraqi would have had no problem finding the "right" people to justify the practices he wished to adopt from Sufism.

This argument reminds us once again that the issue of ʿirfan versus Sufism was ultimately more about religious authority than theology. It also gives us an understanding of the impulse to attribute sayr va suluk texts, with their detailed instructions on zikr formulas and other similar material, to respected Shiʿi scholars such as Bidabadi and Bahr al-ʿUlum, who were known for their impeccable piety. Doing so created much-needed space for the next generation of ʿirfan-minded ulama, people like Mulla ʿAbd al-Samad Hamadani, Kashif Dizfuli, and Mulla Ahmad Niraqi, to speak more explicitly and in greater detail about such practices.

Mulla Ahmad Niraqi (d. 1829), who inherited many of his father's traits as a polymath and a mystically minded religious scholar, has, for example, an extensive discussion of hidden zikr in his *Kitab al-khazaʾin* (*The Book of Treasures*, completed after 1813).‡ This marvelous kashkul work contains passages from many sources on a variety of topics, from technical details of the astrolabe, numerology, and mathematical problems to more quotidian but admittedly important problems including how to heal someone bitten by a dog and premature ejaculation. Not surprisingly, in spite of the fact that many passages in the text are taken from or inspired by Sufi literature, Niraqi Jr. is successful in completely avoiding the term *Sufism* and its related cognates, using in their place the phrase *ahl-i ʿirfan*. As is customary in this genre,

* Niraqi, *Mushkilat al-ʿulum*, 368.
† Niraqi, *Mushkilat al-ʿulum*, 368.
‡ Niraqi, *Khazaʾin*, 422.

the author sometimes quotes extensively from unique sources at his disposal that he believes deserve to be preserved for later generations. An important source used by Niraqi Jr. in his discussion of hidden zikr is the Nurbakhshi literature preserved in the network's khanaqah in Kashan, which was also the resting place of the charismatic master Asadullah Quhpaʾi (d. 1638), otherwise known as Qazi Asad. We know that Niraqi's hometown, Niraq (which is located close to Isfahan), and the city of his residence, Kashan, were both strong Nurbakhshi strongholds. Among Niraqi's contemporaries was an active Nurbakhshi shaykh, ʿAbd al-Vahhab Naʾini (d. 1797), a disciple of Muhammad-Taqi Shahi, whom I mentioned as a contemporary and companion of Nayrizi.* Although information about the situation of Nurbakhshi khanaqah in Kashan during the eighteenth century is lacking, it is clear that Nurbakhshi literature, including the writings of Mirza Muhammad Bidguli (d. after 1665),† otherwise known as Muhaqqiq Ardabili,‡ was available to both Mulla Muhammad Mahdi and to his son Mulla Ahmad.§

In *Khazaʾin,* Niraqi Jr. lays out different techniques of hidden zikr that have reached him through various Sufi sources.** The bulk of his exposition is taken almost verbatim from Muhaqqiq Ardabili's *Tazkirat al-zakirin.* This is followed by the lineage of the latter's Nurbakhshi spiritual masters,†† which is followed in turn by another discussion of the seven levels of zikr. After this concludes, we find a substantial quote from *Hadiyya al-khayr* by Hasan b. Qasim Nurbakhsh, grandson of the founder of the Nurbakhshi Sufi network. The quotation includes technical details concerning the specific motions involved in the practice of zikr.‡‡ This extensive (and approving) quotation of Nurbakhshi sources, especially in the context of the kashkul genre, does not mean that Niraqi was affiliated with that Sufi network or that the

* Naʾini was based in his hometown as a Sufi shaykh and was buried there near the tomb of another Nurbakhshi master, Sayyid Muhammad Lahsavi Nurbakhsi (d. 903). See Maʿsum-ʿAli Shah, *Taraʾiq al-haqaʾiq,* 3:159 and 215–16.

† See Shamlu, *Qisas al-khaqani,* 2:197.

‡ As his title indicates, he was at the same time an erudite Twelver religious scholar. This was a boon to Niraqi in his reliance on Bidguli's authority on the issue of zikr.

§ Niraqi Sr. mentions the two Sufi networks of Nurbakhshiyya and Naqshbandiyya in his "Qurrat al-ʿuyun." See Niraqi, "Qurrat al-ʿuyun," 549.

** Niraqi, *Khazaʾin,* 405–6.

†† Ardabili Bidguli, *Tazkirat al-zakirin* MS, 50–53 and 89–95. This work has been published recently thanks to the efforts of Afshin Atefi, but at the time of writing I do not yet have access to the printed version. Cf. Niraqi, *Khazaʾin,* 407.

‡‡ Niraqi, *Khazaʾin,* 408–11. Interestingly, all the Nurbakhshi treatises mentioned are still held in the library of the Sultani madrasa, one of the most beautiful monuments dating from the Safavid period and the place where both Niraqis taught for many years.

Nurbakhshis had a corporate presence at the time in Kashan. It does, however, strongly suggest that he viewed the Nurbakhshis as part of the larger Twelver heritage and their Sufi pursuit a legitimate one. From his perspective, they could be counted among the true ʿarifin.

The inclusion of hidden zikr among the legitimate spiritual practices of Twelver Shiʿism is significant, but it is also important to note how Niraqi's discussion of this practice marks a meaningful shift in the way controversial Sufi practices were treated. Figures discussed earlier in this book, such as Muʿazzin, Najib, and Darabi, dedicated a considerable portion of their writings to defending practices including vocal zikr, the use of music and dance in conjunction with it, and the occasional trance. Mystically minded ulama of the late eighteenth century such as the Niraqis, however, seem to have been less interested in these conspicuous communal practices. Instead, they focused on practices such as hidden zikr, which, in addition to being performed in silence with less fanfare, is an individual practice that does not necessarily need to happen in a communal setting. As ʿirfan found a new institutional home in the madrasa, it adapted to etiquette of the ulama, who found it beneath their dignity to engage in ceremonies such as samaʿ, which might involve unimaginable breaches of decorum including losing control in front of one's students (something any young *talib* would likely find very entertaining!).

Lest I be accused of idle speculation, I would like to draw my reader's attention to a fascinating story from a mid-seventeenth-century source mentioned earlier, Muhaqqiq Ardabili's *Tazkirat al-zakirin*. It contains a vivid account of how dervishes felt the need to restrain themselves in their own zikr sessions in deference to some visiting ulama: "One night," recounts Ardabili, "we were on a retreat in the courtyard of the Haji Dusa (or Dusar) Mosque in the village of Bidgul in the presence of our master (Qazi Asad, peace be upon him). As was customary, when it came time to gather, I attended the samaʿ session. That particular night, many people were there from the city to visit the master, some exoteric ulama among them. Although my heart began to convulse from the effects of the zikr and yearning [*shawq*], my previous acquaintance with the visitors overshadowed that mood. Diffidence [*haya*] overwhelmed me, and I decided to distract my soul from trance [*vajd*] and presence [*huzur*]. At the time of yearning [*shawq*], I forced myself to return from ecstasy [*hal*], not making a single move, clamping shut my mouth while convulsing from within until the session was over and the people dispersed."*

This fascinating report reflects the dynamics of the mid-seventeenth cen-

* Ardabili Bidguli, *Tazkirat al-zakirin* MS, 65–66.

tury, when the Sufi shaykh still had the social capital to attract a large following and to induce the ulama to come and visit him at the khanaqah. By Niraqi's time, the situation had changed dramatically. In the late and post-Safavid era, social capital was invested mainly in the madrasa, which was home to the standard-bearers of the newly emerged tradition of Shiʿi ʿirfan. The elder Niraqi's arguments might well be applied to Sufi practices beyond the hidden zikr, but many such practices were nonetheless incompatible with the etiquette practiced by an institution housed in the madrasa. By the end of the eighteenth century, even the Zahabis, one of the few surviving Sufi network that retained some of the important organizational and communal elements of the old Sufi tradition, had abandoned the practice of vocal zikr and samaʿ, and their qutb no longer donned the dervish cloak. Instead, he was a trainee of the madrasa and, socially speaking, an esteemed member of the ulama.

In conclusion, it is worth mentioning that Niraqi Jr., like Bidabadi, was suspicious of the claims to spiritual authority inherent in the category of spiritual master. He spends several pages in *Khaza'in* detailing the qualifications requisite for master and disciple. The list in its entirety is taken verbatim from classical Sufi sources such as *Mirsad al-ʿibad.* At the end of the list he confirms the necessity of all such qualifications, but he includes a compelling reminder that only the infallible imams embody the qualities of a spiritual master. Thus, he says, it is "imperative to take murshid and shaykh from the imams."* He adds that it is extremely difficult for any novice to distinguish between a true master and a charlatan. Finding guidance in the teachings of the imams is a safer and less treacherous path, says Niraqi, and therefore there is no reason for the novice to go to anyone other than the imams for spiritual leadership.† Additionally, although Niraqi Jr. endorses the controversial Sufi meditational technique of visualizing the face of the shaykh and meditating upon it, he immediately qualifies his endorsement by making it clear that "shaykh" in the context of this practice can only be one of the imams.‡

A similar position on the religious legitimacy of hidden zikr is found in a widely read work of ʿirfan by Mulla ʿAbd al-Samad Hamadani, another prominent ʿirfan-minded religious scholar of the second half of the eighteenth century. In his *Bahr al-maʿarif,* Hamadani defends the legitimacy of this practice in much the same manner as Niraqi Sr., arguing that such practices do

* Niraqi, *Khaza'in,* 501.
† Niraqi, *Khaza'in,* 498.
‡ Niraqi, *Khaza'in,* 506.

not need to be found in hadith literature with a verifiable chain of transmission to be legitimate. Rather, it suffices to have the word of a trustworthy master who says that such a practice has been handed down to him generation by generation from the imams. Hamadani continues his discussion of hidden zikr by offering a detailed account of the specific gestures and movements entailed in that practice, followed by the spiritual chain of transmission through which he claims to have received such a formula. In contrast to Niraqi Jr.'s reliance on the Nurbakhshi lineage, Hamadani relies on a chain of transmission that goes back to Shah Niʿmatullah Vali (d. 1431), the purported founder of the Niʿmatullahi Sufi network.* This is a result of Hamadani's close relationship, and even possible affiliation, with Niʿmatullahi masters of his time who had been sent from India to revive Sufism in the Shiʿi realm of Iran and Iraq. A proper understanding of the developments of Sufism and ʿirfan during the nineteenth century is impossible without taking into account this development.

The Niʿmatullahi Revival

In the final decade of the eighteenth century, a significant event rocked the mystical landscape of Persia. Three centuries after disappearance of the Niʿmatullahi network from Persia and the migration of its leaders to India, the Sufi network was reintroduced into Iran. A detailed analysis of this event and the related cultural, social, and intellectual developments in the nineteenth century would fill a voluminous book, but here I offer a brief overview and a few observations in the hope that scholars researching this issue will find points of engagement and connection with my own study.

The Niʿmatullahi network is named for one of the most celebrated masters in classical Persian Sufism, Shah Niʿmatullah Vali. It began as a dynamic spiritual movement in Iran, but with the departure of Niʿmatullahi's prominent successor, Shah Khalilullah (d. 1455), to India and the premature death of the latter's son, Mir Shams al-Din (d. 1450), the network declined rapidly in Persia and by 1450 was little more than a moribund family tradition. The network flourished in India, however, where its spiritual center was located in the Deccan.

More than three centuries later, with the power of the clerical hierocracy in Iran weakened in the aftermath of the Safavid downfall, the Niʿmatullahis of India decided to send missionaries to Iran to renew their network there and give life to organized Sufism, which had fallen into near obsolescence. Shah Tahir Dakani and, later, Maʿsum-ʿAli Shah (d. 1796 or 1797) were sent

* Hamadani, *Bahr al-maʿarif,* 1:233–34.

to Iran by Sayyid ʿAli-Riza Shah (d. 1799), the shaykh of the Niʿmatullahi khanaqah in India.* Zayn al-ʿAbidin Shirvani, a contemporary historian and traveler and a Niʿmatullahi himself, describes in his writings the situation of organized Sufism before the arrival of these emissaries:

> For nearly sixty years [after the fall of Isfahan] the country of Iran was empty of mystical knowledge [*maʿarif-i ʿirfan*], and no one had heard the name of the tariqa . . . except for a few dervishes [fuqara] in the holy city of Mashhad from the Nurbakhshi path and some in Shiraz from the Zahabi path who were hidden in obscure corners. If there were some in other places, they avoided publicity. . . . The name of the tariqa in Iran had become [as hard to find] as alchemy and the Simurgh [a mythical bird] until the reviver of the esteemed lineage and the illuminator of the Razavi tariqa, the martyr in the way of God, Sayyid Maʿsum-ʿAli Shah, may he rest in peace, came from the Deccan to Iran upon the orders of the perfect shaykh, Shah ʿAli-Riza Vali, toward the end of the reign of Karim Khan.†

When Maʿsum-ʿAli Shah arrived in Shiraz in 1776–1777, the city was a thriving and peaceful environment under the rule of Karim Khan, the Zand ruler who is said to have had a cordial relationship with the Zahabi Sufis of Shiraz and especially with Nayrizi's successor, Aqa Muhammad Hashim Darvish (d. 1784).‡ In the relatively secure and prosperous environment provided by the Zand dynasty and the figure of Karim Khan, the Zahabis took advantage of the cordial relationship between the ruling party and the Zahabi upper echelon to secure their stronghold in Shiraz. The economic situation and social standing of the network improved even more dramatically after Darvish Hashim's daughter wed Mirza ʿAbd al-Nabi Sharifi (d. 1815), who became Hashim's successor as pole of the Zahabi network. Sharifi's family were the custodians of the shrine of Shah Chiragh, the city's most important religious site and the recipient of large religious endowments and donations.§

* For a brief account of Niʿmatullahi history, see Algar and Page, "Niʿmat-Allāhiyya."

† Shirvani, *Hada'iq al-siyaha* MS, 39.

‡ See, for example, Sharifi Shirazi, *Tarikh-i hayat,* 22–23, and Darvish Shirazi, *Manahil al-tahqiq,* 4–5. Lewisohn mistakenly identifies his death date as 1776. See Lewisohn, "Modern Persian Sufism, Part II," 37. Lewisohn also mistakenly claims that Darvish Shirazi was the first to put the spiritual genealogy of his order in verse. In fact, it was Najib al-Din Riza Isfahani who did so. See Tabrizi Isfahani, *Sabʿ al-masani,* 345–85. For 1784 as Darvish Hashim's death date see Nayyiri's research in Darvish Shirazi, *Manahil al-tahqiq,* 57. Nayyeri's introduction to *Manahil al-tahqiq* is the most comprehensive and accurate account we have of Darvish Shirazi's life and works.

§ Khavari, *Zahabiyya,* 344–48.

Unlike their Zahabi brethren, Maʿsum and his close disciples did not receive a friendly welcome from the political establishment or the clerical hierocracy. The Niʿmatullahis' problems with the Zand authorities were likely related to the network's alliance with the Qajars, who were locked in a power struggle with the Zand dynasty.* Additionally, they may have been perceived as having their own political ambitions.† The ulama's objections to the Niʿmatullahis, however, had partly to do with the latter's "foreign" and unorthodox outlook, practices, and teachings. The contrast between the way Zahabis and Niʿmatullahis were received speaks clearly to how extensively the Safavid nomos had changed the profile of a Sufi network. By this time, Zahabi shaykhs had given up their distinctive Sufi garb and embraced the standard attire of the ulama in order to put to rest the suspicions of religious puritans. The unremarkable scholarly appearance of the Zahabi masters stood in stark contrast to the wild sight of the passionate Sufi fresh from India, decked out in dervish cloaks with all their associated paraphernalia and with flowing hair uncut like a Qalandar's.‡

Maʿsum's charismatic personality led to the conversion of several men who became extremely devout disciples, and their musical expertise, beautiful voices, and attractive miens seem to have added to the appeal of the movement.§ The disciples came from extremely diverse sociocultural backgrounds. Some had been trained in the madrasa, while others were uneducated. Among the former was Maʿsum's first disciple, Fayz-ʿAli Shah (d. 1784), who is said to have been a Nurbakhshi Sufi prior to joining his master.** Another learned disciple was Nur-ʿAli Shah, who is described as being very handsome and as having exquisite taste and facility in composing poetry. Mushtaq-ʿAli Shah (d. 1791) was a professional instrumentalist and vocalist.†† These men traveled extensively in Iran and Mesopotamia, including to the

* Amanat, *Resurrection and Renewal,* 75.

† Van den Bos, *Mystic Regimes,* 59–60.

‡ Maʿsum-ʿAli Shah, *Taraʾiq al-haqaʾiq,* 3:175.

§ Royce, "Mir Maʿsum ʿAli Shah," 102.

** See Malcolm, *History of Persia,* 2:295 (footnote). This is yet more evidence of the fact that the Nurbakhshi Sufi network had a considerable presence in major Iranian cities including Mashhad, Shiraz, and Kashan. See also Royce, "Mir Maʿsum ʿAli Shah," 95–96. Royce's unpublished dissertation remains, I believe, the most accurate scholarly account of the career of Maʿsum in Iran. Several other pieces of scholarship were produced later. A summary of what can be found in Niʿmatullahi and other sympathetic sources is provided in Lewisohn, "Modern Persian Sufism, Part I." A more critical reading can be accessed in Amanat, *Resurrection and Renewal,* 71–80.

†† See Maʿsum-ʿAli Shah, *Taraʾiq al-haqaʾiq,* 3:175 and 194–95. On the popularity of his music see Royce, "Mir Maʿsum ʿali Shah," 108.

holy city of Karbala, and were reportedly extremely successful in attracting a large number of followers in a short span of time.*

The Niʿmatullahis' purportedly antinomian behavior and rapid success alarmed the ulama, and, as a result, a second anti-Sufi campaign was launched. A survey of bibliographical compendiums such as Aqa Bozorg's *al-Zariʿa* shows a dramatic spike in the composition of anti-Sufi treatises beginning in the last decade of the eighteenth century and continuing into the second decade of the nineteenth century.†

It is interesting to note that, unlike the first anti-Sufi campaign of the Safavid period, in which Akhbari-leaning ulama took the lead, this time the overwhelming majority of attacks were penned by Usuli ulama.‡ This is primarily a result of the severe setbacks suffered by the Akhbari school in the ʿAtabat, which can be attributed mainly to the efforts of the renowned Usuli mujtahid Muhammad-Baqir Bihbahani, otherwise known as Vahid Bihbahani. In Algar's words, "Before Behbahani's appearance on the scene, the Ak̲baris were so assured in their dominance of Karbala that no one dared openly to carry books of Oṣuli *feqh*, but by the end of his life he had almost

* Malcolm, *History of Persia,* 2:295, 298, and 299. Amanat's analysis of Malcolm's account is also helpful. See Amanat, *Resurrection and Renewal,* 80.

† Here is a partial bibliography of anti-Sufi works written between 1795 and 1820:

Mirza Abu al-Qasim Qummi, several small treatises gathered in *Jamiʿ al-shattat* (completed in 1798). See Tehrani, *al-Zariʿa,* 5:59–60. In 1814 he wrote another treatise addressed to Fath-ʿAli Shah in response to a prominent pro-Sufi member of the Qajar court. See Mirza Abu al-Qasim Qummi, *Risala-yi radd-i sufiyya* MS.

Aqa Muhammad-ʿAli Bihbahani (d. 1801), *al-Khayratiyya fi ibtal tariqat al-sufiyya* (compiled between 1796–1799), and *Qatʿ al-maqal fi radd-i ahl al-zilal.*

Aqa Muhammad-Jaʿfar Kirmanshahi (eldest son of Aqa Muhammad-ʿAli, d. 1843), *Fazayih al-sufiyya* (completed in 1807).

Aqa Mahmud Kirmanshahi (the fourth son of Aqa Muhammad-ʿAli, d. 1852), *Tanbih al-ghafilin va iqaz al-raqidin* (completed in 1813).

Mirza Muhammad-Riza Qazvini, *al-Mataʿin al-mudhnibiyya fi radd al-sufiyya* (completed in 1820). See Tehrani, *al-Zariʿa,* 21:139.

Muhammad-Kazim Hazarjaribi (d. ca. 1816–22), *Irshad al-munsifin va ilzam al-mulhidin.* For an interesting description of him see Shirvani, *Bustan al-siyaha,* 2:1433. Like Mir Lawhi, Shirvani says, Hazarjaribi was known as "Kazim Laʿnati." Also see Tehrani, *al-Zariʿa,* 1:523.

Mir Muhammad-Taqi Kashmiri, *al-Radd ʿala al-sufiyya.* See Tehrani, *al-Zariʿa,* 10:206.

Mawla Hasan b. Muhammad-ʿAli Yazdi, *al-Radd ʿala al-sufiyya* (completed in 1815). See Tehrani, *al-Zariʿa,* 10:206.

‡ A similar dynamic between the Usuli ulama and the Sufis was developing around the same time in the Shiʿi communities of North India. See Cole, *North Indian Shiʿism,* 152–58.

completely uprooted Akbari influence from the *ʿatabat*."* Bihbahani's son, Muhammad Baqir, and two of his grandsons were all Usuli mujtahids, and each played a major role in the wave of opposition to Sufism that swept across Iran.

Another major difference between the first and second campaigns was that the second was not confined to rhetoric. Vahid Bihbahani's persecution of Akhbaris using techniques such as takfir and even brutal violence (he is said to have been constantly accompanied by a cadre of *mirghazabs* who doled out corporal and capital punishment)† served as an example for anti-Sufi jurists, many of whom were Bihbahani's students. They employed all means possible to persecute the newly arrived Sufis and stem the rapid rise to popularity of Maʿsum and his initial circle of Niʿmatullahi dervishes. Sources tell us that some of Maʿsum's opponents exploited the title of shah (king) in his name to make authorities suspicious that he was pursuing an undercover political agenda.‡ Between 1791 and 1802, several prominent Niʿmatullahis were murdered, and Muhammad-ʿAli Bihbahani (d. 1801) went down in history as the Sufi Killer (*sufi-kush*) for his involvement in some of these killings.§ Mushtaq-ʿAli and one of his disciples, Jaʿfar-ʿAli, were beaten and stoned to death in 1791 by a mob in Kirman that attacked them after being stirred up by a puritan preacher. Maʿsum-ʿAli was detained and murdered on the order of Bihbahani in Kirmanshah in 1796 or 1797, and Bihbahani was also involved in the murder of Muzaffar-ʿAli Shah, a prominent disciple of Mushtaq-ʿAli in 1800. Nur-ʿAli Shah was also poisoned in Mosul in 1797, most probably by the agents of the Sufi Killer. Muʿattar-ʿAli Shah, another disciple of Mushtaq, was beaten to death in 1802.**

The final difference in this anti-Sufi campaign that I would like to mention is the direct role of the state. As Amanat has observed, "the . . . persecution of Niʿmatullahis was the first successful case of the ulama's vigorous campaign to involve the government in the task of eradicating religious dissent."†† The previous anti-Sufi campaign, as we saw, was carried out with the tacit approval of the Safavid state, but the state did not play a direct role. This was not the case with the Qajar dynasty, which rose to power in Iran in 1794, and state involvement in Sufi persecution increased further with the

* Algar, "Behbahānī, Moḥammad-Bāqer."

† Algar, *Religion and State in Iran,* 35–36.

‡ Maʿsum-ʿAli Shah, *Taraʾiq al-haqaʾiq,* 3:172.

§ See Algar, "Behbahānī, Moḥammad-ʿAlī."

** Like his father, he is "reputed to have remarked to a colleague, Shaikh Jaʿfar Najafi, 'I am constantly obliged to carry out various sentences of execution and corporal punishment [hadd].'" Algar, "Behbahānī, Moḥammad-ʿAlī."

†† Amanat, *Resurrection and Renewal,* 78.

1797 coronation of the second Qajar king, Fath-ʿAli Shah, who had a warm relationship with the Shiʿite hierocracy. Shirvani includes an interesting report in *Bustan al-siyaha* that gives us a sense of Fath-ʿAli's hostility toward Sufis. According to this story, the king, who respected Shirvani, summoned the latter to his presence twice in the year 1230 (1814–1815). The monarch advised him to cut his ties with Sufism because of concerns that the king had for Shirvani's safety: "[I]n my country," the king says, "all kinds of nations live in peace and tranquility except for dervishes and the sect of Sufis. Why do you not relinquish your dervishhood and relax under the shadow of our mercy? Because our relationship with the Sufis is not friendly . . . all the populace has become enemies of the dervishes and hostile toward Sufis, and they will bother you."* The powerful collaboration between state and religious hierocracy that had functioned so effectively to preserve and promote the interests of both against rival social entities had been reinstituted. The only difference was that the hierocracy, having had more than a hundred years to refine its power structures, was in a much stronger position vis-à-vis the newly established Qajar dynasty than it had been vis-à-vis the Safavids. The Qajars had a greater need than their predecessors for the ulama to function as underwriters of their rule and help establish the dynasty's legitimacy in the eyes of the public.†

The contrast between the brutal persecution experienced by the Niʿmatullahis and the relatively peaceful and prosperous situation of the Zahabis in the same period demonstrates the extent to which the lifestyle of people who identified with organized Sufism had transformed in the past century and a half in conformance to the religious norms and modes of piety of Safavid Shiʿism. Niʿmatullahi leaders fresh out of India in the late eighteenth century and early nineteenth century adhered to Sufi teachings, used Sufi language, and clung to Sufi institutions and practices that had long disappeared from the Iranian landscape. They did not have the long history of interaction with the ulama and cultural forces of Iran that gave the Zahabis an understanding of how to survive in a religious environment where the clerical hierocracy had powerful resources to systematically suppress rival religious visions. Mystically minded thinkers such as Darabi were so acculturated into the new nomos that they could articulate doctrines giving deputyship of the Hidden Imam to the ulama, while retaining space for esotericism by stipulating that those ulama be masters of both exoteric and esoteric aspects of religion. Not so the Niʿmatullahis, who directly challenged "the theoretical

* Shirvani, *Bustan al-siyaha,* 2:1284.

† For a detailed analysis of the relationship between the ulama and the state during the Qajar period, see Algar, *Religion and State in Iran,* 1–109.

foundations of the collective deputyship of the ulama. In their view, the qutb, the spiritual and secular leader of the Sufi network, rather than the ulama in their entirety should be considered to be the special representatives of the Hidden Imam."*

It took the newcomer Niʿmatullahis some time to come to terms with the reality of the hostile environment toward Sufis in Iran. After a couple of decades, however, as their masters worked to make the network more conformist and orthodox-friendly, they gradually adjusted to the new cultural landscape. Unlike the early masters, who had little or no education in the religious disciplines taught in madrasas, later masters routinely went through madrasa training and achieved advanced levels of knowledge in exoteric matters. This "was reflected in a moderated imagery, and in the fact that each of the network's qutbs would now also be a mulla."† In the process, however, Niʿmatullahis ceased to be an influential religious force among the populace. After the initial phase of hostility and persecution, the Niʿmatullahi Sufi worldview ultimately became a subordinate mode of piety whose reach was confined to a limited social network, an elite Sufi in-group well that some scholars have characterized as aristocratic‡ because several prominent members of the Qajar family, including Crown Prince ʿAbbas Mirza (d. 1833), joined the network.§ The Niʿmatullahi presence in court circles gave the network political impact beyond its numbers, and Niʿmatullahis were important interlocutors in elite religious and political circles. As modern Western ideas spread through different levels of Iranian society beginning in the second half of the nineteenth century, members of the network were at the center of some of the most hotly contested debates.

It is important to remember, however, that the network did not have a unified position on these debates. The history of the Niʿmatullahi network in late nineteenth-century Iran was one of widespread and bitter infighting between several branches of the Niʿmatullahi establishment.** As a result, different groups of Niʿmatullahis came to answer vexing questions of the time, especially those related to the introduction of modern, Western ideas into Iran, in different ways. Some branches supported the old tradition of kingship, for example, but others pioneered modern intellectual and political concepts such as democracy and secularism. Their response to the category of

* Scharbrodt, "Quṭb as Special Representative," 41.

† Van den Bos, *Mystic Regimes,* 62.

‡ On the use of "aristocratic," see Van den Bos, *Mystic Regimes,* 62, note 89.

§ For an anthropologically informed analysis of this important development, see Van den Bos, *Mystic Regimes,* 52–67.

** For a brief account of these splits, see Van den Bos, *Mystic Regimes,* 76–80. A much more detailed account can be found in Lewisohn, "Modern Persian Sufism, Part II."

ʿirfan was also varied. More traditional branches such as the Gunabadis preferred the use of Sufism, considering it a more sacred term than *ʿirfan,* but others embraced the latter designation under the influence of modernity.

Conclusion

As mentioned earlier, my account of post-Safavid developments in ʿirfan only scratch the surface. In addition to the Niʿmatullahi revival, which I treated briefly, any serious research into alternative models of spirituality and piety in nineteenth-century Iran cannot overlook the single most transformative event in the religious history of early modern Iran: the emergence of the Babi sect and its eventual formulation as the Bahaʾi religion. While neither of these important religious movements can be analyzed in detail in this book, I would like to make some broad observation about how the developments related to the emergence of ʿirfan are in fact connected to the religious turmoil of the nineteenth-century Iran.

Damavandi's claims to have received initiation and spiritual direction from Muhammad and Imam Husayn and his assertions that he was given special knowledge by the Mahdi in his dreams and visions, discussed earlier, represent a highly significant and creative attempt to fill in the void that was left in the aftermath of the stigmatization of the concept of the pir as a socially grounded and institutionally defined guide as defined in traditional Sufi networks. In his recourse to this form of otherworldly, mysterious, and abstract master/disciple relationship imagined between the seeker and the invisible pantheon of the fourteen immaculates and his messianic/mystical flirtations with the idea of the Mahdi, Damavandi can be considered a pioneer who was followed by later generations. His unorthodox ideas, for example, bear a striking resemblance to the controversial teachings of Shaykh Ahmad Ahsaʾi (d. 1826), another mystically minded Twelver religious scholar active a half-century after Damavandi. As MacEoin explains, Ahsaʾi, like Damavandi, had dreams and visions of the imams. More specifically, "he dreamt that he was taught verses by Imam Ḥasan, to enable him to call on the imams whenever he required an answer to any problem." On two occasions, once with Imam Hasan and once with Muhammad, he claimed to have undergone what appears to have been a form of initiatory ritual, involving the drinking of saliva from the mouth of the imam or Prophet. This belief that his knowledge was directly granted him by the Prophet and the imams distinguishes Ahsaʾi from contemporary religious leaders. The role of the imams as spiritual guides is familiar in Shiʿism, but Ahsaʾi seems to have taken this concept to an extreme degree. He claimed that, because he derived his knowledge directly from the Prophet and the imams in dreams, error could not find its way into his words and he could easily answer any criticism leveled against him.* The development of the Shaykhi concept of the "Perfect Shiʿa" who functioned as the "gate" or *bab* to the Hidden Imam can be understood in this light as a logical step forward in finding a replacement for the traditional Sufi concept of the "Perfect murshid."

The highly destablizing potentials of such intense speculations about the relationship between the Shiʿa and the imams, which usually carried strong messianic overtones, from the idea of buruz to that of the bab, was not lost on the Shiʿi mujtahids. Nor were the Usulis oblivious to the fact that the Akhbari approach provided more fertile grounds to nurture and nourish the seeds of such unruly ideas. The brutal and sometimes violent persecution and marginalization of the Akhbari scholars by the Usulis was a reflection of the high stakes they thought were involved in this debate. This was a fight over the future of Shiʿism and some unresolved social and epistemological problems left by the marginalization of Sufism.

The Usulis might have been successful in marginalizing Akhbari scholars in the madrasas of Najaf and Karbala, among other places, but they initially did little to address the roots of the problem that made such ideas so popular: the social vacuum left by the inability of the mujtahids to offer charismatic leadership, to act as intermediaries between heaven and earth and to satisfy the religious and social needs of the populace for an enchanted world where the divine is immanent. The huge success of the Niʿmatullahi revival in the early decades of the nineteenth century and the rapid growth of the Babi movement in the middle of the century, which shook the sacred canopy of Twelver Shiʿism to its foundation, can both be seen as attempts to offer this solution and to counter the established, orderly, yet disenchanted worldview offered by the rationalist-Usuli mujtahid.

Only after the Usulis suppressed these revolts against the established nomos were they truly able to rule over official Twelver Shiʿi discourse. There is no question that the mujtahid's alliance with the Qajar dynasty, both parties being highly invested in preserving the emerging order after the tumultuous decades of the interregnum, was key in their success in quashing religious dissent. The result was the emergence, for the first time in the history of Shiʿism, of a single *marjaʿ-i taqlid* recognized by the overwhelming majority of all Twelvers in Iran, Iraq, and beyond. The Usuli jurist who achieved this status was Shaykh Murtaza Ansari (d. 1864),† and his ascendance marked the unprecedented concentration of jurisprudential religious authority in a single figure. The religious profile of Shaykh Ansari and how he was remembered by the subsequent generations, however, is proof that something

* See MacEoin, "Ahsa'i."

† Algar, *Religion and State*, 162–65.

important had been learned in the process of suppressing religious dissent: that the early nineteenth-century division-of-labor model represented by the relationship between Mirza Qummi and Aqa Muhammad Bidabadi was not enough to preserve the authority and legitimacy of the mujtahid as a charismatic leader in the eyes of the public. The figure of Shaykh Ansari, therefore, brought together both the enormous economic power invested in the office of the marjaʿ and the extraordinary charisma of a saintly figure. Stories about his extreme piety, highly ascetic life, miraculous deeds, and meetings with the Hidden Imam quickly spread among the people. In view of his asceticism and exemplary moral character, later hagiographers portrayed him as a successor to the lineage of ʿirfan-minded ulama discussed earlier. Specifically, he is said to have sought spiritual advice from Kashif Dizfuli, who referred Ansari to Sayyid ʿAli Shustari, who is said to have been the teacher of the famous moralist and ʿirfan-minded religious scholar Mulla Husayn-Quli Hamadani.* Such stories appear to have little historical basis, but we know that Ansari studied for a time under Niraqi Jr., and it is quite possible that he was influenced by the latter's mystical proclivities. As a foundational figure, he projected an image of extreme piety and asceticism that was a clear departure from the division-of-labor model discussed in the case of Mirza Abu al-Qasim Qummi and Aqa Muhammad Bidabadi. Unlike the former, Ansari did not delegate the responsibility of spiritual guidance to an ʿirfan-minded contemporary. As the sole marjaʿ, he was seen as both a mujtahid *and* a saintly figure bestowed with miracles, a friend of the imams about whose secret meetings with the Hidden Imam people speculated. It is only at this important historical moment that one can begin to speak of the emergence of "the cult of the mujtahid," as Lewisohn calls it.† Zarrinkub captures well the significant change in the profile of the mujtahids:

> Some of these jurists' reputation for holiness and extraordinary purity, along with their simultaneous rejection of Sufis and accusations that [the Sufis'] earlier masters were Sunni and that they even lacked affection for the family of the Prophet, caused the mass populace, which had previously gravitated toward the Sufis because of the famous miracles attributed to them, to move toward the jurists and mujtahids of the time. Attributing the same kind of miracles to the prominent jurists and mujtahids gradually obtained for them the reputation that had been [reserved] for the Sufi shaykhs of previous eras. Therefore, any discussion

* The story is reproduced in full, with additional useful information, in Saduqi Soha, *Tarikh-i hukama,* 211–13.

† Lewisohn, "Sufism and the School of Iṣfahān." As mentioned already, Lewisohn mistakenly projected this later development onto the Safavid era.

> of Sufism in this era . . . without paying attention to the role that such jurists and ascetics played in distracting the minds of people from the miracles attributed to the Sufis . . . will be incomplete. This is especially the case because such jurists, even without [explicitly] claiming the position of [spiritual] guidance and masterhood [*qutbiyyat*] the way Sufis had customarily done, in reality did attain such a position among their followers.*

In many ways the relationship between the marjaʿ and his followers is reminiscent of that between the Sufi pir and his disciples in the khanaqah. A major difference, however, is the concentrated nature of the marjaʿ's power. Where there existed countless Sufi shaykhs, only a handful of marjaʿs exist at any given time. The result is an unprecedented centralization of religious authority. Ansari's own life was markedly unpolitical, however, and it was left to his students and later generations, influenced by his theoretical innovations in the methodology of jurisprudence, to realize the political power of his thought. The first major example of this power being successfully harnessed was in the Tobacco Protest of 1891–1892, when a prominent student of Ansari, Mirza Hasan Shirazi (d. 1896), issued a statement in his capacity as a marjaʿ that propelled the populace into revolt. Nearly a century later, Khomeini harnessed that power to propel a much more portentous movement: the revolution of 1979.

* Zarrinkub, *Dunbala,* 311.

6 The Modernization of ʿIrfan

At the end of the nineteenth century, ʿirfan occupied a semantic domain independent of the Sufism from which it had developed and against which it had been defined. It was not until the twentieth century, however, that the concept gained traction beyond a small circle of mystically minded ulama whose engagement with ʿirfan was confined to their writings and the corners of the madrasa where they taught. Prior to that time, none of the major Persian, Arabic, or Turkish dictionaries dedicated a separate entry to ʿirfan. It was occasionally mentioned under *maʿrifa* or the root ʿ-r-f as a cognate meaning *knowledge, insight,* or *culture.** Persian dictionaries authored later in the nineteenth century or early in the twentieth began to have separate entries for ʿirfan, but with similar general definitions that did not yet reflect its semantic independence vis-à-vis Sufism,† which still had close to a semantic monopoly as a reference to the mystical aspects of Islam. *Farhang-i nafisi,* a Persian dictionary compiled in the second decade of the twentieth century, provides two different meanings for *ʿirfan.* The first definition is "knowledge of the exalted God," and the second is the more general definition of "knowing something after ignorance."‡ In the same dictionary, the term *tasavvuf* is defined as "the

* The Persian dictionary *Ghiyas al-lughat,* for example, which was first printed in 1826, gives us two major meanings for ʿirfan: "knowledge," and "knowledge of God." See *Ghiyas al-lughat,* s.v. "Maʿrifa."

† The *Persian-English Dictionary* of Francis Steingass (d. 1903), published for the first time in 1892, defines *ʿirfan* as "Knowing, discerning; confessing, owning, admitting; knowledge, learning, science; name of a celebrated female singer; *-ahli ʿirfan,* Learned men, scholars" (see Steingass, *A Comprehensive Persian-English Dictionary,* s.v. "ʿIrfan"). The same dictionary defines *tasavvuf* as "Mysticism, Sufism; devoting oneself to contemplation; contemplation" (s.v. "Tasavvuf").

‡ *Farhang-i nafisi,* s.v. "ʿIrfan." The author of this dictionary, ʿAli-Akbar Nafisi (d. 1924), who was also known as Nazim al-Atibba, was a famous physician and intellectual of the late Qajar period. For more information of the compilation of this dictionary and its publication, as well as a brief biography of the compiler, see Foruqi, "Preface."

name for the school of a group of people of truth who are purified from the desires of their carnal soul and consider worldly entities to be manifestations of God."*

Toward the end of the nineteenth century, as modernist ideas spread rapidly and were being debated heatedly by Iranian intellectuals, ʿirfan expanded beyond its home in the madrasa, where it was the descriptive category for spirituality preferred by a group of ulama unwilling to completely discard Sufi ideas and ideals. It came onto the radar of a group of modern intellectuals who shared the ulama's disdain for popular manifestations of Sufism, seeing them as remnants of a backwardness that kept the nation from progressing toward the promised land of modernity. ʿIrfan provided a discursive space amenable to both groups, allowing intellectuals to express their religious aspirations and esoteric tendencies without contradicting modern modes of thinking, just as it allowed clerics to follow their mystical proclivities without transgressing the norms of Shiʿi orthodoxy. The story of ʿirfan in the twentieth century, then, split into two quite different narratives, one related to small circles of mystically minded ulama of the madrasa and the other to equally small circles of modernist intellectuals and literary figures. The two narratives were not completely independent, however. They crossed paths at multiple junctures and influenced each other in unexpected ways. As a result of these interactions and developments, ʿirfan became a much more visible concept and a familiar term in broader Iranian society. This was a significant step. Whereas earlier discussions of ʿirfan had been carried out under the literary hegemony of Sufism and were usually reactionary in nature, in the twentieth century ʿirfan achieved such discursive prominence and semantic autonomy that it came to overshadow Sufism. It no longer needed to be defined in contrast to Sufism. On the contrary, Sufism, primarily represented by the marginalized Niʿmatullahis, was forced to situate itself in relationship to the central concept of ʿirfan as advocated not only by mystically minded ulama but also by modernist intellectuals and belles-lettrists.

By way of a concrete example, I would like to point to an important and famous history of Sufism published at the turn of the twentieth century in Iran: *Taraʾiq al-haqaʾiq*. The book, now a classic, was authored by the erudite Niʿmatullahi Sufi Mohammad Maʿsum Shirazi (d. 1926), otherwise known as Maʿsum-ʿAli Shah, and printed in lithograph edition in 1900. The book opens with a brief preface by Mohammad-Hoseyn Foruqi (d. 1907), a modern-minded, progressive man of letters known as Zoka al-Molk. Foruqi was the editor of Iran's first nongovernmental newspaper, *Tarbiyat*, which began publication in 1894. He was also a teacher of literature and later the chair of

* *Farhang-i nafisi*, s.v. "Tasavvuf."

the College of Political Science (Madrasa-yi ʿulum-i siyasi), the first such institution ever established in Iran.* What is remarkable about this preface is that in it, Foruqi deliberately avoids any reference to Sufism. Instead, he repeatedly uses terms like *ʿarif* and *ʿirfan,* opening his remarks with a definition of the latter.† More important, he warns that this new concept of ʿirfan, if not accompanied by "reasoning and trustworthy evidence, has no place among the learned and critical generation of the age of discovery."‡ These remarks stand in stark contrast to the content of the book itself. As an author, Maʿsum-ʿAli Shah was fully immersed in traditional Sufi discourse. His long introduction begins with a section on the nature of knowledge, followed, in a familiar pattern, by a section defining the terms *Sufi* and *Sufism.*§ He explicitly equates Shiʿism with Sufism,** and he rarely uses the term *ʿirfan.* When he does, it is in a manner that accords with the traditional role such concepts played in Sufi literature (that is, he uses it in reference to unmediated knowledge of God).††

Such visible contrasts in vocabulary are not exceptional in literature from this tumultuous time in Iranian history. Modernism had begun to impact the social, religious, and political realms, and it created gaping chasms in intellectual discourse. The emergence of a new class of educated, modernist Iran intellectuals was at the core of such tensions. Many educated Iranians of means traveled to Europe for extended periods of time. Some stayed there for decades or even permanently, but the vast majority retained connections with their land of origin and contributed to its intellectual, cultural, and political developments insofar as they were able. Some among them were active in introducing alternative modes of spirituality such as theosophy, spiritism, magnetic sleep, and the religious symbolism of freemasonry to an Iranian audience hungry for new ideas that had the potential to transform modern human life.‡‡ These expatriates saw more potential in ʿirfan than in Sufism,

* For a brief biography see Afshar and Azimi, "Forūgī."

† The same pattern can be seen in his introduction to ʿAttar's *Mantiq al-tayr,* published in 1902. See Foruqi, Introduction, 2–15.

‡ Maʿsum-ʿAli Shah, *Taraʾiq al-haqaʾiq,* 1:8.

§ *Maʿsum-ʿAli Shah, Taraʾiq al-haqaʾiq,* 1:99ff.

** Maʿsum-ʿAli Shah, *Taraʾiq al-haqaʾiq,* 1:156.

†† Nonetheless, the fact that Zoka al-Molk wrote this preface to *Taraʿiq* shows that the traditional Sufi discourse offered in the hundreds of pages following the preface was not necessarily seen as incompatible with the "evidence" that the "critical generation of the age of discovery" required. That is, a substantial continuity was assumed between the past and the future. At issue was discerning the "correct" version of the past, which could be carried, with a newly minted vocabulary, into the future.

‡‡ This is a highly underresearched area. For a brief discussion of spiritism see Doostdar, "Empirical Spirits." On freemasonry, see Bayat, "Freemasonry."

latching onto the former as a concept that could be broadened and used to refer to a more universalist,* individualistic, egalitarian, and accessible mode of spirituality that, from their perspective, was well suited to serve the generation of science and democracy.

Increasing rates of literacy; the widespread availability of books, journals, and newspapers that accompanied the emergence of modern print, a new Western-inspired public education system; and the emergence of an educated Iranian middle class all helped facilitate a new phase in the development of ʿirfan that I call the "modernization of ʿirfan." In this period, ʿirfan gained a new semantic dimension, one that was universal and democratic in scope and pluralistic and individualistic in nature. This new notion of ʿirfan developed mostly independent of the nineteenth century, madrasa-based notion of ʿirfan centered on the mystical philosophy of Ibn ʿArabi. Some thinkers, however, tried to synthesize what they considered to be the best aspects of both notions into a tradition suited to the needs of modernity. A comprehensive overview of the religious landscape of Iran as it relates to the story of ʿirfan is beyond the scope of this study, but I would like to offer a window into these developments by focusing on ʿAbbas Keyvan Qazvini and how his conception of ʿirfan as a modern concept in contrast to Sufism has influenced ʿirfanian discourse to this day.

Keyvan Qazvini

Keyvan Qazvini (d. 1938) was born in Qazvin in 1861. His early learning took place in his hometown, and in 1883 he moved to Tehran as a young adult to continue his education.† Sometime after he began his studies in the capital, he became interested in the less commonly taught disciplines of philosophy and speculative mysticism, and he learned about organized Sufism as well. Economic necessity impelled him to begin preaching during Ramadan, and his talents as a public speaker gradually made a name for him.‡ He searched ardently for a perfect spiritual master, meeting several Niʿmatullahi masters, including Safi-ʿAli Shah (d. 1899). Eventually, however, he cast his lot with another branch of the Sufi network headed by Soltan-ʿAli Shah (d. 1909).§ In 1889 he elected to continue his studies further by moving to Najaf, the

* I am indebted to Alireza Doostdar, who gave me a better understanding of the importance of this universalist feature of modern ʿirfanian discourse as part of a broader cultural development related to modernism and science in twentieth-century Iran.

† Keyvan, *Keyvan-nama,* 2:51–52, and Samiʿi, "Keyvan Qazvini," 1429.

‡ Samiʿi, "Keyvan Qazvini," 1466–67. Keyvan's talents as a preacher are described vividly by Samiʿi, and independent sources confirm his fame in this regard. See Eʿtesam, *Bi rivayat-i saʿid nafisi,* 588.

§ Keyvan, *Keyvan-nama,* 2:118ff.

most important center of Shiʿi learning. According to his autobiography, he was recognized in Najaf by Mirza Habibullah Rashti (d. 1894) for his extraordinary preaching and deep knowledge, which earned him the honorary title of *ayatullah*.* Keyvan relates that he maintained his Niʿmatullahi affiliation throughout this time and spent a total of more than three decades of his life as an active Sufi, initially in the capacity of a novice and then, for seventeen years or so, as a missionary. He deployed his public-speaking skills in the service of three of the Gunabadi-Niʿmatullahi poles, namely Soltan-ʿAli Shah, Nur-ʿAli Shah II (d. 1918), and, eventually, Saleh-ʿAli Shah (d. 1966). According to sympathetic sources, he was promoted and given the honorary Sufi title of Mansur-ʿAli Shah and was an "itinerant shaykh" (*shaykh-i sayyar*).† Keyvan himself claimed that many people recruited by him during his extensive travels regarded him as their pole.‡

Despite his service to the Sufi network, Keyvan gradually grew disillusioned with the Niʿmatullahi leadership, eventually raising explicit objections to Saleh-ʿAli Shah, which led to his excommunication in 1926.§ Keyvan attributed his break with the order to dishonesty, fraudulent claims, and corruption,** but it is not unlikely that a combination of financial disputes, unmet personal ambitions, and bitter infighting between different branches had a role in straining his relationship with the Niʿmatullahi leadership. Whatever the reasons, Keyvan turned his talent for public speaking and his gifts as a writer into effective weapons against the Niʿmatullahi pole and organized Sufism in general.†† His works betray a personal grudge against Saleh-ʿAli Shah and the higher echelons of the Niʿmatullahi network, but they also reveal a deep engagement with fundamental questions regarding the role of religion and tradition in a world that was careening toward modernism at a dizzying speed.‡‡

* We are told by his student that he attained the highest level of religious education (*ijtihad*) there, but this remains unconfirmed by independent sources. See Samiʿi, "Keyvan Qazvini," 1461. For Keyvan's own description of his travel to Iraq and his fame as a preacher see Keyvan, *Keyvan-nama,* 2:91ff.

† Samiʿi, "Keyvan Qazvini," 1465–66. See also Van den Bos, *Mystic Regimes,* 81. Niʿmatullahis dispute the validity or even meaningfulness of this title. See Parishanzade, *Gushayish-i raz,* 19.

‡ See, for example, Keyvan, *Keyvan-nama,* 3:64.

§ Keyvan, *Razgusha,* 85.

** Keyvan, *Keyvan-nama,* 2:106.

†† For a list of his works see Modarresi Chahardehi, *Sayri dar tasavvuf,* 222–24.

‡‡ Accounts of Keyvan's life, especially related to the years he spent as a Niʿmatullahi adept, differ according to whether they were written by a friendly source or a hostile Niʿimatullahi one. For a fairly balanced biography, see Samiʿi and Saduqi Soha,

Before proceeding with my analysis I should clarify that Keyvan did not write in a systematic, scholarly manner, nor was he an unbiased observer. Some of his written legacy consists of transcripts of sermons and other public remarks, and factual inaccuracies and a stream-of-consciousness quality can be found across his writings. His work is also replete with vitriolic polemics against his personal enemies and characterized by self-centeredness and ideological hyperbole. Despite the personal enmities that prejudice certain sections of his accounts, I believe his extraordinary background made him a unique and astute observer of the religious landscape of Iran in the early twentieth century. He had an intimate inside view of organized Sufi networks, and he spent many years as a student of religious disciplines in the madrasa. He rubbed shoulders with high-ranking ulama and had close contact with ordinary people in his capacity as a preacher. His observations and comments are unusually detailed, making them a treasure trove of raw information and a valuable window into broader religious dynamics in his time in Iran, especially as they relate to the developments of ʿirfanian discourse.

I begin with an example drawn from *Keyvan-nama,* his autobiography. The section that interests me starts with a tangential remark that sparks a long discussion of the classification of disciplines of knowledge in Iran. Only the third division, the one composed of "mathematics, natural sciences, philosophy, and ʿirfan," is relevant to our purposes. Keyvan is quick to note that the mujtahids of his hometown disapproved of the fields of knowledge in this third classification, especially philosophy and ʿirfan, and that they sometimes declared the teachers of such disciplines to be unbelievers. The laity, Keyvan says, in their overzealous enthusiasm, took such declarations to heart and considered proponents of these disciplines to be ritually impure. He then adds a fascinating and somewhat amusing story from his childhood. "It was not," he says, "as if everyone in Qazvin considered every philosopher to be a bad person or an unbeliever. But the bottom line is that they did not pay nearly as much money to philosophers as they paid to jurists. Additionally, they would do everything in their power to prohibit their sons from studying philosophy. Once, a religious student was leaving Qazvin for Isfahan to continue his studies. When it came time to say goodbye, his mother wept and said, 'You know I would die for you!* Study whatever you want, but don't embarrass me in front of the neighbors by studying the book of *Asfar!*'"†

Du risala, 125–52. Van den Bos offers a brief overview of Qazvini's life and a useful analysis of his work in Van den Bos, *Mystic Regimes,* 81–86.

* A loose translation of *qadan alim,* a Turkish expression of affection (Qazvin had and still has a significant Turkish-speaking population).

† Keyvan, *Keyvan-nama,* 1:54.

Keyvan himself does not seem to have heeded such advice, stating explicitly that he traveled to Tehran in 1882 to study philosophy and ʿirfan, which, along with astronomy, astrology, geometry, alchemy, and a handful of other disciplines, were deemed occult sciences (*ʿulum-i ghariba*) by their opponents at the time.* It is dangerous to read too much into a single anecdote, but other similar reports confirm Keyvan's take on the situation. One of these is given by Seyyed Hasan Meskhan Tabasi (d. 1949), a student of a well-known philosopher of the Qajar era, Jahangir Khan Qashqaʾi (d. 1910):

> When I came to Isfahan [around 1896], the natural sciences and mathematics were totally abandoned, and literature was in a dismal situation. In spite of the crowdedness of the madrasas, no attention was paid to such disciplines. All the efforts were focused on fiqh and usul. . . . The custom of takfir was not entirely abandoned, but it did not happen frequently. Thanks to the efforts of people like Mulla ʿAli Nuri [d. 1830] and Jahangir Khan Qashqaʾi, the horror that people had for the rational disciplines in the time of Haji Kalbasi† was to some extent turned into familiarity. That is to say, if a person was observant in attending communal prayers, attended the sessions eulogizing the imams [*majalis rawza*], and studied fiqh and usul, he was able in his spare time to study disciplines that religious students of the time referred to as "occult disciplines." . . . [Gradually] the proponents of such disciplines increased and [people's] ears became somewhat accustomed to the type of arguments offered by mathematicians and philosophers, so much so that after three years Jahangir Khan came out of his cell in the Sadr Madrasa and taught *Sharh-i manzuma* [of Mulla Hadi Sabzavari] to almost a hundred and thirty people in the courtyard of the Jarchi Madrasa, and no one complained. Modernism [*tajaddud*] had already entered, or was very close to entering, the madrasas of Isfahan. One of the problems of that time was knowing how to use the astrolabe, and even more difficult, to know the principles upon which it was built. . . . This technology was so abandoned at the time that I could find only one person called Mirza Gholam-Hoseyn [who understood it]. This knowledgeable man was unique in his knowledge of the astrolabe . . . and he could make the best ones, but at the time his passion for alchemy and the other expensive and difficult experiments he was involved in did not let him finish this work. Some among us were not willing to study with Mirza in public, and he did not teach in secret. Instead, he would intentionally sit in

* Keyvan, *Keyvan-nama,* 81.

† Mirza Muhammad-Ibrahim Kalbasi (d. 1845), a student of Bidabadi. See Saduqi Soha, *Tarikh-i hukama,* 153.

> the veranda [*ivan*] of the madrasa and teach. Therefore, he did not have many students. . . . In any case, I learned such disciplines from him and promoted them and moved from Isfahan to Khurasan. . . . In the madrasas of Mashhad in that era people had no inclination toward the rational disciplines . . . if someone was accused of knowing philosophy, he would be considered successful if he escaped with his life. . . . This brief account is related to the period between 1896 and 1906, when a new era had been ushered in and new ideas had emerged in all classes of people in Iran. I had my own share, and I began to study French, the natural sciences, and European literature. I travelled abroad twice, once staying almost a year in Cairo. On the second trip, I stayed three years in Paris. During these trips I saw many places and met learned men from a variety of nations.*

This account adds some fascinating perspective to my earlier considerations. ʿIrfan-minded scholars such as Bidabadi, the Niraqis, and, later, Mulla Hadi Sabzavari may have commanded respect for their charisma and exemplary piety, but they had to exercise great caution about coming out publicly as advocates of controversial philosophers and Sufis such as Mulla Sadra and Ibn ʿArabi. This sheds light on Bidabadi's thoroughgoing reluctance to explicitly assume the role of spiritual guide to the seekers who approached him. More important, Meshkan's account reveals that the increased freedom to teach disciplines such as mathematics, the natural sciences, Islamic philosophy, and (as Keyvan implies) ʿirfan was closely tied to the penetration of modernism into the madrasa and beyond. It seems that as the ulama in control of the madrasa curriculum faced the increasing popularity of modern Western philosophical ideas among the younger generation, they became more open to the rational disciplines, at least as the lesser of two evils.

The urgent desire to be modern, to catch up with the West, and to be part of the new world order that is obvious toward the end of Meshkan's account is something that pervades many Iranian writings of this era. Meshkan was not alone in his desire to learn European languages and to travel. Iranians who traveled, studied, and/or lived in Europe came home with a plethora of new ideas, mainly in the realm of politics but also in religion. They spread these ideas through a growing number of newly established newspapers and magazines. One of the most attractive features of modernism was the scope of its discourse. Science, technology, democracy, human rights, individual agency, autonomy, and freedom were all concepts without borders, or so they

* Meshkan Tabasi, "Naql az kitab-i gulzar," 67–69; reproduced in Saduqi Soha, *Tarikh-i hukama*, 327–28.

seemed to enthralled Iranian intellectuals who saw tribalism, sectarianism, authoritarianism, ritualism, superstition, and many other kinds of particularistic thinking as major impediments to progress.

Of course, modernist intellectuals' views differed widely when it came to the proper role of religion in their utopian conceptions of an ideal modern Iran. At one end of the spectrum were figures such as Fath-'Ali Akhundzade (d. 1878), a dyed-in-the-wool atheist who harbored great hostility toward any form of religion. Mirza Malkom Khan (d. 1908) and others were less strident in their opposition to religion, which expressed itself in the derision of religious institutions.* Others were reformists of various sorts who were inspired by Afghani (d. 1897) and who believed that religion, in its proper form, could play a positive role in moving a nation toward enlightenment. Despite these differences, nearly all were united in their criticism of Sufism. Its alleged teachings of withdrawal from the world were considered a source of stagnancy and laziness among Muslims.

Intellectuals may have differed sharply on matters of religion, but their writings contain common themes that impacted religious developments in Iran. Two of those are unity (of Iran as a nation) and universalism (Iranians as citizens of the modern global community).† Perhaps the most clear and radical example of how universalism as an ideal inspired religious developments in Iran is the Baha'i religion. At its inception, the messianic movement initiated by Sayyid 'Ali-Muhammad Shirazi (d. 1850), otherwise known as the Bab, was not influenced in any explicit way by the cultural forces of modernism, though the economic realities of the New World Order, as Hodgson put it,‡ had begun to have significant impact. After this initial period, however, Babi leaders were forced into exile abroad, a formative event that put the movement into conversation with Western ideas and ideals and helped transform it into the world religion now known as the Baha'i faith. It is not coincidence that the fundamental principles of the Baha'i message as propagated by 'Abd al-Baha (d. 1921) in his journeys to Europe and North American in the early twentieth century strongly resonated with and were sometimes identical to the aspirations of modernist Iranian intellectuals (including Keyvan Qazvini). Similar viewpoints on the necessity of independent investigation of reality (the opposite of *taqlid* or blind imitation), on the unity of mankind, on true religion as a source of unity and harmony, and on the complementary nature of religion and science do not point to Baha'i influence on

* For an analysis of Malkom's take of religion and its role in the Iranian society, see Algar, MĪRZĀ MALKUM KHĀN.

† Ridgeon, *Religion and Politics*, 15.

‡ See the third volume of Hodgson's *Venture of Islam*.

intellectuals (though that existed in some cases) as much as they do to the tremendous influence that Western ideas, especially those with universalist appeal, had in shaping the religious, social, and political worldviews of the Iranian elite at the time.*

The universalism, individualism, and egalitarianism in Keyvan's writings must be understood against this backdrop. He reminds his reader many times that his ideas "are based on human thought with no regard to race, nationality, science, or religion. People of all places are my audience without any exception."† In a comment characteristically long on self-confidence and short on humility, he invites "thinkers around the world" to read and criticize his writings.‡ In order to facilitate this goal, which was hampered by the fact that he knew no European languages, he sent many of his books to his friend Mohammad Qazvini (d. 1949), a prominent Iranian scholar based in Paris, and asked the latter to discuss them with the European thinkers and seek their feedback.§

In Keyvan's writings, the concept of religion (*din*) plays a much more important role than Islam or Shiʿism. As he speaks of religion in a universal way, however, he struggles with the fact that different religions and sects have competing truth claims. Ultimately he attributes the fighting, persecution, and wars stemming from religious differences to the fact that human beings have forgotten the true essence of religion. Drawing on his Islamic religious education, he argues that religion manifests itself on multiple levels of reality. True religion, like a universal archetype, operates at the highest level of reality. Differentiation happens only as we descend to the world of manifestations, just as existence (vujud) is differentiated into various forms and manifestations called *mahiyya* or "quiddity." Therefore, religions are not different from one another in their essence, their true being, which is composed of the higher principle of unity.** Pointing to this metaphysical scheme, he invites his readers to put aside what divides them (*ma bi-hi al-imtiaz*) and to focus on what unites them (*ma bi-hi al-ishtirak*). Keyvan

* Another later manifestation of such universalism can be seen in the "New Global Unity" (*vahdat-i navin-i jahani*) school established by Heshmatollah Dolatshahi (d. 1980), an aristocrat from Kermanshah who was exposed to modernist ideas through literature brought back to Iran by his father from his frequent travels to Europe. For a brief account of Dolatshahi's worldview and activities see Modarresi Chahardehi, *Sayr-i dar tasavvuf*, 263–73 ; also see Doostdar, "Fantasies of Reason," 204.

† Keyvan, *ʿIrfan-nama*, 17.

‡ Keyvan, *Keyvan-nama*, 3:1.

§ Keyvan, *Keyvan-nama*, 2:97.

** Keyvan, *Keyvan-nama*, 3:6–16.

sees it as quite natural that each religion's adherents believe themselves to be closest to the true essence of religion, and he remarks that only at the end of time, when the universal messiah appears, will the stupidity of all these fights be revealed.* His contention is not that all different religions will be wiped out to make way for a universal religion. Rather, people will have a proper understanding of the place and function of what divides them and will never prioritize it over what unites them.

Keyvan, Sufism, and ʿIrfan

Keyvan's harsh criticisms of organized Sufism go hand in hand with his desire to find a universal, accessible, and egalitarian religious vocabulary suitable for a modern-minded audience. As a deeply religious person, however, he takes great pains to devise a plan that does not throw the baby out with the bathwater. First, he carefully differentiates between the mystically minded groups of his time, using an original and insightful tripartite classification to evaluate their relationship with what he considers to be the center of Sufism. This classification system is informed by his long years of familiarity with different religious groups. Aspects of it may seem arbitrary, but it gives us some understanding of the spiritual landscape of Iran at the time.†

Like any good phenomenologist, Keyvan begins with a list of commonalities that he claims all the groups share. These are (1) a general aversion for exotericism and an inclination toward the esoteric aspects of religion; (2) an endorsement Rumi's *Masnavi* with their hearts even if they deny it in public to avoid being labeled; (3) a focus on improving ethical character (akhlaq) and pursuing the goal of universal peace (*sulh-i kull*); (4) an avoidance of worldly pleasures (*khush-guzarani*); and (5) a tendency toward exaggeration (ghuluvv) when it comes to the nature and powers of the imams, the saints, and spiritual masters.‡ These commonalities are interesting in and of themselves, but the qualities that differentiate the groups are more pertinent here. Keyvan recognizes three distinct approaches to Sufism among the mystically

* While some of this might seem similar to the traditional inclusivist view found in the Qur'an (e.g. 3:19), Keyvan uses a markedly nonconfessional vocabulary that makes his position closer to that of a pluralist than an inclusivist. He points out in many instances that Shiʿism does not have a particular hold on truth compared to Sunnism, going so far as to say that those who make the most fuss about how right they are will probably be in more trouble when the messiah comes.

† This classification has surprisingly received no major scholarly attention. It has been quoted in only two works by Persian scholars of Sufism, and with no analysis. See Karbasi-zade, *Hakim-i muta'allih*, 206, and Saduqi Soha, *Tarikh-i hukama*, 214–15.

‡ Keyvan, *Razgusha*, 134–35.

minded people of his time, whom he divides accordingly into three separate groups:

(I) Those in between. This group is farthest away from what Keyvan considers the center of Sufism, and it is composed of people who stand "in between" (*barzakh*) exoteric and esoteric interpretations of religion.* A major marker of this group is that they are terrified of (*vahshat darand*) being called Sufis.

(II) Those at the outset. Moving from the fringes toward the center of Sufism, we come to the second group, which is located at the starting point or beginning of Sufism (*bidayat-i tasavvuf*). This group, while not particularly interested or invested in taking on the title of Sufism, is not terrified of the designation.†

(III) Those at the center. Finally we reach the third group, which is located at the center of Sufism (*markaz-i tasavvuf*). This group is composed of members of traditional Sufi networks best exemplified (Keyvan believes) by the Niʿmatullahi order. This group considers the term *Sufi* "sacred," saying that it is difficult to find even one person among the masters of each age who is worthy of the designation.‡

The first and second groups, according to Keyvan, are separated by only one major difference: the first does not have special instructions for hidden zikr, while the second does. This is significant, Keyvan tells us, because receiving specific instructions for hidden zikr is a prerequisite for becoming an official member of a Sufi network.§ We have seen how hidden zikr and the question of whether it constituted bidʿa were major issues of debate among ʿirfan-minded people. Despite arguments to the contrary from a minority of religious scholars such as Niraqi Sr., many among the ʿirfan-minded ulama, even later generations in the nineteenth century, considered such instructions illegitimate. This is especially true of Mulla Husayn-Quli Hamadani (d. 1893) and the Najafi lineage of ʿirfan teachers who came to be known as the "moralists" or *akhlaqiyyun* and whom Keyvan classifies as being on the fringes of Sufism.**

* *Barzakh bayn-i qishr va lubb.*

† He recounts how one of his spiritual masters, Adine-yi Esfahani, told him how he had been scared of becoming a Sufi, but after a dream he was convinced that there was no need to be afraid of the term *Sufi* anymore. See Keyvan, *Razgusha,* 140.

‡ Keyvan, *Razgusha,* 140.

§ Keyvan, *Razgusha,* 239.

** In fact, Keyvan claims to have been a student of Mulla Husayn-Quli. Another prominent scholar Keyvan classifies under the first group is Mulla Fath-ʿAli Sultanabadi (d. 1900). See Saduqi Soha, *Tarikh-i hukama,* 211–15 and 237–57.

The group at the outset of Sufism, according to Keyvan, is composed of members of the ulama who, because of their familiarity and friendly relationships with some Sufi masters, are more accustomed to the traditional world of Sufism. Nonetheless, they see themselves as following an independent Shiʿi spiritual tradition, which is marked by a distinctive discourse that allows them to distance themselves from traditional Sufi discourse. Keyvan includes among them his contemporary, Molla Mohammad-Javad Adine-yi Esfahani (d. 1921),* as well as Aqa Muhammad Bidabadi. It appears that Bidabadi is classified in the second rather than the first group because he was (wrongly) credited with writing the *Sayr va suluk* treatise.† The treatise includes special instructions on performing hidden zikr, which, for Keyvan, is *the* criterion of differentiation between the two groups.‡

Though they differ in regards to hidden zikr, both the first and second groups share an unwavering adherence to the tenants of Twelver Shiʿism. Unlike the organized Sufi networks at the center of Sufism, there is nothing in particular about the beliefs of the first two groups that deviates from the established norms of orthodoxy of the time. Keyvan's categorization gives us a better sense of the type of people who contributed to the formation of ʿirfan as a category; it was among the people in the first two groups that ʿirfanian discourse flourished.

Differences between the third group and the previous two groups run much deeper. Keyvan enumerates six principal distinctions that mark those at the center of Sufism. These have to do with strict rules, a well-organized hierarchy, various formalities, and a set technical vocabulary. Those at the center use terms like *shah* and *qutb,* and they perform elaborate initiation rites to secure membership. Disciples are required to adhere to a single spiritual master, and initiates are not free to act as missionaries unless given permission by the shaykh. None of these things are true for the first two groups, who are defined by their lack of such practices.§ The absence of Zahabiyya from Keyvan's discussion of the group at the center of Sufism is noteworthy. He knew the network well,** but he may not have included them in the third

* Keyvan claims to have been his student for some, saying that he had received special instructions from him on how to perform a difficult form of the hidden zikr. Esfahani was among the most prominent teachers of the mystical philosophy of Mulla Sadra in his time after his teacher Jahangir Khan in Isfahan. See Saduqi Soha, *Tarikh-i hukama,* 334–35.

† I briefly discussed this attribution in the previous chapter. See pages 167–173, especially note ** on page 173.

‡ Keyvan, *Razgusha,* 138.

§ Keyvan, *Razgusha,* 140–42.

** In his autobiography, Keyvan provides an extensive account of his trip to Shiraz, saying he stayed there for two months and had the opportunity to become

group because of their lack of enthusiasm for being called Sufis.* Additionally, Zahabi vocal zikr sessions resemble Shiʿi sessions eulogizing the imams more than they resemble traditional Sufi zikrs.†

Keyvan puts his tripartite categorization into use in many places, including when he narrates the story of his flirtation with and his eventual conversion to Sufism. After moving to Tehran, he says, he decided to take lessons in philosophy despite its unpopularity among the religious students:

> [I]n the midst of taking lessons in philosophy, I considered making inquiries into ʿirfan and Sufism. . . . I had fear in my heart for the term Sufism, and found ʿirfan more approachable. I told myself, "ʿIrfan will be enough to get you out of your exoteric and biased [mindset],' and I did not dare to think about Sufism. What I meant by ʿirfan was a nuanced discipline of knowledge expressed in a particular vocabulary, something that in my book *ʿIrfan-nama* I have called speculative ʿirfan [*ʿirfan-i ʿilmi*] in contrast to Sufism, which is called practical ʿirfan. . . . At the time, Aqa [Muhammad-]Riza Qumsha'i [d. 1888] was famous for his *Fusus* lessons in Tehran, but I still did not have the courage to go to his lessons out of the fear that I would inevitably become a Sufi. I did not mind taking *al-Isharat* lessons, because the Shaykh [Ibn Sina] used the term ʿarif rather than Sufi . . . then I sought out someone representative of the in-between path, and after a year . . . I found Haj Mir Mohammad- ʿAli. He was a perfect jurist, but he had chosen seclusion, and even though the mosque was near his home, he did not go there. He led the communal prayers in his home and sometimes gave sermons to people there. I joined him and left everyone else. He ordered me to perform very difficult rituals of worship, mortification, and vocal zikr, and he told me that his path was received from Aqa Hasan Najmabadi. . . . I performed those rituals for a couple of years until the fear in my heart for Sufism was not as strong. Then I found an order made up of those at the outset

---

familiar with multiple Sufi organizations, all of which, according to him, were one another's enemies. He observes that the general attitude of the jurists in Shiraz was much more positive toward Sufism than was that of jurists in some other cities in Iran. See Keyvan, *Keyvan-nama*, 3:62–63.

* In this they followed the lead of Qutb al-Din Nayrizi, who preferred the term *fuqara*. In more recent times Zahabis have referred to their fellow members as *akhavan* or, simply, *brothers*.

† The Zahabi zikr sessions, which are open to the public, consist of someone reciting the poetry of Zahabi masters, the content of which is overwhelmingly in praise of the imams. Meanwhile, all other members, dressed in black robes and holding rosaries in their hands, sit in silence and listen. I was able to observe one such zikr session in the summer of 2014 during my visit to Khanaqah-i Ahmadi in Shiraz.

> of Sufism, and they accepted me and trained me. . . . [Despite objections from Haj Mir Mohammad], I did not leave this order. Instead, thanks to a couple of connections, and still totally convinced of the path of the jurists and philosophers, I gradually became familiar with the Sufi orders at the center [of Sufism].*

Only after making these distinctions does Keyvan unleash his harsh criticisms, which are aimed mainly against the third group: those at the center of organized Sufism who adhere to its institutions and rituals. He directs his ire at the vices of corrupt Sufi social institutions and hierarchies,† criticizing the endless feuds between different Sufi networks and the absolutist nature of the master/disciple relationship, which often led to scandalous exploitation of the disciples by opportunistic masters. In place of these institutions and hierarchies, he advocates for a more pluralist, individualist, and universal understanding of Sufism. One of Keyvan's students, in fact, claims that his teacher was the first person to come up with the idea of "individualist Sufism."‡

At this crucial juncture, the term *ʿirfan* takes center stage in Keyvan's discourse. While promoting his own distinct vision of the true essence of religion, Keyvan engages in a fascinating effort to define ʿirfan as a universal concept, unbound by particular religious creeds or institutions. In order to do that, he makes a crucial distinction between two kinds of Sufism: *haqiqi* (true) and *marsum* (customary). From Keyvan's perspective, most of what is associated with organized and institutionalized forms of Sufism fits under the second, nongenuine Sufism. He speaks sympathetically, however, about what he considers to be genuine Sufism, which, according to him, is devoid of all the corruption and superstition of customary Sufism. ʿIrfan, he says, is a broader concept that encompasses genuine Sufism. From one perspective, it can be divided into two branches—speculative (*ʿilmi*) and practical (*ʿamali*).§ Genuine Sufism, he says, can be categorized under the practical branch of ʿirfan, while speculative ʿirfan can be understood to refer to Ibn ʿArabi and

* Keyvan, *Keyvan-nama,* 2:115–16.

† His critique of the Niʿmatullahi network is detailed in his *Razgusha* and *Bihinsukhan.* His criticism of organized forms of Sufism in general is best found in his *ʿIrfan-nama* and *Ustuvar.*

‡ Keyvan, *Sharh rubaʿiyyat,* 10.

§ Here Keyvan takes a dichotomy introduced by students of Ibn ʿArabi, specifically Mulla Muhammad b. Hamza Fanari (d. 1431), who divided Sufism into issues of spiritual quest (*ʿilm al-suluk or ʿilm manazil al-akhira*) and issues of reality and visions (*ʿilm al-haqaʾiq or ʿilm bi-Allah*). Keyvan, however, replaces the mother category with ʿirfan. See Yazdanpanah, *Mabani va usul,* 64.

his school of thought. On the basis of this terminology, he considers Mulla Sadra the founder of the synthesis between philosophy and ʿirfan.*

Keyvan's concept of ʿirfan is much broader than the school of Ibn ʿArabi and cannot be reduced to the sum of the practical and the speculative branches. That is to say, this is a universal conception that could encompass many paths. This in turn means that both the madrasa-based (speculative) and khanaqah-based (practical) versions of ʿirfan/Sufism are particular and local and thus less important than this new hegemonic notion. In an effort to be more precise, Keyvan enumerates three distinct meanings of ʿirfan. First, there is the popular sense of the term, which refers to someone who is talented and resourceful in what he does. Second is a more technical meaning, prevalent among some of the ulama, in which *ʿirfan* is used in contradistinction to *philosophy*. In this context, the latter term usually refers to the Peripatetic school of philosophy, whereas the former is associated with mystical intuition as a complementary epistemological basis of philosophy, which is characteristic of the Illuminationist school of philosophy and some Sufi philosophers as well. Last but not least, in the realm of religion, ʿirfan is used in contradistinction to literalism and exotericism. According to Keyvan, an ʿarif is one who prioritizes intention, ethics, and internal moods and inclinations in religion, whereas a *qishri* person (literally, a person concerned with the crust) sees exoteric actions as more important signs of religiosity.† Keyvan devotes the bulk of his attention to expand the third meaning. This is a critical juncture: ʿirfan as conceptualized in the madrasas of the time was heavily focused on the second meaning. The way Keyvan expanded and enriched the semantic field of ʿirfan on the basis of the third meaning is an original contribution that had a lasting impact on later generations and their understanding of the term.

The differences between customary Sufism and genuine Sufism/ʿirfan are many. Among the most important are that (1) ʿirfan (or genuine Sufism) lacks hierarchical structures, having neither orders nor master/disciple relationships; (2) ʿirfan has no place for secretive or inaccessible language and teachings; and, most important, (3) the genuine impulse of ʿirfan is not confined to a specific set of beliefs, practices, customs, or organizations.‡ This final distinctive feature of ʿirfan makes it a perfect vehicle for Keyvan's universalism. "[A]lthough nowadays we know of no Sufis with traditional titles

* Keyvan, *Razgusha*, 125.

† Keyvan, *ʿIrfan-nama*, 33–35.

‡ Keyvan, *ʿIrfan-nama*, 35, and *Razgusha*, 326–27.

and organizations outside the world of Islam," he says, "genuine Sufis can be found not only within the Islamic world, but within every religion."*

Who might these Sufis of other religions be? Does Keyvan have specific figures or groups in mind? Are they medieval Christian mystics or Jewish adherents to the Kabala tradition, and, if so, would Keyvan be disillusioned by the institutions and hierarchies in which they participate? Keyvan does not elaborate much on this point, but a footnote to the text opens up a window into his worldview and hints at his conception of who might be considered a true Sufi. The note is peculiar and brief, and in it Keyvan points to the Theosophical Society as an example of "universal ʿirfan, which is not bound to any specific religion."† Theosophy is, in fact, mentioned numerous times throughout his writings, and it is clear that he was impressed with the group's philosophy and international popularity.‡

Keyvan's references to the Theosophical Society, founded by Helena Blavatsky (d. 1891), will come as no surprise to anyone familiar with the early twentieth-century religious landscape of Iran. The society was well known among the Iranian elite thanks to the efforts of Hoseyn Kazemzade Iranshahr (d. 1962), a Tabriz-born nationalist who lived as an expatriate in Europe.§ Iranshahr had a deep and personal interest in alternative spiritualities, and at some point in the mid-1920s he joined the Theosophical Society.** As the chief editor of *Iranshahr*, the magazine he published from 1922 to 1927, he introduced his readership in Iran to this school of thought, predicting passionately that theosophy would be the future of all forms of religion.†† Interestingly, he chose to translate the word *theosophy* as "theoretical Sufism" (*tasavvuf -i ʿilmi*) rather than as *ʿirfan*. Moreover, he translated "Christian mysticism" as "Jesus' Sufism" (*tasavvuf -i ʿisawi*) rather than as "*ʿirfan-i ʿisawi*"

* Keyvan, *ʿIrfan-nama,* 35.

† Ibid.

‡ For another example, see Keyvan, *Keyvan-nama,* 2:88.

§ For his autobiography, which is rich in fascinating historical detail, see Kazemzade Iranshahr, *Asar va ahval.* For a more succinct account based on primary sources see Behnam, "Irānšahr." His fascinating life and career beg for further scholarly attention. For his views on the West, see Borujerdi, "'The West.'"

** His early inclination toward mysticism is evident in his conversion to a vegetarian diet at the age of twenty-five. See Kazemzade Iranshahr, *Asar va ahval,* 205.

†† Kazemzade Iranshahr, "Ti'usufi," 641–59 and 705–16. Other "experimental" philosophies and alternative modes of spirituality, such as hypnosis and spiritualism, were also in the air. For a fascinating account of one such figure, Khalil Saqafi (d. 1944), who was well versed in the "science of spirit" and established the Iranian Society for the Empirical Study of the Spirit (*anjuman-i maʿrifat al-ruh tajrubati iran*), see Doostdar, "Fantasies of Reason," 195–204.

or "*ʿirfan-i masihi.*"* These semantic choices clearly demonstrate that, at the time, ʿirfan was not the default choice for Persian speakers when it came to talking about modern, universalist modes of spirituality. However, when he spoke of the Ecole Mystique Esotérique, which he established in 1942 for his European disciples, he translated the name of the group as *maktab-i ʿirfan-i batini,* which as far as I know is one of the earliest instances where the term *mystique* is translated into Persian as *ʿirfan.*†

To return to the role of ʿirfan in Keyvan's worldview, his writings leave no doubt that for him, ʿirfan was the essence of true religion. This led him to define the concept in the broadest way possible:

> [ʿIrfan] is neither an official field of knowledge . . . nor is it a religion or a branch of a specific religion that is biased or defensive against other religions and denominations or that sets its goal on the same level as other religions' goal, making every attempt to promote [that goal] and to falsify the other [religions]. On the contrary, it is an all-encompassing way of knowledge that can turn to any science, religion, or philosophy, benefiting from them as they benefit from it, so that eventually it becomes intimately entwined with them. . . . Therefore, ʿirfan is not only the basis of science and religion, but also their ornament and perfection, and it is the means by which they resolve their differences and reconcile their hostilities.‡ . . . The purported necessary connection between ʿirfan and Sufism is baseless. [Rather,] the relationship between the two is partial overlap. Neither all ʿarifs are Sufis, nor all Sufis, ʿarifs.§

The main characteristics of ʿirfan, based on this definition and other remarks by Keyvan in his writings, are that (1) it is a highly individualistic form of spirituality; (2) it is universal and pluralistic in nature; and (3) it is amenable to reason and knowledge and compatible with science. All of these characteristics, of course, are emblematic of the modern-minded approach to spirituality that resonated with so many of the enlightened scholars of the time. Keyvan's emphasis on the compatibility of ʿirfan with all types of philosophy, knowledge, and religion should be understood against the backdrop of a deep soul-searching among learned Iranians of the time, intellectuals who sought to identify cultural elements responsible for the "backwardness" of their country and who were hungry for a science-friendly worldview that

* Kazemzade Iranshahr, "Tiʾusufi," 708–9.

† Kazemzade Iranshahr, *Asar va ahval,* 203–4.

‡ Keyvan, *ʿIrfan-nama,* 28, and *Razgusha,* 72.

§ Keyvan, *Razgusha,* 124.

would help the nation progress. Thinkers like Keyvan who valued religion sought to free it of the corrupt institutions, hierarchies, and dogmas they believed were harmful, stripping it to its core to reveal what its true essence could offer a society entering the modern world. Keyvan's words reflect this impulse and the influence of Western currents of thought. He wrote, "I *protest* against the form of Sufi orders and against the title of qutb and the institution of master/disciple. I want to distinguish between two kinds of Sufism as Protestants made a distinction between two aspects of Christianity, saying 'we do accept the essence of Christian religion as sacred and necessary to abide by, but refuse the Pope's arbitrary interference in matters of dogma.' "* It is significant that the word "protest" in the quotation is not a translation. Keyvan himself deliberately used this exact word, transliterated from English into Persian script. This can be seen as an attempt to emphasize the familiarity of the author with a modern, Western culture and its lexicon as well as the deep similarity he saw between his reformist ideas and objection to traditional Sufism and the Protestant Reformation. Keyvan's enchantment with the modern world is perhaps nowhere more explicit than in the 1930 version of his *ʿIrfan-nama,* in which he used the Gregorian calendar, the measure of the modern age.†

The influence of Keyvan's attempts at categorization on later Iranian intellectuals has thus far gone unnoticed and unexplored by scholars. Like Darabi, Damavandi, and other marginalized figures whose role in the intellectual history of ʿirfan I have emphasized, Keyvan has perhaps been neglected because of his status as a preacher and the unspoken assumption that men of the pulpit do not make original contributions. Evidence suggests, however, that he influenced elite and popular discourse on ʿirfan in subsequent generations. I first came across such evidence in the transcription of a radio program dating from 1960, when the national channel Radio Iran aired a series titled *Jalva-ha-yi ʿirfan-i iran* (*Manifestations of Iranian ʿIrfan*). In one of the broadcasts, Jalaloddin Homaʾi (d. 1980), a well-known professor of Persian literature and Sufism, offered the following definition of ʿirfan:

> ʿIrfan, in its widest meaning, is not a science or a discipline [fann]... On the contrary, it can be said that it is compatible with all kinds of sciences and disciplines and does not belong to a specific religion or sect ... it is compatible with all religions and sects. It is a misconception to think that the terms ʿarif or Sufi or ʿirfan are the same as Sufism ... in

* Keyvan, *Razgusha,* 342–43.

† Most appropriately, his prominent student Nuroddin Modarresi Chahardehi (d. 1997) referred to his master not as his shaykh but as "the great philosopher." Van den Bos, *Mystic Regimes,* 84.

> principle, it is Sufism that should be considered one of the branches of ʿirfan. Sufism is a type of spiritual quest [suluk] that originates from the fountain or ʿirfan. [By contrast,] ʿirfan is a more general concept that includes Sufism and other sects [*nihla-ha*]. . . . It is possible for a person to be an ʿarif but not a Sufi.*

Although Homaʾi did not provide us with his sources, his definition of ʿirfan is nearly identical to that of Keyvan, and there is little doubt that he was indebted to the latter. Homaʾi was not the only one to adopt this modern conception of ʿirfan. The definition was well received among the literati, quickly making its way into the most comprehensive Persian lexicon of the time, *Lughat-nama-yi dihkhuda.* This authoritative Persian dictionary, which cemented the status of the scholar and lexicographer ʿAli-Akbar Dehkhoda (d. 1956) as one the most influential literary figures of the twentieth century, remains the gold standard today. Its lengthy entry on ʿirfan lists three major meanings. First, we read that ʿirfan can be used as a synonym for Sufism. Second, we are told that it can mean maʿrifa, or knowledge of the Divine. According to the entry, this maʿrifa "can be attained either through rational reasoning or mystical visions." Finally, the dictionary declares that ʿirfan, in its broadest sense, is "finding out the true reality of things through visions." In clarifying this latter meaning, the entry adds that "Sufism is just one manifestation of ʿirfan . . . it is only a specific sect, a particular spiritual path that stems from the fountain of ʿirfan. The latter is a universal and comprehensive term that includes Sufism . . . it is possible, then, for an ʿarif not to be a Sufi and vice versa."†

Keyvan may have been among the earliest thinkers to articulate a notion of ʿirfan suited to the modern era and amenable to subsequent generations of intellectuals, but he was inspired by some of the figures discussed earlier. A crucial link between the late Safavid period and the early modern period, I believe, is Shah Muhammad Darabi. As mentioned before and evidenced by the textual tradition, Darabi's *Latifa-yi ghaybi,* a commentary on the ghazals of Hafez, was the most frequently read of his works in subsequent centuries. Its popularity did not diminish as Iran entered the age of modern print. If anything, it increased. *Latifa* was among the publications of Dar al-Funun, the first institution of higher education in Iran established on the Western model.‡ Several decades later a pioneering literary journal of the time, *Armaghan,* published the entire text in serial form, spreading it across select

* Homaʾi, "Jilva-ha-yi ʿirfan," 16–17.

† Amanat, Introduction to *The Persian Revolution.* "ʿIrfan."

‡ *Latifa* was published in 1886 by Dar al-Funun.

issues throughout 1925 and 1926.* I have found no specific mention of Darabi in Keyvan's writing, but his impulse to put ʿirfan at the center of his effort to redefine the mystical tradition of Islam is reminiscent of Darabi's presentation of Hafez's cosmopolitan, anti-institutional, antihypocritical mode of piety as ʿirfan. Hafez, Darabi tells us in numerous places in his commentary, was the "head of the chain of the lords of ʿirfan." The success and the rapid pace at which Keyvan's definition moved from the margins to the center, where it was accepted and used by literary giants of the mid-twentieth century, may have occurred in part because *Latifa* paved the way for Keyvan's innovation.

Renewed interest in Darabi's commentary on Hafez in the early modern period was part of a broader cultural and literary phenomenon of the early twentieth century in which figures like Hafez, Rumi, Khayyam, and ʿAttar were reimagined and rebranded as icons worthy of national pride. This was just one piece of the process of modern nation-building that consumed political and cultural activists in the first half of the twentieth century. To understand this process, it is helpful to consider the history of orientalism and how it influenced the self-image of Iranian intellectuals.

Orientalism, Mysticism, and ʿirfan

Europeans "discovered" Sufism only at the turn of the nineteenth century, when colonial officers of the East India Company encountered wild-looking "fakirs" and "dervishes," as they called them, in India.† This "discovery" fed into elite Europeans' growing interest in the ancient "wisdom traditions" of the East, an interest that led to the translation of huge numbers of important ancient texts previously unavailable in European languages. Following Edward Said's groundbreaking work, many scholars have written about how this engagement with the "mystic East" was a colonial project the results of which reaffirmed the underlying power dynamics between the colonizers and the colonized.‡ While this is certainly an important part of the picture, a complementary trajectory of scholarship that I find more relevant to my analysis shifts the center of attention to the internal political and intellectual

* Curiously, the editor of *Armaghan,* the famous poet and man of letters Mohammad-Hasan Vahid Dastgerdi (d. 1942), stated that the text was sent to him for publication by the renowned Niʿmatullahi Sufi of the time, Mirza ʿAbdol-Hoseyn Zu al-Riyasatayn (d. 1943). He mistakenly attributed *Latifa* to the latter in spite of the fact that Darabi's name is mentioned a couple of pages later in the text as the author. See Darabi, "Latifa-yi ghaybi," 207. (Darabi's name is on page 213.)

† Ernst, *The Shambhala Guide to Sufism,* 3–4.

‡ See, for example, King, *Orientalism and Religion.*

struggles of Europe. It focuses on the role such a romantic image of the East played in helping European intellectuals navigate questions about their own national identities during the nineteenth century.* Additionally, such romantic flirtation with the East, dubbed by Raymond Schwab the "Oriental Renaissance," was an important element of a critical response some Western intellectuals were formulating in reaction to the hegemony of rationalism and scientism during the nineteenth century. This critical response culminated in the intellectual movement known as Romanticism, which was exemplified by English Romantic poets such as William Blake (d. 1827), Samuel T. Coleridge (d. 1834), and William Wordsworth (d. 1850), as well as by German theologians and idealists including Friedrich Schleiermacher (d. 1834), Georg W. F. Hegel (1831), and Friedrich W. J. Schelling (d. 1874).

Influenced in part by the Romantic movement, orientalists such as Sir William Jones (d. 1794) and Sir John Malcolm (d. 1833), who can be credited with the Western discovery of Sufism, conceptualized Sufism as yet another ancient mystical tradition originating from the East. These orientalists were initially reluctant to see Sufism as part of the Islamic tradition, partly because or the sources on which they relied and partly because of the intense biases they harbored against Islam. Additionally, they labored under the misguided Romantic notion that all mysticism came from India. Pantheism underlay all Eastern mystical traditions, they believed, and this commonality was emphasized and the contexts out of which mystical traditions emerged were deemphasized or denied altogether. Ernst notes that this perspective "made [Sufism's] Islamic connections interesting but incidental."† This can be seen in Jones's description: "Such in part . . . is the wild and enthusiastick religion of the modern *Persian* poets, especially of the sweet HAFIZ and the great Maulavi [Rumi]: such is the system of the *Vedanti* philosophers and best lyrick poets of India, and, as it was a system of highest antiquity in both nations, it may be added to the many other proofs of an immemorial affinity between them."‡ A similar disregard for Sufism's place within the Islamic tradition can be seen in the perspective of James W. Graham, an officer on Malcolm's staff who wrote in 1819, "With regard to the religion (if it can be so termed in general acceptation of that word) or rather the doctrine and tenets of the sect of Sufis, it is requisite to observe, first, that any person, or a person of any religion or sect, may be a *Sufi:* the mystery lies in this;—a total disengagement of the mind from all temporal concerns and worldly pursuits; an

* See, for example, Leask, *British Romantic Writers,* and Germana, *Orient of Europe.*

† Ernst, *The Shambhala Guide to Sufism,* 10–11.

‡ Ernst, *The Shambhala Guide to Sufism,* 10.

entire throwing off not only of every superstition, doubt, or the like, but of the practical mode of worship, ceremonies, &c. laid down in every religion."* This statement foreshadows Keyvan's words almost a century later about the universal impulse of genuine Sufism/ʿirfan.

Orientalists saw Persian poets such as Rumi and Hafez as some of the best representatives of a pantheistic, universal religion. Franklin Lewis noted that as portions of the poets' work were translated into various European languages in the early nineteenth century, a pantheon of Persian poets was constructed in the Western imagination, consisting of Hafez, Saʿdi, Ferdowsi, and Jami. "By the last quarter of the nineteenth century," Lewis observed, "with Edward FitzGerald's astonishingly successful translating of Khayyam following upon Jones, Goethe and Emerson's earlier fascination for Hafez, Persian poetry enjoyed a highly favorable reputation in the West."† As part and parcel of the Romantic conception of the East as the source of universal and salvific wisdom, these translations, at least initially, said less about the original texts and their cultural contexts than they did about the cultural needs and sociopolitical dynamics of their target audiences. Gradually, however, as scores of orientalists made their way through enormous troves of primary sources over the course of the nineteenth century, the simplistic and biased understandings of the early part of the century gave way to nuanced scholarly narratives that did better justice to the sources and their contexts.

Romantic perceptions of Sufism and Perisan poetry persisted, however. In the late nineteenth and early twentieth centuries, they appeared on the radar of a small group of secularist Iranian intellectuals enchanted with modernism. It is difficult to overemphasize the role such circles had in shaping the way Iranians imagined their own cultural identity. As nationalism swept through the region in the early twentieth century, this international network of Iranians, with their familiarity with European languages and access to modern means of communication such as newspapers and literary journals, was at the heart of efforts to forge a national identity for the newly emerging nation-state. When it came to the cultural and religious aspects of this national identity, these intellectuals were highly conscious of how the important "others," the Europeans, viewed Iran and Persian culture.‡

* Ernst, *The Shambhala Guide to Sufism,* 13.

† Lewis, *Rumi,* 574.

‡ Just as an example, *Danishkada* included a series of translations of European orientalist works under the title of "We as Viewed by Others" by S. M. Khorasani. See Danishkada nos. 2, 4, 6, and 9. Another fascinating example comes from the account Kasravi gives of a purported conversation he had with Muhammad-ʿAli Foruqi, the prime minister at the time in 1935, which best illuminates this

European perspectives were spread via the work of Iranian expats in Europe and via translations of European writings done by individual Iranians or through institutions such as Dar al-Funun or the official Office of Translation. Educated Iranians began to see their own history and culture through the lens of European orientalists. When it came to ʿirfan and mysticism, the popularity in orientalist circles of Sufi literature in general and Persian poets such as Hafez and Rumi in particular was reflected in the writings of Iranians, who celebrated the legacy of Sufism as part of the national identity of Iran. There was, however, a major exception. Orientalist fascination with all that was Eastern may have been boundless, but Iranian intellectuals' rationalist-modernist framework left them with little patience with what they saw as the backward, superstitious, and irrational elements of organized Sufism. They criticized the involvement of the religious hierocracy in political and social affairs. Citizens of a modern Muslim nation, they believed, should not take inspiration from nondemocratic, hierarchical institutions of the khanaqah and the madrasa. An individualistic mode of piety was more appropriate for a modern, secular Iran.

The new ʿirfan, with its free-spiritedness and open-mindedness, offered inspiration for such a mode of piety. It thus became part of the conceptual arsenal of intellectuals and literary figures who were trying to establish, for future generations, what the Iranian nation was all about. ʿIrfan was rooted in the past and held promise for the future. It could be traced back to inspirational figures such as Hafez, and Sufi figures in the literary canon, such as Rumi, Jami, Shabistari, and ʿAttar, who came to be promoted as embodiments of Iran's national identity.

One example of this is the relationship many intellectuals of Iran in the turn of the century had with the prominent British orientalist Edward G. Browne (d. 1926) and his works. Browne was deeply influenced by the romanticism of the Victorian era, and he was fascinated by what he considered the "pantheistic" doctrines of the Sufis.* His love for Iran and all things Persian knew no bounds, but his highest regard was reserved for Persian poets,

frustration with the elevation of figures like Hafez and Rumi to the status of "national poets." "One day," he relates, "I went to the palace . . . [and] we spoke at length. [Foruqi] said, 'In Europe [people] associate Iran with Saʿdi, Hafez, Mawlavi, and Khayyam.' I replied . . . 'Why don't they associate Iran with its ancient history? Why don't they associate Iran with Shah ʿAbbas or Nadir Shah?' Is [European praise] reason enough for us to teach all the misguided evil and thoroughly harmful teachings of Saʿdi and others to our children?'" (translation taken, with minor alterations, from Ridgeon, "Aḥmad Kasravī's Criticisms," 227).

* Amanat, Introduction to *The Persian Revolution,* XI, and Ridgeon, "Aḥmad Kasravī's Criticisms," 224.

whose effect on his life he expressed in a profoundly personal way. "As a young doctor at St. Bartholomew's hospital in London," he related, "I witnessed much that made me wonder at man's clinging to life. . . . Never before or since have I realized so clearly the immortality, greatness, and virtue of the spirit of man, or the misery of its earthly environment: it seemed to me like a prince in rags, ignorant alike of his birth and his rights, but to whom is reserved a glorious heritage. No wonder, then, that the Pantheistic idealism of the Masnavi took hold of me, or that such words . . . of Hafiz thrilled me to the very soul."* Browne's words are just one example of a broader pattern of Eastern figures acting as cures for the sick souls of European orientalists.†

Browne's romantic involvement with all things Persian was accompanied by exceptional erudition and an impressive command of Islamicate history and culture. The biggest symbol of his scholarly legacy is his four-volume magnum opus, *A Literary History of Persia.* Published between 1902 and 1924, it represents the first successful attempt in English to write a comprehensive narrative of the literary, intellectual, and social history of Iran. It remains authoritative to this day.‡ Throughout his career, and as a passionate and active supporter of Iran's constitutionalist movement of the early twentieth century, Browne had extensive contact with and a noticeable influence on the new class of Iranian intellectuals, scholars, political activists, and men of letters. As he worked to finish his *Literary History,* he sent completed volumes to Iran for his colleagues to read.§ As soon as the ink was dry on the final volume, a Persian translation was commissioned.** As such, Browne's *Literary History* became yet another mirror in which the Iranian literati looked to find out about their own history and literature.

Browne's influence on the Iranian political and literary elite was not limited to literary encounters. Prominent figures including Mohammad Qazvini, Kazemzade Iranshahr, Seyyed Hasan Taqizade (d. 1970), and Mohammad-ʿAli Tarbiyat (d. 1940) had extensive contact with Browne during their stay or exile in Europe.†† This small circle of modern-minded literati also kept in

* Amanat, Introduction to *The Persian Revolution.*

† It could be argued that the same romantic influence sparked his interest in the study of the early Babi movement and the Baha'i religion as well. See Bosworth, "E. G. Browne," 119.

‡ Lewis, *Rumi,* 530.

§ Kasravi, *Dar piramun-i adabiyyat.*

** To give just one relevant example, by the summer of 1925, just a year after Browne finished his magnum opus, ʿAli-Asghar Hikmat, a senior staff member in the ministry of Maʿarif in the postwar Pahlavi government, commissioned a number of prominent Iranian academics to translate the work. See Yasemi, "Dibacha," 4-15.

†† Qazvini, *Bist maqala,* 14; Kazemzade Iranshahr, *Asar va ahval,* 109–19.

close contact, reading and commenting on one another's works. As a senior scholar, Qazvini had a close working relationship with the younger generation of modern-minded Iranian belles-lettrists such as Saʿid Nafisi (d. 1966), Rashid Yasemi (d. 1951), ʿAbbas Eqbal Ashtiyani (d. 1956), and Mohammad-Taqi Bahar (d. 1951), who established Iran's first literary association and published the pioneering journal *Danishkada.* This close-knit circle of friends and colleagues extended beyond the borders of Iran. During Qazvini's stay in Berlin during the tumultuous years of World War I, for example, a small literary circle was formed that lasted for five years, thanks to the efforts of a prominent modernist politician and proponent of the constitutionalist movement, Taqizadeh. Included in this circle were luminaries such as Tarbiyat, Iranishahr, and the young Mohammad-ʿAli Jamalzade (d. 1997).*

Keyvan, who was himself enchanted with modernism, sought to have his ideas heard by the intellectual powerhouses in these circles. He regularly corresponded with Qazvini while the latter was in Paris, sending monographs to him and asking for comments not only from Qazvini but also from the European intellectuals he hoped Qazvini would convince to read his works. ʿAbbas Eqbal, a prominent historian of the time, seems to have had some contact with Keyvan based on the preface that he wrote to accompany the latter's commentary on Khayyam's quatrains. However, Yasemi was by far the closest friend Keyvan had among the early twentieth-century literary elite. He wrote about how he "discovered" Keyvan and was immediately and deeply impressed with his open-mindedness and erudition.† Yasemi visited Keyvan frequently in the last decade of the latter's life, engaging in regular scholarly conversations with him. Yasemi claims that *ʿIrfan-nama,* the text in which Keyvan laid out his views on ʿirfan and its distinction from Sufism, was written at his request.‡ This provides even more evidence that Keyvan's definition of ʿirfan found its way into literary circles through his communication with scholars such as Qazvini, Eqbal, and Yasemi.

Not all modernist intellectuals of Iran agreed, however, that even a domesticated version of Sufism, best represented by Rumi and Hafez and called ʿirfan or whatever else, could be a healthy contributing factor to their imagined prosperous, modern, and progressive nation of Iran. The most outspoken of these dissenters was Ahmad Kasravi (d. 1946), whose opposition to Sufism and the orientalist agenda of promoting poets such as Hafez and Rumi has already been covered by several scholars.§ Although Kasravi's suspicion of the

* Qazvini, *Bist maqala,* 18–20.

† Yasemi's introduction to Keyvan, *ʿIrfan-nama,* 21–26.

‡ Yasemi's introduction to Keyvan, *ʿIrfan-nama,* 26.

§ See, for example, Ridgeon, *The Sufi Castigator* and "Aḥmad Kasravī's Criticisms."

colonial agenda hidden beneath the disguise of orientalism was later picked up by Iranian intellectuals influenced by the rise of leftist movements across the globe, including Jalal Al-e Ahmad (d. 1969) and ʿAli Shariʿati (d. 1977), his wholesale rejection of Persian poetry and the legacy of Sufism did not gain much traction.

Morteza Motahhari (d. 1980) and ʿIrfan

The influence of Keyvan's definition of ʿirfan was not confined to secularist literati who considered individualistic spirituality more appropriate for a modern nation than a socially and politically active religion. In fact, it was a group of neotraditionalist ulama that played the major role in promoting ʿirfan in the 1970s. These clerics were mostly favorably inclined toward the revolutionary ideas of Khomeini, and their support helped lead to the appointment of a "perfect ʿarif" as the Supreme Leader.* Prominent among them was Morteza Motahhari Farimani, a student of Khomeini who later came to be recognized as the foremost ideologue of the Islamic Revolution. Motahhari was a hybrid figure. He had extensive madrasa training and was deeply invested in the Islamic rational disciplines, but at the same time he had an abiding interest in modern Western thought and scientific knowledge and methodology. He took the challenge of modernism very seriously. Like Keyvan, however, he did not know any European languages, and he educated himself on various aspects of Western philosophy and social thought via translations and conversations with modern-minded intellectuals of his time. He was eager to present Islam in a way that was accessible and attractive to an educated generation of young Iranians trained in engineering and the sciences at Iran's modern institutions of higher education.

Motahhari's systematic thinking and clarity of writing is best exemplified in his *Islam and Iran: A Historical Survey of Mutual Services,* a well-received and popular book that he wrote at the request of his friend Seyyed Hossein Nasr prior to the revolution. He discusses an array of Islamic disciplines, including Qurʾanic commentary, hadith studies, grammar, philosophy, ethics, and jurisprudence, but he also dedicates an entire chapter to ʿirfan and Sufism.† His opening remarks in this detailed chapter are highly relevant to our purposes and deserve to be quoted at length:

* The term *neotraditionalist* refers to a certain group of the ulama who strongly desired continuity with the past but also appreciated the depth of the Western challenge, were deeply influenced by the scientific discourse, and selectively adopted Western ideas and practices. For an interesting example, see Doostdar's discussion of Makarem Shirazi's position in favor of scientific skepticism and empirical evidence in "Empirical Spirits."

† This chapter was added to later editions of *Khadamat.*

> ʿIrfan is one of the disciplines that originated and developed within the realm of Islamic culture, attaining a high level of sophistication. But before we can begin to discuss ʿirfan, we must realize that it can be approached from two viewpoints: the social and the cultural. Unlike the scholars of other Islamic disciplines—such as the Qurʾanic commentators, the scholars of hadith, the jurists, the theologians, the philosophers, the men of literature, and the poets—the ʿurafa are a group of scholars who have not only developed their own discipline of knowledge, that of ʿirfan, and produced great scholars and important books, but have also given rise within the Islamic world to a distinct social grouping. In this the ʿurafa are unique; for the scholars of the other Islamic disciplines—such as the jurists, for instance—form solely academic groupings and are not viewed as a social group distinct from the rest of society.
>
> In view of this distinction the folk of ʿirfan, when referred to as belonging to a certain discipline of knowledge, are called ʿurafa and when referred to as a social group are generally called Sufis [*mutasavvifa*]. The ʿurafa and Sufis are not regarded as forming a separate sect in Islam, nor do they claim themselves to be such. They are found within every Islamic school and sect, yet at the same time, they coalesce to form a distinct social group. The factors that set them apart from the rest of Islamic society are a distinctive chain of ideas and opinions, a special code governing their social intercourse, dress and even, sometimes, the way they wear their hair and beards, and their living communally in khanaqahs.
>
> Of course, there are and have always been ʿurafa—particularly amongst the Shiʿa—who bear none of these external signs to distinguish them socially from others; yet, at the same time, they have been profoundly involved in the ʿirfanian spiritual quest [*sayr va suluk*]. *It is these who are the real ʿurafa; not those who have invented for themselves hundreds of special mannerisms and customs and have brought innovations into being.**

It is clear that the distinction that Motahhari makes here is based on the dichotomy Keyvan created between "genuine Sufism/ʿirfan" and socially organized forms of Sufism. Additionally, Motahhari's insistence that there has always been ʿirfan among the Shiʿa and that the concept applies only to them is consistent with the previous trend in regard to Darabi, Nayrizi, and others. Motahhari goes on to say that he is not interested in the social and sectarian

* *Motahhari, Khadamat,* 542–43 (emphasis added).

aspects of ʿirfan, that is, what is categorized as Sufism. Rather, he wants to discuss ʿirfan as a distinct discipline of knowledge in Islamic culture. Then he adds a classification that should be familiar to us from Keyvan:

> ʿIrfan itself, as a discipline of knowledge, has two branches: the practical and the theoretical [*nazari*]. The practical aspect of ʿirfan describes and explains the relationship and responsibilities human beings bear toward themselves, toward the world, and toward God. Here, ʿirfan is similar to ethics [akhlaq], both of them being practical sciences. . . . The practical teaching of ʿirfan is also called the itinerary of the spiritual quest. Here, the wayfarer who desires to reach the goal of the sublime peak of humanity—that is to say, tawhid—is told where to set off, the ordered stages and stations that he must traverse, the states and conditions he will undergo at these stations, and the events that will befall him. Needless to say, *all these stages and stations must be passed under the guidance and supervision of a mature and perfect example of humanity who, having traveled this path, is aware of the manners and ways of each station.* If not, and there is no perfect human being to guide him on his path, he is in danger of going astray. The ʿarifin have spoken of the perfect man who must necessarily accompany the novice as the "Bird of Heaven" or *ta'ir-i quds* and Khizr.*

At this point, Motahhari quotes two verses taken from Hafez that reference Khizr and *ta'ir-i quds.*† I would like to make two significant points with regard to the preceding quotation. First of all, this classification, although inspired by Keyvan, takes an additional step—one we might call the final step—toward exorcising the "demon" of Sufism from Shiʿi discourse. For Motahhari, unlike Keyvan, there is no longer something called "genuine Sufism" that constitutes the "practical branch" of ʿirfan. Instead, Sufism has been reduced to the social institutions of traditional Sufism and the paraphernalia

* Motahhari, *Khadamat,* 542–44. Translations taken, with some modifications, from this online source: http://english.aviny.com/books/motahari/al-tawhid/irfan.aspx. In another treatise, Motahhari says that theoretical ʿirfan is "concerned with ontology, and discusses God, the world, and the human being. This aspect of ʿirfan resembles divine philosophy [*falsafa-yi ilahi*], which also seeks to explain and interpret being. Like divine philosophy, ʿirfan [as a discipline] has its own subject, essential principles, and problems, but whereas philosophy relies solely upon rational principles for its arguments, ʿirfan bases its deductions on principles discovered through mystical unveiling [*kashf*] and then reverts to the language of reason to explain them." Motahhari, *Majmuʿa asar,* 23:29.

† *Himmatam badraq-yi rah kun iy ta'ir-i quds, ki daraz ast rah-i maqsad va man nau safaram; Tark-i in marhala bi hamrahi-yi khizr makun, zulumat ast bitars az khatar-i gumrahi.*

that made Sufis distinct as a social group. Anything related to matters of spirituality and the journey toward God through purification of the soul, detachment from the world, and meditation on the final goal of tawhid is detached from Sufism and properly understood under the discipline of sayr va suluk and akhlaq, and ʿirfan-minded ulama are its guardians and exponents.

Second, it is remarkable how Motahhari meticulously avoids terms like *murshid* or *pir* despite his insistence that the spiritual path cannot be trodden without a guide. In place of these words he uses the obscure phrase *taʾir-quds* and the name Khizr, who is usually considered the hidden spiritual master of people with no formal ties to a Sufi shaykh. It is no accident that both of these terms are taken from Hafez's *Divan*. As an ʿirfan-minded religious scholar deeply engaged with modernism, Motahhari was not only in conversation with secular and religious literati of his time who valorized Hafez for their own reasons but also deeply aware of a tradition of ʿirfan-minded ulama writing poetry in the style of Hafez. These cleric-poets ranged from Shaykh Bahaʾi, to Mulla Hadi Sabzavari, to Motahhari's own philosophy teacher, Allame Tabatabaʾi. Motahhari himself had a deep engagement with the poet's ghazals, as his extensive commentary on the latter's *Divan* demonstrates.*

The extent of Motahhari's engagement with Hafez is evidenced by a series of lectures he delivered in the newly established department of theology at the University of Tehran, where he spoke in detail about the poet and ʿirfan. The lectures were later transcribed, edited, and published in the form of a book titled *ʿIrfan-i Hafez*. The central question to which Motahhari dedicates the entire introduction is "whether Hafez was really a ʿarif or not." This question references two competing contemporary representations of Hafez. From Motahhari's perspective, the wrong representation had prevailed in the media of his time. "If you read the overwhelming majority of the articles that are written nowadays about Hafez in journals, magazines, newspapers, and even some of the books recently published on Hafez, he is presented as anything but an ʿarif," he says. The trend, Motahhari claims, was to represent Hafez as an Epicurean, an antinomian hedonist poet who could not have cared less about any religion but the universal religion of love.† Although Motahhari does not name names here, in another treatise he explicitly singles out the renowned poet Ahmad Shamlu (d. 2000) as one of the most outspoken advocates of this wrong representation of Hafez.

* His marginalia on the *Divan* were published after his death in a book titled *Ayina-yi jam*. A remarkable feature of his commentary is that he ranks ghazals, based on the themes and vocabulary used, with phrases like "highly ʿirfani," "moderately ʿirfani," "containing ʿirfani allusions," and "mediocre and ʿirfani."

† Motahhari, *ʿIrfan-i Hafez*, 19. See Motahhari, *Ayina-yi jam*, x.

For Motahhari, Hafez was first and foremost a gnostic, "a flower among the many flowers of the garden of Islamic knowledge," someone who had "the lifestyle of the ulama and, at the same time that he was an ʿarif . . . was more known [in his own time] as a religious scholar."* The intellectual figure on whose shoulders Hafez stood, according to Motahhari, was none other than Ibn ʿArabi. Motahhari claimed that many of the major Persian Sufi poets such as Rumi, Mahmud Shabistari (d. 1340), and Shams Maghribi (d. 1277) were students of the school of Ibn ʿArabi.† The centrality of Ibn ʿArabi to his understanding of ʿirfan reflects the deep influence of the madrasa-based notion of ʿirfan on his views. The exclusive emphasis on Ibn ʿArabi in this version of ʿirfan marginalizes or overlooks an equally strong lineage of Sufism in which the concept of love (ʿishq), rather than knowledge of God (maʿrifa), plays the most fundamental role. Ecstatic and passionate Sufis such as Ahmad Ghazali (d. 1126), Ruzbihan Baqli (d. 1209), and Rumi, among others, are considered the standard bearers of the parallel tradition of ʿishq-based Sufism. This tradition was never as successfully absorbed into orthodox Shiʿi discourse as Ibn ʿArabi's school. Instead, it remained central to khanaqah-based forms of Sufism, from whence it captured the attention of some of the modern-minded literati of the twentieth century, who saw in it an expression of their secularist, anticlerical, spiritual, and/or humanistic aspirations. Motahhari's attempts to portray Hafez as a "flower of the garden of Islamic knowledge" and a student of Ibn ʿArabi and to read Hafez in a completely symbolic fashion was another step in the process of domesticating traditional Sufi discourse, this time by a modern, madrasa-trained, ʿirfan-minded religious scholar. Motahhari's symbolic treatment of Hafez followed a long tradition among ʿirfan-minded ulama, some already mentioned, whose reading of Sufi love poetry was completely detached from bodily desires.‡ Khomeini's *Divan,* published after his death, bears a striking resemblance to that of Hafez in both vocabulary and theme, and it could well be considered the final "official" step in recognizing this tradition, though the process of domestication remains far from finished.

Motahhari's take on whether Hafez can be considered an ʿarif can be fruitfully compared to that of the eminent scholar Ehsan Yarshater, a secularist contemporary of Motahhari. In his erudite introduction to *Encyclopedia Iranica*'s long entry on Hafez, Yarshater dedicates a long passage to answering this question:

> Hafez very often is called an ʿārif. The application of this term depends on what is meant by it. If by ʿārif is meant a person of wisdom

* Motahhari, *ʿIrfan-i Hafez,* 26 and 52.

† Ibid., 42–58.

‡ Motahhari, *ʿIrfan-i Hafez,* 50–52.

> and insight, broad-mindedness and understanding, given to reflection on human destiny, the transience of life, and the vanity of our worldly concerns, a man who would not go for the dogmatic rigidity of formal religion and the intervention of self-appointed guardians of faith in the daily lives of believers, but would prefer the devotion of truly pious men and sets high value on purity of heart and kindliness towards others rather than pretentious observation of religious ordinances—in other words, a benevolent sage—there is no reason to deny that epithet to Hafez. . . . On the other hand, if by ʿārif is meant a "mystic," that is, a person who believes in the theory and practice of Sufism, is attached to a certain Order or the circle of a Sufi mentor [pir] or a khānaqāh, or allows the clarity of his mind to be clouded by the irrational and obfuscated by the woolly thinking of some Sufis and their belief in miraculous deeds ascribed to their saints, then the epithet is a misnomer. While it is clear that Hafez distinguishes sincere, self-effacing, and godly mystics from the false ones, he does not belong to any Sufi school of thought, but chooses to be entirely free and independent of any such attachment. . . . Confusing Hafez's lack of fanaticism, his broad world view, and his contemplative and moral musings with "mysticism" implies a subjective interpretation of his poetry.*

The contrast is quite remarkable: to Motahhari, Hafez was a religious scholar, someone who had "the lifestyle the ulama" and was "a flower of the garden of Islamic knowledge." To Yarshater, Hafez was "a man who would not go for the dogmatic rigidity of formal religion and the intervention of self-appointed guardians of faith in the daily lives of believers." Obviously, the concern with whether Hafez was a true ʿarif and, more important, what constitutes a true ʿarif more generally is less about the poet himself and more about competing views on the nature and function of religion in modern Iran. Despite the remarkable contrast in their views, however, Yarshater and Motahhari are united in their observation that Hafez was as far as one can get from organized Sufism. In both idealizations the poet stands in ultimate contrast to Sufism, as a person who would never allow "the clarity of his mind to be clouded by the irrational and obfuscated by the woolly thinking of some Sufis and their belief in miraculous deeds ascribed to their saints."

To conclude, a common thread links the different ways the concept of ʿirfan has been deployed by modern Iranians. Whether they were traditional and madrasa-based, neotraditional and revolutionary, or modernist and secular, all have used ʿirfan in apposition to Sufism. Each group has had

* Yarshater, "Hafez I. An Overview."

different reasons for resenting the traditional mode of Sufi piety, but all have domesticated and appropriated its rich and multifaceted discourse for their own purposes. The result has been an equally rich and multifaceted concept called ʿirfan, the origins and development of which have been the subject of this book.

Epilogue

ʿIrfan as Mysticism?

I wish to close this book with a few words about ʿirfan as mysticism. Throughout this work, I have avoided translating *ʿirfan* as *mysticism.* This is not because I object to such a translation in principle. Rather, in a book dedicated to the complex intellectual and social phenomena that led to the emergence and development of ʿirfan as a category and given my extensive engagement with primary sources, I thought using the original term would make it easier for the reader to follow the story with less distraction. In modern Persian discourse, however, *mysticism* has been translated as *ʿirfan* for quite a while now. As mentioned, Kazemzade Iranshahr's translation of the French term *mystique* into *ʿirfan* in the early 1940s might be one of the earliest examples of what is now a standard practice in translation.* The universal, nonsectarian, and individualistic notion of ʿirfan promoted by the literary figures of the mid-twentieth century gained increasing popularity as Iran witnessed exponential growth in literacy rates among its nascent modern middle-class population.† As increasing numbers of books written in European languages, especially those on psychological and self-help topics, were translated into Persian, translators used the term *ʿirfan* naturally as an equivalent to *mysticism.* The work of the prominent American philosopher and psychologist William James played a role in this regard. He was already known in Iran‡ when his classic work *The Varieties of Religious Experience* became available to the public in partial Persian translation in 1964.§

* Kazemzade Iranshahr, *Asar va ahval,* 203–4.

† For the emergence of a middle class in Iran in the first half of the twentieth century, see Schayegh, *Who Is Knowledgeable, Is Strong,* 53–72.

‡ For example, translations from his works in psychology appeared in the Iranian journal *Mehr* as early as 1938. See Sanaʿi, "Mabahis maʿrifat al-nafsi."

§ It is noteworthy that Motahhari was aware of this translation and thus aware of the vocabulary of "religious experience" and "mysticism." For example, he notes that "among the modern psychologists, there is one person who has some knowledge in this area (maybe there are more; he is the only one I know). He is the famous American philosopher and psychologist William James . . . he wrote a book

Din va ravan (Religion and the Psyche) contained six lectures translated from *Varieties,* including James's discussion of mysticism. In the Persian translation, *ʿirfan* is chosen as the term equivalent to *mysticism,* though at times the term *Sufism* appears in conjunction with it.* By the time Baha'oddin Khorramshahi offered his masterful translation of Walter T. Stace's (d. 1967) *Mysticism and Philosophy,* which appeared on bookstore shelves in postrevolutionary Iran, the vocabulary of "religious experience" had been fully absorbed into Persian discourse.†

The choice of intellectuals and scholars to translate *mysticism* as *ʿirfan* might be criticized or dismissed on the grounds that these translators were ignorant of the complex history of the English term and the story of its emergence in the West in the late nineteenth century, when scholars such as James and Emerson used it as a universal concept referring to what they saw as the "common spiritual core" of different religions.‡ This notion, it has been argued, is characterized by a privatization often considered a prominent feature of a distinctively modern and Western religious consciousness shaped by particular social and political contexts that cannot be generalized to other cultures.§ Richard King deals with this aspect of mysticism to some extent in his *Orientalism and Religion.* Speaking of what he sees as distinctive features of modern Western notions of mysticism, King says, "[T]he privatization of mysticism—that is, the increasing tendency to locate the mystical in the psychological realm of personal experiences— serves to exclude it from political

---

with an original title of something like *Religious Experiences* [*sic*]. Part of this book is translated into Persian under the tile of *Religion and Psyche.* This man himself was an ʿirfan-minded religious person, he was both ʿirfan-minded and a psychologist . . . he deeply believed in mystical psychic states." See Motahhari, *ʿIrfan-i Hafez,* 12–13.

* While Qa'emi uses *ʿirfan* as an independent equivalent term for *mysticism,* he sometimes pays lip service to established conventions of the past and, to make the meaning clear, pairs *ʿirfan* with the term *Sufism* (saying "*ʿirfan va tasavvuf*"). This did not happen in later translations. For example, a couple of years later, in 1970, the prominent translator Najaf Daryabadari (d. 2014) translated a collection of articles by the British philosopher Bertrand Russell, including "Logic and Mysticism," which was translated as *ʿIrfan va mantiq* with no reference to Sufism at all.

† It is hard to overemphasize the influence that James and Stace, through these translations, have had in introducing and establishing of the vocabulary of religious experience in Persian with strong perennialist undertones. Many of the monographs and articles that have appeared in subsequent decades take the basically perennialist view that mysticism has an unchanging essence that runs through all religious traditions.

‡ For a rich and fascinating analysis of the sociocultural background that gave rise to the concept of mysticism, see Schmidt, "The Making of Modern 'Mysticism.'"

§ King, *Orientalism and Religion,* 13.

issues such as social justice. Mysticism thus has become seen as a personal matter of cultivating inner states of tranquility and equanimity, which, rather than seeking to transform the world, serve to accommodate the individual to the status quo through the alleviation of anxiety and stress. . . . In this way, mysticism has been thoroughly domesticated . . . [it] has become at once decontextualized, . . . elitist, . . . antisocial, . . . [and] otherworldly."*

King, like many other scholars of religion who concentrate on postcolonial studies, is primarily focused on Eastern religions, especially Hinduism and Buddhism. But the case studies in his work and that of many others are used to draw broad conclusions about how concepts such as religion and mysticism, as categories deeply embedded in the history of Western colonialism, should either be abandoned completely in scholarly discourse or not applied in comparative analysis and cross-cultural classifications. There is no question that such studies, which reexamine the historical contingencies that shape our seemingly solid categories, need to be taken seriously. In fact, they *have been* taken seriously by scholars, and for good reason.

What makes me uncomfortable with this scholarly trend, however, is its exclusive attention to the modern West and its emphasis on the utter distinction between the West and the rest and between the modern and the premodern. These dichotomies are supposed to be destabilized in postcolonial and postmodern frames of thought, but somehow they always manage to sneak their way back in, as can be evidenced in, for example, Fitzgerald's *The Ideology of Religious Studies.*† This, I believe, has partly to do with the current state of the study of religion and the default position of prioritizing Western phenomena in religious theorizing.‡

In their attempt to break away from the status quo by focusing on Eastern rather than Western religious phenomena, deconstructionists easily fall into a reactionary discourse that reproduces the same binary thinking and modes of power and dominion that they supposedly reject. In their determination to fight the perceived imperialistic agenda of religious studies as a Western discipline of knowledge and to indict the scholars of religion for their sins in this regard, the agency of the "other" is too easily dismissed as a form of "resistance" or "adaptation." It is as if other cultures and civilizations have never been smart enough or imperialist enough, for that matter, to think of comparisons and classifications or to impose their constructed categories on others. But we know that other cultures have also used comparative analyses, that they have objectified their own others. We know that

* King, *Orientalism and Religion,* 21ff.

† *Fitzgerald, Ideology of Religious Studies.*

‡ Orsi, *Cambridge Companion,* 3–12.

Western colonialism was not the first colonialism and that comparison has long been an imperial enterprise.* Only by taking these things into account can we overcome recent moves in the humanities toward the ghettoization of the Western world of ideas.

Additionally, although the enormous transformation of human life in the modern period originated in the West, it has long since ceased to be a particularly Western phenomenon. The modern condition is and has been for quite a while a global phenomenon. It occurs in a variety of local, national, and international forms, but these share common features that distinguish themselves from premodern ways of organizing individual and social life. They share in common a prioritization of an "imminent," this-worldly framework for understanding and pursuing the ultimate goal of "human flourishing," to use Charles Taylor's terminology.† The efforts of modern-minded Iranian intellectuals and scholars to introduce the concept of ʿirfan as a signifier for an individualistic, universal, rational, science-friendly, and egalitarian mode of piety detailed here are only one example of the many ways the modern condition manifests itself. What is significant about these efforts, however, is that they were not simply a wholesale importation of a Western idea or ideal. Rather, they were creative efforts to tap into poignant symbols already present and well developed across the long history of a rich Persianate and, more broadly, Islamicate civilization and to reimagine those symbols as elements of Iran's new identity as a modern nation.

The concept of ʿirfan was chosen, I argue, not by chance but because it already carried with it some of the most important features of the modern concept of mysticism. It emerged, as we saw, as a depoliticized and decontextualized alternative to Sufism, stripped of the extensive social network that supported traditional Sufi organizations centered around the khanaqah. This is not, of course, to say that the post-Safavid concept of ʿirfan was devoid of authoritative and hegemonic systems that controlled its function. The ʿirfanian quest was possible for the adept only if he or she operated within the established norms of Twelver orthodoxy. But the fact remains that the intimate and highly hierarchical personal relationship between master and disciple was transformed into a symbolic and highly abstract form of relationship in which a significant amount of agency was transferred to the adept, broadening the range of interpretive choices when it came to texts, dreams, and traditions relevant to his or her spiritual quest.

To return to the controversial example of Hafez, there is no denying

* Doniger, "Comparisons," 63–74.

† Taylor, *A Secular Age.*

that strong resentment toward formalized and institutionalized forms of religiosity pervades his poems. There is nothing exclusively modern about the refusal to be limited to the confines of dominant modes of piety or about reaching for a more universal, free-spirited, and perhaps individualist spirituality. As Sufi institutions developed and worship became more formalized, or, to put it in Hodgson's terms, as the early Sufi tradition of intensive interiorization re-exteriorized its results,* focus often shifted to institutional formalities, outward signs of piety, and the nuances of outward performance. As a result of their popularity, Sufi shaykhs were able to secure huge financial resources—mostly in the form of pious endowments and donations—and to forge political connections with local and regional powers. As these worldly matters influenced the rank and file of those affiliated with the khanaqah, the problems of hypocrisy (*riya*) and dissimulation (*tazvir*) became the objects of important cultural critique. Hafez's vehement criticism of such traits should be understood in this context. Like Rumi, he preferred the antinomian Qalandar, the bandit (*rind*)† whose hallmark is an absolute indifference to social status and outward appearance and a disregard for the sham piety of ascetics and Sufis and the superficial and dishonest spirituality trumpeted by their ceremonious attire. Hafez decried such hypocrisy, saying:

> Not all Sufi coin is pure and unadulterated,
> How many cloaks deserve to be thrown in the fire!
> If only the touchstone of experience were in our midst,
> So that those who are adulterated might be embarrassed.
> Those brought up in the lap of luxury will not find their way to the
>   friend,
> The lover's path is for the *rind* who throws caution to the wind.
> Hafez' old cloak and prayer mat will go to the wine-seller,
> If his wine comes from the hand of the moon-faced cup-bearer.‡

Hafiz portrays the ʿarif as part and parcel of the Sufi world, a world from which he can (and must) redeem himself.§ In order to find such redemption, he needs only to burn the Sufi cloak:

* Hodgson, *Venture of Islam,* 2:218.

† The *rind,* a word variously translated in English as "rake, ruffian, pious rogue, brigand, libertine, lout, debauché," is the very antithesis of establishment propriety. For more on Hafez's depiction of rind and Qalandar see Lewis, "Hafez viii. Hafez and Rendi."

‡ Ghazal 155. My references to ghazals follow the numbering in Khanlari's critical edition of Hafez's *Divan.*

§ Lewis, "Hafez viii. Hafez and Rendi."

O ʿarif wayfarer, set fire to the cloak,
Apply yourself, and become the leader of the *rinds* of the world.*

Similarly, deemphasizing the need for a spiritual master and the more individualistic model of spiritual quest to which that leads is not uniquely modern. Hafez consistently spoke of an adept's need for a guide in the spiritual journey but noted that the adept's discourse could not be reduced to an essentially Sufi, institutional one. The spiritual guide of Hafez's poetry is the *pir-i mughan,* the Zoroastrian master based in the tavern (*kharabat*). Much ink has been spilled in the effort to identify this figure as a real human being, a Sufi shaykh of a specific khanaqah, but Hafez's elusive, highly symbolic language refuses all attempts to reduce this abstract idea to a particular social reality or concrete hierarchical relationship.†

My point is simple. In response to the quotation from King's work, I say that there is nothing uniquely modern or Western about something being decontextualized, elitist, individualistic, depoliticized, anti-institution, otherworldly, or domesticated. ʿIrfan carried similar connotations even at its earliest stages of development, many years before the advent of modernity in Persia. And its development in the modern period was not simply the result of a scholarly and/or imperial will to make it, in the words of King, "amenable to simplistic comparative analysis." Nor was ʿirfan the conceptual product of foreign agents seeking to declaw Sufism and make it "irreconcilable with the goals of political and social transformation," turning it into an antirevolutionary opiate, so to speak. It is true that Sufism was domesticated and even violently suppressed. But concurrent with—though quite independent from—that suppression and domestication, ʿirfan flourished as a distinct notion of the mystical quest with its own rational, elitist, and otherworldly flavor.

In other words, while there is no doubt that certain aspects of the contemporary notion of ʿirfan, such as the idea that it could be detached from a particular religious context and the emphasis on its compatibility with empirical science and technology, developed in response to and were influenced by the process of modernization in Iran, other elements have been in the

* Ghazal 267.

† Motahhari considers Hafez's lack of reference to a specific spiritual guide as a sign that his mode of piety was close to that of orthodox Shiʿi ʿarifin, rather than traditional Sufis (see Motahhari, *ʿIrfan-i Hafez,* 22–23), Pourjavady, on the other hand, argues that Hafez's reference to a "rose-colored master" (see ghazal 199) is better understood not as referring to a human guide but as a symbolic reference to the abstract divine reality, the active intellect that manifests itself to the wayfarer to guide him along the path, much as we saw in Ibn Sina's *Hayy ibn Yaqzan* (see Pourjavady, *Ishraq va ʿirfan,* 166–77).

making since the seventeenth century as part of the internal dynamics of Persian-Shiʿi culture. If ʿirfan as a category referring to a privatized, reason-friendly, egalitarian, and universal concept resembles the concept of mysticism, it is not because it was transplanted into the soil of Iranian culture by so-called Westoxificated puppets of imperialism or by reactionary fundamentalists who, despite their rhetoric, were deeply embedded in modernity. Nations experienced huge transformations in the process of modernization, but creating a wall between the modern and the premodern does a remarkable disservice to our ability to understand these important transitions. There was transformation and rupture, but there was also continuity. No nation has become modern in a vacuum, and Iran is no exception. In proposing ʿirfan as an alternative to Sufism, modern Iranian intellectuals appropriated an already well-developed notion that they found to be an apt expression of their aspirations.

BIBLIOGRAPHY

Manuscripts

ʿAmilī, ʿAlī b. Muḥammad b. al-Ḥasan b. Zayn al-Dīn. *al-Sihām al-māriqa fī aghrāż al zanādiqa.* 1086h. No. 1968. Kitābkhāna-yi markazī va markaz-i asnād-i dānishgāh-i Tehran.

Anonymous. *Silsila-yi* sidīriyya-yi nūrbakhshiyya-yi hamadāniyya. n.d. No. 4689/2. Kitābkhāna-yi markazī va markaz-i asnād-i dānishgāh-i Tehran.

Ardabīlī Bīdgulī, Mīrzā Muḥammad (Muḥaqqiq). *Tazkirat al-ẓākirīn.* 1194h. No. 345. Kitābkhāna-yi madrasa-yi namāzī.

Balkhī, Shaqīq b. Ibrāhīm. *Miṣbāḥ al-sharīʿa va miftāḥ al-ḥaqīqa / Min taṣānīf al-Shaqīq al-Balkhī.* 711h. MS Arab 124. Hougton Library, Harvard University. Available at http://nrs.harvard.edu/urn-3:FHCL.HOUGH:1580067.

Damāvandī, ʿAbd al-Raḥīm. *Fuyūżāt al-ḥusayniyya fi tafṣīl al-insān al-kāmil ʿalā al-Qurʿān.* 1188–1206h. No. 1952, f. 62b-66b. Kitābkhāna-yi Buzurg-i ḥażrat āyat allāh al-ʿuẓmā marʿashī najafī.

———. *Ḥall-i rumūz rażaviyya dar sharḥ-i ḥadīs ra's al-jālūt.* 1188–1206h. No. 1952, f. 60a-62a. Kitābkhāna-yi Buzurg-i ḥażrat āyat allāh al-ʿuẓmā marʿashī najafī.

———. *Sharḥ-i kalām-i ʿalavī.* 1188–1206h. No. 1952, f. 70a-78a. Kitābkhāna-yi Buzurg-i ḥażrat āyat allāh al-ʿuẓmā marʿashī najafī.

———. *al-Tawḥīd.* 1188–1206h. No. 1952, f. 66b-69b. Kitābkhāna-yi Buzurg-i ḥażrat āyat allāh al-ʿuẓmā marʿashī najafī.

Dārābī, Shāh Muḥammad. *Faraḥ al-sālikīn.* 1246h. No. 5925. Kitābkhāna, mūza, va markaz-i asnād-i majlis-i shūrā-yi islāmī.

———. *Maslak-i ahl-i ʿirfān.* n.d. No. 23251. Kitābkhāna-yi āstān-i quds rażavī.

———. *Miʿrāj al-kamāl.* n.d. No. 7205. Kitābkhāna-yi āstān-i quds rażavī.

———. *Risāla fī taḥqīq ʿālam al-misāl.* n.d. No. 10819. Kitābkhāna-yi āstān-i quds rażavī.

ʿIṣām, Muḥammad b. Niẓām al-Dīn. *Naṣīḥat al-kirām va fażīḥat al-liʾām.* 1083h. No. 10369. Kitābkhāna, mūza, va markaz-i asnād-i majlis-i shūrā-yi islāmī.

Khājūʾī, Ismāʿīl. *Radd-i sūfiyān.* n.d. No. 869/2. Kitābkhāna-yi dānishgāh-i Isfahān.

———. *Vahdat-i vujūd.* n.d. No. 5084. Kitābkhāna-yi Buzurg-i ḥażrat āyat allāh al-ʿuẓmā marʿashī najafī.

Khārazmī, Kamāl al-Dīn Ḥusayn. *Ādāb al-murīdīn.* 936h. No. 10043. Kitābkhāna, mūza, va markaz-i asnād-i majlis-i shūrā-yi islāmī.

Lawḥī, Mir Muḥammad. *Arbaʿīn.* n.d. No. 0356. Caro Minasian Collection of Persian and Arabic Manuscripts. Department of Special Collections. Library of the University of California, Los Angeles.

———. *Kifāyat al-muhtadī fi maʿrifat al-mahdī.* 1083h. No. 1154. Kitābkhāna-yi markazi va markaz-i asnād-i dānishgāh-i Tehran.

Mu'azzin Khurāsānī (Mashhadī Sabzavārī), Muḥammad ʿAlī. *Dīvān.* n.d. No. 8983/1. Kitābkhāna, mūza, va markaz-i asnād-i majlis-i shūrā-yi islāmī.

———. *Tuḥfa-yi ʿAbbāsī.* (MS1). n.d. No. 17760. Kitābkhāna, mūza, va markaz-i asnād-i majlis-i shūrā-yi islāmī.

———. *Tuḥfa-yi ʿAbbāsī.* (MS2). 1077h. No. 590. Caro Minasian Collection of Persian and Arabic Manuscripts. Department of Special Collections. Library of the University of California, Los Angeles.

Nayrīzī, Sayyid Quṭb al-Dīn Muḥammad. *Qasida-yi ʿishqiyya.* n.d. No. 4889, f. 72b-114a. Kitābkhāna, mūza, va markaz-i asnād-i majlis-i shūrā-yi islāmī.

———. *Risāla-yi juz' va kull.* n.d. No. 4889, f. 14a-18a. Kitābkhāna, mūza, va markaz-i asnād-i majlis-i shūrā-yi islāmī.

Qummī, Mīrzā Abu al-Qāsim. *Risāla-yi radd-i ṣufiyya dar javāb-i mīrzā ʿabd al-vahhāb munshī al-mamālik.* 1230h. No. 5348, Kitābkhāna, mūza, va markaz-i asnād-i majlis-i shūrā-yi islāmī.

Qummī, Muḥammad Ṭāhir. *Bahjat al-dārayn.* 1055h. No. Ar. 5431. The Chester Beatty Library.

———. *al-Favā'id al-dīniyya.* n.d. No. 2749. Kitābkhāna-yi markazi va markaz-i asnād-i dānishgāh-i Tehran.

———. *Ḥikmat al-ʿārifīn.* 1079h. No. 13822. Kitābkhāna, mūza, va markaz-i asnād-i majlis-i shūrā-yi islāmī.

———. *Radd-i ṣūfiyān.* n.d. No. 5468. Kitābkhāna-yi markazi va markaz-i asnād-i dānishgāh-i Tehran.

Shīrvānī, Zayn al-ʿĀbidīn. *Ḥadā'iq al-siyāḥa.* 1244h. No. 15848. Kitābkhāna, mūza, va markaz-i asnād-i majlis-i shūrā-yi islāmī.

Ṭabīb Tunikābunī, Muḥammad Mu'min. *Tabṣīrat al-mu'minīn.* 1215h. No. 3928. Kitābkhāna, mūza, va markaz-i asnād-i majlis-i shūrā-yi islāmī.

Tabrīzī Isfahānī (Zargar), Najīb al-Dīn Riżā. *Nūr al-hidāya.* 1230h. No. 4978. Kitābkhāna, mūza, va markaz-i asnād-i majlis-i shūrā-yi islāmī.

———. *Sabʿ al-maṣānī.* n.d. No. 2901. Kitābkhāna, mūza, va markaz-i asnād-i majlis-i shūrā-yi islāmī.

Zāhidī, Ḥusayn. *Bayān al-asrār.* n.d. No. 3043/1. Kitābkhāna, mūza, va markaz-i asnād-i majlis-i shūrā-yi islāmī.

Other Sources

Abisaab, Rula Jurdi. *Converting Persia: Religion and Power in the Safavid Empire.* London: I. B. Tauris, 2004.

ʿAbu al-Khayr, Muḥammad b. Abū Saʿīd. *Asrār al-tawḥīd fī maqāmāt al-shaykh abī saʿīd.* Edited by Ahmad Bahmanyar. Tehran: Kitābkhāna-yi ṭahūrī, 1978.

Adang, Camilla. *Muslim Writers on Judaism and the Hebrew Bible: From Ibn Rabban to Ibn Hazm.* Islamic Philosophy, Theology, and Science 22. Leiden: E. J. Brill, 1996.

Afandī, ʿAbdullāh b. ʿIsā. *Riyāż al-ʿulamā va-ḥiyāż al-fużalā.* Qum: Maktabat āyat allāh al-marʿashī al-ʿāmma, 1981.

Aflākī, Shams al-Dīn Aḥmad. *Manāqib al-ʿārifīn.* Edited by Tahsin Yazıcı. Türk Tarih Kurumu Yayınları. III. Dizi; Sa. 3. Ankara: Chāpkhāna-yi anjuman-i tārīkh-i turk, 1959.

Afshar, Iraj, and Fakhreddin ʿAzimi. "FORŪGĪ, MOḤAMMAD-ʿALĪ ḎOKĀʾ-AL-MOLK." In *Encyclopedia Iranica,* edited by Ehsan Yarshater. Accessed July 2, 2015, http://www.iranicaonline.org/articles/forugi-mohammad-ali.

Afshar, Iraj, and Mohammad-Taqi Daneshpazhuh. *Fihrist-i kitābhā-yi kitābkhāna-yi markazī-i dānishgāh-i Tehran.* 10 vols. Tehran: Dānishgāh-i Tehran: Intishārāt-i kitābkhāna-yi markazī va markaz-i asnād, 1965.

ʿAlavī ʿAmilī, Aḥmad. "Iẓhār al-ḥaqq va miʿyār al-ṣidq." In *Miraṣ-i islāmī-yi irān,* edited by Rasul Jaʿfariyan, 2:260–68. Qum: Kitābkhāna-yi ḥażrat-i āyat allāh al-ʿuẓmā marʿashī najafī, 1994.

Algar, Hamid. "BEHBAHĀNĪ, MOḤAMMAD-ʿALĪ." In *Encyclopedia Iranica,* edited by Ehsan Yarshater. Accessed July 2, 2015, http://www.iranicaonline.org/articles /behbahani-aqa-mohammad-ali-b.

———. "BEHBAHĀNĪ, MOḤMMAD-BĀQER." In *Encyclopedia Iranica,* edited by Ehsan Yarshater. Accessed July 2, 2015, http://www.iranicaonline.org/articles /behbahani-aqa-sayyed-mohmmad-baqer-shiite-mojtahed-and-champion-of-the -osuli-school-in-shiite-law-feqh.

———. "Naqshbandīs and Safavids: A Contribution to the Religious History of Iran and Her Neighbors." In *Safavid Iran and Her Neighbors,* edited by Michel M Mazzaoui, 7–48. Salt Lake City: University of Utah Press, 2003.

———. *Religion and State in Iran, 1785–1906: The Role of the Ulama in the Qajar Period.* Berkeley: University of California Press, 1980.

Algar, Hamid, and J. Burton-Page. "Niʿmat-Allāhiyya." In *Encyclopaedia of Islam,* second edition, edited by P. Bearman, Th. Bianquis, C. E. Bosworth, E. van Donzel, and W. P. Heinrichs. Brill Online. Accessed July 2, 2015, http://referenceworks .brillonline.com/entries/encyclopaedia-of-islam-2/nimat-allahiyya-COM_0865.

Amanat, Abbas. Introduction to *The Persian Revolution of 1905–1909,* by Edward Granville Browne, edited by Abbas Amanat, i–xxvii. Washington, D.C.: Mage, 2006.

———. *Resurrection and Renewal: The Making of the Babi Movement in Iran, 1844–1850.* Ithaca: Cornell University Press, 1989.

ʿĀmilī, Sayyid Muḥsin Amīn. *Aʿyān al-shīʿa.* 11 vols. Beirut: Dar al-Taʿāruf, 1986.

ʿAmili (Shahīd Ṣānī), Zayn al-Dīn b. ʿAlī. *Munyat al-murīd fī adab al-mufīd va al-mustafīd.* Edited by Reza Mokhtari. Beirut: al-Amīra li al-ṭibāʿa va al-nashr va al-tawzīʿ, 2006.

———. *Ṭabaqāt aʿlām al-shīʿa.* Edited by Ali-Naqi Monzavi. 6 vols. Qum: Muʾassasa ismāʿīlīyān, 1990.

Aminrazavi, Mehdi. "Islamic Philosophy in the Modern Islamic World: Persia." In *History of Islamic Philosophy,* edited by Seyyed Hossein Nasr and Oliver Leaman, 1037–50. Routledge History of World Philosophies. London: Routledge, 1996.

Amir-Moezzi, Mohammad Ali. *The Divine Guide in Early Shiʿism: The Sources of Esotericism in Islam.* Albany: State University of New York Press, 1994.

———. *The Spirituality of Shiʿi Islam: Beliefs and Practices.* London: I. B. Tauris, 2011.

Amir-Moezzi, Mohammad Ali, and Hasan Ansari. "Muḥammad b. Yaʿqūb al-Kulaynī (m. 328 ou 329/939–40 ou 940-41) et son Kitāb al-Kāfī: une introduction." *Studia Iranica* 38 ii (2009): 191–247.

Anawati, Georges C. *Muʾallafāt Ibn Sīnā.* Cairo: Dār al-maʿārif, 1950.

———. "Polémique, apologie et dialogue Islamo-chrétiens: positions classiques médiévales et positions contemporaines." *Euntes Docete* 22 (1969): 375–452.

Anzali, Ata. "The Emergence of the Ẕahabiyya in Safavid Iran." *Journal of Sufi Studies* 2, no. 2 (2013): 149–75.

———. "Khānaqāh-i nūrbakhshiyya dar sidīr (maʿrūf bi buqʿa-yi Pīr-i Istīr)." *ʿIrfān-i Irān* 39 (2015): 35–56.

———. "Opposition to Sufism in Safavid Iran: A Debate Between Mulla Muhammad-Tahir Qummi and Mulla Muhammad-Taqi Majlisi." In *Empires of the Near East and India: Source Studies of the Safavid, Ottoman, and Mughal Literary Communities,* edited by Hani Khafipour. New York: Columbia University Press (forthcoming 2017).

———. *Sākhtgirāʾī, sunnat va ʿirfān.* Qum: Anjuman-i maʿārif-i islāmī, 2005.

Anzali, Ata, and S. M. Hadi Gerami. *Opposition to Philosophy in Safavid Iran: Mulla Muhammad-Tahir Qummi's Hikmat al-ʿArifin.* Leiden: Brill (forthcoming 2017).

Aqa Nuri, ʿAli. *ʿĀrifān-i musalmān va sharīʿat-i islām.* Qum: Nashr-i dānishgāh-i adyān, 2008.

ʿArab, ʿAlireza. *Taṣavvuf va ʿirfān az dīdgāh-i ʿulamā-yi mutaʾakhkhir-i shiʿa.* Tehran: Intishārāt-i żāmin-i āhū, 2009.

Arjomand, Said Amir. *The Shadow of God and the Hidden Imam: Religion, Political Order, and Societal Change in Shiʿite Iran from the Beginning to 1890.* Publications of the Center for Middle Eastern Studies, 17. Chicago: University of Chicago Press, 1984.

Arnaldez, R. "Maʿrifa." In *Encyclopaedia of Islam,* second edition, edited by P. Bearman, Th. Bianquis, C. E. Bosworth, E. van Donzel, and W. P. Heinrichs. Brill Online. Accessed July 2, 2015, http://referenceworks.brillonline.com/entries/encyclopaedia-of-islam-2/marifa-COM_0686.

Asad, Talal, *Genealogies of Religion: Discipline and Reasons of Power in Christianity and Islam.* Baltimore: Johns Hopkins University Press, 1993.

ʿĀshiqī, ʿAlī Ḥasan Khān. *Ṣubḥ-i gulshan.* Bhopal: Fayz-i manbā-yi ranq-i āriyai, 1878. Available at http://hdl.handle.net/2027/uc1.b3819092.

Ashkevari, Sadeq. "ʿĀlam al-miṣāl: muʿarrifī-yi pazhūhishī az ʿaṣr-i ṣafavī." *Iṭṭilāʿāt-i ḥikmat va maʿrifat* 73 (2012): 34–35.

———. "Introduction." In *Taẕkira-yi laṭāʾif al-khayāl* by Shāh Muḥammad Dārābī, edited by Yusef Beyg-Babapour, ix–lxxii. Qum: Majmaʿ-i zakhāʾir-i islāmī, 2012.

Ashtiyani, Jalal al-Din. Introduction (I) to *Risāla-i nūriyya dar ʿālam-i miṣāl* by Bahāʾī Lāhījī, edited by Jalal al-Din Ashtiyani. Tehran: Ḥawza-yi hunarī-yi sāzmān-i tablīghāt-i islāmī, daftar-i muṭālaʿāt-i dīnī-yi hunar, 1993.

———. Introduction (II) to *Sharḥ risālat al-mashāʿir Mullā Ṣadrā* by Muḥammad Jaʿfar b. Muḥammad Ṣādiq Lāhījānī, edited by Jalal al-Din Ashtiyani. Qum: Maktab al-iʿlām al-islāmī, n.d.

———. Introduction (III) to *al-Shavāhid al-rubūbiyya fī al-manāhij al-sulūkiyya* by

Ṣadr al-Dīn Shīrāzī, edited by Jalal al-Din Ashtiyani. Mashhad: Markaz-i nashr-i dānishgāhī, 1981.

———. *Sharḥ-i ḥāl va ārāyi falsafī-yi mullā ṣadrā.* Tehran: Nahżat-i zanān-i musalmān, 1981.

ʿAṭṭār, Farīd al-Dīn. *The Tadhkiratu'l-Awliya (Memoirs of the Saints).* Edited by Reynold A. Nicholson. Persian Historical Texts, 3, 5. London: Luzac, 1905.

Babaie, Sussan. *Slaves of the Shah: New Elites of Safavid Iran.* Library of Middle East History, 3. London: I. B. Tauris, 2004.

Babayan, Kathryn. *Mystics, Monarchs, and Messiahs: Cultural Landscapes of Early Modern Iran.* Harvard Middle Eastern Monographs, 35. Cambridge, Mass.: Harvard University Press, 2002.

———. "The Safavid Synthesis: From Qizilbash Islam to Imamite Shiʿism." *Iranian Studies* 27, no. 1/4 (January 1, 1994): 135–61.

———. "The Waning of the Qizilbash: The Spiritual and the Temporal in Seventeenth Century Iran." Ph.D. diss., Princeton University, 1993.

Bahari Hamadani, Mohammad, *Taẕkirat a-muttaqīn.* Tehran: Kitāb-furūshī Tihrānī, 1944.

Baḥr al-ʿUlūm, Muḥammad Mahdī b. Murtażā. *Risālat al-sayr va al-sulūk.* Edited by Mohammad Hoseyn Hoseyni Tehrani. Dawra-yi ʿulūm va maʿārif-i islām, 4. Beirut: Dār al-maḥajja al-bayżāʾ, 2001.

Barbaro, Giosofat, Ambrogio Contarini, William Thomas, Eugene Armand Roy, and Henry Edward John Stanley. *Travels to Tana and Persia.* Harvard College Library Preservation Microfilm Program, 02724. London: Printed for the Hakluyt Society, 1873.

Bashir, Shahzad. *Fazlallah Astarabadi and the Hurufis.* Makers of the Muslim World. Oxford: Oneworld, 2005.

———. *Messianic Hopes and Mystical Vision: The Nūrbakhshīya Between Medieval and Modern Islam.* Studies in Comparative Religion. Columbia, S.C.: University of South Carolina Press, 2003.

———. "Shah Ismaʿil and the Qizilbash: Cannibalism in the Religious History of Early Safavid Iran." *History of Religions* 45, no. 3 (February 1, 2006): 234–56.

———. *Sufi Bodies: Religion and Society in Medieval Islam.* New York: Columbia University Press, 2011.

Bayat, Mongol. "Freemasonry and the Constitutional Revolution in Iran: 1905–1911." In *Freemasonry and Fraternalism in the Middle East,* edited by Andreas Önnerfors and Dorothe Sommer, 109–50. Sheffield: University of Sheffield, 2009.

Behdad, Sohrab, and Farhad Nomani. "What a Revolution! Thirty Years of Social Class Reshuffling in Iran." *Comparative Studies of South Asia, Africa and the Middle East* 29, no. 1 (2009): 84–104.

Behnam, Jamshid. "IRĀNŠAHR, ḤOSAYN KĀẒEMZĀDA." In *Encyclopedia Iranica,* edited by Ehsan Yarshater. Accessed July 2, 2015, http://www.iranicaonline.org/articles/iransahr-hosayn-kazemzada.

Berger, Peter. *The Sacred Canopy: Elements of a Sociological Theory of Religion.* Princeton, N.J.: Anchor, 1990.

Bihbahānī, Āqā Muḥammad-ʿAlī, *Khayrātiyya dar ibṭāl-i ṭarīqa-yi ṣūfiyya*. Qum: Anṣāriyān, 1992.

Boroujerdi, Mehrzad. "'The West' in the Eyes of the Iranian Intellectuals of the Interwar Years (1919–1939)." *Comparative Studies of South Asia, Africa, and the Middle East* 26, no. 3(2006): 391–401.

Bosworth, Edmund C. "E. G. Browne and His 'A Year amongst the Persians.'" *Iran* 33 (January 1, 1995): 115–22. DOI: 10.2307/4299929.

Böwering, Gerhard. "Early Sufism between Persecution and Heresy," In *Islamic Mysticism Contested: Thirteen Centuries of Controversies and Polemics*, edited by Frederick de Jong and Bernd Radtke. Leiden: Brill, 1999.

———. "ʿERFĀN (1)." In *Encyclopedia Iranica*, edited by Ehsan Yarshater. Accessed July 2, 2015, http://www.iranicaonline.org/articles/erfan-1.

Browne, Edward Granville. *A Literary History of Persia*. Cambridge: Cambridge University Press, 1928.

Cavusoglu, Semiramis. "The Kâdîzâdeli Movement: An Attempt of Seriat-Minded Reform in the Ottoman Empire." Ph.D. diss., Princeton University, 1990.

Chardin, John. *Safarnāma-i shārdan: matn-i kāmil*. Translated by Eqbal Yaghmaʾi. 5 vols. Tehran: Tūs, 1993.

———. *Voyages du Chevalier Chardin en Perse, et autres lieux de l'Orient, enrichis d'un grand nombre de belles figures en taille-douce, représentant les antiquités et les choses remarquables du pays*. Paris: Le Normant, 1811. http://nrs.harvard.edu/urn-3:HUL.FIG:004370194.

Chelkowski, Peter. "TAʿZIA." In *Encyclopedia Iranica*, edited by Ehsan Yarshater. Accessed July 2, 2015, http://www.iranicaonline.org/articles/tazia.

Chittick, William C. *The Sufi Path of Knowledge: Ibn al-ʿArabi's Metaphysics of Imagination*. Albany: State University of New York Press, 1989.

Clayer, Nathalie. "Tekke." In *Encyclopaedia of Islam*, second edition, edited by P. Bearman, Th. Bianquis, C. E. Bosworth, E. van Donzel, and W. P. Heinrichs. Brill Online. Accessed June 28, 2012, http://referenceworks.brillonline.com.ezproxy.rice.edu/entries/encyclopaedia-of-islam-2/tekke-SIM_7486.

Cole, Juan R. I. "Ideology, Ethics, and Philosophical Discourse in Eighteenth Century Iran." *Iranian Studies* 22, no. 1 (January 1, 1989): 7–34.

———. *Roots of North Indian Shiʿism in Iran and Iraq: Religion and State in Awadh, 1722–1859*. Berkeley: University of California Press, 1988.

Corbin, Henry. *Avicenna and the Visionary Recital*. Irving, Tex.: Spring Publications, 1980.

———. "Confessions extatiques de Mīr Dāmād, maître de théologie Ispahan." In *Mélanges Louis Massignon*. Damascus: Institut Français de Damas, 1956.

———. *History of Islamic Philosophy*. London: Kegan Paul International, 1993.

Dabashi, Hamid. "Mīr Dāmād and the Founding of 'the School of Iṣfahān.'" In *History of Islamic Philosophy*, edited by Seyyed Hossein Nasr and Oliver Leaman, 597–634. Routledge History of World Philosophies. London: Routledge, 1996.

———. *Theology of Discontent: The Ideological Foundation of the Islamic Revolution in Iran*. New Brunswick, N.J.: Transaction Publishers, 2006.

Dabbagh, Soroush. "Ṭarḥvāra-yi az 'irfān-i mudirn: tanhā-yī ma'navī." Accessed March 29, 2016, http://www.begin.soroushdabagh.com/pdf/183.pdf. Accessed June 3, 2015.

Dāmād, Muḥammad Bāqir ibn Muḥammad. *Jaẕavāt va mavāqīt*. Edited by 'Ali Avjabi. 'Ulūm va ma'ārif-i islāmī, 35. Tehran: Mīrāṣ-i maktūb, 2001.

———. *al-Ravāshiḥ al-samāviyya fī sharḥ al-aḥādīṣ al-imāmiyya*. Tehran: s.n., 1894.

Damāvandī, 'Abd al-Raḥīm. "Miftāḥ-i asrār al-ḥusaynī." In *Anthologie des philosophes iraniens: depuis le XVIIe siècle jusqu'à nos jours,* edited by Jalal al-Din Ashtiyani and Henry Corbin, 4:575–790. Bibliothèque iranienne, 18–19. Tehran: Département d'iranologie de l'Institut franco-iranien de recherche, 1971.

Dārābī, Muḥammad b. Muḥammad. "Laṭīfa-yi ghaybī." *Armaqan* 3–4 (1925): 207–17.

———. *Laṭīfa-yi ghaybī*. Shiraz: Kitābkhāna-yi aḥmadī, 1978.

———. "Maqāmāt al-sālikīn." In *Ghinā, mūsīqī*, edited by Sayyed Ja'far Nabavi, 1: 283–496. Mīrāṣ-i fiqhī. Qum: Mu'assisa-yi būstān-i kitāb (Markaz-i intishārāt daftar-i tablīghāt-i islāmī), 2008.

———. *Riyāż al-'ārifīn fī sharḥ ṣaḥīfat sayyid al-sājidīn*. Edited by Hoseyn Dargahi and Mohammad-Taqi Shari'atmadari. Tehran: Dār al-usva, 2000.

———. *Taẕkira-yi laṭā'if al-khayāl*. Edited by Yusef Bayg-Babapur and Sadeq Ashkevari. 2 vols. Majma'-i ẕakhā'ir-i islāmī, 2012.

Dargahi, Hoseyn, and Hasan Taromi. "Pīshguftār-i muṣaḥḥihān." In Muḥammad-Ṭāhir Qummī, *Safīnat al-najāt*. Edited by Hoseyn Dargahi and Hasan Taromi. Tehran: Intishārāt-i nīk ma'ārif, 1994.

Darvīsh Shīrāzī, Muḥammad Hāshim. *Manāhil al-taḥqīq*. Edited by Mohammad-Yusef Nayyeri. Shiraz: Daryā-yi nūr, 2003.

Dashtakī Shīrāzī, Ghiyāṣ al-Dīn Manṣūr. *Ghiyāṣ al-dīn manṣūr dashtakī va falsafa-yi 'irfān: manāzil al-sā'irīn va maqāmāt al-'ārifīn*. Edited by Ghasem Kakaie. Tehran: Intishārāt-i farhangistān-i hunar, 2008.

Davānī, Jalāl al-Dīn. *Naqd-i niyāzī: Dar sharḥ-i dū bayt va yak ghazal az khāja Ḥāfiẓ Shīrāzī*. Edited by Hoseyn Mo'allem. Tehran: Amīr Kabīr, 1994.

Dehkhoda, 'Alī-Akbar. *Lughatnāma-yi dihkhuda*. Edited by Mohammad Mo'in and Ja'far Shahidi. Tehran: Mu'assasa-yi intishārāt va chāp-i dānishgāh-i Tehran, 1993–.

De Jong, F., and Bernard Radtke, eds. *Islamic Mysticism Contested: Thirteen Centuries of Controversies and Polemics*. Islamic History and Civilization. Studies and Texts, 29. Leiden: Brill, 1999.

Derayati, Mostafa. *Fihristvāra-i dastnivishtahā-yi īrān (Dinā)*. 12 vols. Tehran: Kitābkhāna, mūza va markaz-i asnād-i majlis-i shūrā-yi islāmī, 2010.

DeWeese, Devin. "The Eclipse of the Kubravīya in Central Asia." *Iranian Studies* 21, no. 1/2 (January 1, 1988): 45–83.

Dihdār Shīrāzī, Muḥammad b. Maḥmūd. *Rasā'il-i dihdār*. Edited by Mohammad-Hoseyn Akbari Savi. Mīrāṣ-i maktūb, 1. Tehran: Nuqṭa, 1996.

Doniger, Wendy. "Post-modern and -colonial -structural Comparisons." In *A Magic Still Dwells: Comparative Religion in the Postmodern Age,* edited by Kimberley C. Patton and Benjamin C. Ray, 63–74. Berkeley: University of California Press, 2000.

Doostdar, Alireza. "Empirical Spirits: Islam, Spiritism, and the Virtues of Science in Iran." *Comparative Studies in Society and History* 58, no. 2 (April 2016): 322–49.

———. "Fantasies of Reason: Science, 'Superstition,' and the Supernatural in Iran." Ph.D. diss., Harvard University, 2012.

Ernst, Carl W. "Jalal al-Din Davani's Interpretation of Hafiz." In *Hafiz and the Religion of Love in Classical Persian Poetry,* edited by Leonard Lewisohn, 197–211. Iran and the Persianate World. London: I. B. Tauris in association with Iran Heritage Foundation, 2010.

———. *The Shambhala Guide to Sufism.* Boston, Mass.: Shambhala, 1997.

Estakhri, Ehsanollah. *Uṣūl-i taṣavvuf.* Tehran: Kānūn-i maʿrifat, 1960.

Eʿtesam, ʿAlireza. *Bi ravāyat-i saʿīd nafīsī: Khāṭirāt-i siyāsī, adabī, javānī.* Tehran: Markaz, 2002.

Farhani Monfared, Mahdi. *Muhājarat-i ʿulamā-yi shīʿa az jabal ʿāmil bi irān dar ʿaṣr-i ṣafavī.* Tehran: Amīr Kabīr, 1998.

Fasāʾī, Ḥasan ibn Ḥasan Ḥusaynī. *Fārsnāma-yi nāṣirī.* Edited by Mansur Rastegar Fasaʾi. 2 vols. Tehran: Amīr Kabīr, 1989.

Fatemi, Hasan. "Kuhan-tarīn sharḥ-i ḥāl-hā-yi mullā muḥammad madhī nirāqī." *Kitāb-i māh-i dīn* 53–54 (2002): 26–30.

Fayż Kāshānī, Muḥammad ibn Murtażā. *Kalimāt maknūna min ʿulūm ahl al-ḥikma va al-maʿrifa,* n.p, n.d.

———. *Uṣūl al-maʿārif.* Edited by Jalal al-Din Ashtiyani. Mashhad: Muʾassasa-yi chāp va intishārāt-i dānishgāh-i firdawsī, 1975.

———. *al-Vāfī.* Edited by Ziya al-Din Hoseyni. 26 vols. Isfahan: Maktabat al-imām amīr al-muʾminīn ʿalī al-ʿāmma, 1986.

Felek, Ozgen, and Alexander D. Knysh, eds. *Dreams and Visions in Islamic Societies.* Albany: State University of New York Press, 2012.

Findiriskī, Abū al-Qāsim ibn Mīrzā Buzurg. *Risāla-yi ṣanāʿiyya.* Edited by Hasan Jamshidi. Falsafa va ʿirfān, 152. Qum: Muʾassasa-yi būstān-i kitāb, 2008.

Fitzgerald, Timothy. *The Ideology of Religious Studies.* New York: Oxford University Press, 2000.

Forman, Robert K. C. *Mysticism, Mind, Consciousness.* Albany: State University of New York Press, 1999.

Foruqi, Mohammad-ʿAli. Preface to *Farhang-i nafīsī,* by ʿAli-Akbar Nafisi, 1: i-xii. Tehran: Kitābfurūshī khayyām (chap-i ufsit-i marvī), 1976.

———. Introduction to *Manṭiq al-ṭayr* by Farīd al-Dīn ʿAṭṭār Nīshābūrī. Tehran: lithograph edition (Najm al-dawla), 1902.

Germana, Nicholas A. *The Orient of Europe: The Mythical Image of India and Competing Images of German National Identity.* Newcastle: Cambridge Scholars, 2009.

Ghaffari, Hoseyn. "Taṣavvuf ya ʿirfān? Pāsukhī bar maqāla-yi pārāduks-i taṣavvuf nazd-i asātīd va shāgirdān-i mullā ṣadrā." *Falsafa, majalla-yi dānishkada-yi adabiyyāt va ʿulūm-i insānī dānishgāh-i Tehran* 12 (2006): 109–26.

Gharaviyan, Mohsen, and Mahdi Nasiri. *Munāẓara-yi janjālī nasiri va gharaviyan darbāra-yi ʿirfān va dīn.* Debate televised by Islamic Republic of Iran Broadcasting (IRIB4) on October 5, 2011. Accessed March 29, 2016, http://www.youtube.com/watch?v=I-DZIQHdfsg&feature=youtube_gdata_player.

Giladi, Avner. "On the Origins of Two Key Terms in Gazālī's *Iḥyā' ʿulūm al-dīn.*" *Arabica* 36, no. 1 (1989): 81–93.

Gleave, Robert. "Continuity and Originality in Shiʿi Thought: The Relationship between the *Akhbāriyya* and the *Maktab-i Tafkīk.*" In *Shiʿi Trends and Dynamics in Modern Times,* edited by Dennis Hermann and Sabrina Mervin. Beirut: Orient-Institut/Ergon Verlag, 2010.

———. *Scripturalist Islam: The History and Doctrines of the Akhbārī Shīʿī School.* Islamic Philosophy, Theology, and Science, 72. Leiden: Brill, 2007.

———. "Scripturalist Sufism and Scripturalist Anti-Sufism: Theology and Mysticism amongst the Shiʿi Akhbariyya." In *Sufism and Theology,* edited by Ayman Shihadeh, 158–76. Edinburgh: Edinburgh University Press, 2007.

Goichon, A. M. "Ḥayy b. Yaḳẓān." In *Encyclopaedia of Islam,* second edition, edited by P. Bearman, Th. Bianquis, C. E. Bosworth, E. van Donzel, and W. P. Heinrichs. Brill Online. Accessed July 2, 2015, http://referenceworks.brillonline.com/entries/encyclopaedia-of-islam-2/hayy-b-yakzan-COM_0281.

Golchin Maʿani, Ahmad. *Tārīkh-i taẕkira-hā-yi fārsī,*. Publications de l'Université de Tehran, 1236/1. Tehran: Dānishgāh-i Tehran, 1969.

Goli-Zavare, Gholam-Reza. "Mullā Muḥammad-Ṭāhir Qummī." In *Sitāragān-i ḥaram: akhtarān-i ḥarīm-i maʿṣūma (s)* 14:132–74. Qum: Zā'ir, 1998–.

Graham, Terry. "The Niʿmatu'llāhī Order under Safavid Suppression and in Indian Exile." In *The Heritage of Sufism,* edited byLeonard Lewisohn and David Morgan, 3:178–200. Oxford: Oneworld, 1999.

Gramlich, Richard. *Die Schiitischen Derwischorden Persiens.* Abhandlungen Für Die Kunde Des Morgenlandes, 36. Marburg: Deutsche Morgenländische Gesellschaft, 1965.

Green, Nile. *Sufism: A Global History.* Chichester, West Sussex: Wiley-Blackwell, 2012.

Gutas, Dimitri. "Avicenna V. Mysticism." In *Encyclopedia Iranica,* edited by Ehsan Yarshater. Accessed July 2, 2015, http://www.iranicaonline.org/articles/avicenna-v.

———. "Intellect without Limits: The Absence of Mysticism in Avicenna." In *Intellect et imagination dans la philosophie médiévale,* edited by M. Cândida-Pacheco and J. Francisco-Meirinhos, 1: 351–72. Turnhout: Brepols, 2006.

Hafez, Shams al-Dīn Muḥammad. *Dīvān-i ḥāfiẓ khāja shams al-dīn muḥammad.* Edited by Parviz Natel Khanlari. Tehran: Khārazmī, 1983.

Hamadānī, ʿAbd al-Ṣamad. *Baḥr al-maʿārif.* Edited by Hoseyn Vali Ostad. 3 vols. Tehran: Intishārāt-i ḥikmat, 1991– .

Ḥamavī, Muḥammad b. Isḥāq. *Anīs al-mu'minīn.* Edited by Hashem Mohaddes. Tehran: Vaḥid-i taḥqīqāt-i islāmī, bunyād-i biʿṣat, 1984.

Hanegraaff, Wouter J. *Dictionary of Gnosis and Western Esotericism.* Leiden: Brill, 2006.

Haqiqi, Ranjbar. "Sayrī dar ʿirfān va taṣavvuf." *Kayhān-i andīsha* 54 (1994): 99–116.

Ḥazīn Lāhījī, Muḥammad-ʿAlī. *Tārīkh va safarnāma-i ḥazīn*. Edited by ʿAli Davani. Tehran: Markaz-i asnād-i inqilāb-i islāmī, 1996.

———. *Tazkirat al-muʿāṣirīn*. Edited by Maʿsume Salek. Mīrāṣ-i maktūb, zabān va adabīyyfāt-i fārsī, 2. Tehran: Nashr-i sāya, 1996.

———. *The Life of Sheikh Mohammed Ali Hazin*. Translated by Francis C. Belfour. London: Oriental translation fund, 1831.

Hodgson, Marshall G. S. *The Venture of Islam: Conscience and History in a World Civilization*. 3 vols. Chicago: University of Chicago Press, 1974.

Homa'i, Jalal al-Din. "Jilva-hā-yi ʿirfān-i irān: az barnāma-hā-yi marz-hā-yi dānish." *Rādyu irān: Nashriya-yi idāra-yi kull-i intishārāt va rādyū* 44 (1960): 16–17.

Hoseyni, Ahmad. *Fihrist-i nuskha-hā-yi khaṭṭī-i kitābkhāna-i ʿumūmī-yi ḥazrat āyat allāh al-ʿuẓmā najafī marʿashī*. 40 vols. Qum: Chāpkhāna-i mihr-i ustuvār, 1975– .

Hoseyni, Ziya' al-Din. Introduction to *al-Vāfī* by Muḥammad b. Murtażā Fayż Kāshānī. Edited by Ziya al-Din Hoseyni. Isfahan: Maktabat al-imām amīr al-mu'minīn ʿalī al-ʿāmma, 1986.

Ḥurr ʿĀmilī, Muḥammad ibn al-Ḥasan. *Amal al-āmil*. Edited by Ahmad Hoseyni. 2 vols. Qum: Dār al-kitāb al-islāmī, 1983.

———. *al-Iṣnā ʿashariyya fī al-radd ʿalā al-ṣūfīyya*. Iran: Darūdī, 1987.

———. "Risāla fī al-ghinā." In *Ghinā, mūsīqī*, edited by Reza Mokhtari, 1:101–84. Mīrāṣ-i fiqhī. Qum: Mu'assisa-yi būstān-i kitāb (markaz-i intishārāt daftar-i tablīghāt-i islāmī), 2008.

Hujvīrī, Abu al-Ḥasan ʿAlī, *Kashf al-maḥjūb*. Edited by Valentine Zhokovski. Tehran: Ṭahūrī, 1996.

Ibn ʿArabī. *al-Futūḥāt al-makkiyya*. Edited by ʿUṣmān Yaḥyā and Ibrāhīm Maẕkūr. 12 vols. Monumenta Classica. Cairo: al-Hay'a al-miṣrīya al-ʿāmma li al-kitāb, 1972.

Ibn Bābūya Qummī, Muḥammad b. ʿAlī. *al-Amālī*. Edited by Mohammad-Baqer Kamara'ī. Tehran: Kitābkhāna-yi islāmīyya, 1983.

Ibn Sīnā (Avicenna), Abī ʿAlī Ḥusayn b. ʿAbdullāh. *al-Ishārāt va al-tanbīhāt*. 3 vols. Tehran: Maṭbaʿat al-ḥaydarī, 1958.

Ibn Ṭāvūs Ḥillī, ʿAlī b. Mūsā, *Al-amān min akhṭār al-asfār va al-azmān*. Qum: Mu'assisat āl al-Bayt li iḥyā' al-turāṣ, 1988.

Iṣṭahbānātī, ʿAlī-Naqī. *Burhān al-murtāżīn*. Edited by Mohammad Hortamani. Isfahan: Muqīm, 2003.

Jaʿfariyan, Rasul. Introduction to *Tarjama-yi anājīl-i arbaʿa*, by Muḥammad-Bāqir Khātūnābādī, edited by Rasul Jaʿfariyan, Mirāṣ-i maktub, 31. Tehran: Nashr-i nuqta, 1996.

———. *Qiṣṣakhānān dar tārīkh-i islām va irān: Murūrī bar jarayān-i qiṣṣakhānī, abʿād va taṭṭavur-i ān dar tārīkh-i irān va islām*. Iran: Dalīl, 1999.

———. *Ṣafavīyya dar ʿarṣa-yi dīn, farhang va siyāsat*. 3 vols. Pizhūhishkada-yi ḥawza va dānishgāh, 37–39. Qum: Pizhūhishkada-i ḥawza va dānishgāh, 2000.

———. "Si risāla dar bāb-i Abū Muslim va Abū Muslim nāma-hā." In *Mīrāṣ-i islāmī-i īrān*, 2:247–301. Qum: Kitābkhāna-yi ḥażrat-i āyat allāh al-ʿuẓmā marʿashī najafī, 1995.

———. *Tārīkh-i tashayyuʿ dar irān az āghāz tā qarn-i dahum-i hijrī.* 2 vols. Qum: Anṣarīyān, 1996.

Jantzen, Grace. *Power, Gender, and Christian Mysticism.* Cambridge Studies in Ideology and Religion, 8. Cambridge: Cambridge University Press, 1995.

Javdan, Mohammad. "ʿĀlimān-i shīʿa va taṣavvuf." *Haft āsīmān* 22 (2004): 207–28.

Jazāʾirī, Niʿmatullah b. ʿAbdullāh. *al-Anvār al-nuʿmāniyya.* 4 vols. Tabriz: Kitābjī ḥaqīqat, 1959.

Johnson, Benton. "Church and Sect Revisited." *Journal for the Scientific Study of Religion* 10, no. 2 (1971): 124–37.

———. "On Church and Sect." *American Sociological Review; Official Journal of the American Sociological Association* 28, no. 4 (1963): 539–49.

Kakaie, Ghasem, Introduction to *Ghiyāṣ al-dīn manṣūr dashtakī va falsafa-yi ʿirfān: manāzil al-sāʾirīn va maqāmāt al-ʿārifīn* by Ghiyāṣ al-Dīn Manṣūr Dashtakī Shīrāzī. Edited by Ghasem Kakaie. Tehran: Intishārāt-i farhangistān-i hunar, 2008.

——— and ʿAli Movahhedian ʿAttar, "Niqāhī padīdār-shināsāna bi kārburd-hā-yi mafhūmī-yi ʿirfān [A Phenomenological look at the conceptual uses of the term ʿirfān]." *Anjuman-i maʿārif-i islāmī* 2 (Spring, 1995): 26–43.

Karamustafa, Ahmet T. *Sufism: The Formative Period.* New Edinburgh Islamic Surveys. Edinburgh: Edinburgh University Press, 2007.

Karbalāʾī Tabrīzī, Ḥusayn. *Rawżāt al-jinān va jannāt al-janān.* Edited by Jaʿfar Soltan al-Quraʾi. 2 vols. Majmūʿa-yi mutūn-i fārsī. Tehran: Bungāh-i tarjuma va nashr-i kitāb, 1965.

Karbasi-zade, ʿAlī. *Ḥakīm-i mutaʾallih Bīdābādī: Iḥyāgar-i ḥikmat-i shīʿī dar qarn-i davāzdahum-i hijrī.* Tehran: Pizhūhishgāh-i ʿulūm-i insānī va muṭālaʿāt-i farhangī, 2002.

Kāshif Dizfūlī, Ṣadr al-Dīn. *Mirʾāt al-ghayb: bi hamrāh-i ḥaqq al-ḥaqīqa li arbāb al-ṭarīqa.* Edited by Nahidossadat Pezeshki. Tehran: Bāztāb, 2006.

Kasravi, Ahmad, *Dar pīrāmūn-i adabiyyāt.* Edited by ʿAzizullah Alizade. Tehran: Āfarīnish, 1999.

Katz, Steven T. "The 'Conservative' Character of Mysticism." In *Mysticism and Religious Traditions,* edited by Steven T. Katz, 3–60. New York: Oxford University Press, 1983.

———. "Language, Epistemology, and Mysticism." In *Mysticism and Philosophical Analysis,* edited by Steven T. Katz, 22–74. New York: Oxford University Press, 1978.

Kazemzade Iranshahr, Hoseyn. *Āṣār va aḥvāl-i kazemzade iranshahr.* Tehran: Eqbal, 1971.

———. "Tiʾusufī." *Iranshahr* 11 (1927): 641–59 and *Iranshahr* 12, (1927): 705–716.

Keyvan Qazvini, ʿAbbas. *ʿIrfān-nāma.* Tehran: Āfarīnish, 2009.

———. *Keyvan-nama,* n.p, n.d.

———. *Rāzgushā, bihīn sukhan, ustuvār.* Edited by Mahmud ʿAbbasi. Tehran: n.p., 1997.

———. *Sharḥ-i rubāiyyat-i Khayyām.* Tehran: Intishārāt-i fatḥī, 1984.

Khajavi, Mohammad. Introduction to *Risāla-yi rūḥiyya va manhaj al-taḥrīr,* by Sayyid

Quṭb al-Dīn Muḥammad Nayrīzī, edited by Mohammad Khajavi, 15–33. Shiraz: Kitābkhāna-yi aḥmadī, 1977.

Khānsārī, Muḥammad-Bāqir. *Rawżāt al-jannāt fī aḥwāl al-ʿulamāʾ va al-sādāt.* Edited by Mohammad-ʿAli Rowzati Esfahani. 8 vols. Tehran: Maktabat ismāʿīliyān, 1962.

Khātūnābādī, Muḥammad-Bāqir. *Tarjama-yi anājil-i arbaʿa.* Edited by Rasul Jaʿfariyan. Mīrāṣ-i maktūb, 31. Tehran: Nashr-i nuqṭa, 1996.

Khavari, Asadollah. *Ẕahabiyya: Taṣavvuf-i ʿilmī, āṣār-i adabī.* Tehran: Intishārāt-i dānishgāh-i Tehran, 1983.

Khomeini, Ruhollah. *Sharḥ-i chihil ḥadīṣ: (arbaʿīn ḥadīṣ).* Chāp-i 21. Tehran: Muʾassasa-yi tanẓīm va nashr-i āṣār-i imām khumaynī, 1999.

———. *Sirr al-ṣalāt: miʿrāj al-sālikīn va ṣalāt al-ʿārifīn.* Tehran: Muʾassasa-yi tanẓīm va nashr-i āṣār-i ḥażrat imām khumaynī, 1998.

Khorasani, Molla Hashem. *Muntakhab al-tavārīkh.* Mashhad: Kitābkhāna-yi ʿilmī: 1931.

Khorasani, S. M. "Mā az naẓar-i dīgarān." *Dānishkada* 2 (1918): 79–85.

Khuyī, Abū al-Qāsim Amīn al-Sharīʿa. *Mīzān al-ṣavāb dar sharḥ-i faṣl al-khiṭāb.* Edited by Mohammad Khajavi. 3 vols. Tehran: Mawlā, 2004.

King, Richard. *Orientalism and Religion: Post-colonial Theory, India and "the Mystic East."* London: Routledge, 1999.

Kirmānshāhī, Āqā Muḥammad-Jaʿfar, *Fażāyiḥ al-ṣūfiyya.* Qum: Anṣāriyān, 1993.

Kirmānshāhī, Āqā Mahmūd, *Tanbīh al-ghāfilīn va īqāẓ al-rāqidīn.* Edited by ʿAli Davani. Tehran: Rahnimūn: 2006.

Kiyā, Ṣādiq. *Nuqtaviyān yā pasikhānīyān.* Īrān kūda 13. Tehran: Anjuman-i irān, 1951.

Knysh, Alexander. "ʿIrfan' Revisited: Khomeini and the Legacy of Islamic Mystical Philosophy." *Middle East Journal* 46, no. 4 (October 1, 1992): 631–53.

Kripal, Jeffrey J., et al. *Comparing Religions.* Malden, Mass.: Wiley-Blackwell, 2014.

Kulaynī, Muḥammad b. Yaʿqūb. *al-Uṣūl min al-kāfī.* Edited by ʿAli-Akbar Ghaffari. 8 vols. Tehran: Dār al-kutub al-Islāmiyya, 1957.

Lāhījī, ʿAbd al-Razzāq. *Gawhar-i murād.* Edited by Zeyn al-ʿAbedin Qorbani. Tehran: Sāzmān-i chāp va intishārāt-i vizārat-i farhang va irshād-i islāmī, 1993.

Lawḥī, Mir Muḥammad. "Salvat al-Shīʿa." In *Mīrāṣ-i islāmī-i īrān,* edited by Sheykh Ahmad ʿAbedi, 2:339–59. Iran: Kitābkhāna-yi ḥażrat-i āyat allāh al-ʿuẓmā marʿashī najafī, 1995.

———. "Uṣūl fuṣūl al-tawżīḥ." In *Ṣafavīyya dar ʿarṣa-yi dīn, farhang va siyāsat,* edited by Rasul jaʿfariyan, 3:616–46. Pizhūhishkada-yi ḥawza va dānishgāh, 37–39. Qum: Pizhūhishkada-i ḥawza va dānishgāh, 2000.

Lawrence, Bruce B. *Defenders of God: The Fundamentalist Revolt against the Modern Age.* Studies in Comparative Religion. Columbia: University of South Carolina Press, 1995.

Lawson, Todd. "The Hidden Words of Fayḍ Kāshānī." In *Iran, questions et connaissances: Actes du IVe Congrès européen des études iraniennes,* edited by Philip Huyse and Maria Szuppe, 427–447. Studia Iranica 25–27. Paris: Association pour l'avancement des études iraniennes, 2002.

Le Gall, Dina. *A Culture of Sufism: Naqshbandīs in the Ottoman World, 1450–1700.* SUNY

Series in Medieval Middle East History. Albany: State University of New York Press, 2005.

Leask, Nigel. *British Romantic Writers and the East: Anxieties of Empire.* Cambridge Studies in Romanticism. Cambridge: Cambridge University Press, 1992.

Lewis, Franklin. "HAFEZ viii. HAFEZ AND RENDI." In *Encyclopedia Iranica,* edited by Ehsan Yarshater. Accessed July 2, 2015, http://www.iranicaonline.org/articles/hafez-vii-viii.

———. *Rumi: Past and Present, East and West.* Oxford: Oneworld, 2000.

Lewisohn, Leonard. "An Introduction to the History of Modern Persian Sufism, Part I: The Niʿmatullāhī Order: Persecution, Revival and Schism." *Bulletin of the School of Oriental and African Studies, University of London* 61, no. 3 (January 1, 1998): 437–64.

———. "An Introduction to the History of Modern Persian Sufism, Part II: A Socio-Cultural Profile of Sufism, from the Dhahabī Revival to the Present Day." *Bulletin of the School of Oriental and African Studies, University of London* 62, no. 1 (January 1, 1999): 36–59.

———. "Sufism and the School of Iṣfahān: Taṣawwuf and ʿIrfān in Late Safavid Iran: ʿAbd al-Razzāq Lahījī and Fayḍ-i Kāshānī on the Relation of Taṣawwuf, Ḥikmat and ʿIrfān." In *The Heritage of Sufism,* edited by Leonard Lewisohn and David Morgan, 3:63–134. Oxford: Oneworld, 1999.

———. "Sufism and Theology in the Confessions of Ṣā'in al-Dīn Turka Iṣfahānī (d. 830/1437)." In *Sufism and Theology,* edited by Ayman Shihadeh, 63–82. Edinburgh: Edinburgh University Press, 2007.

Luizard, Pierre-Jean. "Les confréries soufies en Iraq aux dix-neuvième et vingtième siècles face au Chiisme doudecimain et au Wahhabisme." In *Islamic Mysticism Contested: Thirteen Centuries of Controversies and Polemics,* edited by F. de Jong and Bernard Radtke, 283–315. Islamic History and Civilization, Studies and Texts, 0929–2403, 29. Leiden: Brill, 1999.

MacEoin, D. M. "AḤSĀ'Ī, SHAIKH AḤMAD" In *Encyclopedia Iranica,* edited by Ehsan Yarshater. Accessed July 2, 2015, http://www.iranicaonline.org/articles/ahsai-shaikh-ahmad.

Madani, Reza. *Irfān-i islāmī va ʿirfān iltiqāṭī: barrasī va naqd-i ʿaqāyid-i firqa-yi gunābādīyya.* Tehran: Rāh-i nīkān, 2008.

Madelung, Wilferd. "Nasir al-Din Tusi's Ethics: Between Philosophy, Shiʿism and Sufism." Accessed March 29, 2016, akdn2stg.prod.acquia-sites.com/sites/default/files/Nasir%20al-Din%20Tusi%27s%20Ethics%20-%20final-886228271.pdf.

Mahdavi, Mosleh al-Din. *Zindagī-nāma-yi ʿallāma majlisī.* Tehran: Dabīrkhāna-yi hamāyish-i buzurgdāsht-i ʿallāma majlisī, Bakhsh-i intishārāt, 1999.

Majlisī, Muḥammad Bāqir ibn Muḥammad Taqī. *Biḥār al-anvār.* Edited by ʿAbd al-Zahra ʿAlavi. Tehran: Dār al-kutub al-islāmīyya, 1997.

Majlisī, Muḥammad-Taqī, *Lavāmīʿ Ṣāhibqirānī.* Qum: Ismāʿīliyān, 1994.

Malcolm, John. *The History of Persia, from the Most Early Period to the Present Time: Containing an Account of the Religion, Government, Usages, and Character of the Inhabitants of That Kingdom.* London: Murray, 1829. http://nrs.harvard.edu/urn-3:HUL.FIG:005948666. Accessed April 4th, 2015.

Malekiyan, Mostafa. *Dīn, ma'navīyyat va rawshanfikrī-i dīnī: si guft va gū bā Mostafa Malekiyan.* Tehran: Nashr-i pāyān, 2008.

———. *Hadiṣ-i arizūmandī: justār-hā-yi dar 'aqlāniyyat va ma'naviyyat.* Bīnish-i ma'navi 41. Tehran: Nigāh-i mu'āṣir, 2010.

Massignon, Louis. *Essay on the Origins of the Technical Language of Islamic Mysticism.* Notre Dame, Ind.: University of Notre Dame Press, 1997.

Ma'sum-'Alī Shāh, Muḥammad Ma'ṣūm Shīrāzī. *Ṭarā'iq al-ḥaqā'iq.* Edited by Mohammad-Ja'far Mahjub. 3 vols. Tehran: Kitābkhāna-yi bārānī, 1960.

Masuzawa, Tomoko. *The Invention of World Religions, Or, How European Universalism Was Preserved in the Language of Pluralism.* Chicago: University of Chicago Press, 2005.

Matthee, Rudolph P. *Persia in Crisis: Safavid Decline and the Fall of Isfahan.* International Library of Iranian Studies, 17. London: I. B. Tauris, 2012.

McChesney, R. D. "The Central Asian Haj-Pilgrimage in the Time of the Early Modern Empires." In *Safavid Iran and Her Neighbors,* edited by Michel M Mazzaoui, 129–56. Salt Lake City: University of Utah Press, 2003.

Melvin-Koushki, Matthew. "The Quest for a Universal Science: The Occult Philosophy of Ṣā'in al-Dīn Turka Iṣfahānī (1369–1432) and Intellectual Millenarianism in Early Timurid Iran." Ph.D. diss., Yale University, 2012.

Meshkan Tabasi, Seyyed Hasan. "Naql az kitāb-i gulzār-i ma'ānī." *Armaqan* 1–2 (1949): 67–69.

Michot, Jean R. "La pandémie avicennienne au VIe/XIIe siècle, présentation, editio princeps et traduction de l'introduction du *Livre de l'advenue du monde (Kitāb Ḥudūth Al-'ālam) d'Ibn Ghaylān al-Balkhī.*" *Arabica* 40, no. 3 (November 1, 1993): 287–344.

Modarresi Chahardahi, Nur al-Din. *Sayrī dar taṣavvuf: dar sharḥ-i ḥāl-i mashāyikh va aqṭāb.* Tehran: Kitābfurūshī-yi ishrāqī, 1982.

Modarressi Tabataba'i, Hossein. "Si maktūb az Āqā Muḥammad Bīdābādī dar sayr va sulūk." *Vaḥīd* 246–247 (1978): 35–42.

———."Du risāla az Āqā Muḥammad Bīdābādī dar sayr va sulūk," *Vahid* 115 (1973): 394–97.

———. "Mukātabāt-i Fayż va Qāżī Sa'īd Qummī," *Vahid* 117 (1973): 667–78.

———. "Panj nāma az Fatḥ-'Alī Shāh bi Mīrzā-yi Qummī," *Barrasī-hā-yi tārīkhī* 59 (1975): 245–76.

———. *An Introduction to Shī'ī Law: A Bibliographical Study.* St. Antony's Middle East Monographs, 16. London: Ithaca Press, 1984.

Molé, Marijan, *Les Kubrawiya entre sunnisme et shiisme aux hitieme et neuvieme siecles de l'hegira,* in *REI* (1961) 61–142.

Morier, James J. *The adventures of Ḥājī Bābā of Ispahan.* 2nd ed. Calcutta: Asiatic Society of Bengal, 1924.

Motahhari, Morteza. *'Irfān-i Ḥāfiẓ,* Tehran: Intishārāt-i Ṣadrā, 1999.

———. *Khadamāt-i mutaqābil-i islām va irān.* Tehran: Intishārāt-i Ṣadrā, 1983.

———. *Majmū'a-yi āṣār,* 23 *(jild-i duvvum az bakhsh-i akhlāq va 'irfān).* Tehran, Intishārāt-i ṣadrā, 2005.

Motahhari, Morteza, and Ḥāfiẓ. *Āyīna-i jām: dīvān-i Ḥāfiẓ hamrāh bā yād-dāsht-hā-yi ustād muṭahharī.* Tehran: Intishārāt-i ṣadrā, 1999.

Mottahedeh, Roy P. *The Mantle of the Prophet: Religion and Politics in Iran.* New York: Simon and Schuster, 1985.

Movahhedian ʿAttar, ʿAli. *Mafūm-i ʿirfān.* Qum: Nashr-i dānishgāh-i adyān, 2009.

Mu'aẓẓin Khurāsānī, Muḥammad-ʿAli. *Tuḥfah-yi ʿAbbāsī: The Golden Chain of Sufism in Shīʿite Islam.* Translated by Mohammad Hassan Faghfoory. Lanham, Md.: University Press of America, 2008.

Mu'min Mashhadī, Muḥammad. *Tafsīr-i Muḥammad Mu'min Mashhadī bar juz'-i sīyum-i qur'ān-i majīd.* Edited by ʿAli Mohaddes. Majmūʿa-yi mīrāṣ-i irān va islām. Tehran: Markaz-i intishārāt-i ʿilmī va farhangī, 1983.

Musavi Bojnordi, ʿAli. "Imām Khomeini va mukhālafān-i ḥawzavī-ash." *Ṣāmin,* March 29, 2010. Accessed July 2, 2015, http://mousavibojnordi.blogfa.com/post-9.aspx.

Nafisi, ʿAli-Akbar. *Farhang-i nafīsī.* 5 vols. Tehran: Kitābfurūshī khayyām (Chap-i ufsit-i marvi), 1976.

Nakash, Yitzhak. "An Attempt to Trace the Origin of the Rituals of ʿĀshūrā'." *Die Welt Des Islams* 33, no. 2 (November 1, 1993): 161–81.

Nasr, Seyyed Hossein. *The Garden of Truth: The Vision and Practice of Sufism, Islam's Mystical Tradition.* New York: Harper One, 2007.

———. *Islamic Philosophy from Its Origin to the Present: Philosophy in the Land of Prophecy.* SUNY Series in Islam. Albany: State University of New York Press, 2006.

———. "Shiʿism and Sufism: Their Relationship in Essence and in History." *Religious Studies* 6, no. 3 (1970): 229–42.

———. "Religion in Safavid Persia." *Iranian Studies* 7, no. 1/2 (1974): 271–86.

———. "Spiritual Movements, Philosophy and Theology in the Safavid Period." In *The Cambridge History of Iran: Timurid and Safavid Periods,* edited by Peter Jackson and Laurence Lockhart, 6:656–97. Cambridge: Cambridge University Press, 2008. http://nrs.harvard.edu/urn-3:hul.ebookbatch.CAMHI_batch:9780511467783. Accessed June 2, 2015,

———, and Ramin Jahanbegloo. *Dar just-va-jū-yi amr-i qudsī: guft-va-gū-yi Rāmīn Jahānbiglū bā Sayyid Ḥusayn Nasr.* Tehran: Nay, 2006.

Naṣrābādī Iṣfahānī, Muḥammad Ṭāhir. *Taẕkira-yi Naṣrābādī:taẕkirat al-shuʿarā bi inżimām-i rasā'il, munsha'āt va ashʿār.* Edited by Mohsen Naji Nasrabadi. Tehran: Asāṭīr, 1999.

Nayrīzī, Sayyid Quṭb al-Dīn Muḥammad. "Risāla-yi vaḥdat-i ʿadadī." In *Tabāshīr al-ḥikma: sharḥ-i ḥadīṣ-i nūr muḥammadī,* by Mīrzā Abū al-Qāsim Ḥusaynī Sharīfī Shīrāzī (Rāz-i Shīrāzī), 98–101. Shiraz: Khānaqāh-i aḥmadī, 1973.

Nayrīzī, Umm Salma. *Jamiʿ al-kulliyyat.* Edited by Mahdi Eftekhar. Qum: Bakhshāyish, 2007.

Newman, Andrew J. "Fayd al-Kashani and the Rejection of the Clergy/State Alliance: Friday Prayer as Politics in the Safavid Period." In *The Most Learned of the Shiʿa: The Institution of the Marjaʿ Taqlid,* edited by Linda S. Walbridge, 34–52. Oxford: Oxford University Press, 2001.

———. "The Myth of the Clerical Migration to Safawid Iran: Arab Shiite Opposition to ʿAlī al-Karakī and Safawid Shiism." *Die Welt Des Islams* 33, no. 1. New Series (April 1, 1993): 66–112.

———. "The Recovery of the Past: Ibn Babawayh, Baqir al-Majlisi and Safavid Medical Discourse." *Iran: Journal of the British Institute of Persian Studies* 50 (2012): 109–27.

———. *Safavid Iran: Rebirth of a Persian Empire*. Library of Middle East History, 5. London: I. B. Tauris, 2006.

———. "Sufism and Anti-Sufism in Safavid Iran: The Authorship of the 'Ḥadīqat al-Shīʿa' Revisited." *Iran* 37 (January 1, 1999): 95–108.

Nicholson, Reynold A. *Studies in Islamic Mysticism*. Cambridge: Cambridge University Press, 1967.

Nirāqī, Aḥmad ibn Muḥammad Mahdī. *al-Khazāʾin*. Edited by ʿAli-Akbar Ghaffari. Tehran: Kitābfurūshī-i ʿilmiyya, 1960.

Nirāqī, Muḥammad-Mahdī b. Abī Ẓarr. *al-Lumʿa al-ilāhīya va al-kalimāt al-vajīza*. Edited by Jalal al-Din Ashtiyani. Mashhad: Anjuman-i falsafa, 1978.

———. *Jāmiʿ al-saʿādāt*. Edited by Mohammad Kalantar. 3 vols. Najaf: Dār al-nuʿmān li al- ṭibāʿa va al-nashr, n.d.

———. Mushkilāt al-ʿulūm. Tehran: Muʾassasa-yi muṭālaʿāt va taḥqīqāt-i farhangī. vābasta bi vizārat-i farhang va āmūzish-i ʿālī, 1988.

———. "Qurrat al-ʿUyūn." In *Muntakhabātī az āṣār-i ḥukamā-yi ilāhī-yi irān az ʿaṣr-i Mīr Dāmād va Mīr Findiriskī tā zamān-ī ḥāẓir* 4. Edited by Jalal al-Din Ashtiyani. Qum : Daftar-i tablīghāt-i islāmī-yi ḥawza-yi ʿilmiyya-yi Qum, 1999.

Nongbri, Brent. *Before Religion: A History of a Modern Concept*. New Haven, Conn.: Yale University Press, 2013.

Orsi, Robert A. *The Cambridge Companion to Religious Studies*. Cambridge Companions to Religion. Cambridge: Cambridge University Press, 2012.

Parishanzade, Abolhasan. *Gushāyish-i rāz: pāsukh bih kitāb-i rāzgushā-yi Keyvan Qazvini*. Tehran: Ḥaqīqat, 1998.

Parvizi Zahabi, Shams al-Din. *Taẕkirat al-awliyā*, Tabriz: Riżāʿī, 1953.

Pazouki, Shahram. "Pārāduks-i taṣavvuf nazd-i asātīd va shāgirdān-i mullā ṣadrā." *Falsafa, majalla-yi dānishkada-yi adabiyyāt va ʿulūm-i insānī dānishgāh-i Tehran* 12 (2006): 93–108.

Perry, John R. "ḤAZIN LĀHIJI." In *Encyclopedia Iranica*, edited by Ehsan Yarshater. Accessed July 2, 2015, http://www.iranicaonline.org/articles/hazin-lahiji.

———. *Karim Khan Zand*. Makers of the Muslim World. Oxford: Oneworld, 2006.

Pourjavady, Nasrollah. *Ishrāq va ʿirfān: maqāla-hā va naqd-hā*. Markaz-i nashr-i dānishgāhī, 3. Tehran: Markaz-i nashr-i dānishgāhī, 2001.

pseudo-Ardabīlī. *Ḥadīqat al-shīʿa*. Edited by Sadeq Hasanzade and ʿAli-Akbar Zamaninezhad. 2 vols. Qum: Anṣāriyān, 1998.

Qazvīnī, ʿAbd al-Nabī b. Muḥammad. *Tatmīm amal al-āmil*. Edited by Ahmad Hoseyni. Qum: Maktabat Āyat Allāh al-Marʿashī, 1987.

Qazvini, Mirza Mohammad b. ʿAbd al-Vahhāb. *Bīst maqāla: az maqālāt-i tārīkhī va intiqādī va adabī*. Tehran: Maṭbaʿa-yi majlis, 1934.

Qazvīnī, Muḥammad Ṭāhir Vaḥīd al-Zamān. *ʿAbbās-nāma*. Edited by Ebrahim Dehqan. Arak: Dāvūdī, 1951.

———. *Tārīkh-i jahānārā-yi ʿabbāsī*. Edited by Saʿid Mir Mohammad Sadeq and Ehsan Eshraqi. Tehran: Pizhūhishgāh-i ʿulūm-i insānī va muṭālaʿāt-i farhangī, 1994.

Quinn, Sholeh Alysia. "Coronation Narratives in Safavid Chronicles." In *History and Historiography of Post-Mongol Central Asia and the Middle East: Studies in Honor of John E. Woods*, edited by Judith Pfeiffer and Ernest Tucker, 311–31. Wiesbaden: Harrassowitz, 2006.

Qummī, Mīrzā Abu al-Qāsim. *Jāmiʿ al-shattāt*. n.p.: Aḥmad āqa tājir kitābfurūsh, 1892.

———. *Si risāla dar naqd-i ʿirfān*. Edited by Hoseyn Latifi, ʿAli Jabbar Golbaghi Masule, and ʿAbdullah Ghofrani. Mashhad: Bunyād-i pizhūhish-hā-yi islāmī, 2009.

Qummī, Muḥammad Ṭāhir. "Mūnis al-abrār dar radd-i sūfiyān," edited by Mohammad-Reza Arjomand. In *Mīrāṣ-i islāmī-i īrān*, 7:423–437. Qum: Kitābkhāna-yi Ḥażrat-i Āyat Allāh al-ʿUẓmā Marʿashī Najafī, 1998.

———. *Safīnat al-najāt*. Edited by Hoseyn Dargahi and Hasan Taromi. Tehran: Intishārāt-i nīk-i maʿārif, 1984.

———. *Shish risāla-yi fārsī*. Edited by Jalal al-Din Hoseyni Ormavi (Mohaddes). Tehran: Muṣṭafavī, 1960.

———. *Tuḥfat al-akhyār*. Tehran: Chāp-i muṣavvar, 1958.

Rahimi, Babak. *Theater State and the Formation of Early Modern Public Sphere in Iran: Studies on Safavid Muharram Rituals, 1590–1641 C.E.* Iran Studies, 5. Leiden: Brill, 2012.

Rāmpūrī, Ghiyāṣ al-Dīn Muḥammad. *Ghiyāṣ al-lughāt*. Edited by Mansur Sarvat. Tehran: Amīr Kabīr, 1984.

Rażavī Mashhadī, Muḥammad-Zamān. "Ṣaḥīfat al-rīshād." In *Mīrāṣ-i islāmī-i īrān*, edited by Rasul Jaʿfariyan, 2:268–72. Iran: Kitābkhāna-yi ḥażrat-i āyat allāh al-ʿuẓmā marʿashī najafī, 1994.

Rāzī, ʿAbdullāh Najm al-Dīn b. Muḥammad. *Mirṣād al-ʿibād*. Edited by Mohammad-Amin Riyahi. Majmūʿa-yi mutūn-i fārsī, 46. Tehran: Bungāh-i tarjuma va nashr-i kitāb, 1973.

Rāzī, Fakhr al-Dīn Muḥammad b. ʿUmar. *al-Tafsīr al-kabīr*. Beirut: Dār iḥyāʾ al-turāṣ al-ʿarabī, n.d.

Ridgeon, Lloyd V. J. "Aḥmad Kasravī's Criticisms of Edward Granville Browne." *Iran* 42 (January 1, 2004): 219–33.

———. *Religion and Politics in Modern Iran: A Reader*. London: I. B. Tauris, 2005.

———. *Sufi Castigator: Ahmad Kasravi and the Iranian Mystical Tradition*. Routledge Sufi Series, 19. London: Routledge, 2006.

Ritter, Helmot. "Abū Saʿīd Faḍl Allāh b. Abi 'l-Khayr." In *Encyclopaedia of Islam*, second edition, edited by P. Bearman, Th. Bianquis, C. E. Bosworth, E. van Donzel, and W. P. Heinrichs. Brill Online. Accessed July 2, 2015, http://referenceworks.brillonline.com/entries/encyclopaedia-of-islam-2/abu-said-fadl-allah-b-abi-l-khayr-SIM_0245.

Rizvi, Sajjad H. *Mullā Ṣadrā Shīrāzī: His Life and Works and the Sources for Safavid*

Philosophy. Journal of Semitic Studies Supplement, 18. Oxford: Oxford University Press on behalf of the University of Manchester, 2007.

———. "'Only the Imam Knows Best': The Maktab-e Tafkīk's Attack on the Legitimacy of Philosophy in Iran." *Journal of the Royal Asiatic Society* (Third Series) 2, (2012): 487–503.

———. "Philosophy as a Way of Life in the World of Islam: Applying Hadot to the Study of Mullā Ṣadrā Shīrāzī (d. 1635)." *Bulletin of the School of Oriental and African Studies* 75, no. 01 (2012): 33–45.

———. "A Sufi Theology Fit for a Shīʿī King: The Gawhar-i Murād of ʿAbd al-Razzāq Lāhījī (d. 1072/1661–2)." In *Sufism and Theology*, edited by Shihadeh Aymen, 83–88. Edinburgh: Edinburgh University Press, 2007.

Roknzade Adamiyyat, Mohammad Hoseyn. *Dānishmandān va sukhansarāyān-i fārs*. 5 vols. Tehran: Kitābfurūshīhā-yi islāmīyya va khayyām, 1958.

Royce, William Ronald. "Mir Maʿsum ʿali Shah and the Niʿmat Allahi Revival 1776–77 to 1796–97: A Study of Sufism and Its Opponents in Late Eighteenth Century Iran." Ph.D. diss., Princeton University, 1979.

Rūmi, Jalāl al-Dīn Muḥammad. *Maṣnavī-i maʿnavī*, edited by Reynold Nicholson. 4 vols. Tehran: Amīr Kabīr, 1984.

Rusta, Mohammad-Reza. *Tafāvut-i ʿirfān va taṣavvuf*. Tehran: Rāh-i nīkān, 2009.

Sabzavārī, Muḥammad-Bāqir, *Rawżat al-anvār ʿabbāsī*. Edited by Esmaʿil Changizi. Tehran: Markaz-i pazhīhishī-yi mīrāṣ-i maktūb, 2004.

Sadeghi-Boroujerdi, Eskandar. "Mostafa Malekian: Spirituality, Siyasat-Zadegi and (A)political Self-Improvement." *Digest of Middle East Studies, Domes* 23:2 (2014): 279–311.

Sadra'i Khuyi, ʿAlī. *Āshnā-yi ḥaqq: sharḥ-i aḥvāl va afkār-i āqā muḥammad bīdābādī*. Qum: Nahāvandī, 2000.

———. *Taẕkarat al-sālikīn: nāma-hā-yi ʿirfānī-i āqā muḥammad bīdābādī*. Qum: Intishārāt-i khuyī, 2011.

———. "Tawḥīd-nāma." In *Mīrāṣ-i islamī-i īrān*, 4:113–21. Edited by Rasul Jaʿfariyan. Qum: Kitābkhāna-yi ḥażrat-i āyatullāh al-ʿuẓmā marʿashī najafī, 1997.

Saduqi Soha, Manuchehr. *Tārīkh-i ḥukamā va ʿurafā-yi muta'akhkhir*. Tehran: Ḥikmat, 2002.

———. "Yagānagī ya dugānagī-yi taṣavvuf bā ʿirfān." *Kayhān-i andīsha* 54 (1994): 86–90.

Safa, Zabihollah. "Ishāra-yi kūtāh bi dāstān guzārī va dāstān guzārān tā dawrān-i ṣafavī." *Irān-shināsī* 3 (1999): p 463–471.

———. *Tārīkh-i adabīyāt dar īrān*. Vol. 5. Tehran: Firdawsī bā hamkārī-i adīb, 1984.

Safi-ʿAli Shah, Hasan. *ʿIrfān al-ḥaqq*. Tehran: Muhamadī, 1954.

Samiʿi, Keyvan. "Hāj Mullā ʿAbbās Keyvan Qazvini." *Vahid* 83 (1970): 1425–29.

———and Manuchehr Saduqi Soha. *Dū risāla dar tārīkh-i jadīd-i taṣavvuf-i irān*. Tehran: Pāzhang, 1991.

Sanaʿi, Mahmud. "Mabāḥiṣ maʿrifat al-nafsī: nīrū-ha-yi insān." *Mihr* 57 (1938): 1128–34.

Sargent, John. *A Memoir of the Rev. Henry Martyn, B.D.: Late Fellow of St. John's College,*

Cambridge, and the Chaplain to the Honourable East India Company. Boston: Perkins & Marvin, 1831.

Sarrāj, Abū Naṣr. *al-Lumaʿ fi al-taṣavvuf.* Edited by Reynold Nicholson. Leiden: Brill, 1914.

Scharbrodt, Oliver. "The Quṭb as Special Representative of the Hidden Imam: The Conflation of Shiʿi and Sufi Vilāyat in the Niʿmatullāhī Order." In *Shiʿi Trends and Dynamics in Modern Times (XVIIIth–XXth Centuries),* edited by Denis Hermann and Sabrina Mervin, 33–49. Bibliothèque Iranienne, 72. Beirut: Orient-Institut, 2010.

Schayegh, Cyrus. *Who Is Knowledgeable, Is Strong: Science, Class, and the Formation of Modern Iranian Society, 1900–1950.* Berkeley: Univerity of California Press, 2009.

Schimmel, Annemarie. *Mystical Dimensions of Islam.* Chapel Hill: University of North Carolina Press, 1975.

Schmidt, L. E. "The Making of Modern 'Mysticism.'" *Journal of the American Academy of Religion* 71, no. 2 (June 1, 2003): 273–302.

Sefatgol, Mansur. *Sākhtār-i nihād va andīsha-i dīnī dar irān-i ʿaṣr-i ṣafavī: Tārīkh-i taḥavvulāt-i dīnī-i īrān dar sadahā-yi dahum tā davāzdahum-i hijrī-i qamarī.* Tehran: Rasā, 2002.

Shāmlū, Valī Qulī b. Dāvūd Qulī. *Qiṣaṣ al-khāqānī.* Edited by Hasan Sadat Naseri. Tehran: Sāzmān-i chāp va intishārāt-i vizārat-i farhang va irshād-i islāmī, 1992.

Shariʿat Musavi, Mustafa. Introduction to *Kifāyat al-muhtadī fī maʿrīfat al-mahdī ʿalay-hi al-salām* by Mīr Lawḥī Sabzavārī, edited by Mustafa Shariʿat Musavi, 17–179. Qum: Dār al-tafsīr, 2005.

Sharīfī Shīrāzī (Rāz-i Shīrāzī), Mīrzā Abū al-Qāsim. "Yak qismat az tārikh-i ḥayāt va karāmāt-i Ḥażrat-i Sayyid Quṭb al-Dīn Muḥammad Shīrāzī." In *Tazkirat al-awliyā,* edited by Shams al-Dīn Ẓahabī Parvīzī. Tabriz: Rizāʿī, 1953.

Shepard, William. *Introducing Islam.* New York: Routledge, 2009.

Shīrāzī (Mulla Sadra), Ṣadr al-Dīn Muḥammad b. Ibrāhīm. *Breaking the Idols of Ignorance: Admonition of the Soi-Disant Sufi.* Translated by Mahdi Dasht Bozorgi and Sayyed Khalil Toussi. London: ICAS Press, 2008.

———. *al-Ḥikma al-mutaʿālīya fī al-asfār al-arbaʿa al-ʿaqlīyya.* Tehran: Shirkat dār al-maʿārif al-islāmīyya, 1958.

———. *Kasr aṣnām al-jāhilīyya.* Edited by Mohsen Jahangiri. Tehran: Bunyād ḥikmat-i islāmī-i ṣadrā, 2002.

———. *Risāla-yi si aṣl.* Edited by Seyyed Hossein Nasr. Tehran: Mawlā, 1961.

———. *al-Shavāhid al-rubūbiyya fī al-manāhij al-sulūkiyya.* Edited by Jalal al-Dīn Ashtiyani. Mashhad: Markaz-i nashr-i dānishgāhi, 1981.

Shirazi, Ziya' al-Din. *Fihrist-i kitābkhāna-yi madrasa-yi ʿāli-yi sipahsālār.* Tehran: Chāpkhāna-yi dānishgāh-i Tehran, 1926.

Shīrvānī, Zayn al-ʿĀbidīn. *Bustān al-siyāḥa.* 3 vols. Edited by Manizhe Mahmudi. Tehran: Intishārāt-i ḥaqīqat, 2010.

———. *Riyāż al-siyāḥa.* Edited by Hamid Rabbani. Tehran: Kitābfurūrūshī-yi Saʿdī, 1960.

Shūshtarī, Nūrallāh b. ʿAbdullāh. *Majālis al-muʾminīn*. Tehran: Kitābfurūshī-yi islāmīyya, 1998.

Smith, Jonathan Z. "Religion, Religions, Religious." In *Critical Terms for Religious Studies*, edited by Mark C. Taylor. Chicago: University of Chicago Press, 1998.

Soanes, Catherine, and Angus Stevenson, eds. *Oxford Dictionary of English*, 2nd edition. Oxford: Oxford University Press, 2003.

Sobieroj, F. "The Muʿtazila and Sūfism." In *Islamic Mysticism Contested*, edited by Fredrick de Jong and Bernd Radtke, 68–92. Leiden: Brill, 1999.

Stanfield-Johnson, Rosemary. "The Tabarraʾiyan and the Early Safavids." *Iranian Studies* 37, no. 1 (March 1, 2004): 47–71.

Steingass, Francis Joseph, et al. *A Comprehensive Persian-English Dictionary: Including the Arabic Words and Phrases to Be Met with in Persian Literature*. London: K. Paul, Trench, Trubner & Co., 1930.

Stewart, Devin. "Notes on the Migration of ʿĀmilī Scholars to Safavid Iran." *Journal of Near Eastern Studies* 55, no. 2 (April 1, 1996): 81–103.

Stewart, Devin J. *Islamic Legal Orthodoxy: Twelver Shiite Responses to the Sunni Legal System*. Salt Lake City: University of Utah Press, 1998.

Subtelny, Maria. "KĀŠEFI, KAMĀL-AL-DIN ḤOSAYN WĀʿEẒ." In *Encyclopedia Iranica*, edited by Ehsan Yarshater. Accessed July 2, 2015, http://www.iranicaonline.org/articles/kasefi_kamal.

Sulamī, ʿAbd al-Raḥmān. *Ṭabaqāt al-ṣūfiyya*. Edited by Muṣṭafā ʿAbd al-Qādir ʿAṭā. Beirut: Dār al-kutub al-ʿilmiyya, 2003.

Sviri, Sara. "Ḥakīm Tirmidhī and the Malāmatī Movement in Early Sufism." In *The Heritage of Sufism*, edited by Leonard Lewisohn and David Morgan, 1:583–613. Oxford: Oneworld, 1999.

Swatos, William. "CHURCH-SECT THEORY." In *Encyclopedia of Religion and Society*, edited by William H. Swatos and Peter Kivisto. Online edition. Accessed July 2, 2015, http://hirr.hartsem.edu/ency/cstheory.htm.

Tabande, Nur-ʿAli. *Āshinā-yi bā ʿirfān va taṣavvuf*. Tehran: Intishārāt-i ḥaqīqat, 2001.

Tabrīzī Isfahānī, Najīb al-Dīn Riżā. *Nūr al-hidāya*. Tehran: Chāpkhāna-yi ʿilmī, 1946.

———. *Sabʿ al-maṣānī*. Tehran: Intishārāt-i khāniqāh-i aḥmadī, 1981.

Tadayyon, Mahdi. "Ḥadīqat al-shīʿa yā kāshif al-ḥaqq." *Maʿārif* 6 (1985): 105–21.

Ṭāliqānī, ʿAbd al-Muṭṭalib b. Yaḥyā. "Khulāṣat al-favāʾid." In *Mīrāṣ-i islāmī-i īrān*, edited by Rasul Jaʿfariyan, 2:273–302. Qum: Kitābkhāna-yi ḥażrat-i āyat allāh al-ʿuẓmā marʿashī najafī, 1994.

Tavana, Jaʿfar. *Sarchashma-hā-yi taṣavvuf*. Tehran: Rāh-i nīkān, 1997.

Taylor, Charles. *A Secular Age*. Cambridge, Mass: Belknap Press of Harvard University Press, 2007.

Tehrani, Javad. *ʿArif va ṣūfī chi migūyand*. Tehran: Nashr-i āfāq, 2011.

Tehrani, Mohammad-Mohsen (Aqa Bozorg). *al-Ẕarīʿa ilā taṣānīf al-shīʿa*. 25 vols. Beirut: Dār al-ażvāʾ, 1983.

———. *Ṭabaqāt aʿlām al-shīʿa*. 17 vols. Beirut: Dar iḥyā al-turāth al-ʿarabī, 2009.

Tucker, Ernest S. *Nadir Shah's Quest for Legitimacy in Post-Safavid Iran*. Gainesville: University Press of Florida, 2006.

Ṭūsī, Naṣīr al-Dīn Muḥammad b. Muḥammad. *Awṣāf al-ashrāf.* Edited by Mohammad Modarresi. Tehran: Kitābfurūshi-yi islāmiyya, n.d.

Tustarī, ʿAbdullāh b. Nūr al-Dīn. *al-Ijāza al-kabīra.* Edited by Mohammad Samami Ha'eri. Qum: Maktabat al-marʿashī, 1989.

Van den Bos, Matthijs. *Mystic Regimes: Sufism and the State in Iran, from the Late Qajar Era to the Islamic Republic.* Leiden: Brill, 2002.

Varzi, Roxanne. *Warring Souls: Youth, Media, and Martyrdom in Post-Revolution Iran.* Durham, N.C.: Duke University Press, 2006.

Von Ess, Josef. "Sufism and Its Opponents: Reflections on Topoi, Tribulations and Transformations." In *Islamic Mysticism Contested: Thirteen Centuries of Controversies and Polemics,* edited by Frederick de Jong and Bernd Radtke. Leiden: Brill, 1999.

Yarshater, Ehsan. "Hafez I. An Overview." In *Encyclopedia Iranica,* edited by Ehsan Yarshater. Accessed July 2, 2015, http://www.iranicaonline.org/articles/hafez-i.

Yasemi, Rashid. "Dībācha [preface]." In *Tārīkh-i adabiyyāt-i īrān az āghāz-i ʿahd-i ṣafaviyya tā zaman-i ḥāẓir* 4 by Edward G. Browne. Translated by Rashid Yasemi. Tehran: 1937.

Yazdanpanah, Yadollah. *Mabānī va uṣūl- ʿirfān-i nazarī.* Edited by Ata Anzali. Qum: Intishārāt-i mu'assasa-yi āmūzishī va pazhūhishī-yi Imām Khomeini, 2009.

Zāhidī, Ḥusayn. *Silsilat al-nasab ṣafaviyya: nasab-nāma-yi pādishāhān-i bā ʿaẓimat-i ṣafavi.* Publications Iranschähr, 6. Berlin: Çaphana-i Iransahr, 1964.

Zakeri, ʿAli Akbar, "Akhbārī-garī, paydāiysh va payāmad-hā." *Hawza* 89–90 (1997–8): 315–369.

Zanūzī, Muḥammad. *Riyāż al-janna.* Edited by ʿAli Rafiʿi and ʿAli Sadra'i. 5 vols. Qum: Min makhṭūṭāt maktabat Āyat Allāh al-Marʿashī al-ʿāmma, 1991.

Zargar, Cyrus Ali. "Revealing Revisions: Fayd Al-Kāshānī's Four Versions of Al-Kalimāt Al-Maknūna." *Iranian Studies* 47, no. 2 (January 3, 2014): 241–62.

Zarrinkub, ʿAbd al-Hoseyn. *Dunbāla-yi just-va-jū dar taṣavvuf-i irān.* Tehran: Amīr Kabīr, 1983.

Zilfi, Madeline C. "The Kadizadelis: Discordant Revivalism in Seventeenth-Century Istanbul." *Journal of Near Eastern Studies* 45, no. 4 (October 1, 1986): 251–69.

INDEX

CPSIA information can be obtained
at www.ICGtesting.com
Printed in the USA
BVOW03*1402190817
492434BV00002B/4/P